IN AEDIBVS
VATICA
NIS

I would like to dedicate this book
to my children Vanessa and Eraklis, whom I adore,
so that they may know the whole story...

A.H.D.

The GREEKS

The Triumphant Journey

The GREEKS

The Triumphant Journey

From the Ancient Greeks
and the Greek Revolution of 1821,
to Greek Americans

ΕΘΝΙΚΟΣ ΚΗΡΥΞ ♦ The National Herald

NEW YORK 2001

*This book is made possible due to the generous support
of the "Stavros S. Niarchos" Foundation
to which we are deeply grateful.*

ISBN 960-87119-0-8

Layout – Printing: M. ROMANOS Ltd – Athens, Greece – Tel: 011 301-99 46 244 – Fax: 011 301-99 48 943

CONTENTS

INTRODUCTION

From the start, I saw the role of The National Herald not only as informative but educational as well. It is in this spirit that we undertook the publication of this book.

This is a collection of essays and documents concerning some of the most important events in the long history of Greek people. As far as I know, it is the first book that contains some of the most important readings available about the Greeks' triumphant journey through the ages along with commentary by some of the greatest scholars of our times. Due to the vastness of the material, we decided to concentrate on three particular periods: Ancient Greece, the Revolution of 1821 that led to the establishment of the modern Greek State, and the early years of the Greek immigrant experience in the New World.

It is my firm belief that the establishment and subsequent progress of the Greek American community will prove to be by far the most significant event in the long history of the Greek people since 1821.

This book consists mostly, but not entirely, of material contained in three special issues published and distributed mainly by the National Herald.

Like those three special issues, this book, too, became possible due to the generous support of the "Stavros S. Niarchos" Foundation, which is widely recognized for its unprecedented commitment and service to the ideals of Hellenism – a dedication befitting a great foundation.

In particular, I owe a great debt of gratitude to Andreas K. Drakopoulos, a member of the Board of Directors of the Foundation, for his support and encouragement. Mr. Drakopoulos is an asset not only to the Foundation but also to Hellenism worldwide.

A lot of people worked on this project. I want to recognize especially Eleni Papadakis-Demetriades, Managing Editor of special issues at The National Herald, for her efficiency and hard work in preparing the three special issues that preceded the book.

Harilaos Daskalothanassis, the Managing Editor of the National Herald, for his thoughtfulness and advise.

My sister and Advertising Manager of the newspaper Veta Diamataris-Papadopoulos for her invaluable contribution in every and all projects undertaken by the newspaper.

Myron Romanos, the Athenian publisher, who put his heart and mind into this book.

Last but not least, I want to thank my wife Litsa for her unyielding and boundless love and support not only throughout this project but in everything that I do. I could not possibly imagine what life would be like without her.

Antonis H. Diamataris, Publisher

GREECE IN THE AMERICAN IMAGINATION

By Steve Frangos

Without question the three periods of Greek history most familiar to the average American are the Classical Age, the 1821 War of Independence, and the Great Migration of Greeks to the New World from the1870s to the 1920s. But it must be admitted that the average American, at this moment in history, really doesn't know all that much about Greek culture and society. The most that can be claimed is that nearly every American one speaks to, once they learn you are Greek, always say they know some individual Greek or Greek family. In most instances, that Greek or small group of Greeks has so impressed this American that he or she smiles as they tell you what a fine person or family those Greeks back home really are! The symbolic importance of this nearly universal feeling among average Americans, at this point in time, cannot be over-emphasized.

Unfortunately it is also a feature of the contemporary Greek American experience that whatever the average American does know about Greece, ancient, medieval or modern, has, more often than not, come directly from this association with these Greeks of his or her acquaintance.

It was not always this way. There was a time when a sound education in America used to mean a close familiarity with the Classics. It was this exposure to the past that ultimately led to the renewed interest in the living Greeks. For between 1821 and 1829, the average American, became caught up in that era's "Grecian Fever," as support for the Greek Revolution was then called. In that time of turmoil, whether because of nationwide relief work, or because of the much-publicized departure of notable Americans to fight with the embattled Greeks, or even due to the arrival of some forty Greek orphans and refugees to American shores, at least three generations of Americans came to know of the Grecian Cause for Freedom.

The War of Independence did more than free the Greeks from the Ottoman yoke. It came as a bolt of lighting crashing down onto the quietude of American readings and understandings of Classical Greece. The cultural consequences of the Greek Revolution on the American imagination have yet to be fully assessed. Clearly this volume of essays hopes, in its sweep of topics and time periods, to bridge something of that gap in histories, cultures and understandings of the past we collectively share.

While it is true that cultural historians have always known that Greece holds a unique place in the American mind, only a few detailed studies have documented the dynamic nature of this ongoing process. Over the centuries Americans have created their own ideas of what Greek culture and history mean to them as a people. These indigenous American notions of what it means to be Greek see regular expression in an amazingly diverse range of ideas, actions, and physical structures. American intellectuals readily identify Greek influences our own political system, architecture, theatre (in all the various senses of dramatic themes, performance styles and the physical structure in which one witnesses a play), popular culture and other realms of everyday life. These American notions of things Greek are not restricted simply to the Classical World but also to the very birth of the Greek nation-state. As a consequence, Greeks arriving to American shores, unlike other ethnic groups, have and must continue to address these decidedly non-Greek expressions and cultural forms. An extraordinary two-way exchange has developed.

Yet we must quickly stress that the fundamental feature of this exchange is that it has not always been fully reciprocal. These duelling viewpoints see expression regularly as in the most recent case of the so-called Macedonian Question, which was but the latest and perhaps, most unfortunate example of this enduring divide. Earlier exchanges during the two world wars, the Greek civil war and the dictatorship of 1967-74 could also be cited as times when the attention of America was once again directed towards its ever changing relationship with Greece.

It is interesting to note that regardless of the circumstances Greeks always put a premium on education. If Americans--as the argument goes--only knew the actual history and the on-ground reality of the Greek position, then they would see our side of the argument. The fallacy in this argument is that Americans, ultimately, have the same cultural and political interests that Greeks do. Which history has proven, time and again, they most certainly do not.

So how do we re-engage the Americans around us into this exchange of ideas? As it has so often in the past, the publisher and writers of the Ethnikos Keryx, have stepped forward to offer a sweeping presentation of Greek culture and history from Classical Times to our own present existence in America. This volume is composed mostly of material from three special issue supplements published by The National Herald. The first, Ancient Greece and its Contributions to Civilization which, was a survey of the Age of Pericles and its lasting inheritance to the West. The next drew together in words and pictures not just the facts of various moments of The Greek Revolution of 1821 but the significance of conflict in global terms. The last special supplement, The Greek Epic in America: The Early Immigrants reported on the establishment and ongoing concerns of a variety of Greek communities across the United States.

Just like this present volume, all these special editions were made possible though the generous support of the Stavros S. Niarchos Foundation.

For those interested in the history of the Greek press in North America this compiled volume is in no way innovative in format but in fact is something of a tradition for the Ethnikos Keryx. Started in 1915, the Ethnikos Keryx, by no later than 1925, had issued at least four octavo size volumes that offered the best of the articles from the pages of the newspaper. In the last of these volumes, "Apo tin zoin kai drasin tou apantahou Ellinismou" (From The Life and Activities of the Hellenic World: the advancing Greek people in Hellas, Egypt, Europe and America; letters, arts, sciences, industry, commerce, the accomplishments of the Greeks in America, New York: National Herald, Volume 11 No. 4, 1925) the newspaper's editorial staff, under the indomitable editorship of Demetrios Callimachos, gathered 416 pages of essays, documents, and illustrations to make their case for the, then, current state of modern Greek culture.

Since the 1920s, the Ethnikos Keryx has regularly issued volumes, in English as well as Greek, whose sole purpose is to reach out to the American public at large. Undoubtedly the reason for producing this long series of publications is because it has worked to amazing effect on the local and personal level across the nation. It can be well argued that the general American public holds the Greek community in such high esteem because, since the 1870s, the Greeks have never been afraid to seek out their neighbors directly. Over candy counters, at the back table of diners, under the tents at the local Hellenic festivals, on the street corners and byways of small towns and great cities Greeks meet their American neighbors head-on in good fellowship and open discussion. While it is true that no systematic studies now exist on how the average American perceives the Greeks, still it is clearly the case, that aside from some understandable criticism of the Greek zeal for boosterism, in the end, it is the daily example of Greeks in the American mainstream that has carried the day.

If all this is true, then why do I say the average American, at this point in time, really does not know much Greek history at all? Greeks err because they assume Americans have the same overall regard for history as they do. Americans most certainly do not. As even the most cursory examination of the public record will show after high school few Americans ever read history again. With that being said need I point out that topics related to the historical connections between American and Greek societies must – except in those times of crisis –remain largely forgotten?

This does not mean that Americans do not actively seek out history books. Writers such as Howard Zinn and his A Peoples History of the United States (New York: Harper Perennial, 1980), James W.

Loewens Lies My Teacher Told Me: Everything Your American History Textbook Got Wrong (New York: Simon & Schuster, 1995), or Ray Raphaels A Peoples History of the American Revolution (New York: New Press, 2000) became national best sellers. What we need to do is provide the average American reader with examples, and many exist, of when Greek society and its considerable history and American daily life have resulted in that unique combination that only exists here on American shores.

It is the mandate of the Greek American press to not simply bring critical issues of the day to the attention of our community but in fact carry these issues and arguments outward to the wider American community. And sometimes we have to repeat ourselves. Where the Greek-American community has failed is in not educating American society at large – in a sustained fashion – to the wider historical, cultural and social realities of being Greek in the Modern World. Greek-Americans are quite literally at the height of their wealth, education and social status in this country. While no reliable demographic figures exist it is safe to claim that more Greeks hold university positions than at any other time in our history in this country. But still there is no university that offers a full sweep of courses from Classical Greece, through the Hellenic period, Roman to Byzantine times, the Turkokratia, the Modern era and the Greek-American and wider Diaspora experiences. Why?

Part of the reason surely lies in the fact that by and large we are now complaisant consumers. The hypnotic lull of our better-than-middle-class status has caused us to disengage from the collective interests of the Greek community. Certainly we go to church, visit our relatives on holidays, spend time with our Greek friends. But is that all we have become? Moving from one coffee clutch or dinner dance to another?

So, in the final analysis, how can we be sure the average American will know of this volume? First, we can be certain that Greek-Americans around the country will do as they have always done: engage their neighbors in open discussion. This volume, as those that have gone before, will be pressed into the hands of friends and Philhellenes around the country and so disseminated in this time-honored fashion. Secondly, and certainly not so well know even to the average Greek-American, let alone their native born American counterparts, the ethnic press is not over looked by the federal government. As Greek-American research into the files of the Office of Strategic Services during World War II documents, our press, along with many others in the United States, is closely read.

The ideals first generated by the society and culture of Greece as well as those created by the American imagination about Greece are still very much in a state of tense interaction. The final influence of this collection of essays and articles will only be judged by how well, or how poorly, they change the hearts and minds of those who ultimately read the following pages.

εκρόπιου

Ancient Greece and its contribution to civilization

Chronology of Ancient Greece

(all dates B.C.)

circa 1600	Island of Thera explodes, causing a tidal wave that inundates coastal settlements in the Aegean, and cripples the civilization of Crete.
circa 1300	Theseus establishes the city of Athens.
circa 1250	Troy falls to Agamemnon and his Greek army after a ten-year siege.
circa 1200	Dorians set up states in the southern Peloponnese, Crete, and Rhodes.
circa 800	Lycurgus institutes reforms in Sparta, Homer's epics, the Iliad and the Odyssey are compiled.
776	First Olympiad.
730	Sparta conquers Messene.
594	Solon gives Athens a constitutional democracy, and wipes out all debts.
560-27	Tyranny of Pisistratus and his sons in Athens. Eventually this tyranny is ended by Cleisthenes.
490	Battle of Marathon. Athens defeats an invading army of Persians.
480	King Xerxes of Persia invades Greece, and overcomes the heroic resistance of a vastly outnumbered Spartan force at the Battle of Thermopylae. Athens is destroyed. At the Battle of Salamis, the Persian navy is defeated by the Greeks, so Xerxes decides to go home and leave the rest of the war to his lieutenant, Mardonius.
479	Battle of Plataea. The allied Greeks defeat the Persians under Mardonius, and the Persian invasion is over.
477	Athens assumes leadership of Delian League, which is an alliance of the city-states and islands of Greece against the Persians.
464	Earthquake in Sparta; helots revolt.
461	Kimon is ostracized from Athens.
454	Treasury of the Delian League is transferred to Athens.
443	Thucydides ostracized, leaving Pericles in total control of Athens. The Athenians use the treasury of the Delian League to build the Parthenon and other monuments to their greatness.
431	Peloponnesian War begins. Athens and Sparta struggle for hegemony in the Greek World.
429	Pericles dies of the plague in Athens.
421	Peace of Nicias begins, temporarily ending the Peloponnesian War.

415	Peace of Nicias ends, and Athens invades Sicily.
413	Nicias and the Athenian army surrender in Sicily.
405	Dionysius I becomes tyrant of Syracuse.
404	Peloponnesian War ends when Athens surrenders to Sparta. Tyranny of The Thirty begins in Athens.
401-399	Greek mercenaries, including Xenophon, fight their way through the Persian Empire to the Black Sea (March of the Ten Thousand).
399	The philosopher Socrates is sentenced to death in Athens for his unpopular attitude.
396	Agesilaus invades the Persian Empire.
395	War breaks out among the Greeks, Agesilaus returns to Sparta.
387	King of Persia arranges peace among the Greeks.
382	Sparta seizes Thebes by surprise attack.
379	Pelopidas, et al., liberate Thebes.
371	Spartan power is crushed by Thebes at the Battle of Leuctra.
369	City of Megalopolis is founded by Thebans to shut in Sparta.
367	Dionysius I dies; Dionysius II becomes tyrant of Syracuse.
362	Battle of Mantinea; Epaminondas dies.
357	Dion liberates Syracuse.
344	Timoleon goes to liberate Sicily.
341	Timoleon defeats the Carthaginians and liberates Sicily.
338	Battle of Chaeronea. King Philip of Macedonia defeats the combined armies of the Greeks and becomes the ruler of Greece.
336	Alexander the Great becomes king of Macedonia after Philip is assassinated.
335	Alexander obliterates Thebes.
333	Battle of Issus. Alexander defeats the army of Persia and takes control of the western half of the Persian empire.
331	Battle of Gaugamela (Arbela). Alexander defeats King Darius of Persia and takes control of the whole Persian Empire as well as all of Greece. Greek language and civilization spread from Egypt to India.
326	Battle of the Hydaspes. Alexander's invasion of India ends.
323	Alexander enters Babylon and dies.
318	The Athenians sentence Phocion to death.
301	Alexander's successors fight at the Battle of Ipsus.
281-75	Pyrrhus fights in Italy and Sicily.
245	Agis attempts reform in Sparta.
241	Agis is executed by the rich of Sparta.
222	Royal lines of Sparta end.
197	Rome defeats Macedonia.
146	Rome obliterates Corinth, Greece becomes conquered Roman territory.

The Athenian Constitution

By Aristotle

Following is an exposition on the Athenian system of government by the philosopher Aristotle:

SECTION I

Part 3

...Now the ancient constitution, as it existed before the time of Draco, was organized as follows. The magistrates were elected according to qualifications of birth and wealth. At first they governed for life, but subsequently for terms of ten years. The first magistrates, both in date and in importance, were the King, the Polemarch, and the Archon. The earliest of these offices was that of the King, which existed from ancestral antiquity. To this was added, secondly, the office of Polemarch, on account of some of the kings proving feeble in war; for it was on this account that Ion was invited to accept the post on an occasion of pressing need. The last of the three offices was that of the Archon, which most authorities state to have come into existence in the time of Medon. Others assign it to the time of Acastus, and adduce as proof the fact that the nine Archons swear to execute their oaths 'as in the days of Acastus, which seems to suggest that it was in his time that the descendants of Codrus retired from the kingship in return for the prerogatives conferred upon the Archon. Whichever way it may be, the difference in date is small; but that it was the last of these magistracies to be created is shown by the fact that the Archon has no part in the ancestral sacrifices, as the King and the Polemarch have, but exclusively in those of later origin. So it is only at a comparatively late date that the office of Archon has become of great importance, through the dignity conferred by these later additions. The Thesmothetae were many years afterwards, when these offices had already become annual, with the object that they might publicly record all legal decisions, and act as guardians of them with a view to determining the issues between litigants. Accordingly their office, alone of those which have been mentioned, was never of more than annual duration.

A sketch of the completed Acropolis and its environs.

Part 4

Such, then, is the relative chronological precedence of these offices. At that time the nine Archons did not all live together. The King occupied the building now known as the Boculium, near the Prytaneum, as may be seen from the fact that even to the present day the marriage of the King's wife to Dionysus takes place there. The Archon lived in the Prytaneum, the Polemarch in the Epilyceum. The latter building was formerly called the Polemarcheum, but after Epilycus, during his term of office as Polemarch, had rebuilt it and fitted it up, it was called the Epilyceum.

The Thesmothetae occupied the Thesmotheteum. In the time of Solon, however, they all came together into the Thesmotheteum. They had power to decide cases finally on their own authority, not, as now, merely to hold a preliminary hearing. Such then was the arrangement of the magistracies. The Council of Areopagus had as its constitutionally assigned duty the protection of the laws; but in point of fact it administered the greater and most important part of the government of the state, and inflicted personal punishments and fines summarily upon all who misbehaved themselves. This was the natural consequence of the facts that the Archons were elected under qualifications of birth and wealth, and that the Areopagus was composed of those who had served as Archons; for which latter reason the membership of the Areopagus is the only office which has continued to be a life-magistracy to the present day.

Such was, in outline, the first constitution, but not very long after the events above recorded, in the archonship of Aristaichmus, Draco enacted his ordinances. Now his constitution had the following form. The franchise was given to all who could furnish themselves with a military equipment. The nine Archons and the Treasurers were elected by this body from persons possessing an unencumbered property of not less than ten minas, the less important officials from those who could furnish themselves with a military equipment, and the generals [*Strategi*] and commanders of the cavalry [*Hipparchi*] from those who could show an unencumbered property of not less than a hundred minas, and had children born in lawful wedlock over ten years of age. These officers were required to hold to bail the Prytanes, the Strategi, and the Hipparchi of the preceding year until their accounts had been audited, taking four securities of the same class as that to which the Strategi and the Hipparchi belonged. There was also to be a Council, consisting of four hundred and one members, elected by lot from among those who possessed the franchise. Both for this and for the other magistracies the lot was cast among those who were over thirty years of age; and no one might hold office twice until every one else had had his turn, after which they were to cast the lot afresh. If any member of the Council failed to attend when there was a sitting of the Council or of the Assembly, he paid a fine, to the amount of three drachmas if he was a Pentacosiomedimnus, two if he was a Knight, and One if he was a Zeugites. The Council of Areopagus was guardian of the laws, and kept watch over the magistrates to see that they executed their offices in accordance with the laws. Any person who felt himself wronged might lay an information before the Council of Areopagus, on declaring what law was broken by the wrong done to him. But, as has been said before, loans were secured upon the persons of the debtors, and the land was in the hands of a few.

Part 6

...As soon as he was at the head of affairs, Solon liberated the people once and for all, by prohibiting all loans on the security of the debtor's person: and in addition he made laws by which he cancelled all debts, public and private. This measure is commonly called the Seisachtheia [= removal of burdens], since thereby the people had their loads removed from them. In connection with it some persons try to traduce the character of Solon. It so happened that, when he was about to enact the Seisachtheia, he communicated his intention to some members of the upper class, whereupon, as the partisans of the popular party say, his friends stole a march on him; while those who wish to attack his character maintain that he too had a share in the fraud himself. For these persons borrowed money and bought up a large amount of land, and so when, a short time afterwards, all debts were cancelled, they became wealthy; and this, they say, was the origin of the families which were afterwards looked on as having been wealthy from primeval times. However, the story of the popular party is by far the most probable. A man who was so moderate and public-spirited in all his other actions, that when it was within his power to put his fellow-citizens beneath his feet and establish himself as tyrant, he preferred instead to incur the hostility of both parties by placing his honor and the general welfare above his personal aggrandizement, is not likely to have consented to defile his hands by such a petty and palpable fraud. That he had this absolute power is, in the first place, indicated by the desperate condition the country; moreover, he mentions it himself repeatedly in his poems, and it is universally admitted. We are therefore bound to consider this accusation to be false.

Part 7

Next Solon drew up a constitution and enacted new laws; and the ordinances of Draco ceased to be used, with the exception of those relating to murder. The laws were inscribed on the wooden stands, and set up in the King's Porch, and all swore to obey them; and the nine Archons made oath upon the stone, declaring that they would dedicate a golden statue if they should transgress any of them. This is the origin of the oath to that effect which they take to the present day. Solon ratified his laws for a hundred years; and the following was the fashion in which he organized the constitution. He divided the population according to property into four classes, just as it had been divided before, namely, Pentacosiomedimni, Knights, Zeugitae, and Thetes.

The various magistracies, namely, the nine Archons, the Treasurers, the Commissioners for Public Contracts (Poletae), the Eleven, and Clerks (Colacretae), he assigned to the Pentacosiomedimni, the Knights, and the Zeugitae, giving offices to each class in proportion to the value of their rateable property. To who ranked among the Thetes he gave nothing but a place in the Assembly and in the juries. A man had to rank as a Pentacosiomedimnus if he made, from his own land, five hundred measures, whether liquid or solid. Those ranked as Knights who made three hundred measures, or, as some say, those who were able to maintain a horse. In support of the latter definition they adduce the name of the class, which may be supposed to be derived from this fact, and also some votive offerings of early times; for in the Acropolis there is a votive offering, a statue of Diphilus, bearing this inscription:

The son of Diphilus, Athenion height,
Raised from the Thetes and become a knight,
Did to the gods this sculptured charger bring,

For his promotion a thank-offering. And a horse stands in evidence beside the man, implying that this was what was meant by belonging to the rank of Knight. At the same time it seems reasonable to suppose that this class, like the Pentacosiomedimni, was defined by the possession of an income of a certain number of measures. Those ranked as Zeugitae who made two hundred measures, liquid or solid; and the rest ranked as Thetes, and were not eligible for any office. Hence it is that even at the present day, when a candidate for any office is asked to what class he belongs, no one would think of saying that he belonged to the Thetes.

The amphora of Dipylon (8th century B.C., National Archaeological Museum of Athens)

Part 8

The elections to the various offices Solon enacted should be by lot, out of candidates selected by each of the tribes. Each tribe selected ten candidates for the nine archonships, and among these the lot was cast. Hence it is still the custom for each tribe to choose ten candidates by lot, and then the lot is again cast among these. A proof that Solon regulated the elections to office according to the property classes may be found in the law still in force with regard to the Treasurers, which enacts that they shall be chosen from the *Pentacosiomedimni*. Such was Solon's legislation with respect to the nine Archons; whereas in early times the Council of Areopagus summoned suitable persons according to its own judgement and appointed them for the year to the several offices.

There were four tribes, as before, and four tribe-kings. Each tribe was divided into three *Trittyes* [=Thirds], with twelve Naucraries in each; and the Naucraries had officers of their own, called *Naucrari*, whose duty it was to superintend the current receipts and expenditure. Hence, among the laws of Solon now obsolete, it is repeatedly written that the Naucrari are to receive and to spend out of the Naucraric fund. Solon also appointed a Council of four hundred, a hundred from each tribe; but he assigned to the Council of the Areopagus the duty of superintending the laws, acting as before as the guardian of the constitution in general. It kept watch over the affairs of the state in most of the more important matters, and corrected offenders, with full powers to inflict either fines or personal punishment. The money received in fines it brought up into the Acropolis, without assigning the reason for the mulct. It also tried those who conspired for the overthrow of the state, Solon having enacted a process of impeachment to deal with such offenders.

Further, since he saw the state often engaged in internal disputes, while many of the citizens from sheer indifference accepted whatever might turn up, he made a law with express reference to such persons, enacting that any one who, in a time civil factions, did not take up arms with either party, should lose his rights as a citizen and cease to have any part in the state.

Part 9

...There are three points in the constitution of Solon which appear to be its most democratic features: first and most important, the prohibition of loans on the security of the debtor's person; secondly, the right of every person who so willed to claim redress on behalf of any one to whom wrong was being done; thirdly, the institution of the appeal to the jury courts; and it is to this last, they say, that the masses have owed their strength most of all, since, when the democracy is master of the voting-power, it is master of the constitution. Moreover, since the laws were not drawn up in simple and explicit terms (but like the one concerning inheritances and wards of state), disputes inevitably occurred, and the courts had to decide in every matter, whether public or private. Some persons in fact believe that Solon deliberately made the laws indefinite, in order that the final decision might be in the hands of the people. This, however, is not probable, and the reason no doubt was that it is impossible to attain ideal perfection when framing a law in general terms; for we must judge of his intentions, not from the actual results in the present day, but from the general tenor of the rest of his legislation.

Part 11

...When he had completed his organization of the constitution in the manner that has been described, he found himself beset by people coming to him and harassing him concerning his laws, criticizing here and questioning there, till, as he wished neither to alter what he had decided on nor yet to be an object of ill will to every one by remaining in Athens, he set off on a journey to Egypt, with the combined objects of trade and travel, giving out that he should not return for ten years. He considered that there was no call for him to expound the laws personally, but that every one should obey them just as they were written. Moreover, his position at this time was unpleasant. Many members of the upper class had been estranged from him on account of his abolition of debts, and both parties were alienated through their disappointment at the condition of things which he had created. The mass of the people had expected him to make a complete redistribution of all property, and the upper class hoped he would restore everything to its former position, or, at any rate, make but a small change. Solon, however, had resisted both classes. He might have made himself a despot by attaching himself to whichever party he chose, but he preferred, though at the cost of incurring the enmity of both, to be the saviour of his country and the ideal lawgiver.

A bust of the Athenian admiral Themistocles

Part 12

The truth of this view of Solon's policy is established alike by common consent, and by the mention he has himself made of the matter in his poems.

Thus:

I gave to the mass of the people such rank as befitted their need,
I took not away their honor, and I granted naught to their greed;
While those who were rich in power, who in wealth were glorious and great,
I bethought me that naught should befall them unworthy their splendor and state;
So I stood with my shield outstretched, and both were sale in its sight,
And I would not that either should triumph, when the triumph was not with right.

Again he declares how the mass of the people ought to be treated:

But thus will the people best the voice of their leaders obey, When neither too slack is the rein, nor violence holdeth the sway; For indulgence breedeth a child, the presumption that spurns control,

When riches too great are poured upon men of unbalanced soul.

And again elsewhere he speaks about the persons who wished to redistribute the land:

So they came in search of plunder, and their cravings knew no bound, Every one among them deeming endless wealth would here be found. And that I with glowing smoothness hid a cruel mind within. Fondly then and vainly dreamt they; now they raise an angry din, And they glare askance in anger, and the light within their eyes Burns with hostile flames upon me. Yet therein no justice lies. All I promised, fully wrought I with the gods at hand to cheer, Naught beyond in folly ventured. Never to my soul was dear With a tyrant's force to govern, nor to see the good and base Side by side in equal portion share the rich home of our race.

Once more he speaks of the abolition of debts and of those who before were in servitude, but were released owing to the Seisachtheia:

Of all the aims for which I summoned forth
The people, was there one I compassed not?
Thou, when slow time brings justice in its train,
O mighty mother of the Olympian gods,
Dark Earth, thou best can't witness, from whose breast
I swept the pillars broadcast planted there,
And made thee free, who hadst been slave of yore.
And many a man whom fraud or law had sold
For from his god-built land, an outcast slave,
I brought again to Athens; yea, and some,
Exiles from home through debt's oppressive load,
Speaking no more the dear Athenian tongue,
But wandering far and wide, I brought again;
And those that here in vilest slavery
Crouched 'neath a master's frown, I set them free.
Thus might and right were yoked in harmony,
Since by the force of law I won my ends
And kept my promise. Equal laws I gave
To evil and to good, with even hand
Drawing straight justice for the lot of each.
But had another held the goad as
One in whose heart was guile and greediness,
He had not kept the people back from strife.
For had I granted, now what pleased the one,
Then what their foes devised in counterpoise,
Of many a man this state had been bereft.
Therefore I showed my might on every side,
Turning at bay like wolf among the hounds.
And again he reviles both parties for their grumblings in the times that followed:
Nay, if one must lay blame where blame is due,
Wer't not for me, the people ne'er had set
Their eyes upon these blessings e'en in dreams:-
While greater men, the men of wealthier life,
Should praise me and should court me as their friend. For had any other man, he says, received this exalted post,
He had not kept the people hack, nor ceased
Till he had robbed the richness of the milk.
But I stood forth a landmark in the midst,
And barred the foes from battle.

Part 13

Such then, were Solon's reasons for his departure from the country. After his retirement the city was still torn by divisions. For four years, indeed, they lived in peace; but in the fifth year after Solon's government they were unable to elect an Archon on account of their dissensions, and again four years later they elected no Archon for the same reason. Subsequently, after a similar period had elapsed, Damasias was elected Archon; and he governed for two years and two months, until he was forcibly expelled from his office. After this, it was agreed, as a compromise, to elect ten Archons, five from the Eupatridae, three from the Agroeci, and two from the Demiurgi, and they ruled for the year following Damasias. It is clear from this that the Archon was at the time the magistrate who possessed the greatest power, since it is always in connection with this office that conflicts are seen to arise. But altogether they were in a continual state of internal disorder. Some found the cause and justification of their discontent in the abolition of debts, because thereby they had been reduced to poverty; others were dissatisfied with the political constitution, because it had undergone a revolutionary change; while with others the motive was found in personal rivalries among themselves. The parties at this time were three in number. First there was the party of the Shore, led by Megacles the son of Alcmeon, which was considered to aim at a moderate form of government; then there were the men of the Plain, who desired an oligarchy and were led by Lycurgus; and thirdly there were the men of the Highlands, at the head of whom was Pisistratus, who was looked on as an extreme democrat. This latter party was reinforced by those who had been deprived of the debts due to them, from motives of poverty, and by those who were not of pure descent, from motives of personal apprehension. A proof of this is seen in the fact that after the tyranny was overthrown a revision was made of the citizen-roll, on the ground that many persons were partaking in the franchise without having a right to it. The names given to the respective parties were derived from the districts in which they held their lands.

Part 14

Pisistratus had the reputation of being an extreme democrat, and he also had distinguished himself greatly in the war with Megara. Taking advantage of this, he wounded himself, and by representing that his injuries had been inflicted on him by his political rivals, he persuaded the people, through a motion proposed by Aristion, to grant him a bodyguard. After he had got these 'club-bearers', as they were called, he made an attack with them on the people and seized the Acropolis. This happened in the archonship of Comeas, thirty-one years after the legislation of Solon. It is related that, when Pisistratus asked for his bodyguard, Solon opposed the request, and declared that in so doing he proved himself wiser than half the people and braver than the rest,-wiser than those who did not see that Pisistratus designed to make himself tyrant, and braver than those who saw it and kept silence. But when all his words availed nothing he carried forth his armor and set it up in front of his house, saying that he had helped his country so far as lay in his power (he was already a very old man), and that he called on all others to do the same. Solon's exhortations, however, proved fruitless, and Pisistratus assumed the sovereignty. His administration was more like a constitutional government than the rule of a tyrant; but before his power was firmly established, the adherents of Megacles and Lycurgus made a coalition and drove him out. This took place in the archonship of Hegesias, five years after the first establishment of his rule. Eleven years later Megacles, being in difficulties in a party struggle, again opened-negotiations with Pisistratus, proposing that the latter should marry his daughter; and on these terms he brought him back to Athens, by a very primitive and simple-minded device. He first spread abroad a rumor that Athena was bringing back Pisistratus, and then, having found a woman of great stature and beauty, named Phye (according to Herodotus, of the deme of Paeania, but as others say a Thracian flower-seller of the deme of Collytus), he dressed her in a garb resembling that of the goddess and brought her into the city with Pisistratus. The latter drove in on a chariot with the woman beside him, and the inhabitants of the city, struck with awe, received him with adoration.

Part 17

...Thus did Pisistratus grow old in the possession of power, and he died a natural death in the archonship of Philoneos, three and thirty years from the time at which he first established himself as tyrant, during nineteen of which he was in possession of power; the rest he spent in exile. It is evident from this that the story is mere gossip which states that Pisistratus was the youthful favorite of Solon and commanded in the war against Megara for the recovery of Salamis. It will not harmonize with their respective ages, as any one may see who will reckon up the years of the life of each of them, and the dates at which they died. After the death of Pisistratus his sons took up the government, and conducted it on the same system. He had two sons by his first and legitimate wife, Hippias and Hipparchus, and two by his Argive consort, Iophon and Hegesistratus, who was surnamed Thessalus. For Pisistratus took a wife from Argos, Timonassa, the daughter of a man of Argos, named Gorgilus; she had previously been the wife of Archinus of Ambracia, one of the descendants of Cypselus. This was the origin of his friendship with the Argives, on account of which a thousand of them were brought over by Hegesistratus and fought on his side in the battle at Pallene. Some authorities say that this marriage took place after his first expulsion from Athens, others while he was in possession of the government.

Part 19

...After this event the tyranny became much harsher. In consequence of his vengeance for his brother, and of the execution and banishment of a large number of persons, Hippias became a distrusted and an embittered man. About three years after the death of Hipparchus, finding his position in the city insecure, he set about fortifying Munichia, with the intention of establishing himself there. While he was still engaged on this work, however, he was expelled by Cleomenes, king of Lacedaemon, in consequence of the Spartans being continually incited by oracles to overthrow the tyranny. These oracles were obtained in the following way. The Athenian exiles, headed by the Alcmeonidae, could not by their own power effect their return, but failed continually in their attempts. Among their other failures, they fortified a post in Attica, Lipsydrium, above Mt. Parnes, and were there joined by some partisans from the city; but they were besieged by the tyrants and reduced to surrender. After this disaster the following became a popular drinking song:

Ah! Lipsydrium, faithless friend!
Lo, what heroes to death didst send,
Nobly born and great in deed!
Well did they prove themselves at need
Of noble sires a noble seed.

Having failed, then, in very other method, they took the contract for rebuilding the temple at Delphi, thereby obtaining ample funds, which they employed to secure the help of the Lacedaemonians. All this time the Pythia kept continually enjoining on the Lacedaemonians who came to consult the oracle, that they must free Athens; till finally she succeeded in impelling the Spartans to that step, although the house of Pisistratus was connected with them by ties of hospitality. The resolution of the Lacedaemonians was, however, at least equally due to the friendship which had been formed between the house of Pisistratus and Argos. Accordingly they first sent Anchimolus by sea at the head of an army; but he was defeated and killed, through the arrival of Cineas of Thessaly to support the sons of Pisistratus with a force of a thousand horsemen. Then, being roused to anger by this disaster, they sent their king, Cleomenes, by land at the head of a larger force; and he, after defeating the Thessalian cavalry when they attempted to intercept his march into Attica, shut up Hippias within what was known as the Pelargic wall and blockaded him there with the assistance of the Athenians. While he was sitting down before the place, it so happened that the sons of the Pisistratidae were captured in an attempt to slip out; upon which the tyrants capitulated on condition of the safety of their children, and surrendered the Acropolis to the Athenians, five days being first allowed them to remove their effects. This took place in the archonship of Harpactides, after they had held the tyranny for about seventeen years since their father's death, or in all, including the period of their father's rule, for nine-and-forty years.

A Mycenean krater, depicting a procession of warriors found on the acropolis of Mycenae (12 th century B.C., Athens Archaeological Museum)

Part 21

...The people, had good reason to place confidence in Cleisthenes. Accordingly, now that he was the popular leader, three years after the expulsion of the tyrants, in the archonship of Isagoras, his first step was to distribute the whole population into ten tribes in place of the existing four, with the object of intermixing the members of the different tribes, and so securing that more persons might have a share in the franchise. From this arose the saying "Do not look at the tribes," addressed to those who wished to scrutinize the lists of the old families. Next he made the Council to consist of five hundred members instead of four hundred, each tribe now contributing fifty, whereas formerly each had sent a hundred. The reason why he did not organize the people into twelve tribes was that he might not have to use the existing division into trittyes; for the four tribes had twelve trittyes, so that he would not have achieved his object of redistributing the population in fresh combinations. Further, he divided the country into thirty groups of demes, ten from the districts about the city, ten from the coast, and ten from the interior. These he called trittyes; and he assigned three of them by lot to each tribe, in such a way that each should have one portion in each of these three localities. All who lived in any given deme he declared fellow-demesmen, to the end that the new citizens might not be exposed by the habitual use of family names, but that men might be officially described by the names of their demes; and accordingly it is by the names of their demes that the Athenians speak of one another. He also instituted Demarchs, who had the same duties as the previously existing Naucrari, – the demes being made to take the place of the naucraries. He gave names to the demes, some from the localities to which they belonged, some from the persons who founded them, since some of the areas no longer corresponded to localities possessing names. On the other hand he allowed every one to retain his family and clan and religious rites according to ancestral custom. The names given to the tribes were the ten which the Pythia appointed out of the hundred selected national heroes.

Part 22

By these reforms the constitution became much more democratic than that of Solon. The laws of Solon had been obliterated by disuse during the period of the tyranny, while Cleisthenes substituted new ones with the object of securing the goodwill of the masses. Among these was the law concerning ostracism. Four year after the establishment of this system, in the archonship of Hermocreon, they first imposed upon the Council of Five Hundred the oath which they take to the present day. Next they began to elect the generals by tribes, one from each tribe, while the Polemarch was the commander of the whole army. Then, eleven years later, in the archonship of Phaenippus they won the battle of Marathon; and two years after this victory, when the people had now gained self-confidence, they for the first time made use of the law of ostracism.

Part 24

...After this, seeing the state growing in confidence and much wealth accumulated, he advised the people to lay hold of the leadership of the league, and to quit the country districts and settle in the city. He pointed out to them that all would be able to gain a living there, some by service in the army, others in the garrisons, others by taking a part in public affairs; and in this way they would secure the leadership. This advice was taken; and when the people had assumed the supreme control they proceeded to treat their allies in a more imperious fashion, with the exception of the Chians, Lesbians, and Samians. These they maintained to protect their empire, leaving their constitutions untouched, and

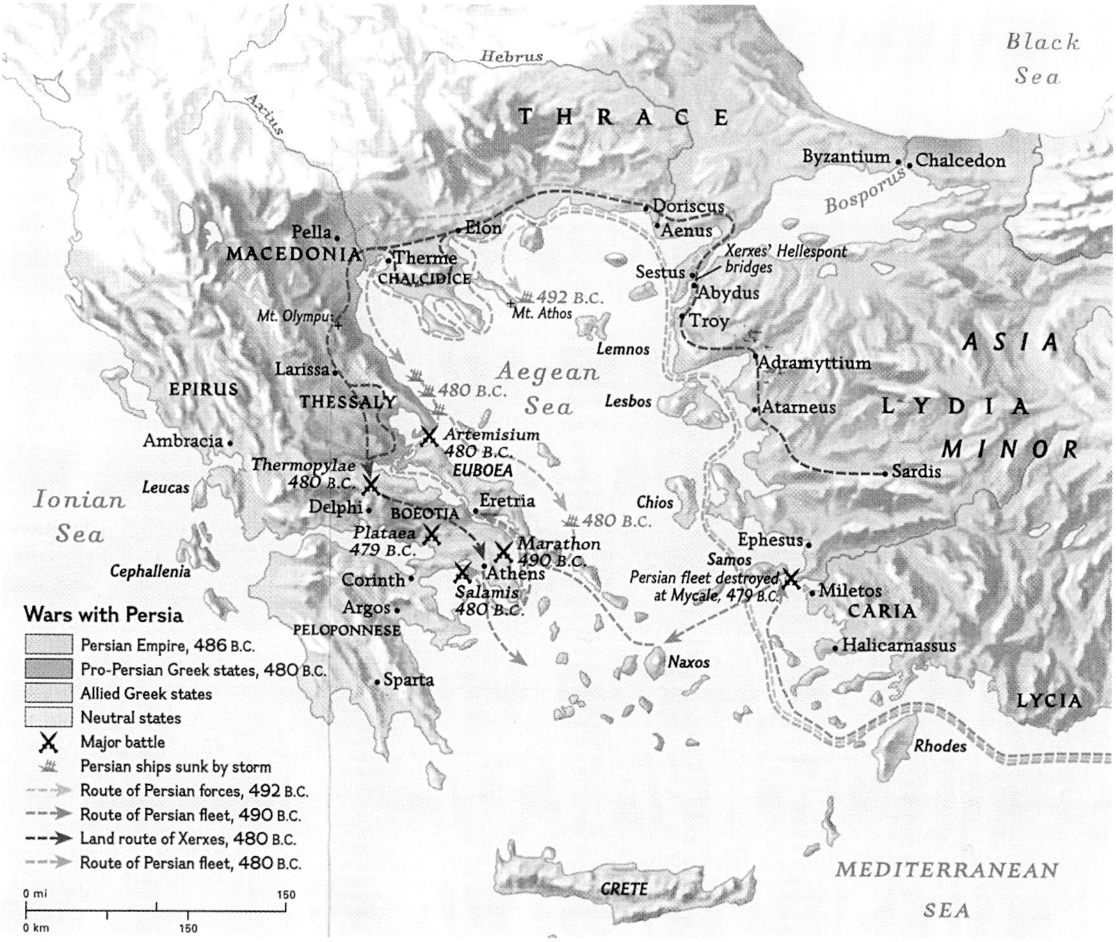

Map of the Persian invasions of Greece

allowing them to retain whatever dominion they then possessed. They also secured an ample maintenance for the mass of the population in the way which Aristides had pointed out to them. Out of the proceeds of the tributes and the taxes and the contributions of the allies more than twenty thousand persons were maintained. There were 6,000 jurymen, 1,600 bowmen, 1,200 Knights, 500 members of the Council, 500 guards of the dockyards, besides fifty guards in the Acropolis. There were some 700 magistrates at home, and some 700 abroad. Further, when they subsequently went to war, there were in addition 2,500 heavy-armed troops, twenty guard-ships, and other ships which collected the tributes, with crews amounting to 2,000 men, selected by lot; and besides these there were the persons maintained at the Prytaneum, and orphans, and gaolers, since all these were supported by the state.

Part 26

...After this revolution the administration of the state became more and more lax, in consequence of the eager rivalry of candidates for popular favor. During this period the moderate party, as it happened, had no real chief, their leader being Cimon son of Miltiades, who was a comparatively young man, and had been late in entering public life; and at the same time the general populace suffered great losses by war. The soldiers for active service were selected at that time from the roll of citizens, and as the generals were men of no military experience, who owed their position solely to their family standing, it continually happened that some two or three thousand of the troops perished on an expedition; and in this way the best men alike of the lower and the upper classes were exhausted. Consequently in most matters of administration less heed was paid to the laws than had formerly been the case. No alteration, however, was made in the method of election of the nine Archons, except that five years after the death of Ephialtes it was decided that the candidates to be submitted to the lot for that office might be selected from the Zeugitae as well as from the higher classes. The first Archon from that class was Mnesitheides. Up to this time all the Archons had been taken from the Pentacosiomedimni and Knights, while the Zeugitae were confined to the ordinary magistracies, save where an evasion of the law was overlooked. Four years later, in the archonship of Lysicrates, thirty "local justices," as they as they were called, were re-established; and two years afterwards, in the archonship of Antidotus, consequence of the great increase in the number of citizens, it was resolved, on the motion of Pericles, that no one should admitted to the franchise who was not of citizen birth by both parents.

Part 27

After this Pericles came forward as popular leader, having first distinguished himself while still a young man by prosecuting Cimon on the audit of his official accounts as general. Under his auspices the constitution became still more democratic. He took away some of the privileges of the Areopagus, and, above all, he turned the policy of the state in the direction of sea power, which caused the masses to acquire confidence in themselves and consequently to take the conduct of affairs more and more into their own hands. Moreover, forty-eight years after the battle of Salamis, in the archonship of Pythodorus, the Peloponnesian war broke out, during which the populace was shut up in the city and became accustomed to gain its livelihood by military service, and so, partly voluntarily and partly involuntarily, determined to assume the administration of the state itself. Pericles was also the first to institute pay for service in the law-courts, as a bid for popular favor to counterbalance the wealth of Cimon. The latter, having private possessions on a regal scale, not only performed the regular public services magnificently, but also maintained a large number of his fellow-demesmen. Any member of the deme of Laciadae could go every day to Cimon's house and there receive a reasonable provision; while his estate was guarded by no fences, so that any one who liked might help himself to the fruit from it. Pericles' private property was quite unequal to this magnificence and accordingly he took the advice of Damonides of Oia (who was commonly supposed to be the person who prompted Pericles in most of his measures, and was therefore subsequently ostracized), which was that, as he was beaten in the matter of private possessions, he should make gifts to the people from their own property; and accordingly he instituted pay for the members of the juries. Some critics accuse him of thereby causing a deterioration in the character of the juries, since it was always the common people who put themselves forward for selection as jurors, rather than the men of better position. Moreover, bribery came into existence after this, the first person to introduce it being

Anytus, after his command at Pylos. He was prosecuted by certain individuals on account of his loss of Pylos, but escaped by bribing the jury.

Part 28

So long, however, as Pericles was leader of the people, things went tolerably well with the state; but when he was dead there was a great change for the worse. Then for the first time did the people choose a leader who was of no reputation among men of good standing, whereas up to this time such men had always been found as leaders of the democracy. The first leader of the people, in the very beginning of things, was Solon, and the second was Pisistratus, both of them men of birth and position. After the overthrow of the tyrants there was Cleisthenes, a member of the house of the Alcmeonidae; and he had no rival opposed to him after the expulsion of the party of Isagoras. After this Xanthippus was the leader of the people, and Miltiades of the upper class. Then came Themistocles and Aristides, and after them Ephialtes as leader of the people, and Cimon son of Miltiades of the wealthier class. Pericles followed as leader of the people, and Thucydides, who was connected by marriage with Cimon, of the opposition. After the death of Pericles, Nicias, who subsequently fell in Sicily, appeared as leader of the aristocracy, and Cleon son of Cleaenetus of the people. The latter seems, more than any one else, to have been the cause of the corruption of the democracy by his wild undertakings; and he was the first to use unseemly shouting and coarse abuse on the Bema, and to harangue the people with his cloak girt up short about him, whereas all his predecessors had spoken decently and in order. These were succeeded by Theramenes son of Hagnon as leader of the one party, and the lyre-maker Cleophon of the people. It was Cleophon who first granted the two obol donation for the theatrical performances, and for some time it continued to be given; but then Callicrates of Paeania ousted him by promising to add a third obol to the sum. Both of these persons were subsequently condemned to death; for the people, even if they are deceived for a time, in the end generally come to detest those who have beguiled them into any unworthy action. After Cleophon the popular leadership was occupied successively by the men who chose to talk the biggest and pander the most to the tastes of the majority, with their eyes fixed only on the interests of the moment. The best statesmen at Athens, after those of early times, seem to have been Nicias, Thucydides, and Theramenes. As to Nicias and Thucydides, nearly every one agrees that they were not merely men of birth and character, but also statesmen, and that they ruled the state with paternal care. On the merits of Theramenes opinion is divided, because it so happened that in his time public affairs were in a very stormy state. But those who give their opinion deliberately find him, not, as his critics falsely assert, overthrowing every kind of constitution, but supporting every kind so long as it did not transgress laws; thus showing that he was able, as every good citizen should be, to live under any form of constitution, while he refused to countenance illegality and was its constant enemy.

Part 29

So long as the fortune of the war continued even, the Athenians preserved the democracy; but after the disaster in Sicily, when the Lacedaemonians had gained the upper hand through their alliance with the king of Persia, they were compelled to abolish the democracy and establish in its place the constitution of the Four Hundred. The speech recommending this course before the vote was made by Melobius, and the motion was proposed by Pythodorus of Anaphlystus; but the real argument which persuaded the majority was the belief that the king of Persia was more likely to form an alliance with them if the constitution were on an oligarchical basis. The motion of Pythodorus was to the following effect. The popular Assembly was to elect twenty persons, over forty years of age, who, in conjunction with the existing ten members of the Committee of Public Safety, after taking an oath that they would frame such measures as they thought best for the state, should then prepare proposals for the public. safety. In addition, any other person might make proposals, so that of all the schemes before them the people might choose the best. Cleitophon concurred with the motion of Pythodorus, but moved that the committee should also investigate the ancient laws enacted by Cleisthenes when he created the democracy, in order that they might have these too before them and so be in a position to decide wisely; his suggestion being that the constitution of Cleisthenes was not really democratic, but closely akin to that of Solon. When the committee was elected, their first proposal was that the Prytanes should be compelled to put to the vote any motion that was offered on behalf of the public safety. Next they abolished all indictments for illegal proposals, all impeachments and pubic prosecutions, in order that every Athenian should be free to give his counsel on the situation, if he chose; and they decreed that if any person imposed a fine on any other for his acts in this respect, or prosecuted him or summoned him before the courts, he should, on an information being laid against him, be summarily arrested and brought before the generals, who should deliver him to the Eleven to be put to death. After these preliminary measures, they drew up the constitution in the following manner. The revenues of the state were not to be spent on any purpose except the war. All magistrates should serve without remuneration for the period of the war, except the nine Archons and the Prytanes for the time being, who should each receive three obols a day. The whole of the rest of the administration was to be committed, for the period of the war, to those Athenians who were most capable of serving the state personally or pecuniarily, to the number of not less than five thousand. This body was to have full powers, to the extent even of making treaties with whosoever they willed; and ten representatives, over forty years of age, were to be elected from each tribe to draw up the list of the Five Thousand, after taking an oath on a full and perfect sacrifice.

A "treasure" of 51 gold staters of kings Phillip II and Alexander III (Corinth excavations by the American School of Classical Studies, 1930)

Part 30

These were the recommendations of the committee; and when they had been ratified the Five Thousand elected from their own number a hundred commissioners to draw up the constitution. They, on their appointment, drew up and produced the following recommendations. There should be a Council, holding office for a year, consisting of men over thirty years of age, serving without pay. To this body should belong the Generals, the nine Archons, the Amphictyonic Registrar (*Hieromnemon*), the Taxiarchs, the Hipparchs, the Phylarch, the commanders of garrisons, the Treasurers of Athena and the other gods, ten in number, the Hellenic Treasurers (*Hellenotamiae*), the Treasurers of the other non-sacred moneys, to the number of twenty, the ten Commissioners of Sacrifices (*Hieropoei*), and the ten Superintendents of the mysteries. All these were to be appointed by the Council from a larger number of selected candidates, chosen from its members for the time being. The other offices were all to be filled by lot, and not from the members of the Council. The Hellenic Treasurers who actually administered the funds should not sit with the Council. As regards the future, four Councils were to be created, of men of the age already mentioned, and one of these was to be chosen by lot to take office at once, while the others were to receive it in turn, in the order decided by the lot. For this purpose the hundred commissioners were to distribute themselves and all the rest as equally as possible into four parts, and cast lots for precedence, and the selected body should hold office for a year. They were to administer that office as seemed to them best, both with reference to the safe custody and due expenditure of the finances, and generally with regard to all other matters to the best of their ability. If they desired to take a larger number of persons into counsel, each member might call in one assistant of his own choice, subject to the same qualification of age. The Council was to sit once every five days, unless there was any special need for more frequent sittings. The casting of the lot for the Council was to be held by the nine Archons; votes on divisions were to be counted by five tellers chosen by lot from the members of the Council, and of these one was to be selected by lot every day to act as president. These five persons were to cast lots for precedence between the parties wishing to appear before the Council, giving the first place to sacred matters, the second to heralds, the third to embassies, and the fourth to all other subjects; but matters concerning the war might be dealt with, on the motion of the generals, whenever there was need, without balloting. Any member of the Council who did not enter the Council-house at the time named should be fined a drachma for each day, unless he was away on leave of absence from the Council.

Part 31

Such was the constitution which they drew up for the time to come, but for the immediate present they devised the following scheme. There should be a Council of Four Hundred, as in the ancient constitution, forty from each tribe, chosen out of candidates of more than thirty years of age, selected by the members of the tribes. This Council should appoint the magistrates and draw up the form of oath which they were to take; and in all that concerned the laws, in the examination of official accounts, and in other matters generally, they might act according to their discretion. They must, however, observe the laws that might be enacted with reference to the constitution of the state, and had no power to alter them nor to pass others.

The generals should be provisionally elected from the whole body of the Five Thousand, but so soon as the Council came into existence it was to hold an examination of military equipment, and thereon elect ten persons, together with a secretary, and the persons thus elected should hold office during the coming year with full powers, and should have the right, whenever they desired it, of joining in the deliberations of the Council.

The Five thousand was also to elect a single Hipparch and ten Phylarchs; but for the future the Council was to elect these officers according to the regulations above laid down. No office, except those of member of the Council and of general, might be held more than once, either by the first occupants or by their successors. With reference to the future distribution of the Four Hundred into the four successive sections, the hundred commissioners must divide them whenever the time comes for the citizens to join in the Council along with the rest.

The Athenian law-giver and archon Solon

Part 34

...The people, however, in a very short time deprived the Five Thousand of their monopoly of the government. Then, six years after the overthrow of the Four Hundred, in the archonship of Callias of Angele, battle of Arginusae took place, of which the results were, first, that the ten generals who had gained the victory were all condemned by a single decision, owing to the people being led astray by persons who aroused their indignation; though, as a matter of fact, some of the generals had actually taken no part in the battle, and others were themselves picked up by other vessels. Secondly, when the Lacedaemonians proposed to evacuate Decelea and make peace on the basis of the existing position, although some of the Athenians supported this proposal, the majority refused to listen to them. In this they were led astray by Cleophon, who appeared in the Assembly drunk and wearing his breastplate, and prevented peace being made, declaring that he would never accept peace unless the Lacedaemonians abandoned their claims on all the cities allied with them. They mismanaged their opportunity then, and in a very short time they learned their mistake. The next year, in the archonship of Alexias, they suffered the disaster of Aegospotami, the consequence of which was that Lysander became master of the city, and set up the Thirty as its governors. He did so in the following manner. One of the terms of peace stipulated that the state should be governed according to "the ancient constitution." Accordingly the popular party tried to preserve the democracy, while that part of the upper class which belonged to the political clubs, together with the exiles who had returned since the peace, aimed at an oligarchy, and those who were not members of any club, though in other respects they considered themselves as good as any other citizens, were anxious to restore the ancient constitution. The latter class included Archinus, Anytus, Cleitophon, Phormisius, and many others, but their most prominent leader was Theramenes. Lysander, however, threw his influence on the side of the oligarchical party, and the popular Assembly was compelled by sheer intimidation to pass a vote establishing the oligarchy. The motion to this effect was proposed by Dracontides of Aphidna.

Part 35

In this way were the Thirty established in power, in the archonship of Pythodorus. As soon, however, as they were masters of the city, they ignored all the resolutions which had been passed relating to the organization of the constitution, but after appointing a Council of Five Hundred and the other magistrates out of a thousand selected candidates, and associating with themselves ten Archons in Piraeus, eleven superintendents of the prison, and three hundred "lash-bearers" as attendants, with the help of these they kept the city under their own control. At first, indeed, they behaved with moderation towards the citizens and pretended to administer the state according to the ancient constitution. In pursuance of this policy they took down from the hill of Areopagus the laws of Ephialtes and Archestratus relating to the Areopagite Council; they also repealed such of the statutes of Solon as were obscure, and abolished the supreme power of the law-courts. In this they claimed to be restoring the constitution and freeing it from obscurities; as, for instance, by making the testator free once for all to leave his property as he pleased, and abolishing the existing limitations in cases of insanity, old age, and undue female influence, in order that no opening might be left for professional accusers. In other matters also their conduct was similar. At first, then, they acted on these lines, and they destroyed the professional accusers and those mischievous and evil-minded persons who, to the great detriment of the democracy, had attached themselves to it in order to curry favor with it. With all of this the city was much pleased, and thought that the Thirty were doing it with the best of motives. But so soon as they had got a firmer hold on the city, they spared no class of citizens, but put to death any persons who were eminent for wealth or birth or character. Herein they aimed at removing all whom they had reason to fear, while they also wished to lay hands on their possessions; and in a short time they put to death not less than fifteen hundred persons.

Part 39

...This reconciliation was effected in the archonship of Eucleides, on the following terms. All persons who, having remained in the city during the troubles, were now anxious to leave it, were to be free to settle at Eleusis, retaining their civil rights and possessing full and independent powers of self-government, and with the free enjoyment of their own personal property. The temple at Eleusis should be common ground for both parties, and should be under the superintendence of the Ceryces, and the Eumolpidae, according to primitive custom. The settlers at Eleusis should not be allowed to enter Athens, nor the people of Athens to enter Eleusis, except at the season of the mysteries, when both parties should be free from these restrictions. The secessionists should pay their share to the fund for the common defense out of their revenues, just like all the other Athenians. If any of the seceding party wished to take a house in Eleusis, the people would help them to obtain the consent of the owner; but if they could not come to terms, they should appoint three valuers on either side, and the owner should receive whatever price they should appoint. Of the inhabitants of Eleusis, those whom the secessionists wished to remain should be allowed to do so. The list of those who desired to secede should be made up within ten days after the taking of the oaths in the case of persons already in the country, and their actual departure should take place within twenty days; persons at present out of the country should have the same terms allowed to them after their return. No one who settled at Eleusis should be capable of holding any office in Athens until he should again register himself on the roll as a resident in the city. Trials for homicide, including all cases in which one party had either killed or wounded another, should be conducted according to ancestral practice. There should be a general amnesty concerning past events towards all persons except the Thirty, the Ten, the Eleven, and the magistrates in Piraeus; and these too should be included if they should submit their accounts in the usual way. Such accounts should be given by the magistrates in Piraeus before a court of citizens rated in Piraeus, and by the magistrates in the city before a court of those rated in the city. On these terms those who wished to do so might secede. Each party was to repay separately the money which it had borrowed for the war.

Part 40

When the reconciliation had taken place on these terms, those who had fought on the side of the Thirty felt considerable apprehensions, and a large number intended to secede. But as they put off entering their names till the last moment, as people will do, Archinus, observing their numbers, and being anxious to retain them as citizens, cut off the remaining days during which the list should have remained open; and in this way many persons were compelled to remain, though they did so very unwillingly until they recovered confidence. This is one point in which Archinus appears to have acted in a most statesmanlike manner, and another was his subsequent prosecution of Thrasybulus on the charge of illegality, for a motion by which he proposed to confer the franchise on all who had taken part in the return from Piraeus, although some of them were notoriously slaves.

And yet a third such action was when one of the returned exiles began to violate the amnesty, whereupon Archinus haled him to the Council and persuaded them to execute him without trial, telling them that now they would have to show whether they wished to preserve the democracy and abide by the oaths they had taken; for if they let this man escape they would encourage others to imitate him, while if they executed him they would make an example for all to learn by. And this was exactly what happened; for after this man had been put to death no one ever again broke the amnesty. On the contrary, the Athenians seem, both in public and in private, to have behaved in the most unprecedentedly admirable and public-spirited way with reference to the preceding troubles. Not only did they blot out all memory of former offenses, but they even repaid to the Lacedaemonians out of the public purse the money which the Thirty had borrowed for the war, although the treaty required each party, the party of the city and the party of Piraeus, to pay its own debts separately. This they did because they thought it was a necessary first step in the direction of restoring harmony; but in other states, so far from the democratic parties making advances from their own possessions, they are rather in the habit of making a general redistribution of the land. A final reconciliation was made with the secessionists at Eleusis two years after the secession, in the archonship of Xenaenetus.

Part 41

...At the time of which we are speaking the people, having secured the control of the state, established the constitution which exists at the present day. Pythodorus was Archon at the time, but the democracy seems to have assumed the supreme power with perfect justice, since it had effected its own return by its own exertions. This was the eleventh change which had taken place in the constitution of Athens. The first modification of the primeval condition of things was when Ion and his companions brought the people together into a community, for then the people was first divided into the four tribes, and the tribe-kings were created. Next, and first after this, having now some semblance of a constitution, was that which took place in the reign of Theseus, consisting in a slight deviation from absolute monarchy.

After this came the constitution formed under Draco, when the first code of laws was drawn up. The third was that which followed the civil war, in the time of Solon; from this the democracy took its rise. The fourth was the tyranny of Pisistratus; the fifth the constitution of Cleisthenes, after the overthrow of the tyrants, of a more democratic character than that of Solon. The sixth was that which followed on the Persian wars, when the Council of Areopagus had the direction of the state. The seventh, succeeding this, was the constitution which Aristides sketched out, and which Ephialtes brought to completion by overthrowing the Areopagite Council; under this the nation, misled by the demagogues, made the most serious mistakes in the interest of its maritime empire. The eighth was the establishment of the Four Hundred, followed by the ninth, the restored democracy. The tenth was the tyranny of the Thirty and the Ten. The eleventh was that which followed the return from Phyle and Piraeus; and this has continued from that day to this, with continual accretions of power to the masses. The democracy has made itself master of everything and administers everything by its votes in the Assembly and by the law-courts, in which it holds the supreme power. Even the jurisdiction of the Council has passed into the hands of the people at large; and this appears to be a judicious change, since small bodies are more open to corruption, whether by actual money or influence, than large ones. At first they refused to allow payment for attendance at the Assembly; but the result was that people did not attend. Consequently, after the Prytanes had tried many devices in vain in order to induce the populace to come and ratify the votes, Agyrrhius, in the first instance, made a provision of one obol a day, which Heracleides of Clazomenae, nicknamed "the king," increased to two obols, and Agyrrhius again to three.

Part 42

The present state of the constitution is as follows. The franchise is open to all who are of citizen birth by both parents. They are enrolled among the demesmen at the age of eighteen. On the occasion of their enrollment the demesmen give their votes on oath, first whether the candidates appear to be of the age prescribed by the law (if not, they are dismissed back into the ranks of the boys), and secondly whether the candidate is free born and of such parentage as the laws require. Then if they decide that he is not a free man, he appeals to the law-courts, and the demesmen appoint five of their own number to act as accusers; if the court decides that he has no right to be enrolled, he is sold by the state as a slave, but if he wins his case he has a right to be enrolled among the demesmen without further question. After this the Council examines those who have been enrolled, and if it comes to the conclusion that any of them is less than eighteen years of age, it fines the demesmen who enrolled him. When the youths (*Ephebi*) have passed this examination, their fathers meet by their tribes, and appoint on oath three of their fellow tribesmen, over forty years of age, who, in their opinion, are the best and most suitable persons to have charge of the youths; and of these the Assembly elects one from each tribe as guardian, together with a director, chosen from the general body of Athenians, to control the while. Under the charge of these persons the youths first of all make the circuit of the temples; then they proceed to Piraeus, and some of them garrison Munichia and some the south shore. The Assembly also elects two trainers, with subordinate instructors, who teach them to fight in heavy armor, to use the bow and javelin, and to discharge a catapult. The guardians receive from the state a drachma apiece for their keep, and the youths four obols apiece. Each guardian receives the allowance for all the members of his tribe and buys the necessary provisions for the common stock (they mess together by tribes), and generally superintends everything. In this way they spend the first year. The next year, after giving a public display of their military evolutions, on the occasion when the Assembly meets in the theatre, they receive a shield and spear from the state; after which they patrol the country and spend their time in the forts. For these two years they are on garrison duty, and wear the military cloak, and during this time they are exempt from all taxes. They also can neither bring an action at law, nor have one brought against them, in order that they may have no excuse for requiring leave of absence; though exception is made in cases of actions concerning inheritances and wards of state, or of any sacrificial ceremony connected with the family. When the two years have elapsed they thereupon take their position among the other citizens. Such is the manner of the enrollment of the citizens and the training of the youths.

Translated by Sir Frederic G. Kenyon

A silver urn where the bones of the deceased were held; from the "Prince's grave" in Vergina. The golden diadem was found in the same grave (Vergina Museum)

Pericles's Funeral Oration

By Thucydides

Pericles delivered this speech at the funeral of soldiers who fell during the first year of the Peloponnesian War. It is related to us by Thucydides, and it includes the author's introduction describing the burial rites of the Athenians.

In the same winter the Athenians, following their annual custom, gave a public funeral for those who had been the first to die in the war. These funerals are held in the following way: two days before the ceremony the bones of the fallen are brought and put in a tent which has been erected, and people make whatever offerings they wish to their own dead. Then there is a funeral procession in which coffins of cypress wood are carried on wagons. There is one coffin for each tribe, which contains the bones of members of that tribe. One empty bier is decorated and carried in the procession: this is for the missing, whose bodies could not be recovered. Everyone who wishes to, both citizens and foreigners, can join in the procession, and the women who are related to the dead are there to make their laments at the tomb. The bones are laid in the public burial place, which is in the most beautiful quarter outside the city walls. Here the Athenians always bury those who have fallen in war. The only exception is those who died at Marathon, who, because their achievement was considered absolutely outstanding, were buried on the battlefield itself.

When the bones have been laid in the earth, a man chosen by the city for his intellectual gifts and for his general reputation makes an appropriate speech in praise of the dead, and after the speech all depart. This is the procedure at these burials, and all through the war, when the time came to do so, the Athenians followed this ancient custom. Now, at the burial of those who were the first to fall in the war Pericles, the son of Xanthippus, was chosen to make the speech. When the moment arrived, he came forward from the tomb and, standing on a high platform, so that he might be heard by as many people as possible in the crowd, he spoke as follows:

"Many of those who have spoken here in the past have praised the institution of this speech at the close of our ceremony. It seemed to them a mark of honor to our soldiers who have fallen in war that a speech should be made over them. I do not agree. These men have shown themselves valiant in action, and it would be enough, I think, for their glories to be proclaimed in action, as you have just seen it done at this funeral organized by the state. Our belief in the courage and manliness of so many should not be hazarded on the goodness or badness of one man's speech. Then it is not easy to speak with a proper sense of balance, when a man's listeners find it difficult to believe in the truth of what one is saying. The man who knows the facts and loves the dead may well think that an oration tells less than what he knows and what he would like to hear: others who do not know so much may feel envy for the dead, and think the orator over-praises them, when he speaks of exploits that are beyond their own capacities. Praise of other people is tolerable only up to a certain point, the point where one still believes that one could do oneself some of the things one is hearing about. Once you get beyond this point, you will find people becoming jealous and incredulous. However, the fact is that this institution was set up and approved by our forefathers, and it is my duty to follow the tradition and do my best to meet the wishes and the expectations of every one of you.

"I shall begin by speaking about our ancestors, since it is only right and proper on such an occasion to pay them the honor of recalling what they did. In this land of ours there have always been the same people living from generation to generation up till now, and they, by their courage and their virtues, have handed it on to us, a free country. They certainly deserve our praise. Even more so do our fathers deserve it. For to the inheritance they had received they added all the empire we have now, and it was not without blood and toil that they handed it down to us of the present generation. And then we ourselves, assembled here today, who are mostly in the prime of life, have, in most directions, added to the power of our empire and have organized our State in such a way that it is perfectly well able to look after itself both in peace and in war.

"I have no wish to make a long speech on subjects familiar to you all: so I shall say nothing about the warlike deeds by which we acquired our power or the battles in which we or our fathers gallantly resisted our enemies, Greek or foreign. What I want to do is, in the first place, to discuss the spirit in which we faced our trials and also our constitution and the way of life which has made us great. After that I shall speak in praise of the dead, believing that this kind of speech is not inappropriate to the present occasion, and that this whole assembly, of citizens and foreigners, may listen to it with advantage.

"Let me say that our system of government does not copy the institutions of our neighbors. It is more the case of our being a model to others, than of our imitating anyone else. Our constitution is called a democracy because power is in the hands not of a minority but of the whole people. When it is a question of settling private disputes, everyone is equal before the law; when it is a question of putting one person before another in positions of public responsibility, what counts is not membership of a particular class, but the actual ability which the man possesses. No one, so long as he has it in him to be of service to the state, is kept in political obscurity because of poverty. And, just as our political life is free and open, so is our day-to-day life in our relations with each other. We do not get into a state with our next-door neighbor if he enjoys himself in his own way, nor do we give him the kind of black looks which, though they do no real harm, still do hurt people's feelings. We are free and tolerant in our private lives; but in public affairs we keep to the law. This is because it commands our deep respect.

"We give our obedience to those whom we put in positions of authority, and we obey the laws themselves, especially those which are for the protection of the oppressed, and those unwritten laws which it is an acknowledged shame to break.

"And here is another point. When our work is over, we are in a position to enjoy all kinds of recreation for our spirits. There are various kinds of contests and sacrifices regularly throughout the year; in our own homes we find a beauty and a good taste which delight us every day and which drive away our cares. Then the greatness of our city brings it about that all the good things from all over the world flow in to us, so that to us it seems just as natural to enjoy foreign goods as our own local products.

"Then there is a great difference between us and our opponents, in our attitude towards military security. Here are some examples: Our city is open to the world, and we have no periodical deportations in order to prevent people observing or finding out secrets which might be of military advantage to the enemy. This is because we rely, not on secret weapons, but on our own real courage and loyalty. There is a difference, too, in our educational systems. The Spartans, from their earliest boyhood, are submitted to the most laborious training in courage; we pass our lives without all these restrictions, and yet are just as ready to face the same dangers as they are. Here is a proof of this: When the Spartans invade our land, they do not come by themselves, but bring all their allies with them; whereas we, when we launch an attack abroad, do the job by ourselves, and, though fighting on foreign soil, do not often fail to defeat opponents who are fighting for their own hearths and homes. As a matter of fact none of our enemies has ever yet been confronted with our total strength, because we have to divide our attention between our navy and the many missions on which our troops are sent on land. Yet, if our enemies engage a detachment of our forces and defeat it, they give themselves credit for having thrown back our entire army; or, if they lose, they claim that they were beaten by us in full strength. There are certain advantages, I think, in our way of meeting danger voluntarily, with an easy mind, instead of with a laborious training, with natural rather than with state-induced courage. We do not have to spend our time practicing to meet sufferings which are still in the future; and when they are actually upon us we show ourselves just as brave as these others who are always in strict training. This is one point in which, I think, our city deserves to be admired. There are also others:

"Our love of what is beautiful does not lead to extravagance; our love of the things of the mind does not make us soft. We regard wealth as something to be properly used, rather than as something to boast about. As for poverty, no one need be ashamed to admit it: the real shame is in not taking practical measures to escape from it. Here each individual is interested not only in his own affairs but in the affairs of the state as well: even those who are mostly occupied with their own business are extremely well-informed on general politics – this is a peculiarity of ours: we do not say that a man who takes no interest in politics is a man who minds his own business; we say that he has no business here at all. We Athenians, in our own persons, take our decisions on policy or submit them to proper discussions: for we do not think that there is an incompatibility between words and deeds; the worst thing is to rush into action before the consequences have been properly debated. And this is another point where we differ from other people. We are capable at the same time of taking risks and of estimating them beforehand. Others are brave out of ignorance; and, when they stop to think, they begin to fear. But the man who can most truly be accounted brave is he who best knows the meaning of what is sweet in life and of what is terrible, and then goes out undeterred to meet what is to come.

"Again, in questions of general good feeling there is a great contrast between us and most other people. We make friends by doing good to others, not by receiving good from them. This makes our friendship all the more reliable, since we want to keep alive the gratitude of those who are in our debt by showing continued goodwill to them: whereas the feelings of one who owes us something lack the same enthusiasm, since he knows that, when he repays our kindness, it will be more like paying back a debt than giving something spontaneously. We are unique in this. When we do kindnesses to others, we do not do them out of any calculations of profit or loss: we do them without afterthought, relying on

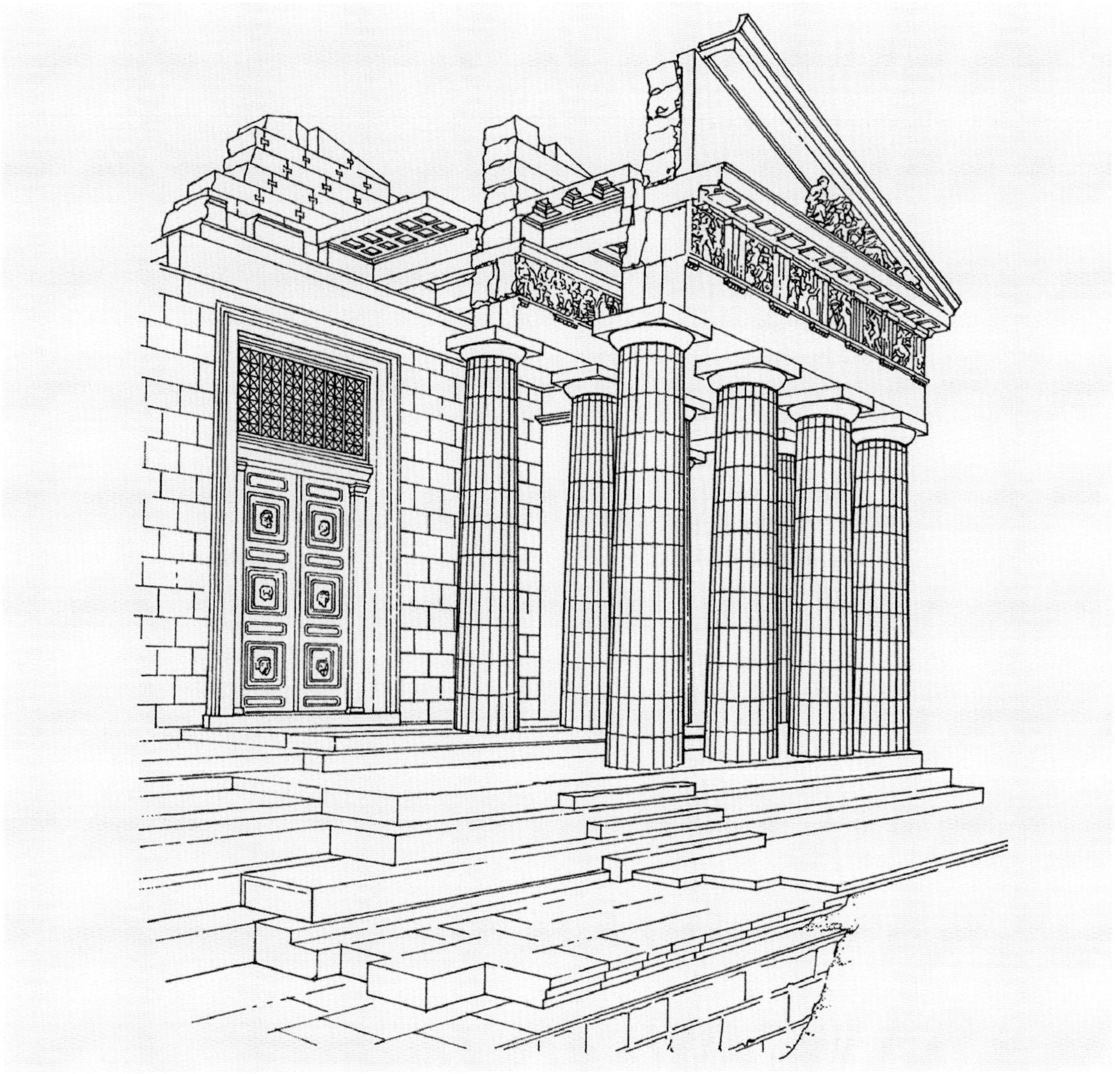

Structure of the temple of Parthenon on Acropolis rock

our free liberality. Taking everything together then, I declare that our city is an education to Greece, and I declare that in my opinion each single one of our citizens, in all the manifold aspects of life, is able to show himself the rightful lord and owner of his own person, and do this, moreover, with exceptional grace and exceptional versatility. And to show that this is no empty boasting for the present occasion, but real tangible fact, you have only to consider the power which our city possesses and which has been won by those very qualities which I have mentioned. Athens, alone of the states we know, comes to her testing time in a greatness that surpasses what was imagined of her. In her case, and in her case alone, no invading enemy is ashamed at being defeated, and no subject can complain of being governed by people unfit for their responsibilities. Mighty indeed are the marks and monuments of our empire which we have left. Future ages will wonder at us, as the present age wonders at us now. We do not need the praises of a Homer, or of anyone else whose words may delight us for the moment, but whose estimation of facts will fall short of what is really true. For our adventurous spirit has forced an entry into every sea and into every land; and everywhere we have left behind us everlasting memorials of good done to our friends or suffering inflicted on our enemies.

"This, then, is the kind of city for which these men, who could not bear the thought of losing her, nobly fought and nobly died. It is only natural that every one of us who survive them should be willing to undergo hardships in her service. And it was for this reason that I have spoken at such length about our city, because I wanted to make it clear that for us there is more at stake than there is for others who lack our advantages; also I wanted my words of praise for the dead to be set in the bright light of evidence. And now the most important of these words has been spoken. I have sung the praises of our city; but it was the courage and gallantry of these men, and of people like them, which made her splendid. Nor would you find it true in the case of many of the Greeks, as it is true of them, that no words can do more than justice to their deeds.

"To me it seems that the consummation which has overtaken these men shows us the meaning of manliness in its first revelation and in its final proof. Some of them, no doubt, had their faults; but what we ought to remember first is their gallant conduct against the enemy in defense of their native land. They have blotted out evil with good, and done more service to the commonwealth than they ever did harm in their private lives. No one of these men weakened because he wanted to go on enjoying his wealth: no one put off the awful day in the hope that he might live to escape his poverty and grow rich. More to be desired than such things, they chose to check the enemy's pride. This, to them, was a risk most glorious, and they accepted it, willing to strike down the enemy and relinquish everything else. As for success or failure, they left that in the doubtful hands of Hope, and when the reality of battle was before their faces, they put their trust in their own selves. In the fighting, they thought it more honorable to stand their ground and suffer death than to give in and save their lives. So they fled from the reproaches of men, abiding with life and limb the brunt of battle; and, in a small moment of time, the climax of their lives, a culmination of glory, not of fear, were swept away from us.

"So and such they were, these men – worthy of their city. We who remain behind may hope to be spared their fate, but must resolve to keep the same daring spirit against the foe. It is not simply a question of estimating the advantages in theory. I could tell you a long story (and you know it as well as I do) about what is to be gained by beating the enemy back. What I would prefer is that you should fix your eyes every day on the greatness of Athens as she really is, and should fall in love with her. When you realize her greatness, then reflect that what made her great was men with a spirit of adventure, men who knew their duty, men who were ashamed to fall below a certain standard. If they ever,failed in an enterprise, they made up their minds that at any rate the city should not find their courage lacking to her, and they gave to her the best contribution that they could. They gave her their lives, to her and to all of us, and for their own selves they won praises that never grow old, the most splendid of sepulchers – not the sepulcher in which their bodies are laid, but where their glory remains eternal in men's minds, always there on the right occasion to stir others to speech or to action. For famous men have the whole earth as their memorial: it is not only the inscriptions on their graves in their own country that mark them out; no, in foreign lands also, not in any visible form but in people's hearts, their memory abides and grows. It is for you to try to be like them. Make up your minds that happiness depends on being freehand freedom depends on being courageous. Let there be no relaxation in face of the perils of the war. The people who have most excuse for despising death are not the wretched and unfortunate, who have no hope of doing well for themselves, but those who run the risk of a complete reversal in their lives, and who would feel the difference most intensely, if things went wrong for them. Any intelligent man would find a humiliation caused by his own slackness more painful to bear than death, when death comes to him unperceived, in battle, and in the confidence of his patriotism.

"For these reasons I shall not commiserate with those parents of the dead, who are present here. Instead I shall try to comfort them. They are well aware that they have grown up in a world where there are many changes and chances. But this is good fortune – for men to end their lives with honor, as these have done, and for you honorably to lament them: their life was set to a measure where death and happiness went hand in hand. I know that it is difficult to convince you of this. When you see other people happy you will often be reminded of what used to make you happy too.

"One does not feel sad at not having some good thing which is outside one's experience: real grief is felt at the loss of something which one is used to. All the same, those of you who are of the right age must bear up and take comfort in the thought of having more children. In your own homes these new children will prevent you from brooding over those who are no more, and they will be a help to-the city, too, both in filling the empty places, and in assuring her security. For it is impossible for a man to put forward fair and honest views about our affairs if he has not, like everyone else, children whose lives may be at stake. As for those of you who are now too old to have children, I would ask you to count as gain the greater part of your life, in which you have been happy, and remember that what remains is not long, and let your hearts be lifted up at the thought of the fair fame of the dead. One's sense of honor, is the only thing that does not grow old, and the last pleasure, when one is worn out with age, is not, as the poet said, making money, but having the respect of one's fellow men.

"As for those of you here who are sons or brothers of the dead, I can see a hard struggle in front of you. Everyone always speaks well of the dead, and, even if you rise to the greatest heights of heroism, it will be a hard thing for you to get the reputation of having come near, let alone equalled, their standard. When one is alive, one is always liable to the jealousy of one's competitors, but when one is out of the way, the honor one receives is sincere and unchallenged.

"Perhaps I should say a word or two on the duties of women to those among you who are now widowed. I can say all I have to say in a short word of advice. Your great glory is not to be inferior to what God has made you, and the greatest glory of a woman is to be least talked about by men, whether they are praising you or criticizing you. I have now, as the law demanded, said what I had to say. For the time being our offerings, to the dead have been made, and for the future their children will be supported at the public expense by the city, until they come of age. This is the crown and prize which she offers, both to the dead and to their children, for the ordeals which they have faced. Where the rewards of valour are the greatest, there you will find also the best and bravest spirits among the people. And now, when you have mourned for your dear ones, you must depart.

A bust of Pericles, Roman copy of a lost original by Cresilas (London, British Museum)

The Republic

By Plato

Following is an excerpt from Plato's famous work The Republic *where the philosopher, through an imaginary discussion between Socrates and his disciples, arrives at what he regards as the perfect system of government:*

SECTION I

THUS, Glaucon, I said, after pursuing a lengthened inquiry we have, not without difficulty, discovered who are true philosophers and who are not.

– Yes, he replied; probably it was not easy to abridge the inquiry.

– Apparently not, I said. However that may be, I think, for my part, that the result would have been brought out still more clearly, if we had to speak of this only, without discussing the many points that still await our notice, if we wish to ascertain wherein the superiority of a righteous over an unrighteous life consists.

– Then what are we to do next?

– We have only to take the step next in order. Since those who are able to apprehend the eternal and immutable, are philosophers while those who are incapable of this and who wander in the region of change and multiformity, are not philosophers, which of the two, tell me, ought to be governors of a state?

– What must I reply, if I am to do justice to the question?

– Ask yourself which of the two are to be thought capable of guarding the laws and customs of states, and let these be appointed guardians.

– You are right.

– Can there be any question as to whether a blind man, or one with quick sight, is the right person to guard and keep any thing?

– There can be no question about it.

– Then do you think that there is a particle of difference between the condition of blind persons, and the state of those who are absolutely destitute of the knowledge of things as they really are, and who possess in their soul no distinct exemplar, and cannot, like painters, fix their eyes on perfect truth as a perpetual standard of reference, to be contemplated with the minutest care, before they proceed to deal with earthly canons about things beautiful and just and good, laying them down where they are required, and where they already exist watching over their preservation?

– No, indeed, there is not much difference.

– Shall we then appoint such persons to the office of guardians, in preference to those who not only have gained a knowledge of each thing in its reality, but in practical skill are not inferior to the former, and come behind them in no other department of excellence?

– Why, if these latter are not wanting in the other qualifications, it would be perfectly absurd to choose any others. For just the point in which they are superior may be said to be the most important of all...

– Well then, I continued, the causes of the prejudice against philosophy, and the injustice of this prejudice, have in my opinion been satisfactorily disposed of, unless you have anything to add.

– No, I have nothing more to say on this head: but which of the constitutions of our time is the one that you call suited to philosophy?

– There is not one that I can call so: nay, what I complain of is precisely this, that no state, as now constituted, is a worthy sphere for a philosophic nature.

– Hence that nature becomes warped and deteriorated. For just as the seed of a rare exotic when sown in a foreign soil, habitually becomes enfeebled and loses its essential character, and eventually passes into a common plant of the country; so this kind of character at the present day, failing to preserve its peculiar virtues, degenerates into tendencies that are not its own: but if it could only find the most perfect constitution, answering to itself as the most perfect of characters, it will then give proof that it is the true divine type; whereas all other kinds of character and of vocation are merely human. Now I make no doubt you will proceed to ask me what this constitution is.

– You are mistaken, he said; what I was going to ask was, whether you were thinking of this constitution, whose organization we have discussed, or of another.

– The same, I replied, in all points but one; and this one point was alluded to during the discussion, when we said that it would be necessary to have constantly present in the state some authority, that should view the constitution in the very light in which you, the legislator, viewed it, when you framed the laws.

– True, it was alluded to.

– But it was not sufficiently developed, because I was alarmed by your objections, which showed that the demonstration of it would be tedious and difficult: for it is by no means the easiest part of the discussion that is left.

– What is that part?

– To show in what way a state may handle philosophy without incurring utter destruction. For we know that all great things are hazardous, and, according to the proverb, beautiful things are indeed hard of attainment.

– Nevertheless, he said, let this point be cleared up, in order that the demonstration may be complete.

– The hindrance, if any, will arise, not from want of will, but from want of power. My zeal, at any rate, you shall see with your own eyes. For observe at once with what reckless zeal I proceed to assert, that a state ought to deal with the pursuit of philosophy on a plan the very reverse of that now in vogue.

– How so?

– At present, those who pursue philosophy at all are mere striplings just emerged from boyhood, who take it up in the intervals of housekeeping and business; and, after just dipping into the most abstruse part of the study, (by which I mean Dialectic), abandon the pursuit altogether, and these are the most advanced philosophers; and ever afterwards, if, on being invited, they consent to listen to others whose attention is devoted to it, they think it a great condescension, because they imagine that philosophy ought to be made a mere secondary occupation; and on the approach of old age, all but a very few are extinguished far more effectually than the sun of Heracleitus, inasmuch as they are not, like it, rekindled.

– And pray what is the right plan? he asked.

– Just the opposite. In youth and boyhood they ought to be put through a course of training in philosophy, suited to their years; and while their bodies are growing up to manhood, especial attention should be paid to them, as a serviceable acquisition in the cause of philosophy. At the approach of that period, during which the mind begins to attain its maturity, the mental exercises ought to be rendered more severe. Finally, when their bodily powers begin to fail, and they are released from public duties and military service, from that time forward they ought to lead a dedicated life, and consecrate themselves to this one pursuit, if they are to live happily on earth, and after death to crown the life they have led with a corresponding destiny in another world.

– Well, indeed, Socrates, I do not doubt your zeal. But I expect most of your hearers, beginning with Thrasymachus, to oppose you with still greater zeal, and express their unqualified dissent.

– Do not make a quarrel between me and Thrasymachus, when we have just become friends; – though I do not mean to say that we were enemies before. I shall leave nothing untried, until I have either won him over to my way of thinking, along with the rest, or have achieved something for their good in that future state, should they ever happen, in a second existence, to encounter similar discussions.

– Truly a trifling adjournment! he exclaimed.

– Rather speak of it as a nothing, compared with all time. However, it need not surprise us that most people disbelieve in my doctrines; for they have never yet seen our present theory realized. No, what is much more likely is, that they have met with proposals somewhat resembling ours, but forced expressly into appearing of a piece with one another, instead of falling spontaneously into agreement, as in the present case. They have never yet seen, in either one or more instances, a man moulded into the most perfect possible conformity and likeness to virtue, both in words and in works, reigning in a state as perfect as himself. Or do you think they have?

– No, indeed I do not.

– And further, my dear friend, they have not listened often enough to discussions of an elevated and liberal tone, confined to the strenuous investigation of truth by all possible means, simply for the sake of knowing it; and which therefore will, both in private disquisitions and in public trials, keep at a

A bust of Plato (Roman copy, 1st century A.D., Berlin Arcaeological Museum)

respectful distance from those subtleties and special pleadings, whose sole aim it is to prolong debate, and elicit applause.

– You are right again.

– It was for these reasons, and in anticipation of these results, that, notwithstanding my fears, I was constrained by the force of truth on a former occasion to assert, that no state, or constitution, or individual either, can ever become perfect, until these few philosophers, who are at present described as useless though not depraved, find themselves accidentally compelled, whether they like it or not, to accept the charge of a state, which in its turn finds itself compelled to be obedient to them; or until the present sovereigns and kings, or their sons, are divinely inspired with a genuine love of genuine philosophy. Now to assert the impossibility of both or either of these contingencies, I for my part pronounce irrational. If they are impossible, we may fairly be held up to derision as mere visionary theorists. Am I not right?

– You are.

– If, then, persons of first-rate philosophical attainments, either in the countless ages that are past have been, or in some foreign clime, far beyond the limits of our horizon, at the present moment are, or hereafter shall be, constrained by some fate to undertake the charge of a state, I am prepared to argue to the death in defence of this assertion, that the constitution described has existed, does exist, and will exist, wherever the Muse aforesaid has become mistress of a state. For its realization is no impossibility, nor are our speculations impracticable; though their difficulty is even by us acknowledged.

– I am of the same opinion, said he.

– But are you prepared to say, that the majority, on the contrary, entertain a different opinion?

– Perhaps so.

– My excellent friend, beware how you bring so heavy a charge against the multitude. No doubt they will change their minds, if you avoid controversy, and endeavour with all gentleness to remove their prejudice against the love of learning, by showing them whom you understand by philosophers, and defining, as we have just done, their nature and cultivation, that they may not suppose you to mean such characters as are uppermost in their own thoughts; or shall you venture to maintain that, even if they look at them from your point of view, they will entertain a different opinion from yours, and return another sort of answer? In other words, do you think that an unmalicious and gentle person can quarrel with one who is not quarrelsome, or feel malice towards one who is not malicious? I will anticipate you with the declaration that, in my opinion, a disposition so perverse may be found in some few cases, but not in the majority of mankind.

– I am myself entirely of your opinion, he replied.

– Then are you not also of my opinion on just this point, that the ill-will which the multitude bear to philosophy is to be traced to those who have forced their way in, like tipsy men, where they had no concern, and who abuse one another and delight in picking quarrels, and are always discoursing about persons, – conduct peculiarly unsuitable to philosophy?

– Very unsuitable.

– For surely, Adeimantus, he who has his thoughts truly set on the things that really exist, cannot even spare time to look down upon the occupations of men, and, by disputing with them, catch the infection of malice and hostility. On the contrary, he devotes all his time to the contemplation of certain well-adjusted and changeless objects; and beholding how they neither wrong nor are wronged by

each other, but are all obedient to order and in harmony with reason, he studies to imitate and resemble them as closely as he can. Or do you think it possible for a man to avoid imitating that with which he reverently associates?
– No, it is impossible.
– Hence the philosopher, by associating with what is godlike and orderly, becomes, as far as is permitted to man, orderly and godlike himself: though here, as everywhere, there is room for misconstruction.
– Indeed, you are right.
– So that, if he ever finds himself compelled to study how he may introduce into the habits of men, both in public and in private life, the things that draw his notice in that higher region, and to mould others as well as himself, do you think that he will prove an indifferent artist in the production of temperance and justice and all public virtue?
– Certainly not.
– Well, but if the multitude are made sensible that our description is a correct one, will they really be angry with the philosophers, and will they discredit our assertion, that a state can only attain to true happiness, if it be delineated by painters who copy the divine original?
– They will not be angry, if they are made sensible of the fact. But pray how do you mean them to sketch it?
– They will take for their canvas, I replied, a state and the moral nature of mankind, and begin by making a clean surface; which is by no means an easy task. However you are aware, that at the very outset they will differ from all other artists in this respect, that they will refuse to meddle with man or city, and hesitate to pencil laws, until they have either found a clear canvas, or made it clear by their own exertions.
– Yes, and they are right.
– In the next place, do you not suppose that they will sketch in outline the form of their constitution?
– Doubtless they will.
– Their next step, I fancy, will be to fill up this outline; and in doing this they will often turn their eyes to this side and to that, first to the ideal forms of justice, beauty, temperance, and the like, and then to the notions current among mankind; and thus, by mingling and combining the results of their studies, they will work in the true human complexion, guided by those realizations of it among men, which, if you remember, even Homer has described as godly

The Socratic philosopher Aristippos of Cyrrene (Rome, Palazzo Spada)

and godlike.
– You are right.
– And, I imagine, they will go on rubbing out here and repainting there, until they have done all in their power to make the moral character of men as pleasing as may be in the eye of heaven.
– Well, certainly their picture will be a very beautiful one.
– Do we then, I continued, make any progress in persuading those assailants, who by your account were marching stoutly to attack us, that such a painter of constitutions is to be found in the man whom we praised lately in their hearing, and who occasioned their displeasure, because we proposed to deliver up our cities into his hands? And do they feel rather less exasperation at being told the same thing now ?
– Yes, much less, if they are wise.
– I think so too; for pray, how will they be able to dispute our position? Can they deny that philosophers are enamoured of real existence and of truth?

– No, it would be indeed ridiculous to do that.
– Well; can they maintain that their character, such as we have described it, is not intimately allied to perfection ?
– No, they cannot.
– Once more; will they tell us that such a character, placed within reach of its appropriate studies, will fail to become as thoroughly good and philosophical as any character can become? Or will they give the preference to those whom we discarded ?
– Surely not.
– Will they then persist in their anger, when I assert that, till the class of philosophers be invested with the supreme authority in a state, such state and its citizens will find no deliverance from evil, and the fabulous constitution which we are describing will not be actually realized?
– Probably they will grow less angry.
– What do you say to our assuming, not merely that they are less angry, but that they are perfectly pacified and convinced, in order that we may shame them into acquiescence, if nothing else will do?
– By all means assume it.
– Well then, let us regard these persons as convinced so far. But, in the next place, will anybody maintain that kings and sovereigns cannot by any possibility beget sons gifted with a philosophic nature ?
– No one in the world will maintain that.
– And can any one assert, that, if born with such a nature, they must necessarily be corrupted? I grant that their preservation is a difficult matter; but I ask, is there any one who will maintain that in the whole course of time not one of all the number can ever be preserved from contamination?
– Who could maintain that ?
– Well but, I continued, one such person, with a submissive state, has it in his power to realize all that is now discredited.
– True, he has.
– For, surely, if a ruler establishes the laws and customs which we have detailed, it is, I presume, not impossible for the citizens to consent to carry them out.
– Certainly not.
– And, pray, would it be a miracle, beyond the verge of possibility, if what we think right were thought right by others also?
– For my part I think not.
– But I believe we have quite convinced ourselves, in the foregoing discussion, that our plan, if possible, is the best.
– Yes, quite.
– So that the conclusion, apparently, to which we are now brought with regard to our legislation, is, that what we propose is best, if it can be realized; and that to realize it is difficult, but certainly not impossible.
– True, that is our conclusion, he said.
– Well, then, this part of the subject having been laboriously completed, shall we proceed to discuss the questions still remaining, in what way, and by the help of what pursuits and studies, we shall secure the presence of a body of men capable of preserving the constitution unimpaired, and what must be the age at which these studies are severally undertaken?
– Let us do so by all means.
– I have gained nothing, I continued, by my old scheme of omitting the troublesome questions involved in the treatment of the women and children, and the appointment of the magistrates; which I was induced to leave out from knowing what odium the perfectly correct method would incur, and how difficult it would be to carry into effect. Notwithstanding all my precautions, the moment has now arrived when these points must be discussed. It is true the question of the women and children has been already settled, but the inquiry concerning the magistrates must be pursued quite afresh. In describing them, we said, if you recollect, that, in order to place their patriotism beyond the reach of suspicion, they must be tested by pleasure and by pain, and proved never to have deserted their principles in the midst of toil and danger and every vicissitude of fortune, on pain of forfeiting their position if their powers of endurance fail; and that whoever comes forth from the trial without a flaw, like gold tried in the fire, must be appointed to office, and receive, during life and after death, privileges and rewards. This was pretty nearly the drift of our language, which, from fear of awakening the question now pending, turned aside and hid its face.
– Your account is quite correct, he said; I remember perfectly.
– Yes, my friend, I shrank from making assertions which I have since hazarded; but now let me venture upon this declaration, that we must make the most perfect philosophers guardians.
– We hear you, he replied.
– Now consider what a small supply of these men you will, in all probability, find. For the various

members of that character, which we described as essential to philosophers, will seldom grow incorporate: in most cases that character grows disjointed.
– What do you mean?
– You are aware that persons endowed with a quick comprehension, a good memory, sagacity, acuteness, and their attendant qualities, do not readily grow up to be at the same time so noble and lofty-minded, as to consent to live a regular, calm, and steady life: on the contrary, such persons are drifted by their acuteness hither and thither, and all steadiness vanishes from their life.
– True.
– On the other hand, those steady and invariable characters, whose trustiness makes one anxious to employ them, and who in war are slow to take alarm, behave in the same way when pursuing their studies; that is to say, they are torpid and stupid, as if they were benumbed, and are constantly dozing and yawning, whenever they have to toil at anything of the kind.
– That is true.
– But we declare that, unless a person possesses a pretty fair amount of both qualifications, he must be debarred all access to the strictest education, to honour, and to government.
– We are right.
– Then do you not anticipate a scanty supply of such characters?
– Most assuredly I do.
– Hence we must not be content with testing their behaviour in the toils, dangers, and pleasures, which we mentioned before; but we must go on to try them in ways which we then omitted, exercising them in a variety of studies, and observing whether their character will be able to support the highest subjects, or whether it will flinch from the trial, like those who flinch under other circumstances.
– No doubt, it is proper to examine them in this way. But pray which do you mean by the highest subjects?
– I presume you remember, that, after separating the soul into three specific parts, we deduced the several natures of justice, temperance, fortitude, and wisdom ?
– Why, if I did not remember, I should deserve not to hear the rest of the discussion.
– Do you also remember the remark which preceded that deduction?
– Pray what was it?
– We remarked, I believe, that to obtain the best possible view of the question, we should have to take a different and a longer route, which would bring us to a thorough insight into the subject: still that it would be possible to subjoin a demonstration of the question, flowing from our previous conclusions. Thereupon you said that such a demonstration would satisfy you; and then followed those investigations, which, to my own mind, were deficient in exactness; but you can tell me whether they contented you.
– Well, to speak for myself, I thought them fair in point of measure; and certainly the rest of the party held the same opinion.
– But, my friend, no measure of such; a subject, which falls perceptibly short of the truth, can be said to be quite fair: for nothing imperfect is a measure of anything: though people sometimes fancy that enough has been done, and that there is no call for further investigation.
– Yes, he said, that is a very common habit, and arises from indolence.
– Yes, but it is a habit remarkably undesirable in the guardian of a state and its laws.
– So I should suppose.
– That being the case, my friend, such a person must go round by that longer route, and must labour as devotedly in his studies as in his bodily exercises. Otherwise, as we were saying just now, he will never reach the goal of that highest science, which is most peculiarly his own.
– What! he exclaimed, are not these the highest? Is there still something higher than justice and those other things which we have discussed?
– Even so, I replied: and here we must not contemplate a rude outline, as we have been doing: on the contrary, we must be satisfied with nothing short of the most complete elaboration. For would it not be ridiculous to exert oneself on other subjects of small value, taking all imaginable pains to bring them to the most exact and spotless perfection; and at the same time to ignore the claim of the highest subjects to a corresponding exactitude of the highest order ?
– The sentiment is a very just one. But do you suppose that any one would let you go without asking what that science is which you call the highest, and of what it treats?
– Certainly not, I replied; so put the question yourself. Assuredly you have heard the answer many a time; but at this moment either you have forgotten it, or else you intend to find me employment by rais-

Female dieties, perhaps Hestia and Dioni with Aphrodite from the eastern pediment of the Parthenon (London, Bristish Museum).

ing objections. I incline to the latter opinion; for you have often been told that the essential Form of the Good is the highest object of science, find that this essence, by blending with just things and all other created objects, renders them useful and advantageous. And at this moment you can scarcely doubt that I am going to assert this, and to assert, besides, that we are not sufficiently acquainted with this essence. And if so – if, I say, we know everything else perfectly, without knowing this, – you are aware that it will profit us nothing; just as it would be equally profitless to possess everything without possessing what is good. Or do you imagine it would be a gain to possess all possessible things, with the single exception of things good; or to apprehend every conceivable object, without apprehending what is good, – in other words, to be destitute of every good and beautiful conception?

– Not I, believe me.

– Moreover, you doubtless know besides, that the chief good is supposed by the multitude to be pleasure, – by the more enlightened, insight?

– Of course I know that.

– And you are aware, my friend, that the advocates of this latter opinion are unable to explain what they mean by insight, and are compelled at last to explain it as insight into that which is good.

– Yes, they are in a ludicrous difficulty.

– They certainly are: since they reproach us with ignorance of that which is good, and then speak to us the next moment as if we knew what it was. For they tell us that the chief good is insight into good, assuming that we understand their meaning, as soon as they have uttered the term 'good'.

– It is perfectly true.

– Again: are not those, whose definition identifies pleasure with good, just as much infected with error as the preceding? For they are forced to admit the existence of evil pleasures, are they not?

– Certainly they are.

– From which it follows, I should suppose, that they must admit the same thing to be both good and evil. Does it not?

– Certainly it does.

– Then is it not evident that this is a subject often and severely disputed?

– Doubtless it is.

– Once more: is it not evident, that though many persons would be ready to do and seem to do, or to possess and seem to possess, what seems just and beautiful, without really being so; yet, when you come to things good, no one is content to acquire what only seems such; on the contrary, everybody seeks the reality, and semblances are here, if nowhere else, treated with universal contempt?

– Yes, that is quite evident.

– This good, then, which every soul pursues, as the end of all its actions, divining its existence, but perplexed and unable to apprehend satisfactorily its nature, or to enjoy that steady confidence in relation to it, which it does enjoy in relation to other things, and therefore doomed to forfeit any advantage which it might have derived from those same things; – are we to maintain that, on a subject of such overwhelming importance, the blindness we have described is a desirable feature in the character of those best members of the state in whose hands everything is to be placed?

– Most certainly not.

– At any rate, if it be not known in what way just things and beautiful things come to be also good, I imagine that such things will not possess a very valuable guardian in the person of him who is ignorant on this point. And I surmise that none will know the just and the beautiful satisfactorily till he knows the good.

– You are right in your surmises.

– Then will not the arrangement of our constitution be perfect, provided it be overlooked by a guardian who is scientifically acquainted with these subjects?

– Unquestionably it will. But pray, Socrates, do you assert the chief good to be science or pleasure

or something different from either?
– Ho, ho, my friend! I saw long ago that you would certainly not put up with the opinions of other people on these subjects.
– Why, Socrates, it appears to me to be positively wrong in one who has devoted so much time to these questions, to be able to state the opinions of others, without being able to state his own.
– Well, I said, do you think it right to speak with an air of information on subjects on which one is not well-informed?
– Certainly not with an air of information; but I think it right to be willing to state one's opinion for what it is worth.
– Well, but have you not noticed that opinions divorced from science are all ill-favoured? At the best they are blind. Or do you conceive that those who, unaided by the pure reason, entertain a correct opinion, are at all superior to blind men, who manage to keep the straight path?
– Not at all superior, he replied.
– Then is it your desire to contemplate objects that are ill-favoured, blind, and crooked, when it is in your power to learn from other people about bright and beautiful things?
– I implore you, Socrates, cried Glaucon, not to hang back, as if you had come to the end. We shall be content even if you only discuss the subject of the chief good in the style in which you discussed justice, temperance, and the rest.
– Yes, my friend, and I likewise should be thoroughly content. But I distrust my own powers, and I feel afraid that my awkward zeal will subject me to ridicule. No, my good sirs: let us put aside, for the present at any rate, all inquiry into the real nature of the chief good. For, methinks, it is beyond the measure of this our enterprize to find the way to what is, after all, only my present opinion on the subject. But I am willing to talk to you about that which appears to be an off-shoot of the chief good, and bears the strongest resemblance to it, provided it is also agreeable to you; but if it is not, I will let it alone.
– Nay, tell us about it, he replied. You shall remain in our debt for an account of the parent.
– I wish that I could pay, and you receive, the parent sum, instead of having content ourselves with the interest springing from it. However, here I present you with the fruit and scion of the essential good. Only take care that I do not involuntarily impose upon you by handing in a forged account of this offspring.
– We will take all the care we can; only proceed.
– I will do so, as soon as we have come to a settlement together, and you have been reminded of certain statements made in a previous part of our conversation, and renewed before now again and again.
– Pray what statements ?
– In the course of the discussion we have distinctly maintained the existence of a multiplicity of things that are beautiful, and good, and so on.
– True, we have.
– And also the existence of an essential beauty, and an essential good, and so on; – reducing all those things which before we regarded as manifold, to a single form and a single entity in each case, and addressing each as an independent being.

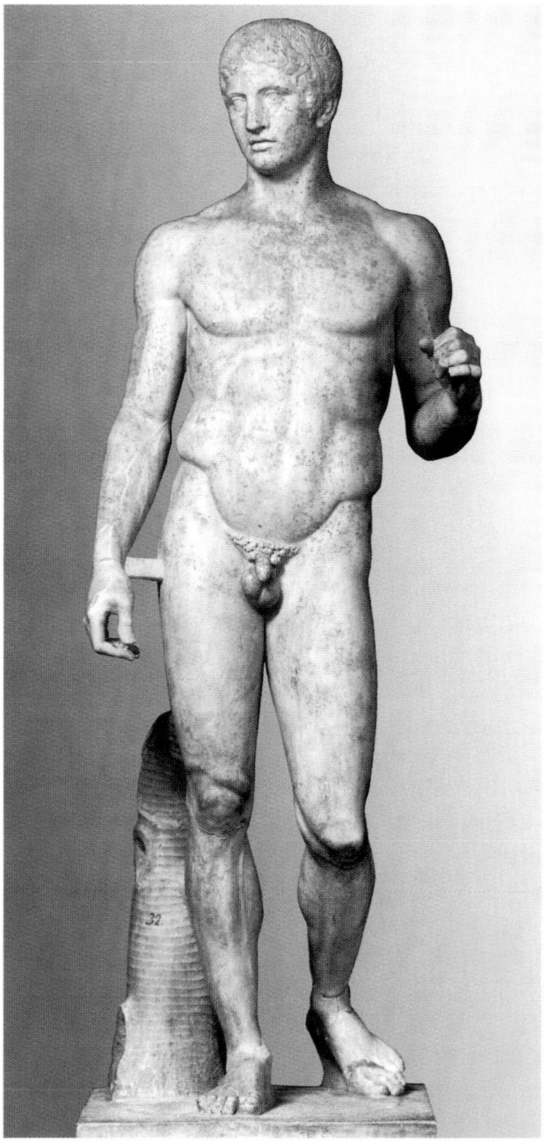

The Doryforos by Polykleitos (Roman copy, Naples, Museo Archeologico Nazionale)

– Just so.
– And we assert that the former address themselves to the eye, and not to the pure reason; whereas the forms address themselves to the reason, and not to the eye.
– Certainly.
– Now with what part of ourselves do we see visible objects?
– With the eyesight.
– In the same way we hear sounds with the hearing, and perceive everything sensible with the other senses, do we not?
– Certainly.
– Then have you noticed with what transcendent costliness the architect of the senses has wrought out the faculty of seeing and being seen?
– Not exactly, he replied.
– Well then, look at it in this light. Is there any other kind of thing, which the ear and the voice require, to enable the one to hear, and the other to be heard, in the absence of which third thing the one will not hear, and the other will not be heard ?
– No, there is not.
– And I believe that very few, if any, of the other senses require any such third thing. Can you mention one that does?
– No, I cannot.
– But do you not perceive that, in the case of vision and visible objects, there is a demand for something additional?
– How so?
– Why, granting that vision is seated in the eye, and that the owner of it is attempting to use it, and that colour is resident in the objects, still, unless there be present a third kind of thing, devoted to this especial purpose, you are aware that the eyesight will see nothing, and the colours will be invisible.
– Pray what is the third thing to which you refer.
– You are right.
– Hence it appears, that of all the pairs aforesaid, the sense of sight, and the faculty of being seen, are coupled by the noblest link, whose nature is anything but insignificant, unless light is an ignoble thing.
– No, indeed; it is very far from being ignoble.
– To whom, then, of the gods in heaven can you refer as the author and dispenser of this blessing? And whose light is it that enables our sight to see so excellently well, and makes visible objects appear?
– There can be but one opinion on the subject, he replied: your question evidently alludes to the sun.
– Then the relation subsisting between the eyesight and this deity is of the following nature, is it not?
– Describe it.
– Neither the sight itself, nor the eye, which is the seat of sight, can be identified with the sun.
– Certainly not.
– And yet, of all the organs of sensation, the eye, methinks, bears the closest resemblance to the sun.
– Yes, quite so.
– Further, is not the faculty which the eye possesses dispensed to it from the sun, and held by it as something adventitious ?
– Certainly it is.
– Then is it not also true, that the sun, though not identical with sight, is nevertheless the cause of sight, and is moreover seen by its aid?
– Yes, quite true.
– Well then, I continued, believe that I meant the sun, when I spoke of the offspring of the chief good, begotten by it in a certain resemblance to itself, – that is to say, bearing the same relation in the visible world to sight and its objects, which the chief good bears in the intellectual world to pure reason and its objects.
– How so? Be so good as to explain it to me more at length.
– Are you aware, that whenever a person makes an end of looking at objects, upon which the light of day is shedding colour, and looks instead at objects coloured by the light of the moon and stars, his eyes grow dim and appear almost blind, as if they were not the sea of distinct vision?
– I am fully aware of it.
– But whenever the same person looks at objects on which the sun is shining, these very eyes, I believe, see clearly, and are evidently the seat of distinct vision?
– Unquestionably it is so.
– Just in the same way understand the condition of the soul to be as follows:

Whenever it‘ has fastened upon an object, over which truth and real existence are shining, it seizes that object by an act of reason, and knows it, and thus proves itself to be possessed of reason: but whenever it has fixed upon objects that are blent with darkness, – the world of birth and death, – then it rests in opinion, and its sight grows dim, as its opinions shift backwards and forwards, and it has the appearance of being destitute of reason.

– True, it has.

– Now, this power, which supplies the objects of real knowledge with the truth that is in them, and which renders to him who knows them the faculty of knowing them, you must consider to be the essential Form of Good, and you must regard it as the origin of science, and of truth, so far as the latter comes within the range of knowledge: and though knowledge and truth are both very beautiful things, you will be right in looking upon good as something distinct from them, and even more beautiful. And just as, in the analogous case, it is right to regard light and vision as resembling the sun, but wrong to identify them with the sun; so, in the case of science and truth, it is right to regard both of them as resembling good, but wrong to identify either of them with good; because, on the contrary, the quality of the good ought to have a still higher value set upon it.

– That implies an inexpressible beauty, if it not only is the source of science and truth, but also surpasses them in beauty; for, I presume, you do not mean by it pleasure.

– Hush! I exclaimed, not a word of that. But you had better examine the illustration further, as follows.

– Show me how.

– I think you will admit that the sun ministers to visible objects, not only the faculty of being seen, but also their vitality, growth, and nutriment, though it is not itself equivalent to vitality.

– Of course it is not.

– Then admit that, in like manner, the objects of knowledge not only derive from the good the gift of being known, but are further endowed by it with a real and essential existence; though the good, far from being identical with real existence, actually transcends it in dignity and power.

– Hereupon Glaucon exclaimed with a very amusing air, 'Good heavens'! what a miraculous superiority!

– Well, I said, you are the person to blame, because you compel me to state my opinions on the subject.

– Nay, let me entreat you not to stop, till you have at all events gone over again your similitude of the sun, if you are leaving anything out.

– Well, to say the truth, I am leaving out a great deal.

– Then pray do not omit even a trifle.

– I fancy I shall leave much unsaid; however, if I can help it under the circumstances, I will not intentionally make any omission.

– Pray do not.

– Now understand that, according to us, there are two powers reigning, one over an intellectual, and the other over a visible region and class of objects; – if I were to use the term "firmament" you might think I was playing on the word. Well then, are you in possession of these as two kinds, – one visible, the other intellectual ?

– Yes, I am.

– Suppose you take a line divided into two unequal parts, – one to represent the visible class of objects, the other the intellectual, – and divide each part again into two segments on the same scale. Then, if you make the lengths of the segments represent degrees of distinctness or indistinctness, one of the two segments of the part which stands for the visible world will represent all images: – meaning by images, first of all, shadows; and, in the next place, reflections in water, and in close – grained, smooth, bright substances, and everything of the kind, if you understand me.

– Yes, I do understand.

– Let the other segment stand for the real objects corresponding to these images, – namely, the animals about us, and the whole world of nature and of art.

– Very good.

– Would you also consent to say that, with reference to this class, there is, in point of truth and untruthfulness, the same distinction between the copy and the original, that there is between what is matter of opinion and what is matter of knowledge?

– Certainly I should.

– Then let us proceed to consider how we must divide that part of the whole line which represents the intellectual world.

– How must we do it?

– Thus: one segment of it will represent what the soul is compelled to investigate by the aid of the segments of the other part, which it employs as images starting from hypotheses, and travelling not to a first principle, but to a conclusion. The other segment will represent the objects of the soul, as it makes its way from an hypothesis to a first principle which is not hypothetical, unaided by those images which the former division employs, and shaping its journey by the sole help of real essential forms.

– I have not understood your description so well as I could wish.

An Athenian tetradrachm circa 440-420 B.C. (Numismatic Museum of Athens)

– Then we will try again. You will understand me more easily when I have made some previous observations. I think you know that the students of subjects like geometry and calculation, assume by way of materials, in each investigation, all odd and even numbers, figures, three kinds of angles, and other similar data. These things they are supposed to know, and having adopted them as hypotheses, they decline to give any account of them, either to themselves or to others, on the assumption that they are self-evident; and, making these their starting point, they proceed to travel through the remainder of the subject, and arrive at last, with perfect unanimity, at that which they have proposed as the object of investigation.

– I am perfectly aware of the fact, he replied.

– Then you also know that they summon to their aid visible forms, and discourse about them, though their thoughts are busy not with these forms, but with their originals, and though they discourse not with a view to the particular square and diameter which they draw, but with a view to the absolute square and the absolute diameter, and so on. For while they employ by way of images those figures and diagrams aforesaid, which again have their shadows and images in water, they are really endeavouring to behold those abstractions which a person can only see with the eye of thought.

– True.

– This, then, was the class of things which I called intellectual; but I said that the soul is constrained to employ hypotheses while engaged in the investigation of them, – not travelling to a first principle, (because it is unable to step out of, and mount above, its hypotheses,) but using, as images, just the copies that are presented by things below, – which copies, as compared with the originals, are vulgarly esteemed distinct and valued accordingly.

– I understand you to be speaking of the subject-matter of the various branches of geometry and the kindred arts.

– Again, by the second segment of the intellectual world understand me to mean all that the mere reasoning process apprehends by the force of dialectic, when it avails itself of hypotheses not as first principles, but as genuine hypotheses, that is to say, as stepping-stones and impulses, whereby it may force its way up to something that is not hypothetical, and arrive at the first principle of every thing, and seize it in its grasp; which done, it turns round, and takes hold of that which takes hold of this first principle, till at last it comes down to a conclusion, calling in the aid of no sensible object whatever, but simply employing abstract, self-subsisting forms, and terminating in the same.

– I do not understand you so well as I could wish, for I believe you to be describing an arduous task; but at any rate I understand that you wish to declare distinctly, that the field of real existence and pure intellect, as contemplated by the science of dialectic, is more certain than the field investigated by what are called the arts, in which hypotheses constitute first principles, which the students are compelled, it is true, to contemplate with the mind and not with the senses; but, at the same time, as they do not come back, in the course of inquiry, to a first principle, but push on from hypothetical premises, you think that they do not exercise pure reason on the questions that engage them, although taken in connection with a first principle these questions come within the domain of the pure reason. And I believe you apply the term understanding, not pure reason, to the mental habit of such people as geometricians, – regarding understanding as something intermediate between opinion and pure reason.

– You have taken in my meaning most satisfactorily; and I beg you will accept these four mental states, as corresponding to the four segments, – namely pure reason corresponding to the highest, understanding to the second, belief to the third, and conjecture to the last; and pray arrange them in gradation, and believe them to partake of distinctness in a degree corresponding to the truth of their respective objects.

– I understand you, said he. I quite agree with you, and will arrange them as you desire.

Demosthenes Attacks His Accuser

WHAT greater crime can an orator be charged with than that his opinions and his language are not the same?"

Here is Demosthenes' *On the Crown* – reputedly the greatest oration by the greatest orator of the ancient world. Judged by modern standards, it is not such a great speech – too obviously self-serving, replete with obscure references, and too long even in this edited form.

But this classic of rhetoric must be judged, and remembered, in the context of its time – delivered in Greece in 330 B.C. – when few men could assemble their thoughts, devise an argumentation strategy, and speak out to persuade their audience as this man did.

Demosthenes of Greece, an agitator and statesman, pitted his lifetime's oratory and ideas of freedom against Philip of Macedon, a general with a lust for world conquest. As Macedonia encroached on Greece, Demosthenes loosed a series of denunciations at Philip (from whose name we get the noun 'philippic'), defining the difference between civilization and barbarism, but the word could not stop the advance of the sword. "We shall go to war, I am told, when it is necessary," said the orator, who perfected the interrogative technique. "If the necessity has not come yet, when will it come?" It came and went; Philip was victorious, and Demosthenes lived his final years in a repressed nation-state.

Friends of the orator wanted to present him with a golden crown as a loser's reward, but the Macedonian party, led by Aeschines, charged that it was an unlawful act to so compensate any official who had not reported fully on his conduct and, worse, that it was an attempt to place a lie in the Athenian archives. After seven years, a trial was held; Aeschines laid out the case against the entire public life of Demosthenes, with an argument that was seen to be a refutation of the honor of Athens and a condemnation of his courageous philippics. Called upon to defend himself and his award of the honorary crown, Demosthenes took his freedom and perhaps his life in his hands to answer the charges.

The technique he chose was to attack his accuser. The device was not new; in the biblical Book of Job, written a couple of centuries earlier, the first words of the accused and angry God were directed at his human challenger: "Who is this that darkens counsel with words devoid of knowledge?" Demosthenes refused to be compared with other Greek patriots; instead, he compared his own career with that of Aeschines, whom he addressed at the start as an "accursed scribbler" and then proceeded to derogate further.

The speech was successful; the one who brought the charges against Demosthenes and his supporters was exiled, and the accused was awarded a crown:

Accursed scribbler! you, to deprive me of the approbation and affection of my countrymen, speak of trophies and battles and ancient deeds, with none of which had this present trial the least concern; but I that rose to counsel the state how to maintain her preeminence! in what spirit was I to mount the hustings? In the spirit of one having unworthy counsel to offer?– I should have deserved to perish!...

Of what a statesman may be responsible for, I allow the utmost scrutiny;

I deprecate it not. What are his functions? To observe things in the beginning, to foresee and foretell them to others – this I have done: again, wherever he finds delays, backwardness, ignorance, jealousies, vices inherent and unavoidable in all communities, to contract them into the narrowest compass, and on the other hand, to promote unanimity and friendship and zeal in the discharge of duty. All this, too, I have performed; and no one can discover the least neglect on my part. Ask any man, by what means Philip achieved most of his successes, and you will be told, by his army, and by his bribing and corrupting men in power. Well, your forces were not under my command or control, so that I cannot be questioned for anything done in that department. But by refusing the price of corruption I have overcome Philip; for as the offer of a bribe, if it be accepted, as vanquished the taker, so the person who refuses it and is not corrupted has vanquished the person offering. Therefore is the commonwealth undefeated as far as I am concerned.

For my part, I regard anyone who reproaches his fellow man with fortune as devoid of sense. He that is best satisfied with his condition, he that deems his fortune excellent, cannot be sure that it will remain so until the evening: how then can it be right to bring it forward, or upbraid another man with it? As Aeschines, however, has on this subject (besides many others) expressed himself with insolence, look, men of Athens, and observe how much more truth and humanity there shall be in my discourse upon fortune than in his.

I hold the fortune of our commonwealth to be good, and so I find the oracles of Dodonaean Jupiter and Pythian Apollo declaring to us. The fortune of all mankind, which now prevails, I consider cruel and dreadful: for what Greek, what barbarian, has not in these times experienced a multitude of evils? That Athens chose the noblest policy, that she fares better than those very Greeks who thought, if they abandoned us, they should abide in prosperity, I reckon as part of her good fortune; if she suffered reverses, if all happened not to us as we desired, I conceive she has had that share of the general fortune which fell to our lot. As to my fortune (personally speaking) or that of any individual among us, it should, as I conceive, be judged of in connection with personal matters.

Such is my opinion upon the subject of fortune, a right and just one, as it appears to me, and I think you will agree with it. Aeschines says that my individual fortune is paramount to that of the commonwealth, the small and mean to the good and great. How can this possibly be?

However, if you are determined, Aeschines, to scrutinize my fortune, compare it with your own, and, if you find my fortune better than yours, cease to revile it. Look, then, from the very beginning. And I pray and entreat that I may not be condemned for bad taste. I don't think any person wise, who insults poverty or who prides himself on having been bred in affluence: but by the slander and malice of this cruel man I am forced into such a discussion, which I will conduct with all the moderation which circumstances allow.

I had the advantage, Aeschines, in my boyhood of going to proper schools, and having such allowance as a boy should have who is to do nothing mean from indigence. Arrived at man's estate, I lived suitably to my breeding; was choirmaster, ship commander, rate-payer; backward in no acts of liberality public or private, but making myself useful to the commonwealth and to my friends. When I entered upon state affairs, I chose such a line of politics that both by my country and by many people of Greece I have been crowned many times, and not even you, my enemies, venture to say that the line I chose was not honorable. Such, then, has been the fortune of my life: I could enlarge upon it, but I forbear, lest what I pride myself in should give offense.

But you, the man of dignity, who spit upon others, look what sort of fortune is yours compared with mine. As a boy you were reared in abject poverty, waiting with your father in his school, grinding the ink, sponging the benches, sweeping the room, doing the duty of a menial rather than a freeborn man. After you were grown up, you attended your mother in the initiations, reading her books and helping in all the ceremonies, at night wrapping the noviciates in fawn skin, swilling, purifying, and scouring them with clay and bran...

But passing over what may be imputed to poverty, I will come to the direct charges against your character. You espoused such a line of politics (when at last you thought of taking to them) that, if your country prospered, you lived the life of a hare, fearing and trembling and ever expecting to be scourged for the crimes of which your conscience accused you, though all have seen how bold you were during the misfortunes of the rest.

A man who took courage at the death of a thousand citizens – what does he deserve at the hands of the living? A great deal more than I could say about him I shall omit; for it is not all I can tell of his turpitude and infamy which I ought to let slip from my tongue, but only what is not disgraceful to myself to mention.

Contrast now the circumstances of your life and mine, gently and with temper, Aeschines; and then ask these people whose fortune they would each of them prefer. You taught reading, I went to school; you performed initiations, I received them; you danced in the chorus, I furnished it; you were assembly clerk, I was a speaker; you acted third parts, I heard you; you broke down, and I hissed; you have worked as a statesman for the enemy, I for my country. I pass by the rest; but this very day I am on my probation for a crown, and am acknowledged to be innocent of all offense; while you are already judged to be a pettifogger, and the question is whether you shall continue that trade or at once be silenced by not getting a fifth part of the votes. A happy fortune, do you see, you have enjoyed, that you should denounce mine as miserable!...

You undertook this cause to exhibit your eloquence and strength of lungs, not to obtain satisfaction for any wrong. But it is not the language of an orator, Aeschines, that has any value, nor yet the tone of his voice, but his adopting the same views with the people, and his hating and loving the same persons that his country does. He that is thus minded will say everything with loyal intention; he that courts persons from whom the commonwealth apprehends danger to herself rides not on the same anchorage with the people and, therefore, has not the same expectation of safety. But – do you see? – I have; for my objects are the same with those of my countrymen; I have no interest separate or distinct. Is that so with you? How can it be – when immediately after the battle you went as ambassador to Philip, who was at that period the author of your country's calamities, notwithstanding that you had before persisted in refusing that office, as all men know?

And who is it that deceives the state? Surely the man who speaks not what he thinks. On whom does the crier pronounce a curse? Surely on such a man. What greater crime can an orator be charged with than that his opinions and his language are not the same? Such is found to be your character. And yet you open your mouth and dare to look these men in the faces! Do you think they don't know you? – or are sunk in such slumber and oblivion as not to remember the speeches which you delivered in the assembly, cursing and swearing that you had nothing to do with Philip, and that I brought that charge against you out of personal enmity without foundation? No sooner came the news of the battle than you forgot all that; you acknowledge and avowed that between Philip and yourself there subsisted a relation of hospitality and friendship – new names these for your contract of hire. For upon what plea of equality or justice could Aeschines, son of Glaucothea, the timbrel player, be the friend or acquaintance of Philip? I cannot see. No! You were hired to ruin the interests of your countrymen; and yet, though you have been caught yourself in open trea-

The large golden larnax, found in the sarcophagus contained in the grave of Phillip II in Vergina

son, and informed against yourself after the fact, you revile and reproach me for things which you will find any man is chargeable with sooner than I.

Many great and glorious enterprises has the commonwealth, Aeschines, undertaken and succeeded in through me; and she did not forget them. Here is the proof. On the election of a person to speak the funeral oration immediately after the event, you were proposed, but the people would not have you, notwithstanding your fine voice, nor Demades, though he had just made the peace, nor Hegemon, nor any other of your party – but me. And when you and Pythocles came forward in a brutal and shameful manner (0, merciful heaven!) and urged the same accusations against me which you now do, and abused me, they elected me all the more. The reason – you are not ignorant of it – yet I will tell you.

The Athenians knew as well the loyalty and zeal with which I conducted their affairs, as the dishonesty of you and your party; for what you denied upon oath in our prosperity, you confessed in the misfortunes of the republic. They considered, therefore, that men who got security for their politics by the public disasters had been their enemies long before, and were then avowedly such. They thought it right also, that the person who was to speak in honor of the fallen and celebrate their valor should not have sat under the same roof or at the same table with their antagonists; that he should not revel there and sing a paean over the calamities of Greece in company with their murderers, and then come here and receive distinction; that he should not with his voice act the mourner of their fate, but that he should lament over them with his heart. This they perceived in themselves and in me, but not in any of you; therefore, they elected me and not you...

There is indeed a retirement just and beneficial to the state, such as you, the bulk of my countrymen, innocently enjoy; that however is not the retirement of Aeschines; far from it. Withdrawing himself from public life when he pleases (and that is often), he watches for the moment when you are tired of a constant speaker, or when some reverse of fortune has befallen you, or anything untoward has happened (and many are the casualties of human life); at such a crisis he springs up an orator, rising from his retreat like a wind; in full voice, with words and phrases collected, he rolls them out audibly and breathlessly, to no advantage or good purpose whatsoever, but to the detriment of some or other of his fellow citizens and to the general disgrace.

Yet from this labor and diligence, Aeschines, if it proceeded from an honest heart, solicitous for your country's welfare, the fruits should have been rich and noble and profitable to all alliances of states, supplies of money, conveniences of commerce, enactment of useful laws, opposition to our declared enemies. All such things were looked for in former times; and many opportunities did the past afford for a good man and true to show himself; during which time you are nowhere to be found, neither first, second, third, fourth, fifth, nor sixth – not in any rank at all – certainly on no service by which your country was exalted. For what alliance has come to the state by your procurement? What succors, what acquisition of good will or credit? What embassy or agency is there of yours, by which the reputation of the country has been increased? What concern domestic, Hellenic, or foreign, of which you have had the management, has improved under it? What galleys? What ammunition? What arsenals? What repair of walls? What cavalry? What in the world are you good for? What assistance in money have you ever given, either to the rich or the poor, out of public spirit or liberality? None...

A tiny ivory bust of Phillip II from the decoration of his cline, also made of ivory, found in his grave in Vergina

My politics and principles, if considered fairly, will be found to resemble those of the illustrious ancients, and to have had the same objects in view, while yours resemble those of their calumniators; for it is certain there were persons in those times, who ran down the living, and praised people dead and gone, with a malignant purpose like yourself...

Two things, men of Athens, are characteristic of a well-disposed citizen – so may I speak of myself and give the least offense: In authority, his constant aim should be the dignity and preeminence of the common-wealth; in all times and circumstances his spirit should be loyal. This depends upon nature; power and might, upon other things. Such a spirit, you will find, I have ever sincerely cherished. Only see. When my person was demanded – when they brought Amphictyonic suits against me – when they menaced – when they promised – when they set these miscreants like wild beasts upon me – never in any way have I abandoned my affection for you. From the very beginning I chose an honest and straight – forward course in politics, to support the honor, the power, the glory of my fatherland, these to exalt, in these to have been my being. I do not walk about the marketplace gay and cheerful because the stranger has prospered, holding out my right hand and congratulating those who I think will report it yonder, and on any news of our own success shudder and groan and stoop to the earth, like these impious men, who rail at Athens, as if in so doing they did not rail at themselves; who look abroad, and if the foreigner thrives by the distresses of Greece, are thankful for it, and say we should keep him so thriving to all time.

Never, 0 ye gods, may those wishes be confirmed by you! If possible, inspire even in these men a better sense and feeling! But if they are indeed incurable, destroy them by themselves; exterminate them on land and sea; and for the rest of us, grant that we may speedily be released from our present fears, and enjoy a lasting deliverance!

The Apology of Socrates

By Plato

Accused of corrupting the city's youth, the philosopher Socrates is brought to trial in front of a jury of fellow Athenians. Here is his apology as passed on to us by his disciple, Plato:

How you have felt, O men of Athens, at hearing the speeches of my accusers, I cannot tell; but I know that their persuasive words almost made me forget who I was – such was the effect of them; and yet they have hardly spoken a word of truth. But many as their falsehoods were, there was one of them which quite amazed me; – I mean when they told you to be upon your guard, and not to let yourselves be deceived by the force of my eloquence. They ought to have been ashamed of saying this, because they were sure to be detected as soon as I opened my lips and displayed my deficiency; they certainly did appear to be most shameless in saying this, unless by the force of eloquence they mean the force of truth; for then I do indeed admit that I am eloquent. But in how different a way from theirs! Well, as I was saying, they have hardly uttered a word, or not more than a word, of truth; but you shall hear from me the whole truth: not, however, delivered after their manner, in a set oration duly ornamented with words and phrases. No indeed! but I shall use the words and arguments which occur to me at the moment; for I am certain that this is right, and that at my time of life I ought not to be appearing before you, O men of Athens, in the character of a juvenile orator – let no one expect this of me. And I must beg of you to grant me one favor, which is this – If you hear me using the same words in my defense which I have been in the habit of using, and which most of you may have heard in the agora, and at the tables of the money-changers, or anywhere else, I would ask you not to be surprised at this, and not to interrupt me. For I am more than seventy years of age, and this is the first time that I have ever appeared in a court of law, and I am quite a stranger to the ways of the place; and therefore I would have you regard me as if I were really a stranger, whom you would excuse if he spoke in his native tongue, and after the fashion of his country; – that I think is not an unfair request. Never mind the manner, which may or may not be good; but think only of the justice of my cause, and give heed to that: let the judge decide justly and the speaker speak truly.

And first, I have to reply to the older charges and to my first accusers, and then I will go to the later ones. For I have had many accusers, who accused me of old, and their false charges have continued during many years; and I am more afraid of them than of Anytus and his associates, who are dangerous, too, in their own way. But far more dangerous are these, who began when you were children, and took possession of your minds with their falsehoods, telling of one Socrates, a wise man, who speculated about the heaven above, and searched into the earth beneath, and made the worse appear the better cause. These are the accusers whom I dread; for they are the circulators of this rumor, and their hearers are too apt to fancy that speculators of this sort do not believe in the gods. And they are many, and their charges against me are of ancient date, and they made them in days when you were impressible – in childhood, or perhaps in youth – and the cause when heard went by default, for there was none to answer. And, hardest of all, their names I do not know and cannot tell; unless in the chance of a comic poet. But the main body of these slanderers who from envy and malice have wrought upon you – and there are some of them who are convinced themselves, and impart their convictions to others – all these, I say, are most difficult to deal with; for I cannot have them up here, and examine them, and therefore I must simply fight with shadows in my own defense, and examine when there is no one who answers. I will ask you then to assume with me, as I was saying, that my opponents are of two kinds – one recent, the other ancient; and I hope that you will see the propriety of my answering the latter first, for these accusations you heard long before the others, and much oftener.

Well, then, I will make my defense, and I will endeavor in the short time which is allowed to do away with this evil opinion of me which you have held for such a long time; and I hope I may succeed, if this be well for you and me, and that my words may find favor with you. But I know that to accomplish this is not easy – I quite see the nature of the task. Let the event be as God wills: in obedience to the law I make my defense.

I will begin at the beginning, and ask what the accusation is which has given rise to this slander of me, and which has encouraged Meletus to proceed against me. What do the slanderers say? They shall be my prosecutors, and I will sum up their words in an affidavit. "Socrates is an evil-doer, and a curious person, who searches into things under the earth and in heaven, and he makes the worse appear the better cause; and he teaches the aforesaid doctrines to others." That is the nature of the accusation, and that is what you have seen yourselves in the comedy of Aristophanes; who has introduced a man whom he calls Socrates, going about and saying that he can walk in the air, and talking a deal of nonsense concerning matters of which I do not pretend to know either much or little – not that I mean to say anything disparaging of anyone who is a student of natural philosophy. I should be very sorry if Meletus could lay that to my charge. But the simple truth is, O Athenians, that I have nothing to do with these studies. Very many of those here present are witnesses to the truth of this, and to them I appeal. Speak then, you who have heard me, and tell your neighbors whether any of you have ever known me hold forth in few words or in many upon matters of this sort. ... You hear their answer. And from what they say of this you will be able to judge of the truth of the rest.

As little foundation is there for the report that I am a teacher, and take money; that is no more true than the other. Although, if a man is able to teach,

Ancient Athenian jury ballots: the ones with a solid axis through them denote guilt; the ones with a hole, innocence.

I honor him for being paid. There is Gorgias of Leontium, and Prodicus of Ceos, and Hippias of Elis, who go the round of the cities, and are able to persuade the young men to leave their own citizens, by whom they might be taught for nothing, and come to them, whom they not only pay, but are thankful if they may be allowed to pay them. There is actually a Parian philosopher residing in Athens, of whom I have heard; and I came to hear of him in this way: – I met a man who has spent a world of money on the Sophists, Callias the son of Hipponicus, and knowing that he had sons, I asked him: "Callias," I said, "if your two sons were foals or calves, there would be no difficulty in finding someone to put over them; we should hire a trainer of horses or a farmer probably who would improve and perfect them in their own proper virtue and excellence; but as they are human beings, whom are you thinking of placing over them? Is there anyone who understands human and political virtue? You must have thought about this as you have sons; is there anyone?" "There is," he said. "Who is he?" said I, "and of what country? and what does he charge?" "Evenus the Parian," he replied; "he is the man, and his charge is five minae." Happy is Evenus, I said to myself, if he really has this wisdom, and teaches at such a modest charge. Had I the same, I should have been very proud and conceited; but the truth is that I have no knowledge of the kind.

I dare say, Athenians, that someone among you will reply, "Why is this, Socrates, and what is the origin of these accusations of you: for there must have been something strange which you have been doing? All this great fame and talk about you would never have arisen if you had been like other men: tell us, then, why this is, as we should be sorry to judge hastily of you." Now I regard this as a fair challenge, and I will endeavor to explain to you the origin of this name of "wise," and of this evil fame. Please to attend then. And although some of you may think I am joking, I declare that I will tell you the entire truth. Men of Athens, this reputation of mine has come of a certain sort of wisdom which I possess. If you ask me what kind of wisdom, I reply, such wisdom as is attainable by man, for to that extent I am inclined to believe that I am wise; whereas the persons of whom I was speaking have a superhuman wisdom, which I may fail to describe, because I have it not myself; and he who says that I have, speaks falsely, and is taking away my charac-

A Hermaic stele with a bust of Socrates (Naples, National Archeological Museum)

ter. And here, O men of Athens, I must beg you not to interrupt me, even if I seem to say something extravagant. For the word which I will speak is not mine. I will refer you to a witness who is worthy of credit, and will tell you about my wisdom – whether I have any, and of what sort – and that witness shall be the god of Delphi. You must have known Chaerephon; he was early a friend of mine, and also a friend of yours, for he shared in the exile of the people, and returned with you. Well, Chaerephon, as you know, was very impetuous in all his doings, and he went to Delphi and boldly asked the oracle to tell him whether – as I was saying, I must beg you not to interrupt – he asked the oracle to tell him whether there was anyone wiser than I was, and the Pythian prophetess answered that there was no man wiser. Chaerephon is dead himself, but his brother, who is in court, will confirm the truth of this story.

Why do I mention this? Because I am going to explain to you why I have such an evil name. When I heard the answer, I said to myself, What can the god mean? and what is the interpretation of this riddle? for I know that I have no wisdom, small or great. What can he mean when he says that I am the wisest of men? And yet he is a god and cannot lie; that would be against his nature. After a long consideration, I at last thought of a method of trying the question. I reflected that if I could only find a man wiser than myself, then I might go to the god with a refutation in my hand. I should say to him, "Here is a man who is wiser than I am; but you said that I was the wisest." Accordingly I went to one who had the reputation of wisdom, and observed to him – his name I need not mention; he was a politician whom I selected for examination – and the result was as follows: When I began to talk with him, I could not help thinking that he was not really wise, although he was thought wise by many, and wiser still by himself; and I went and tried to explain to him that he thought himself wise, but was not really wise; and the consequence was that he hated me, and his enmity was shared by several who were present and heard me. So I left him, saying to myself, as I went away: Well, although I do not suppose that either of us knows anything really beautiful and good, I am better off than he is – for he knows nothing, and thinks that he knows. I neither know nor think that I know. In this latter particular, then, I seem to have slightly the advantage of him. Then I went to another, who had still higher philosophical pretensions, and my conclusion was exactly the same. I made another enemy of him, and of many others besides him."

After this I went to one man after another, being not unconscious of the enmity which I provoked, and I lamented and feared this: but necessity was laid upon me – the word of God, I thought, ought to be considered first. And I said to myself, Go I must to all who appear to know, and find out the meaning of the oracle. And I swear to you, Athenians, by the dog I swear! – for I must tell you the truth – the result of my mission was just this: I found that the men most in repute were all but the most foolish; and that some inferior men were really wiser and better. I will tell you the tale of my wanderings and of the "Herculean" labors, as I may call them, which I endured only to find at last the oracle irrefutable. When I left the politicians, I went to the poets; tragic, dithyrambic, and all sorts. And there,

I said to myself, you will be detected; now you will find out that you are more ignorant than they are. Accordingly, I took them some of the most elaborate passages in their own writings, and asked what was the meaning of them – thinking that they would teach me something. Will you believe me? I am almost ashamed to speak of this, but still I must say that there is hardly a person present who would not have talked better about their poetry than they did themselves. That showed me in an instant that not by wisdom do poets write poetry, but by a sort of genius and inspiration; they are like diviners or soothsayers who also say many fine things, but do not understand the meaning of them. And the poets appeared to me to be much in the same case; and I further observed that upon the strength of their poetry they believed themselves to be the wisest of men in other things in which they were not wise. So I departed, conceiving myself to be superior to them for the same reason that I was superior to the politicians.

At last I went to the artisans, for I was conscious that I knew nothing at all, as I may say, and I was sure that they knew many fine things; and in this I was not mistaken, for they did know many things of which I was ignorant, and in this they certainly were wiser than I was. But I observed that even the good artisans fell into the same error as the poets; because they were good workmen they thought that they also knew all sorts of high matters, and this defect in them overshadowed their wisdom – therefore I asked myself on behalf of the oracle, whether I would like to be as I was, neither having their knowledge nor their ignorance, or like them in both; and I made answer to myself and the oracle that I was better off as I was.

This investigation has led to my having many enemies of the worst and most dangerous kind, and has given occasion also to many calumnies, and I am called wise, for my hearers always imagine that I myself possess the wisdom which I find wanting in others: but the truth is, O men of Athens, that God only is wise; and in this oracle he means to say that the wisdom of men is little or nothing; he is not speaking of Socrates, he is only using my name as an illustration, as if he said, He, O men, is the wisest, who, like Socrates, knows that his wisdom is in truth worth nothing. And so I go my way, obedient to the god, and make inquisition into the wisdom of anyone, whether citizen or stranger, who appears to be wise; and if he is not wise, then in vindication of the oracle I show him that he is not wise; and this occupation quite absorbs me, and I have no time to give either to any public matter of interest or to any concern of my own, but I am in utter poverty by reason of my devotion to the god.

There is another thing: – young men of the richer classes, who have not much to do, come about me of their own accord; they like to hear the pretenders examined, and they often imitate me, and examine others themselves; there are plenty of persons, as they soon enough discover, who think that they know something, but really know little or nothing: and then those who are examined by them instead of being angry with themselves are angry with me: This confounded Socrates, they say; this villainous misleader of youth! – and then if somebody asks them, Why, what evil does he practice or teach? they do not know, and cannot tell; but in order that they may not appear to be at a loss, they repeat the ready-made charges which are used against all philosophers about teaching things up in the clouds and under the earth, and having no gods, and making the worse appear the better cause; for they do not like to confess that their pretense of knowledge has been detected – which is the truth: and as they are numerous and ambitious and energetic, and are all in battle array and have persuasive tongues, they have filled your ears with their loud and inveterate calumnies. And this is the reason why my three accusers, Meletus and Anytus and Lycon, have set upon me; Meletus, who has a quarrel with me on behalf of the poets; Anytus, on behalf of the craftsmen; Lycon, on behalf of the rhetoricians: and as I said at the beginning, I cannot expect to get rid of this mass of calumny all in a moment. And this, O men of Athens, is the truth and the whole truth; I have concealed nothing, I have dissembled nothing. And yet I know that this plainness of speech makes them hate me, and what is their hatred but a proof that I am speaking the truth? – this is the occasion and reason of their slander of me, as you will find out either in this or in any future inquiry.

I have said enough in my defense against the first class of my accusers; I turn to the second class, who are headed by Meletus, that good and patriotic man, as he calls himself. And now I will try to defend myself against them: these new accusers must also have their affidavit read. What do they say? Something of this sort: – That Socrates is a doer of evil, and corrupter of the youth, and he does not believe in the gods of the state, and has other new divinities of his own. That is the sort of charge; and now let us examine the particular counts. He says that I am a doer of evil, who corrupt the youth; but I say, O men of Athens, that Meletus is a doer of evil, and the evil is that he makes a joke of a serious matter, and is too ready at bringing other men to trial from a pretended zeal and interest about matters in which he really never had the smallest interest. And the truth of this I will endeavor to prove.

Come hither, Meletus, and let me ask a question of you. You think a great deal about the improvement of youth?

– Yes, I do.

– Tell the judges, then, who is their improver; for you must know, as you have taken the pains to discover their corrupter, and are citing and accusing me before them. Speak, then, and tell the judges who their improver is. Observe, Meletus, that you are silent, and have nothing to say. But is not this rather disgraceful, and a very considerable proof of what I was saying, that you have no interest in the matter? Speak up, friend, and tell us who their improver is.

– The laws.

– But that, my good sir, is not my meaning. I want to know who the person is, who, in the first place, knows the laws.

– The judges, Socrates, who are present in court.

– What do you mean to say, Meletus, that they are able to instruct and improve youth?

– Certainly they are.

– What, all of them, or some only and not others?

– All of them.

– By the goddess Here, that is good news! There are plenty of improvers, then. And what do you say of the audience, – do they improve them?

– Yes, they do.

– And the senators?

– Yes, the senators improve them.

– But perhaps the members of the citizen assembly corrupt them? – or do they too improve them?

– They improve them.

– Then every Athenian improves and elevates them; all with the exception of myself; and I alone am their corrupter? Is that what you affirm?

– That is what I stoutly affirm.

– I am very unfortunate if that is true. But suppose I ask you a question: Would you say that this also holds true in the case of horses? Does one man do them harm and all the world good? Is not the exact opposite of this true? One man is able to do them good, or at least not many; – the trainer of horses, that is to say, does them good, and others who have to do with them rather injure them? Is not that true, Meletus, of horses, or any other animals? Yes, certainly. Whether you and Anytus say yes or no, that is no matter. Happy indeed would be the condition of youth if they had one corrupter only, and all the rest of the world were their improvers. And you, Meletus, have sufficiently shown that you never had a thought about the young: your carelessness is seen in your not caring about matters spoken of in this very indictment.

– And now, Meletus, I must ask you another question: Which is better, to live among bad citizens, or among good ones? Answer, friend, I say; for that is a question which may be easily answered. Do not the good do their neighbors good, and the bad do them evil?

– Certainly.

– And is there anyone who would rather be injured than benefited by those who live with him? Answer, my good friend; the law requires you to answer – does anyone like to be injured?

– Certainly not.

– And when you accuse me of corrupting and deteriorating the youth, do you allege that I corrupt them intentionally or unintentionally?

– Intentionally, I say.

– But you have just admitted that the good do their neighbors good, and the evil do them evil. Now is that a truth which your superior wisdom has recognized thus early in life, and am I, at my age, in such darkness and ignorance as not to know that if a man with whom I have to live is corrupted by me, I am very likely to be harmed by him, and yet I corrupt him, and intentionally, too; – that is what you are saying, and of that you will never persuade me or any other human being. But either I do not corrupt them, or I corrupt them unintentionally, so that on either view of the case you lie. If my offense is unintentional, the law has no cognizance of unintentional offenses: you ought to have taken me privately, and warned and admonished me; for if I had been better advised, I should have left off doing what I only did unintentionally – no doubt I should; whereas you hated to converse with me or teach me, but you indicted me in this court, which is a place not of instruction, but of punishment.

– I have shown, Athenians, as I was saying, that Meletus has no care at all, great or small, about the matter. But still I should like to know, Meletus, in what I am affirmed to corrupt the young. I suppose you mean, as I infer from your indictment, that I teach them not to acknowledge the gods which the state acknowledges, but some other new divinities or spiritual agencies in their stead. These are the lessons which corrupt the youth, as you say.

– Yes, that I say emphatically.

– Then, by the gods, Meletus, of whom we are speaking, tell me and the court, in somewhat plainer terms, what you mean! for I do not as yet understand whether you affirm that I teach others to acknowledge some gods, and therefore do believe in gods and am not an entire atheist – this you do not lay to my charge; but only that they are not the same gods which the city recognizes – the charge is that they are different gods. Or, do you mean to say that I am an atheist simply, and a teacher of atheism?

– I mean the latter – that you are a complete atheist.

– That is an extraordinary statement, Meletus. Why do you say that? Do you mean that I do not believe in the godhead of the sun or moon, which is the common creed of all men?

– I assure you, judges, that he does not believe in them; for he says that the sun is stone, and the moon earth.

– Friend Meletus, you think that you are accusing Anaxagoras; and you have but a bad opinion of the judges, if you fancy them ignorant to such a degree as not to know that those doctrines are found in the books of Anaxagoras the Clazomenian, who is full of them. And these are the doctrines which the youth are said to learn of Socrates, when there are not infrequently exhibitions of them at the theatre (price of admission one drachma at the most); and they might cheaply purchase them, and laugh at Socrates if he pretends to father such eccentricities. And so, Meletus, you really think that I do not believe in any god?

– I swear by Zeus that you believe absolutely in none at all.

– You are a liar, Meletus, not believed even by yourself. For I cannot help thinking, O men of Athens, that Meletus is reckless and impudent, and that he has written this indictment in a spirit of mere wantonness and youthful bravado. Has he not compounded a riddle, thinking to try me? He said to himself: – I shall see whether this wise Socrates will discover my ingenious contradiction, or whether I shall be able to deceive him and the rest of them. For he certainly does appear to me to contradict himself in the indictment as much as if he said that Socrates is guilty of not believing in the gods, and yet of believing in them – but this surely is a piece of fun.

I should like you, O men of Athens, to join me

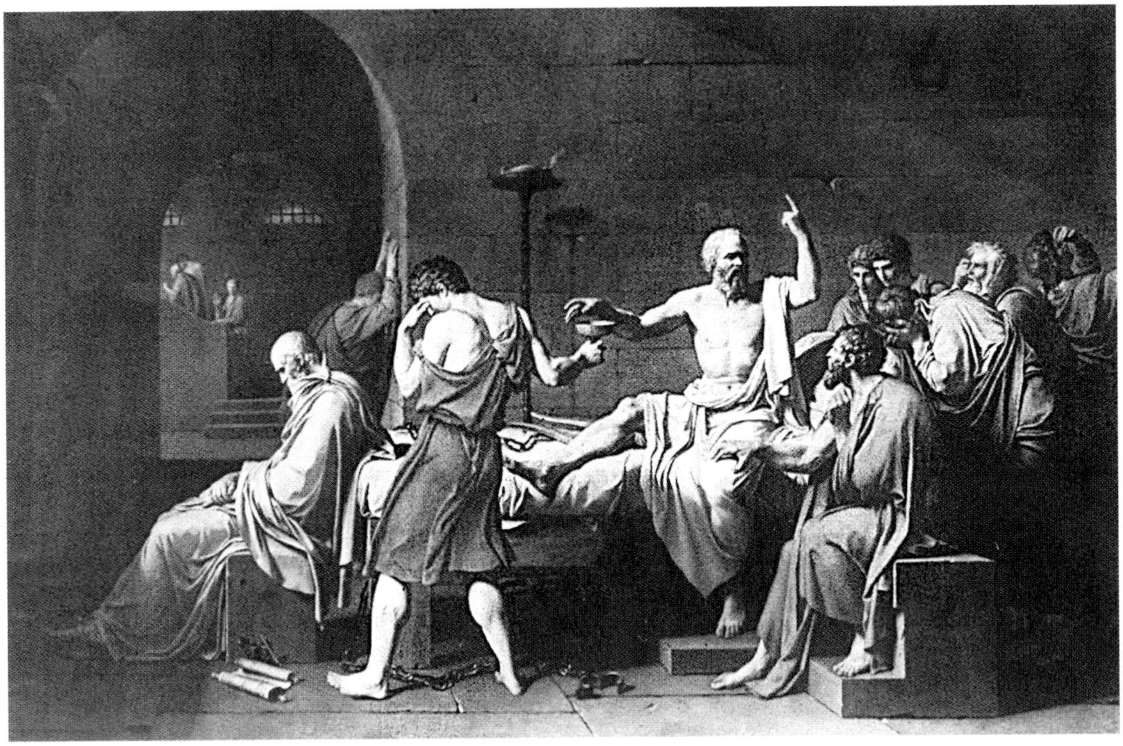

The death of Socrates

in examining what I conceive to be his inconsistency; and do you, Meletus, answer. And I must remind you that you are not to interrupt me if I speak in my accustomed manner.

Did ever man, Meletus, believe in the existence of human things, and not of human beings? ...I wish, men of Athens, that he would answer, and not be always trying to get up an interruption. Did ever any man believe in horsemanship, and not in horses? or in flute-playing, and not in flute-players? No, my friend; I will answer to you and to the court, as you refuse to answer for yourself. There is no man who ever did.

But now please to answer the next question: Can a man believe in spiritual and divine agencies, and not in spirits or demigods?

– He cannot.

– I am glad that I have extracted that answer, by the assistance of the court; nevertheless you swear in the indictment that I teach and believe in divine or spiritual agencies (new or old, no matter for that); at any rate, I believe in spiritual agencies, as you say and swear in the affidavit; but if I believe in divine beings, I must believe in spirits or demigods; – is not that true? Yes, that is true, for I may assume that your silence gives assent to that. Now what are spirits or demigods? are they not either gods or the sons of gods? Is that true?

– Yes, that is true.

– But this is just the ingenious riddle of which I was speaking: the demigods or spirits are gods, and you say first that I don't believe in gods, and then again that I do believe in gods; that is, if I believe in demigods. For if the demigods are the illegitimate sons of gods, whether by the Nymphs or by any other mothers, as is thought, that, as all men will allow, necessarily implies the existence of their parents. You might as well affirm the existence of mules, and deny that of horses and asses. Such nonsense, Meletus, could only have been intended by you as a trial of me. You have put this into the indictment because you had nothing real of which to accuse me. But no one who has a particle of understanding will ever be convinced by you that the same man can believe in divine and superhuman things, and yet not believe that there are gods and demigods and heroes.

I have said enough in answer to the charge of Meletus: any elaborate defense is unnecessary; but as I was saying before, I certainly have many enemies, and this is what will be my destruction if I am

A bust of Antisthenes, a disciple of Socrates (Vatican Museum).

destroyed; of that I am certain; – not Meletus, nor yet Anytus, but the envy and detraction of the world, which has been the death of many good men, and will probably be the death of many more; there is no danger of my being the last of them.

Someone will say: And are you not ashamed, Socrates, of a course of life which is likely to bring you to an untimely end? To him I may fairly answer: There you are mistaken: a man who is good for anything ought not to calculate the chance of living or dying; he ought only to consider whether in doing anything he is doing right or wrong – acting the part of a good man or of a bad. Whereas, according to your view, the heroes who fell at Troy were not good for much, and the son of Thetis above all, who altogether despised danger in comparison with disgrace; and when his goddess mother said to him, in his eagerness to slay Hector, that if he avenged his companion Patroclus, and slew Hector, he would die himself – "Fate," as she said, "waits upon you next after Hector;" he, hearing this, utterly despised danger and death, and instead of fearing them, feared rather to live in dishonor, and not to avenge his friend. "Let me die next," he replies, "and be avenged of my enemy, rather than abide here by the beaked ships, a scorn and a burden of the earth." Had Achilles any thought of death and danger? For wherever a man's place is, whether the place which he has chosen or that in which he has been placed by a commander, there he ought to remain in the hour of danger; he should not think of death or of anything, but of disgrace. And this, O men of Athens, is a true saying.

Strange, indeed, would be my conduct, O men of Athens, if I who, when I was ordered by the generals whom you chose to command me at Potidaea and Amphipolis and Delium, remained where they placed me, like any other man, facing death; if, I say, now, when, as I conceive and imagine, God orders me to fulfil the philosopher's mission of searching into myself and other men, I were to desert my post through fear of death, or any other fear; that would indeed be strange, and I might justly be arraigned in court for denying the existence of the gods, if I disobeyed the oracle because I was afraid of death: then I should be fancying that I was wise when I was not wise. For this fear of death is indeed the pretense of wisdom, and not real wisdom, being the appearance of knowing the unknown; since no one knows whether death, which they in their fear apprehend to be the greatest evil, may not be the greatest good. Is there not here conceit of knowledge, which is a disgraceful sort of ignorance? And this is the point in which, as I think, I am superior to men in general, and in which I might perhaps fancy myself wiser than other men, – that whereas I know but little of the world below, I do not suppose that I know: but I do know that injustice and disobedience to a better, whether God or man, is evil and dishonorable, and I will never fear or avoid a possible good rather than a certain evil. And therefore if you let me go now, and reject the counsels of Anytus, who said that if I were not put to death I ought not to have been prosecuted, and that if I escape now, your sons will all be utterly ruined by listening to my words – if you say to me, Socrates, this time we will not mind Anytus, and will let you off, but upon one condition, that are to inquire and speculate in this way any more, and that if you are caught doing this again you shall die; – if this was the condition on which you let me go, I should reply: Men of Athens, I honor and love you; but I shall obey God rather than you, and while I have life and strength I shall never cease from the practice and teaching of philosophy, exhorting anyone whom I meet after my manner, and convincing him, saying: O my friend, why do you who are a citizen of the great and mighty and wise city of Athens, care so much about laying up the greatest amount of money and honor and reputation, and so little about wisdom and truth and the greatest improvement of the soul, which you never regard or heed at all? Are you not ashamed of this? And if the person with whom I am arguing says: Yes, but I do care; I do not depart or let him go at once; I interrogate and examine and cross-examine him, and if I think that he has no virtue, but only says that he has, I reproach him with undervaluing the greater, and overvaluing the less. And this I should say to everyone whom I meet, young and old, citizen and alien, but especially to the citizens, inasmuch as they are my brethren. For this is the command of God, as I would have you know; and I believe that to this day no greater good has ever happened in the state than my service to the God. For I do nothing but go about persuading you all, old and young alike, not to take thought for your persons and your properties, but first and chiefly to care about the greatest improvement of the soul. I tell you that virtue is not given by money, but that from virtue come money and every other good of man, public as well as private. This is my teaching, and if this is the doctrine which corrupts the youth, my influence is ruinous indeed. But if anyone says that this is not my teaching, he is speaking an untruth. Wherefore, O men of Athens, I say to you, do as Anytus bids or not as Anytus bids, and either acquit me or not; but whatever you do, know that I shall never alter my ways, not even if I have to die many times.

Men of Athens, do not interrupt, but hear me; there was an agreement between us that you should hear me out. And I think that what I am going to say will do you good: for I have something more to say, at which you may be inclined to cry out; but I beg that you will not do this. I would have you know that, if you kill such a one as I am, you will injure yourselves more than you will injure me. Meletus and Anytus will not injure me: they cannot; for it is not in the nature of things that a bad man should injure a better than himself. I do not deny that he may, perhaps, kill him, or drive him into exile, or deprive him of civil rights; and he may imagine, and others may imagine, that he is doing him a great injury: but in that I do not agree with him; for the evil of doing as Anytus is doing – of unjustly taking away another man's life– is greater far. And now, Athenians, I am not going to argue for my own sake, as you may think, but for yours, that you may not sin against the God, or lightly reject his boon by condemning me. For if you kill me you will not easily find another like me, who, if I may use such a ludicrous figure of speech, am a sort of gadfly, given to the state by the God; and the state is like a great and noble steed who is tardy in his motions owing to his very size, and requires to be stirred into life. I am that gadfly which God has given the state and all day long and in all places am always fastening upon you, arousing and persuading and reproaching you. And as you will not easily find another like me, I would advise you to spare me. I dare say that you may feel irritated at being suddenly awakened when you are caught napping; and you may think that if you were to strike me dead, as Anytus advises, which you easily might, then you would sleep on for the remainder of your lives, unless God in his care of you gives you another gadfly. And that I am given to you by God is proved by this: – that if I had been like other men, I should not have neglected all my own concerns, or patiently seen the neglect of them during all these years, and have been doing yours, coming to you individually, like a father or elder brother, exhorting you to regard virtue; this I say, would not be like human nature. And had I gained anything, or if my exhortations had been paid, there would have been some sense in that: but now, as you will perceive, not even the impudence of my accusers dares to say that I have ever exacted or sought pay of anyone; they have no witness of that. And I have a witness of the truth of what I say; my poverty is a sufficient witness.

Plato's Academy. Mosaic from Pompeii, 1st century A.D. (Naples National Archaeological Museum)

Someone may wonder why I go about in private, giving advice and busying myself with the concerns of others, but do not venture to come forward in public and advise the state. I will tell you the reason of this. You have often heard me speak of an oracle or sign which comes to me, and is the divinity which Meletus ridicules in the indictment. This sign I have had ever since I was a child. The sign is a voice which comes to me and always forbids me to do something which I am going to do, but never commands me to do anything, and this is what stands in the way of my being a politician. And rightly, as I think. For I am certain, O men of Athens, that if I had engaged in politics, I should have perished long ago and done no good either to you or to myself. And don't be offended at my telling you the truth: for the truth is that no man who goes to war with you or any other multitude, honestly struggling against the commission of unrighteousness and wrong in the state, will save his life; he who will really fight for the right, if he would live even for a little while, must have a private station and not a public one.

I can give you as proofs of this, not words only, but deeds, which you value more than words. Let me tell you a passage of my own life, which will prove to you that I should never have yielded to injustice from any fear of death, and that if I had not yielded I should have died at once. I will tell you a story – tasteless, perhaps, and commonplace, but nevertheless true. The only office of state which I ever held, O men of Athens, was that of senator; the tribe Antiochis, which is my tribe, had the presidency at the trial of the generals who had not taken up the bodies of the slain after the battle of Arginusae; and you proposed to try them all together, which was illegal, as you all thought afterwards; but at the time I was the only one of the Prytanes who was opposed to the illegality, and I gave my vote against you; and when the orators threatened to impeach and arrest me, and have me taken away, and you called and shouted, I made up my mind that I would run the risk, having law and justice with me, rather than take part in your injustice because I feared imprisonment and death. This happened in the days of the democracy. But when the oligarchy of the Thirty was in power, they sent for me and four others into the rotunda, and bade us bring Leon the Salaminian from Salamis, as they wanted to execute him. This was a specimen of the sort of commands which they were always giving with the view of implicating as many as possible in their crimes; and then I showed, not in words only, but in deed, that, if I may be allowed to use such an expression, I cared not a straw for death, and that my only fear was the fear of doing an unrighteous or unholy thing. For the strong arm of that oppressive power did not frighten me into doing wrong; and when we came out of the rotunda the other four went to Salamis and fetched Leon, but I went quietly home. For which I might have lost my life, had not the power of the Thirty shortly afterwards come to an end. And to this many will witness.

Now do you really imagine that I could have survived all these years, if I had led a public life, supposing that like a good man I had always supported the right and had made justice, as I ought, the first thing? No, indeed, men of Athens, neither I nor any other. But I have been always the same in all my actions, public as well as private, and never have I yielded any base compliance to those who are slanderously termed my disciples or to any other. For the truth is that I have no regular disciples: but if anyone likes to come and hear me while I am pursuing my mission, whether he be young or old, he may freely come. Nor do I converse with those who pay only, and not with those who do not pay; but anyone, whether he be rich or poor, may ask and answer me and listen to my words; and whether he turns out to be a bad man or a good one, that cannot be justly laid to my charge, as I never taught him anything. And if anyone says that he has ever learned or heard anything from me in private which all the world has not heard, I should like you to know that he is speaking an untruth.

But I shall be asked, Why do people delight in continually conversing with you? I have told you already, Athenians, the whole truth about this: they like to hear the cross-examination of the pretenders to wisdom; there is amusement in this. And this is a duty which the God has imposed upon me, as I am assured by oracles, visions, and in every sort of way in which the will of divine power was ever signified to anyone. This is true, O Athenians; or, if not true, would be soon refuted. For if I am really corrupting the youth, and have corrupted some of them already, those of them who have grown up and have become sensible that I gave them bad advice in the days of their youth should come forward as accusers and take their revenge; and if they do not like to come themselves, some of their relatives, fathers, brothers, or other kinsmen, should say what evil their families suffered at my hands. Now is their time. Many of them I see in the court. There is Crito, who is of the same age and of the same deme with myself; and there is Critobulus his son, whom I also see. Then again there is Lysanias of Sphettus, who is the father of Aeschines – he is present; and also there is Antiphon of Cephisus, who is the father of Epignes; and there are the brothers of several who have associated with me. There is Nicostratus the son of Theosdotides, and the brother of Theodotus (now Theodotus himself is dead, and therefore he, at any rate, will not seek to stop him); and there is Paralus the son of Demodocus, who had a brother Theages; and Adeimantus the son of Ariston, whose brother Plato is present; and Aeantodorus, who is the brother of Apollodorus, whom I also see. I might mention a great many others, any of whom Meletus should have produced as witnesses in the course of his speech; and let him still produce them, if he has forgotten – I will make way for him. And let him say, if he has any testimony of the sort which he can produce. Nay, Athenians, the very opposite is the truth. For all these are ready to witness on behalf of the corrupter, of the destroyer of their kindred, as Meletus and Anytus call me; not the corrupted youth only – there might have been a motive for that – but their uncorrupted elder relatives. Why should they too support me with their testimony? Why, indeed, except for the sake of truth and justice, and because they know that I am speaking the truth, and that Meletus is lying.

Well, Athenians, this and the like of this is nearly all the defense which I have to offer. Yet a word more. Perhaps there may be someone who is offended at me, when he calls to mind how he himself, on a similar or even a less serious occasion, had recourse to prayers and supplications with many tears, and how he produced his children in court, which was a moving spectacle, together with a posse of his relations and friends; whereas I, who am probably in danger of my life, will do none of these things. Perhaps this may come into his mind, and he may be set against me, and vote in anger because he is displeased at this. Now if there be such a person among you, which I am far from affirming, I may fairly reply to him: My friend, I am a man, and like other men, a creature of flesh and blood, and not of wood or stone, as Homer says; and I have a family, yes, and sons. O Athenians, three in number, one of whom is growing up, and the two others are still young; and yet I will not bring any of them hither in order to petition you for an acquittal. And why not? Not from any self-will or disregard of you. Whether I am or am not afraid of death is another question, of which I will not now speak. But my reason simply is that I feel such conduct to be discreditable to myself, and you, and the whole state. One who has reached my years, and who has a name for wisdom, whether deserved or not, ought not to debase himself. At any rate, the world has decided that Socrates is in some way superior to other men. And if those among you who are said to be superior in wisdom and courage, and any other virtue, demean themselves in this way, how shameful is their conduct! I have seen men of reputation, when they have been condemned, behaving in the strangest manner: they seemed to fancy that they were going to suffer something dreadful if they died, and that they could be immortal if you only allowed them to live; and I think that they were a dishonor to the state, and that any stranger coming in would say of them that the most eminent men of Athens, to whom the Athenians themselves give honor and command, are no better than women. And I say that these things ought not to be done by those of us who are of reputation; and if they are done, you ought not to permit them; you ought rather to show that you are more inclined to condemn, not the man who is quiet, but the man who gets up a doleful scene, and makes the city ridiculous.

But, setting aside the question of dishonor, there seems to be something wrong in petitioning a judge, and thus procuring an acquittal instead of informing and convincing him. For his duty is, not to make a present of justice, but to give judgment; and he has sworn that he will judge according to the laws, and not according to his own good pleasure; and neither he nor we should get into the habit of perjuring ourselves – there can be no piety in that. Do not then require me to do what I consider dishonorable and impious and wrong, especially now, when I am being tried for impiety on the indictment of Meletus. For if, O men of Athens, by force of persuasion and entreaty, I could overpower your oaths, then I should be teaching you to believe that there are no gods, and convict myself, in my own defense, of not believing in them. But that is not the case; for I do believe that there are gods, and in a far higher sense than that in which any of my accusers believe in them. And to you and to God I commit my cause, to be determined by you as is best for you and me.

[At this point, the jury finds Socrates guilty. Socrates now offers a proposal for his sentence.]

There are many reasons why I am not grieved, O men of Athens, at the vote of condemnation. I expected it, and am only surprised that the votes are so nearly equal; for I had thought that the majority against me would have been far anger; but now, had thirty votes gone over to the other side, I should have been acquitted. And I may say that I have escaped Meletus. And I may say more; for without the assistance of Anytus and Lycon, he would not have had a fifth part of the votes, as the law requires, in which case he would have incurred a fine of a thousand drachmae, as is evident.

And so he proposes death as the penalty. And what shall I propose on my part, O men of Athens?

A copy of a statue of Aphrodite (Paris, Musée du Louvre, Hirmer Archive).

Clearly that which is my due. And what is that which I ought to pay or to receive? What shall be done to the man who has never had the wit to be idle during his whole life; but has been careless of what the many care about – wealth, and family interests, and military offices, and speaking in the assembly, and magistracies, and plots, and parties. Reflecting that I was really too honest a man to follow in this way and live, I did not go where I could do no good to you or to myself; but where I could do the greatest good privately to everyone of you, thither I went, and sought to persuade every man among you that he must look to himself, and seek virtue and wisdom before he looks to his private interests, and look to the state before he looks to the interests of the state; and that this should be the order which he observes in all his actions. What shall be done to such a one? Doubtless some good thing, O men of Athens, if he has his reward; and the good should be of a kind suitable to him. What would be a reward suitable to a poor man who is your benefactor, who desires leisure that he may instruct you? There can be no more fitting reward than maintenance in the Prytaneum, O men of Athens, a reward which he deserves far more than the citizen who has won the prize at Olympia in the horse or chariot race, whether the chariots were drawn by two horses or by many. For I am in want, and he has enough; and he only gives you the appearance of happiness, and I give you the reality. And if I am to estimate the penalty justly, I say that maintenance in the Prytaneum is the just return.

Perhaps you may think that I am braving you in saying this, as in what I said before about the tears and prayers. But that is not the case. I speak rather because I am convinced that I never intentionally wronged anyone, although I cannot convince you of that – for we have had a short conversation only; but if there were a law at Athens, such as there is in other cities, that a capital cause should not be decided in one day, then I believe that I should have convinced you; but now the time is too short. I cannot in a moment refute great slanders; and, as I am convinced that I never wronged another, I will assuredly not wrong myself. I will not say of myself that I deserve any evil, or propose any penalty. Why should I? Because I am afraid of the penalty of death which Meletus proposes? When I do not know whether death is a good or an evil, why should I propose a penalty which would certainly be an evil? Shall I say imprisonment? And why should I

Sketch of an Ionian temple in Ampelokipi in the outskirts of Athens (by Manolis Korres, 1993)

live in prison, and be the slave of the magistrates of the year – of the Eleven? Or shall the penalty be a fine, and imprisonment until the fine is paid? There is the same objection. I should have to lie in prison, for money I have none, and I cannot pay. And if I say exile (and this may possibly be the penalty which you will affix), I must indeed be blinded by the love of life if I were to consider that when you, who are my own citizens, cannot endure my discourses and words, and have found them so grievous and odious that you would fain have done with them, others are likely to endure me. No, indeed, men of Athens, that is not very likely. And what a life should I lead, at my age, wandering from city to city, living in ever-changing exile, and always being driven out! For I am quite sure that into whatever place I go, as here so also there, the young men will come to me; and if I drive them away, their elders will drive me out at their desire: and if I let them come, their fathers and friends will drive me out for their sakes.

Someone will say: Yes, Socrates, but cannot you hold your tongue, and then you may go into a foreign city, and no one will interfere with you? Now I have great difficulty in making you understand my answer to this. For if I tell you that this would be a disobedience to a divine command, and therefore that I cannot hold my tongue, you will not believe that I am serious; and if I say again that the greatest good of man is daily to converse about virtue, and all that concerning which you hear me examining myself and others, and that the life which is unexamined is not worth living – that you are still less likely to believe. And yet what I say is true, although a thing of which it is hard for me to persuade you. Moreover, I am not accustomed to think that I deserve any punishment. Had I money I might have proposed to give you what I had, and have been none the worse. But you see that I have none, and can only ask you to proportion the fine to my means. However, I think that I could afford a minae, and therefore I propose that penalty; Plato, Crito, Critobulus, and Apollodorus, my friends here, bid me say thirty minae, and they will be the sureties. Well then, say thirty minae, let that be the penalty; for that they will be ample security to you.

[At this point, the jury condemns Socrates to death. Socrates then comments on his sentence.]

Not much time will be gained, O Athenians, in

return for the evil name which you will get from the detractors of the city, who will say that you killed Socrates, a wise man; for they will call me wise even although I am not wise when they want to reproach you. If you had waited a little while, your desire would have been fulfiled in the course of nature. For I am far advanced in years, as you may perceive, and not far from death. I am speaking now only to those of you who have condemned me to death. And I have another thing to say to them: You think that I was convicted through deficiency of words – I mean, that if I had thought fit to leave nothing undone, nothing unsaid, I might have gained an acquittal. Not so; the deficiency which led to my conviction was not of words – certainly not. But I had not the boldness or impudence or inclination to address you as you would have liked me to address you, weeping and wailing and lamenting, and saying and doing many things which you have been accustomed to hear from others, and which, as I say, are unworthy of me. But I thought that I ought not to do anything common or mean in the hour of danger: nor do I now repent of the manner of my defense, and I would rather die having spoken after my manner, than speak in your manner and live. For neither in war nor yet at law ought any man to use every way of escaping death. For often in battle there is no doubt that if a man will throw away his arms, and fall on his knees before his pursuers, he may escape death; and in other dangers there are other ways of escaping death, if a man is willing to say and do anything. The difficulty, my friends, is not in avoiding death, but in avoiding unrighteousness; for that runs faster than death. I am old and move slowly, and the slower runner has overtaken me, and my accusers are keen and quick, and the faster runner, who is unrighteousness, has overtaken them. And now I depart hence condemned by you to suffer the penalty of death, and they, too, go their ways condemned by the truth to suffer the penalty of villainy and wrong; and I must abide by my award – let them abide by theirs. I suppose that these things may be regarded as fated, – and I think that they are well.

Iris from the western pediment of the Parthenon, part of the vast Elgin collection of Parthenon sculptures at the British Museum

And now, O men who have condemned me, I would fain prophesy to you; for I am about to die, and that is the hour in which men are gifted with prophetic power. And I prophesy to you who are my murderers, that immediately after my death punishment far heavier than you have inflicted on me will surely await you. Me you have killed because you wanted to escape the accuser, and not to give an account of your lives. But that will not be as you suppose: far otherwise. For I say that there will be more accusers of you than there are now; accusers whom hitherto I have restrained: and as they are younger they will be more severe with you, and you will be more offended at them. For if you think that by killing men you can avoid the accuser censuring your lives, you are mistaken; that is not a way of escape which is either possible or honorable; the easiest and noblest way is not to be crushing others, but to be improving yourselves. This is the prophecy which I utter before my departure, to the judges who have condemned me.

Friends, who would have acquitted me, I would like also to talk with you about this thing which has happened, while the magistrates are busy, and before I go to the place at which I must die. Stay then awhile, for we may as well talk with one another while there is time. You are my friends, and I should like to show you the meaning of this event which has happened to me. O my judges – for you I may truly call judges – I should like to tell you of a wonderful circumstance. Hitherto the familiar oracle within me has constantly been in the habit of opposing me even about trifles, if I was going to make a slip or error about anything; and now as you see there has come upon me that which may be thought, and is generally believed to be, the last and worst evil. But the oracle made no sign of opposition, either as I was leaving my house and going out in the morning, or when I was going up into this court, or while I was speaking, at anything which I was going to say; and yet I have often been stopped in the middle of a speech; but now in nothing I either said or did touching this matter has the oracle opposed me. What do I take to be the explanation of this? I will tell you. I regard this as a proof that what has happened to me is a good, and that those of us who think that death is an evil are in error. This is a great proof to me of what I am saying, for the customary sign would surely have opposed me had I been going to evil and not to good.

Let us reflect in another way, and we shall see that there is great reason to hope that death is a good, for one of two things: – either death is a state of nothingness and utter unconsciousness, or, as men say, there is a change and migration of the soul from this world to another. Now if you suppose that there is no consciousness, but a sleep like the sleep of him who is undisturbed even by the sight of dreams, death will be an unspeakable gain. For if a person were to select the night in which his sleep was undisturbed even by dreams, and were to compare with this the other days and nights of his life, and then were to tell us how many days and nights he had passed in the course of his life better and more pleasantly than this one, I think that any man, I will not say a private man, but even the great king, will not find many such days or nights, when compared with the others. Now if death is like this, I say that to die is gain; for eternity is then only a single night. But if death is the journey to another place, and there, as men say, all the dead are, what good, O my friends and judges, can be greater than this? If indeed when the pilgrim arrives in the world below, he is delivered from the professors of justice in this world, and finds the true judges who are said to give judgment there, Minos and Rhadamanthus and Aeacus and Triptolemus, and other sons of God who were righteous in their own life, that pilgrimage will be worth making. What would not a man give if he might converse with Orpheus and Musaeus and Hesiod and Homer? Nay, if this be true, let me die again and again. I, too, shall have a wonderful interest in a place where I can converse with Palamedes, and Ajax the son of Telamon, and other heroes of old, who have suffered death through an unjust judgment; and there will be no small pleasure, as I think, in comparing my own sufferings with theirs.

Above all, I shall be able to continue my search into true and false knowledge; as in this world, so also in that; I shall find out who is wise, and who pretends to be wise, and is not. What would not a man give, O judges, to be able to examine the leader of the great Trojan expedition; or Odysseus or Sisyphus, or numberless others, men and women too! What infinite delight would there be in conversing with them and asking them questions! For in that world they do not put a man to death for this; certainly not. For besides being happier in that world than in this, they will be immortal, if what is said is true.

Wherefore, O judges, be of good cheer about death, and know this of a truth – that no evil can happen to a good man, either in life or after death. He and his are not neglected by the gods; nor has my own approaching end happened by mere chance. But I see clearly that to die and be released was better for me; and therefore the oracle gave no sign. For which reason also, I am not angry with my accusers, or my condemners; they have done me no harm, although neither of them meant to do me any good; and for this I may gently blame them.

Still I have a favor to ask of them. When my sons are grown up, I would ask you, O my friends, to punish them; and I would have you trouble them, as I have troubled you, if they seem to care about riches, or anything, more than about virtue; or if they pretend to be something when they are really nothing – then reprove them, as I have reproved you, for not caring about that for which they ought to care, and thinking that they are something when they are really nothing. And if you do this, I and my sons will have received justice at your hands.

The hour of departure has arrived, and we go our ways – I to die, and you to live. Which is better God only knows.

Translated by Benjamin Jowet

MEDICINE IN ANCIENT GREECE

*By Ernest A. Kollitides**

Somebody once said that everything we possess we owe either to Nature or to the Ancient Greeks. This is certainly true in the case of medicine and the healing arts. Long before mankind had any concept of medicine, it was nature that was the great healer and it was Hippocrates, the Father of Medicine, who taught us how to help nature and not impede her work. But Greek medicine did not start or end with Hippocrates.

From about 3,000 B.C. the various tribes that were later collectively known as the Greeks were gradually settling on the Aegean islands, the Mediterranean coast of Asia minor, and the Greek mainland. It is almost impossible to know how much medical knowledge the Greeks learned from Egypt or from the remarkable Minoan civilization centered on Crete. We do know, however, that the Mycenean Greeks traded with both of them and the Homeric epics refer to battle wounds and treatments.

According to D.H. Frolich, the Iliad refers to 147 cases of battle wounds of which 106 were spear thrusts, 17 sword slashes, 12 arrow shots, and 12 sling shots. The mortality of these injuries was 77.6 percent. We also learn that the army doctor of King Menelaos of Sparta (the husband of Helen of Troy) extracted an arrow, sucked out the blood, and applied an ointment on the king's wound.

However, none of the medical interventions described in Homer show any hint of Egyptian influence which leads us to conclude that, even if there was some prehistoric outside influence, Greek medicine quickly went its own way. Homer depicts Asclepios as a tribal chief and a skilled healer of injuries, whose sons were called Asclepiads and became physicians, the forerunners of all future healers. He was portrayed with a staff intertwined with two snakes – their skin-shedding symbolizing the renewal of life – a symbol still in use today. Asclepios, who in myth is presented as god, also had two daughters, Hygeia (health) and Panacea (cure-all).

Shrines to Asclepios were built all over Greece, the most famous two on the island of Cos and Epidauros. To their magnificent temples came patients from all over the Greek world and beyond, seeking a cure to all kinds of ailments and, to be sure, some got what they came for. Simple practices such as baths, dieting, massage, and exercise were used at these temples but the main treatment was based on psychotherapy, known as "incubation." After making sacrifices to the god and taking a purification bath, the patient would sleep in the colonnaded terrace, the "avaton" and would either be visited by god Asclepios in a dream, or would be treated by the god's earthly agents, the priests. Ointment and herbal remedies, and even minor surgery, were common at these temples.

Even though the Greeks were more intellectual, and, therefore, less superstitious than Egyptians or Babylonians, the Greek doctors, up until the dawn of 5th century B.C., seemed to have had more faith in religious healing including exorcism, spirits, shamans, and priests than in physical remedies and cures.

All this changed in the post-Hippocratic Age. But even before Hippocrates, the ancient Greek medical world began to stir with the medical findings of Pythagoras and some of his disciples, such as Alcmaeon.

Following is a short list of great and pioneering ancient Greek doctors and their momentous contributions to medicine.

Alcmaeon

Physician, (flourished c. 520 B.C.). Disciple of Pythagoras, was first to conduct scientific dissections of the human body. He differentiated arteries from veins and correctly judged that the brain was the seat of the intellect. He identified the optical nerve and the tubes connecting the ears to the mouth. These are now called Eustachian tubes after the Italian anatomist who "discovered" them 2,000 later.

Hippocrates

Physician, (460-370 B.C.). He is not called the "Father of Medicine" because he was the first physician; clearly, he was not the first. What won him this amply deserved designation was his founding, on the island of Cos, of the most rational and advanced school of medicine of the ancient world. He studied in Athens but, following Greek custom, he travelled widely to Thessaly, Macedonia, and Thrace to broaden his experience. Numerous writings are attributed to him and, until a couple of hundred years ago, he was considered the ultimate medical authority. All doctors pay him homage when they take the "Hippocratic Oath." He urged doctors to maintain high professional and ethical standards and to discover the physical causes of illness.

Unlike all before him, Hippocrates believed that disease was the result of natural rather than supernatural causes. Thus, he signaled the end of the witch-doctor, the sorcerer, the magician, and the exploiting priest and launched the new era of clinical medicine. He established basic principles of dietary and holistic medicine and considered the brain the center of intellect. He relied more on general measures, such as diet, change of air, etc., rather than drugs. He believed that the food intake, which he considered fuel, should be proportional to the individual's physical activity. Unlike other medical schools, the Hippocratic school was never content to just speculate or propose theories, but it also performed excellent clinical experiments. Thus, under supervision, a patient was given different kinds of food [similar to present day test meals] and, following induced vomiting, the inadequately digested ingredients would be eliminated from the patient's diet.

Hippocrates coined many famous maxims, such as "One person's food, is another person's poison;" "Desperate diseases require desperate measures;" "Medicine must be dissociated from the studies of theology and philosophy;" "Do not disturb a patient either during or after a crisis, and try no experiments neither with purges nor with diuretics;" "All diseases occur at all seasons, but some diseases are more apt to occur and to be aggravated at certain seasons;" "In winter occur pleurisy, pneumonia, colds, sore throats, headaches, dizziness, apoplexy." Overuse over the centuries may have made such axioms sound somewhat trite, but at Hippocrates' time they were pioneering, even revolutionary.

Hippocrates, who breathed a new spirit into medicine, really launched modern medicine 2,500 years ago. The Hippocratic collection of books, consisting of 100 volumes, and written by him and other authors inspired by him, collide head-on with the magical rites, the secret incantations, and the bewildering and tortured theology of opportunistic priests of earlier times. They advance scientific observation of symptoms, objective judgement, serene wisdom, and the careful recording of the physical signs of the illness, both to indicate possible treatments and to assist in the recognition of similar diseases in other patients. All of these were essential prerequisites for a good doctor then and now. No wonder he is universally considered the "Father of Medicine."

The lofty goals and the high ideals of the Hippocratic school are clearly evident in the "Hippocratic Oath" that his students had to take upon entering their medical apprenticeship. Perhaps the seedling from the 2,500-year-old plane tree on the island of Cos – under which Hippocrates taught –

A statue of the goddess Hygeia

now growing near the entrance of the New York Hospital provides a fitting transcendental symbolic link between the islands of Manhattan and Cos, each located in a region that, in its own time, provided the best medicine in the world. It was in this hospital that a modern descendant of Hippocrates, the late Dr. George Papanicolaou discovered the famous "Pap-test" that, in the last few decades has saved untold numbers of lives.

Aristotle

Philosopher (384-322 B.C.). This greatest figure in the history of science, though not a physician himself, nevertheless had a remarkable effect on medicine, as he did in just about every other field of knowledge. He dissected and studied many different animals and thus founded the field of biology, zoology, histology, and the science of comparative anatomy and embryology – all related to medicine. His views had an incalculable impact on all branches of science, including medicine.

Herophilos and Erasistratos

Herophilos, an anatomist who flourished from 300 to 250 B.C., and Erasistratos, a physician (c. 304-250 B.C.), pioneered scientific anatomy on dead human bodies to educate their students and to study organs and their function. They correctly divided the brain into cerebrum and cerebellum and studied the reproductive system and its operation. Their work was not surpassed, or even equalled, for at least 1,500 years.

Galen

Physiologist, physician (130-203 A.D.). One of the great physicians of antiquity, Galen studied philosophy in Pergamon and Smyrna and medicine in Alexandria which was then a thriving center for Greek science. Graduating at the age of 28, he was appointed surgeon to a school of gladiators, where he had the opportunity to study wounds. However, he was so confident of his abilities, he moved his practice to Rome where, after a few years, he was hired by the Emperor Marcus Aurelius.

Galen made many contributions to anatomy even though at this time it had become illegal to dissect human bodies and he had to use apes and pigs. He made many discoveries in anatomy and physiology, including the fact that the arteries were filled with blood, not air as it was believed until that time. Unfortunately, he missed the point of the complete circulation of the blood, as did all doctors for the next several hundred years. From the 500 books Galen had written, only 80 survive; the rest were burned in a fire that destroyed his home in Rome.

Galen accepted the Aristotelian view that Nature makes everything on purpose and he set out to justify the form of every structure of the human body. With the knowledge of his time, this was virtually impossible, but he wrote with such confidence that people believed everything he wrote. He often paid tribute to his great predecessor Hippocrates who, because of his personality and medical school, left a much greater legacy than he, even though Galen's reputation and influence continued long after his death.

Dioscorides

Physician-surgeon (Flourished c. 60 A.D.). Dioscorides studied plants as a source of drugs and wrote five books which formed the world's first scientific pharmacopeia containing meticulous botanical and pharmacological prescriptions free of demons, evil spirits, and magic. His books were later translated into Latin and formed the basis of modern botanical research. Notes TIME Magazine in its January 15, 2001 issue cover story: *Drugs of the Future*: "In an age in which so much of medical science is utterly incomprehensible – even to other scientists – it is comforting to remind ourselves from time to time that a lot of what passes for modern medicine is simply the refinement and repackaging of ancient remedies."

Women in Ancient Greek Medicine

One of the earliest scientists to occupy himself with medicine was the philosopher Pythagoras. He and his disciples wrote the first essays on child care but the master's wife and daughters helped. As a matter of fact, they were so good on this subject, they won a debate with the respected physician Euryphon in arguing that a seven-month, or less, foetus was viable.

History tells us that, during their honeymoon on the island of Lesbos, Aristotle's wife Pythias assisted him in studying biology, botany, and physiology. Together they wrote an encyclopedia with their important findings. Pythias was particularly good in embryology, histology, and systematic collection and astute examination of all living things. Their collection and study of eggs of different species led them to make excellent observations and write books on generation and histology and proposed theories on fertilization and embryonic development. She may not have signed any of Aristotle's books, but he never hid the fact that she was his valuable assistant.

Artemisia, who became queen of Caria after the death of her husband Mausolos, was a medical student and a botanist and named many of the flowers she had studied with the names of friends and monarchs, including her own. She was an expert in medicinal herbs and her skill was praised by Strabon, Pliny, and Theophrastos.

In Thessaly, there were women surgeons capable of removing arrow heads and other missiles. Seneca praised the "skillful fingers of his woman doctor" and Greeks recognized the value of women in obstetrics. We learn from Pliny that Sotira and Lais and the Theban Olympias wrote a book on sterility and abortions and Salpe on ophthalmic diseases and that Philista, the sister of king Pyrrhus (318-272 B.C.) was an obstetrix (in Greek *iatromaia*), or midwife.

Women were allowed to study medicine in all Hippocratic schools where obstetrics and gynecology were established branches of medicine. Medical schools in Alexandria taught large classes of men and women. When the Romans conquered Corinth in 146 B.C. they enslaved hundreds of Greek women to be sold in Rome. The medical women brought the highest prices.

In spite of Hippocrates and the medical philosophy of his schools, doctors were not ready yet to discard the supernatural aspects in medicine [I suppose because people in their desperation demanded them], and shortly after his death, the deification of Hippocrates began. Magic and witchcraft were not to be expelled from medicine as readily as Hippocrates had thought. Thus, as R.C. Macfie points out in the *Romance of Medicine*, "he who had performed no magic living was reputed to perform magic dead."

Also, several years after Aristotle's death, biology was considered a rather unimportant part of medicine and the accumulated knowledge stagnated. With the sunset of the Golden Age of Athens many other fields of science suffered the same fate. Similarly, after Galen's death, all serious work in anatomy and physiology came to a halt because of the naive belief that he had discovered and described everything a doctor needed to know and,

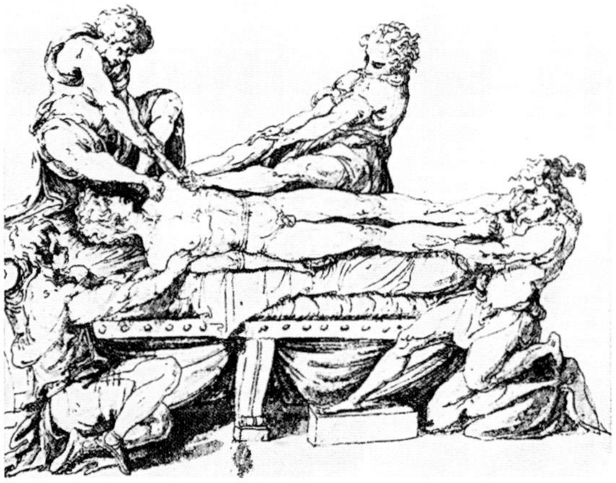

A gravure depicting a dislocated shoulder surgery

therefore, there was no need for further research.

In spite of these and other major setbacks to medicine, Hippocrates's spirit of study, discovery, and treatment managed to survive until it was overcome by the intellectual stagnation of the Middle Ages, especially in Western Europe. Byzantium did a far better job. However, with the fall of Byzantium to the Ottomans, the writings of the ancient Greek doctors were re-introduced into Europe via Italy and they had been imported into Spain by the Arabs. As with the writings of all the other Greek philosophers, they sparked the Renaissance and ancient Greek medicine became the fertile soil upon which our modern medicine grew and advanced.

Dr. Angelique G. Panayotatou of Alexandria writes in her book *L' Hygiene chez les ancient Grecs* (Paris, 1923): "The Hellenic spirit left to all future ages its creative genius. It was the ferment of the social and intellectual organism... Its influence was never one sided, because the Hellenic spirit never expressed itself merely by one idea but by creative acts." She then emphasized that this creative spirit and the belief in hygiene and health carried mankind up to the days of Louis Pasteur (1822-1895) in spite of countless setbacks and fluctuations and an imperfect understanding of the causes of infection or disease.

---

* *Ernest A. Kollitides is a scientist-professional engineer and historian who has published numerous articles and lectured frequently at national and international forums, universities, etc. on scientific, environmental, and historical subjects. He was also asked to address the U.S. Congress in Washington, D.C. on environmental issues. A world traveller, he has visited and studied the historical sites of the ancient Egyptian, Greek, Persian, Roman, and Byzantine worlds.*

THE OATH OF HIPPOCRATES

I SWEAR BY APOLLO THE PHYSICIAN, AND AESCULAPIUS, AND HEALTH, AND ALL-HEAL, AND ALL THE GODS AND GODDESSES, THAT, ACCORDING TO MY ABILITY AND JUDGEMENT, I WILL KEEP THIS OATH AND THIS STIPULATION TO RECKON HIM WHO TAUGHT ME THIS ART EQUALLY DEAR TO ME AS MY PARENTS, TO SHARE MY SUBSTANCE WITH HIM, AND RELIEVE HIS NECESSITIES IF REQUIRED; TO LOOK UPON HIS OFFSPRING IN THE SAME FOOTING AS MY OWN BROTHERS, AND TO TEACH THEM THIS ART, IF THEY SHALL WISH TO LEARN IT, WITHOUT FEE OR STIPULATION; AND THAT BY PRECEPT, LECTURE, AND EVERY OTHER MODE OF INSTRUCTION, I WILL IMPART A KNOWLEDGE OF THE ART TO MY OWN SONS, AND THOSE OF MY TEACHERS, AND TO DISCIPLES BOUND BY A STIPULATION AND OATH ACCORDING TO THE LAW OF MEDICINE, BUT TO NONE OTHERS. I WILL FOLLOW THAT SYSTEM OF REGIMEN WHICH, ACCORDING TO MY ABILITY AND JUDGMENT, I CONSIDER FOR THE BENEFIT OF MY PATIENTS, AND ABSTAIN FROM WHATEVER IS DELETERIOUS AND MISCHIEVOUS. I WILL GIVE NO DEADLY MEDICINE TO ANY ONE IF ASKED, NOR SUGGEST ANY SUCH COUNSEL; AND IN LIKE MANNER I WILL NOT GIVE TO A WOMAN A PESSARY TO PRODUCE ABORTION. WITH PURITY AND WITH HOLINESS I WILL PASS MY LIFE AND PRACTICE MY ART. I WILL NOT CUT PERSONS LABORING UNDER THE STONE, BUT WILL LEAVE THIS TO BE DONE BY MEN WHO ARE PRACTITIONERS OF THIS WORK. INTO WHATEVER HOUSES I ENTER, I WILL GO INTO THEM FOR THE BENEFIT OF THE SICK, AND WILL ABSTAIN FROM EVERY VOLUNTARY ACT OF MISCHIEF AND CORRUPTION; AND, FURTHER FROM THE SEDUCTION OF FEMALES OR MALES, OF FREEMEN AND SLAVES. WHATEVER, IN CONNECTION WITH MY PROFESSIONAL PRACTICE OR NOT, IN CONNECTION WITH IT, I SEE OR HEAR, IN THE LIFE OF MEN, WHICH OUGHT NOT TO BE SPOKEN OF ABROAD, I WILL NOT DIVULGE, AS RECKONING THAT ALL SUCH SHOULD BE KEPT SECRET. WHILE I CONTINUE TO KEEP THIS OATH UNVIOLATED, MAY IT BE GRANTED TO ME TO ENJOY LIFE AND THE PRACTICE OF THE ART, RESPECTED BY ALL MEN, IN ALL TIMES! BUT SHOULD I TRESPASS AND VIOLATE THIS OATH, MAY THE REVERSE BE MY LOT.

Hippocrates, Works trans., Francis Adams (New York; Loeb) vol. I, 299-301.

Ancient Greek Religious Thought Marks Christian Theology

*By Demetrios J. Constantelos**

The first idea I will analyze is spirituality and religious thought. From the outset I should emphasize that I am concerned with the official trend in ancient Greek thought and not with popular religious life. While many persons know of the importance of Greek art, Greek poetry, Greek philosophy, and other aspects of ancient Greek civilization, few realize that Greek religion too repays our study at the present day. The terms theology, enthusiasm, psyche, demon, ecstasy, mystery, theism, atheism, hagiology, hierarchy, and therapy derive from the Greek religious language and experience. A language learned from childhood and transmitted from generation to generation leaves its imprint upon human experience. Ancient Greek religious thought affects us today because it has put its stamp on Christian theology and practice.

One of the distinct characteristics of the evolution of Greek culture is that the lower and more embryonic forms of ideas, whether religious or philosophical, have survived through the ages either by the side or within the higher and more developed. Modern man of the Western heritage, whether a practicing Christian or not, has been nourished on a tradition in which Hebrew monotheism, reformed by Jesus Christ and Paul of Tarsus, is combined with a metaphysical theology derived from Greek philosophers – Parmenides, Plato, and Aristotle. Let us remember that Christianity, Orthodox, Catholic, Episcopal, Baptist, Evangelical, Methodist, Presbyterian, Church, Ecclesiastical, Synagogue, Pope, Patriarch, presbyter, and deacon are terms of Greek origin and transmit Greek ideas, concepts, and experiences. Of course it is easier to write the history of ideas than a history of their application; the history of a religion than a history of its practice; the history of the democratic idea than a history of democracy in action.

The ancient Greeks advised: *"panti theon aition ypertithemen"* that is, set god over all as cause (Pindaros, *Pythian Odes*, 5.25). Thus the first idea we need to explore is the idea of divinity, god. But what did the ancient Greeks mean by god? What was their idea of divinity?

The Greeks provided no specific definition of divinity. Whatever is immortal, is divine; whatever is divine is immortal. Divinity, deity, or god meant not a person but something alive, active, imperishable – energy. Of course one may immediately react and remind us of the Olympian gods and goddesses, and other lesser divinities of Greek mythology. Even though myths and mythology belong to the field of literature rather than religion, we need to underline that even in mythology Greek religion is neither uniform nor strictly defined. Belief in many gods and practices of cultic rites were never absent from popular religion of many ancient (Babylonian, Egyptian, Hittite, Hebrew) and modern people, including the Greeks. But many ancient Greeks interpreted their myths and mythological divinities allegorically. From as early as Minoan and Mycenaean religious myths in the Cyclades, Crete, and mainland Greece, several names of goddesses appear as diverse epithets of the same divinity or diversified forms of the same entity. And lesser gods, such as Hyakinthos, appear in assimilation with the chief of gods – Zeus. Gods and goddesses have been described as a "dual monotheism." It is doubtful whether Homer himself believed in the real existence of the Olympian deities. Homer and Hesiod were accused by ancient Greeks such as Theagenes, Hekataios, Xenophanes, and Protagoras, as the inventors of Greek polytheism. Whatever the case, myths and mythological divinities as emblematic of truths, whether as natural forces or human attributes, were never absent from ancient Greek thought. (Cf. Gilbert Murray, *Five Stages of Greek Religion*, New York: Doubdleday, 1955, pp. 66-72; Jean-Pierre Vernant, *"Greek Religion" in Religions of Antiquity*, ed. by Robert B. Seltzer, New York: Macmillan Co., 1989 164-65).

In the last analysis archaic Greek religion recognized many divine powers in one divine cosmos.

The search for the Arche, the prime cause/mover, became a major concern of the ancient Greeks after the seventh century. Divinity was the source of knowledge because it was perceived as the cause of creation of everything. *"Human nature has no knowledge, but the divine nature has,"* said Heracleitos, (Heracleitos, *Fragments*, no. 78), a belief repeated by many Greek thinkers from Homer to Aristotle. "Begin with god" is an ancient maxim which has survived and is practiced by the modern Greeks.

The idea of divinity went through stages of development, and religion among the ancient Greeks was a constant quest. The fourth century poet and philosopher Menander captured the idea of religion in ancient Greece in the following lines:

By each of us there stands directly from birth a kind of mystagogic spirit to lead us through the labyrinthine mysteries of life
And we must never think this spirit evil, Nor fraught with wickedness to harm our lives,
But always hold God good in everything,
Those who themselves turn base in character and complicate their lives exceedingly,
When they have ruined all through carelessness,
Declare and hold as cause this spirit-guide,
And make him evil, becoming such themselves.

(Menander, *Fragments*, no. 549k; 535, 536)

A detail from the bronze statue of the goddess Athina in military garb found in Piraeus (4th century B.C.)

The idea of divinity not as an exclusive possession, like the god of ancient Israel, but as a universal, all-encompassing being became a central idea of the ancient Greeks. In Homeric times it was acknowledged that *"all people have need of the gods – divinity."* (Homer, *The Odyssey*, Bks 3 and 4. Ennis Rees' translation, NY: Random House, 1960, 34, 63). The Greeks searched for the divinity in the beauty and harmony of the cosmos, the powers and forces of nature, in the logic and conscience of the human being. Thus in ancient Greek religion, the divinity is everywhere – it is a cosmic being expressed in various ways and manners. Zeus, Apollo, Athena, Demeter are names of the same divinity in different actions and as different attributes of the human being. The presence of the divinity everywhere implies the deification of the world. The unity of human nature is achieved through its unity with the *Pneuma* (Spirit) common to all human beings. The spirituality of one person can progress in relationship with the spirituality of other people in a community, like the ancient Greek polis or the Christian *ecclesia* (or church). Spiritual and religious duties are realized within the community and spiritual, religious, and political functions are interwoven.

The idea of divinity became subject to evolution and refinement after the sixth century. The ideas of Thales of Miletos, the first among the Greek philosophers, about divinity and the cosmos, influenced later thinkers including Plato and Aristotle. Thales emphasized the spiritual nature of the cosmos, the ever-presence of the divinity everywhere and in everything. "All things are full of god" he taught. "The whole world is a living organism, filled with souls, and god is the mind behind the cosmos." (G.S. Kirk and J.E. Raven, *The Presocratic Philosophers,* Cambridge: Cambridge University Press, 1975, pp. 94-96). Later thinkers such as Plato emphasized the interrelationship between the physical and the metaphysical. Nature is neither material nor metaphysical; it is an organic whole. And the human being is a part of the whole landscape – an organic whole of the physical and the metaphysical.

From a religion of polytheism, to religious syncretism, through a belief in philosophical monotheism, the Greeks arrived at the belief in an "unknown God," who ultimately was identified with the Logos of the Gospel of John – Jesus the Christ. Their understanding of the Christian God's nature and attributes, God's relationship with the cosmos, Christian theology of the first five centuries in particular was Greek. The so-called Gentile Christianity and the Christian Church of the first five centuries was likewise Greek. In the times of Jesus and later, Gentile corresponded to Greek (Jn 7.35; Rom 3.9, etc.). Gentile stood for the culture and the religion of the Greeks and those influenced by the Greeks.

As a historical religion, Christianity was born in a Hellenistic Judaism and it quickly spread in the Greek world of late antiquity. The Christian scriptures were written entirely in Greek and Greek cities such as Antioch, Ephesus, Philippi, Thessaloniki, and Corinth were the first to be evangelized and receive Christianity. Latin Christianity was an offshoot of Greek Christianity, like a branch which grows from a tree trunk. The early Church was implanted in the Greek-speaking world and expressed itself in the Greek language for many centuries.

The idea of divinity, then, as it evolved in Greek thought, both non-Christian and Christian, is imbedded in contemporary theology which emphasizes the importance of the mystery, incomprehensibility, and God's all-encompassing love. "God is called philios and etaireios, God of love and fellowship, because God brings mankind into union, and desires that all should be friends one with another" in the words of the first century philosopher Dio Chrysostom (Dio Chrysostom, *Orations*, no. 12). The idea of the divinity is closely related with the idea of humanity, what it means to be human.

The second major idea I intend to touch upon is the idea about the human being, the anthropos. *"There are many wonderful things, but none more wonderful than man"* exclaims Sophocles's chorus in the Antigone (Sophocles, *Antigone*, 332). The human person was perceived as a being having its existence in the First Being, the source of everything and present everywhere. Divinity and humanity are two powers in constant interaction and cooperation. The major contributions of the ancient Greeks to Western civilization are based on the conception they had of the human person's ontology – the human person as a spiritual, rational (logical), moral, social, artistic, and creative evolutionary being of infinite value. Human energy was perceived as an innate divine quality, a manifestation of the creator's

Detail from a depiction of the god Apollon from the pediment of the Temple of Zeus in Olympia (Museum of Olympia)

vital energy. The human being represents so to speak the Supreme Being on earth. But the human was understood as a mortal destined for immortality. Only divinity is by itself immortal. The human being is a dependent being and any attempt to ignore or supersede the divinity results in severe consequences.

The two protagonists in the Homeric epics, the Iliad and the Odyssey, represent some of the central ideas of pre-classical Greece. The example of Achilles was used to teach that irrational wrath is futile and destructive, and that self-control is indispensable and a source of rewards. No matter how powerful and how clever, whether an Achilles, Agamemnon, or Odysseus man is not god, an all-powerful being. Pride which would attempt to elevate the human to a divine status was a hubris, an arrogant insult against divinity, and destructive. Laws, whether of the universe, nature, or the state need to be obeyed because all laws are of divine origins.

Man must be himself and play the part he has been assigned to by nature with a sense of humility. The self, which is absent from the Old Testament, is an independent and a dependent entity and it appears balanced and measured. In the Homeric epics we discern a synergy between Divinity and humanity–the principles of religious humanism. In the Odyssey we find the ideal which should be pursued by the human mind in cooperation with the divinity. When Odysseus found himself in a hopeless situation, the divinity in the form of Ino (Leukothea) appeared and urged him not to despair but to move on, assuring him other help (Homer, *The Odyssey*, Bk 5. Rees' transl. pp. 87-91).

Odysseus is the prototype of the man who thinks but who also needs divine assistance. Mind and body are good in themselves and need to be in constant cooperation and harmony. The body must possess valor, endurance, health; the mind must provide intelligence, alertness, ability to function with decision-making and moderation qualities. Presence of mind and inner strength were highly admired in ancient Greece. The human mind, however, should be able to solve not only personal but also universal problems. Man by himself is not the measure of all things, but with supernatural assistance he is. Are these ideas not of contemporary value? Who doubts that these principles cannot affect our lives for the better?

Notwithstanding their understanding of man's limitations, the ancient Greeks advised: "strive always after excellence" aien aristeuein, (Homer, *Iliad*, ch. 6, 208; Ch. 11, 783), using an alert mind and pursuing it through vigorous action. The idea of excellence implied an appreciation of creative intelligence, tireless inquiry, education for the sake of a good life – all harmonized and balanced. *Miden ogan, pan metron ariston*, nothing in excess, moderation in everything, were principles of the educated mind. The people who coined the term harmonia applied it in their personal life – the life of body and soul – thus *nous ygies en somati ygies*, a healthy mind in a healthy body; in the relations between order and freedom, religious unity and rational individualism, nationalism and universalism, individual rights and community obligations. (See Preston H. Epps, *Thoughts from the Greeks*, Columbia, Missouri: University of Missouri Press, 1969 121-130).

A detail from the bronze statue of the god Poseidon found in Artemision, north of the island of Euboea (circa 460 B.C., National Archaeological Museum of Athens)

Whether harmonia remained a yearning of an ideal or became a realized experience, it was born as a result of conflicts and dialogues between thought and experience, faith and reason, mythical symbolism and historical realities. For example, the conflict between monarchy and oligarchy, oligarchy and the demos gave birth to democracy. And democracy is a system which harmonizes extremes and brings equality among people of diverse interests and different talents. The debate between the ideas expressed by Pericles in his famous Funeral Oration and those of Plato's Republic affects our life today. Democracy or Monarchy? Democracy or Dictatorship? Democracy or Oligarchy? are questions of perennial significance.

Several more important and relevant ideas were emphasized in pre-classical Greece. Self-control, fidelity, and trust in married life; hospitality toward all – no matter what the origin, color, or creed of the person in need of hospitality; generosity; righteousness; respect for the elders; but also eros as the beginning of trust between husband and wife. No wonder the Homeric epics were considered a gospel among the ancient Greeks and are studied to the present day as classics, not only as epic poetry but also as sources for the study of the social and moral values of the ancient Greeks.

The human being was perceived as both a spiritual, divinely ordained person, but also as an intellectual earthly being. The later was the result of the presence of reason (*logos*), but reason was not the ultimate in human conduct. There is something deeper and autonomous in the human psyche, a daimonion, a spirit of supernatural origins. Their investigation and study of the nature of the human led them to the conclusion of God's or the Divinity's existence. Thus the affinity between the universal Logos and human logos, the affinity between the Divine and the human. At no times were the ancient Greeks anthropocentric but throughout their long history they combined theocentricism and anthropocentricism, a synergy, if you please, between Divinity and humanity. At no time was Greek civilization only man-centered for it was deity-centered also. Some of their artistic and literary productions were celebrations of both Divinity and humanity. And their earliest, the Ionian, or Pre-Socratic, philosophers believed that their knowledge and wisdom derived from or were gifts of the Divinity. The human being as a spiritual and intellectual being has metaphysical roots. "Men are gods, and gods are men... god in man and man in god" said Herakleitos (Kirk and Raven, *The Presocratic Philosophers*, op.cit., 210). "A mystery indeed" said approvingly the second-century Christian theologian Clement of Alexandria (Clement of Alexandria, *Paidogogos*, bk. 3.1).

The interrelationship between the divine and the human was later expressed by Pindar, the greatest of the Greek Lyric poets who believed that whatever is excellent in the human being is partly inborn, a gift of the gods. He believed that in the realm of the spirit, the divine and the human met (Cf. K. W. Gransder, *"Homer and the Epic" in The Legacy of Greece*, ed. by M.I. Finley, New York: Oxford University Press, 1981, 111).

The idea of the nature of the human achieved a climax in the thought of Socrates, Plato, and Plotinos. All three emphasized the divine destiny of the human being as a soul or spiritual entity. The question was raised "What is man, and What powers and properties distinguish such a nature from any other?" (Plato, *Theaitetos*, 174). As a god-related being, man should not submit to the desires of mortal nature but should seek to take flight from the world of evil to the other, that means "becoming like the divine so far as man can, becoming righteous with the help of wisdom."

"Nothing is more like the divine than any one of us who becomes as righteous as possible. It is here that a man shows his true spirit and power or lack of spirit and nothingness" says Socrates (Ibid., 176a-c). The human as a spiritual being related to the Divinity longs to return to it.

Christianity's notion about the presence of the divine in the human and the ultimate destiny of the human to be eternally in God was not foreign to the ancient Greeks. In the Second Letter of Peter, Christians are called upon to become sharers in the divine nature through faith, courage, self control, and virtue with knowledge (2 Pet 1.5). *"If one knows himself, he will know God; and knowing God, he will be made like God,"* wrote later Clement of Alexandria (Clement of Alexandria, *Paidagogos*, Bk 3.1).

The Pantokrator at the Monastery of Daphni in Athens (second half of the 11th century – Photographic archive of Ekdotiki Athinon)

Indeed there are many common teachings between Greek philosophy and the Christian scriptures. Thus Deacon Agapetos ventured to say:

He who knows himself will know God; and he who knows God will be made like to God; and he will be made like to God who has become worthy of God; and he becomes worthy of God, who does nothing unworthy of God, but he thinks the things that are his, and speaks what he thinks, and does what he speaks.

In summary, Greek ideas in religion, philosophy, art, and politics have profoundly modified the whole trend of modern civilization. Ancient Greece (archaiac, classical, Hellenistic, Roman, and Byzantine) has imposed her thought, standards, literary forms, imagery, visions, and dreams wherever she is known. The extent of the Greek influence is incalculable throughout Europe and its intensity is at its highest in Germany, England, and France.

The Greek religious mind has seen the divine spirit of the Logos unfolding like a flower in all the races on earth. From as early as the Homeric age to the closing of the school of philosophy in Athens by Emperor Justinian in 529, the Greek mind recognized many divine powers in one divine cosmos. Their poets, philosophers, historians possessed the sense of the universal divine presence and the holiness of the universe. What Sophocles said about his native village can be expanded to include the thought of later centuries and of the whole universe: *"all the place is holy, and there is nothing which is without a share of soul."* (Sophocles, *Oedipus at Colonus*, 54c).

The perception of holiness prepared the ground for the development of monotheism under the great Neoplatonist philosophers of the early Christian era which, however, included polytheistic elements. For example, Plotinos sees a multiplicity of god emanating from me One, the Nous or Divine Intellect; the One *"encompasses in himself all things immortal, every intellect, every god, every soul."* (Plotinos, *On the Three Primary Hypostases*, Vl, k4. 10-11).

Daphni Monastery: The Resurrection (11th century – Photographic archive of Ekdotiki Athinon)

The last phase of ancient Greek thought was expressed by Simplikios, the last major of the non-Christian philosophers. In his commentary on the *Enchiridion of Epictetos*, Simplikios writes: *"The Good is source and principle of all beings. For that which all things desire, and touch all things reach up, this is the principle and the goal of all things. And the Good brings forth all things from himself."* (Simplikios, *Commentary on Epicteti Enchiridion*, 5, 4-11).

So, the searching person who aspires to know and unite with this unknown Good, or God, should strive to have a more immediate relationship with more accessible beings created by the unknown god.

Throughout their spiritual life and religious evolution, the Greeks have searched to find the divine presence. And they searched for it in their mountains and valleys, their seas and rivers, their villages and cities, their trees and springs. And they found the divine presence in the likeness of many distinct beings and yet united with the one, the unknowable.

This element is very much alive in Greek Orthodox piety today, as well as in Orthodox theology which sees God's activity in the Incarante Logos. (See the *Prayers of the Blessing of the Waters for Theophany*, Ieratikon, Athens: Ekdosis Apostolikes Diakonias, 1977, pp. 251-55. In English see translation of Joseph Raya and Jose de Vinck, *Byzantine Daily Worship* (Allendale, N.J.: Alleluia Press, 1968, pp. 597-604).

Don't you think that our seas and rivers, our mountains and lakes, our cities and towns, our environment in general would appreciate such an understanding by their modern masters–human beings and technology alike?

To be sure the persistence of ancient Greek ideas and values, including the language itself, is of importance not only for the modern Greeks but also for all the inheritors of the classical tradition. It indicates fidelity to the past but also the legitimacy, its seriousness, and the unity of Western Civilization's historical experience.

---

* *Demetrios J. Constantelos is Charles Cooper Townsend Sr. Distinguished Professor of History and Religious Studies at the Richard Stockton College of New Jersey. He is the author of many books, including* The Greeks. Their Heritage and Its Value Today *[Hellenic College Press, Brookline, MA., 1996] where a larger, more detailed version of this article appears.*

The Greek Revolution of 1821

THE ORIGINS OF THE REVOLUTION

By D.G. Kousoulas

The air over the Greek peninsula was heavy with anticipation throughout the year 1820. In the mountain villages and the small towns in the valleys below, landowners and bishops, peasants, shepherds and artisans, brigands, sailors, and monks traded rumors of things to come. Visitors from the prospering communities of the Greek diaspora as far as Paris, Vienna, and Odessa were bringing tidings of hope.

The day of delivery from Turkish rule, they claimed, was near. Almost four centuries had passed since May 29, 1453, the day the conquering armies of Sultan Mohammed had breached the walls of Constantinople ending more than a thousand years of Byzantine history. In the following centuries, Turkish hegemony spread over the Balkan lands where Byzantium once ruled. The Greeks, who previously held the levers of power in the Byzantine empire, became a vassal people, who were soon reduced to poverty and ignorance. The more fortunate among them fled to Europe and Russia where they planted the communities of Greek diaspora. In the next four hundred years, while Europe was experiencing the exhilarating awakening of the Renaissance and the Enlightenment, the Greeks went through their belated version of the Dark Ages. During this period of adversity they almost lost their sense of identity; to the Turk, they were part of the faceless mass of infidels, and to themselves, Romioi (a corrupted pronunciation of the Greek word for Roman). For the first three centuries of Ottoman rule, little of significance occurred to record in the annals of history. Then, during the closing decades of the eighteenth century, the Greeks re-emerged in history with an increasingly strong awareness of their national heritage and uniqueness.

"The blessing of the flag of Freedom at Aghia Lavra." (By Theodoros Vryzakis, 1856 – Athens, National Gallery).

The Role of the Church

The revival of national spirit was not a sudden flash of inspiration. Many forces had long been at work – some fostered unintentionally by the Turks themselves. The Orthodox Church, probably the most important among those forces, owed the Greek character it had maintained under the Turks to a fortuitous action by Sultan Mohammed. Soon after entering Constantinople, he had appointed a Greek by the name Georgios Scholarios as the new patriarch of the Orthodox Christians in the conquered lands. What the Sultan wanted was to set up a convenient channel of control over his new subjects; at the same time, considering the deep antagonism between Orthodoxy and the Vatican, he was cleverly thinking of erecting a barrier between his Christian subjects and the Catholic West. Yet, his gesture was to have unintended and far-reaching consequences. It reinforced the notion long maintained by the Greeks that they were the heirs of Byzantium, and it vested the Church with administrative and judicial authority over the Christians under Ottoman rule, which was to prove critical for the future. Even in the darkest days, the Church became a focus of identity and a barrier to assimilation with the Turks, while the Orthodox faith and the Greek language – both of which were taught by the clergy – were to serve in the course of time as the sinews of national identity.

Other factors

Several other seemingly unrelated factors paved the way toward a resurgence of the national spirit. Trade was one such factor. The Turkish conquerors regarded trade as being too humble an occupation for proud warriors. Before long, starting with the seventeenth century, Greeks in the occupied lands, working closely with their compatriots in Europe and Russia, had taken over most commercial activities, amassing fortunes in the process and building a tradition of independence and self-assertion that would later play a pivotal role.

Trade went hand in hand with transport. In 1803 Greek shipping was estimated at 131,000 tons – a huge volume for those days – with more than 16,000 sailors aboard. Shipowning families in the islands amassed wealth during the Napoleonic wars when their boats braved the British blockade for a high price.

Moreover, most of the Sultan's navy was manned with crews from the Aegean islands since the Turks generally disliked the sea. When later, at the time of the War of Independence, these sailors deserted the Turkish ships, control of sea communications in the Aegean passed to the Greek insurgents.

On land, the warlike spirit was kept alive by the klephts – the celebrated brigands who harassed the wealthy Turks in Robin Hood style – and the armatoles – local Greeks commissioned by the Ottoman authorities to keep order in their areas but who often took to the mountains and joined the klephts against the Turkish overlords.

Even fate seemed to take a hand. In 1699 the Venetians seized from the Turks most of southern Greece. The Turks returned twenty years later but by then the feudal system they had initially set up was gone, destroyed in the upheaval of the Venetian conquest. Their efforts to revive it failed. A law, which in the past had blocked the transfer of land to infidels, was conveniently ignored by corrupt administrators who, for a price, turned feudal fiefs into private estates. In the eighteenth century, Greek landowners made their appearance in the Peloponnese and in Central Greece. Land ownership became a source of power. Strong ties of dependence were forged between the landlord and the peasants who tilled his lands as sharecroppers. Moreover, the need for safety, and the craggy, mountainous terrain, forced rich and poor alike to live side by side in villages. There were no manorial houses overlooking sprawling fields as in Western Europe; life centered in the villages and the small towns, where religious ritual dominated social life.

The Phanariotes

This provincial, rustic life in the Greek peninsula was worlds apart from that of the sophisticated Phanariotes – named after Constantinople's neighborhood where most of them lived. These Greeks, through one of the curious twist of history, had come to hold many exalted positions in the administration of the Ottoman Empire. To deal with the European rulers, the early Sultans had turned to these worldly and experienced Greeks whose families had occupied important posts even in the days of the Byzantine emperors. In the course of time, the Phanariotes entrenched themselves in the inner circles of the administration and became in their own way indispensable to their Ottoman masters.

Shared Memories

In terms of life style, wealth, education, interests, and aspirations, these various groups had little in common. Yet, shared emotions, appealing myths, and practical considerations would combine in time to forge a nation.

The most overpowering emotional elements were their hostility against the Turks and their mystical faith in the revival of the Byzantine Empire. Later, as they came closer to the moment of insurrection, they visualized a large state embracing all the different Christian people living in the Balkan peninsula with the Greeks being the leading element, just as they had been in the days of Byzantium. This expectation was to prove nothing more than an illusion, but in the years before the revolution it nourished their pride and sense of destiny.

As time went on, the memories of Byzantium began to merge in the imagination of the more sophisticated with the distant echoes of classical Greece. Especially those in Europe were exposed to the growing literature on the glories of ancient Greece. Even the humble Romioi peasants were told by the intellectuals that the marble "stones" were the testimony of a great civilization and that they were the proud descendants of godlike heroes – a notion later encouraged by European humanists and liberals in search of a cause. Thus, history became, after religion, the second major force for building a national identity.

The Tide of Nationalism

By the end of the eighteenth century, especially after the ill-fated campaign instigated by Russia, the tide of nationalism gathered momentum. Not surprisingly, poets and men of letters were the first to embrace the vision of national liberation. But there was no unity of purpose at the outset. The Phanariotes advocated caution; they favored a strategy of increasing infiltration into the Ottoman power structure, confident that in time they would bring the empire under their – and thus Greek – control.

Many wealthy landowners on the mainland were also reluctant to act in a way that might jeopardize the modest improvements they had worked out in their relations with the Turkish authorities. Even the patriarchate in Constantinople and many prominent bishops saw with misgivings the mounting of revolutionary agitation.

Those who opposed a violent uprising could point to the disaster of 1770 when the Russians had instigated a revolt in the Peloponnese only to abandon the Greeks at the critical moment to the tender mercies of the sultan's Albanian soldiers. They could also argue that after the fall of Napoleon conservative forces dominated European politics. The Holy Alliance regarded any revolutionary activity as a criminal plot. Britain, on her part, favored the preservation of the Ottoman Empire as a barrier to Russia's expansion into the Mediterranean.

Swept Away

Yet, the arguments of cold logic were in the end swept away by the forces of revolution. With the opening of the nineteenth century the visionary intellectuals were joined by more practical merchants and sea captains, dedicated monks and proud klephts, patriotic bishops and landowners. The proponents of revolution came together in a secret organization known as Philiki Etairia (Society of Friends) which was formed in 1814 by three Greek merchants in Odessa. To conceal their uninspiring identity, the founders of the organization invented a "supreme authority" which many Greeks assumed to be the Russian czar himself. The society's activists, of course, made no effort to dispel this useful myth. With an elaborate system of ranks, secret rites of initiation, a fearsome oath, and the allusion to supreme backing, this secret society spread far and wide within five years. By 1820 the revolutionary agitation had reached the point where no patriotic Greek could stand aloof, let alone be openly hostile to the idea of revolution.

The Powder Ignites

Alexandros Ypsilantis, a Phanariot who was serving at the time as aide-de-camp to the czar of Russia, led the first move. Fifteen years earlier, the Turks had executed his grandfather and had forced the family into self-exile in Russia. Ypsilantis saw the struggle as a historic mission to restore the Byzantine empire. The fact that his family traced its origin to the Komninos dynasty may have sparked a personal ambition.

Ypsilantis' plan for the revolution called for the eruption of simultaneous uprisings in Greece and in Serbia to split the Sultan's forces.

Moreover, the brewing conflict between the Sultan and Ali Pasha, the ruler of Epirus, would further fragment the Turkish armies. It was a good plan on paper but it failed in its execution. In February 1821, Ypsilantis crossed the river Pruth and entered Moldavia with a small force. Serbia's Milos Obrenovich, however, did not move. The czar, at Laibach, was too busy with his partners in the Holy Alliance making plans to extinguish revolutionary fires in Latin America, Spain and Italy and was in no mood to support Ypsilantis' revolutionary plans. On June 18, Ypsilantis' small detachment was surrounded by the Turks at Dragatsani. Few survived. Ypsilantis escaped in the darkness. He managed to reach Austria, only to be thrown into prison.

The news that Ypsilantis had crossed the Prut in February reached Greece in mid-March. Greek legend has it that on March 25, 1821, Germanos, the metropolitan of Old Patras, raised the standard of revolution at the monastery of Aghia Lavra.

An appealing legend, but a legend no less. Actually, the revolution started with minor, isolated incidents which in less volatile times would have been little more than insignificant clashes between hot-blooded Greeks and isolated Turk settlers. But in March 1821, with the news that Ypsilantis had crossed the Prut, they acted as the spark that sets off the powder keg. The vizier (governor) of Peloponnese summoned to a conference in Tripolis the bishops and other prominent Greeks of the area.

Afraid they might be arrested and held hostage, many refused to go, metropolitan Germanos one of them. On March 22, Theodoros Kolokotronis with his band of fighters launched the first major operation and captured Kalamata, eliminating its weak garrison. The following day he moved toward Karytaina, while other groups seized Kalavrita and surrounded the Turkish garrison in the fortress of Patras.

When the news of Ypsilantis' failure reached Greece in July, it was much too late to turn back. The revolution was on.

---

* *From D.G. Kousoulas' book* Modern Greece: Profile of A Nation.

Revolutionary Proclamation, For Law and Fatherland

[To] the people, descended from the Greeks, who inhabit Rumeli, Asia Minor, the Mediterranean islands, Wallachia and Moldavia, and all who groan under the most unbearable tyranny of the most abominable Ottoman despotism or who have been forced to flee to foreign kingdoms, to escape its insupportable and burdensome yoke. All, I say, Christians and Turks, without any distinction of religion (since all are creatures of God and children of the first man), who think that the tyrant, called the Sultan, wholly given over to his filthy woman-obsessed appetites, surrounded by eunuchs and bloodthirsty and ignorant courtiers, has forgotten and despised humanity, has hardened his heart against innocence, and the most beautiful kingdom in the world [the Byzantine Empire], on all sides praised by the philosophers, has been reduced to a country of such abominable anarchy, where no one of whatever class or religion, is assured either of his life, or of his honor, or of his property; but where the quietest, the most innocent, the most upright citizen, is in danger of becoming, at any moment, a pitiable victim of the tyrant's imagination or of the savage deputies and unworthy magnates of the tyrant and finally (and this happens most frequently) of his most savage imitators, with their evil ways, delighting in unpunishable crime, in the most harsh inhumanity, in murder, without any examination, without any judgement.

O heavens! you are the impartial witness of such evil deeds. O sun! you daily see such beastly effronteries. O earth! you are watered continuously by the streams of innocent blood. Who has the voice to contradict. This until now unfortunate people, I say, seeing that all its miseries and woes, its daily tears, its annihilation, deriving from the bad and most vile government, from the absence of good laws, has resolved, taking courage once again, to look up to the Heavens, to raise up manfully its overburdened neck and, furiously equipping its arms with the weapons of vengeance and despair, to shout out in a great shout before the whole Oikumene, with a thunderous shout, the holy and blameless rights, which are God given, in order to live quietly in the earth.

Therefore, so that all the inhabitants may unanimously and continuously compare, with tireless scrutiny, the activities of the government of the rulers with the objective of social legislation, manfully throwing off the worthless yoke of despotism and embracing the cherished Freedom of their glorious forebears; so that they never allow themselves to be subjected in the future as slaves of the inhuman tyranny; so that each one may have, as a bright mirror before his eyes, the bases of his liberty, his security and his happiness; so that the judges manifestly may know what is their unavoidable obligation towards free citizens being judged; so that the lawmakers and the first people of the government may know the honest standard by which their calling must be measured and inspired for the happiness of the citizens is publicly proclaimed the following public declaration of the cherished rights of man and of the free inhabitants of the empire.

The full text of Rigas Pheraios Velestinlis's revolutionary proclamation, translated by Richard Clogg for his book The Movement for Greek Independence 1770-1821. *The original text is from Riga Pheraiou,* I Elliniki Dimokratia, *ed. G. Papageorgiou (Athens, 1971).*

Revolutionary Conspiracy: The Philiki Etairia

Following are the initiation rituals and the great oath of the Philiki Etairia, translated by Richard Clogg for his book The Movement for Greek Independence 1770-1821 *(Harper & Row, 1976). The original text is from* Documente privind Istoria Rominiei-Racoala din 1821. *Eteria in Principatele Romine, ed. A. Otetea et al., (Bucharest, 1960) IV, pp. 32-9.*

Part I

If you know a Greek who is a true lover of the freedom of his country and is a worthy person, and you know that he is not a member of any other secret society whatever, and that he wishes to be enrolled in our Society, not motivated by curiosity, or other such cause, but by true patriotism, then you can give him an undertaking that you will receive him into the Society.

And first you make him a blood brother, with the holy and sacred Gospel, and with the symbols (if perhaps you find yourself far from the Motherland, that is to say Greece, and you cannot do this through a priest). Then you explain the symbols and words to him, and he is obliged to become the blood brother of whichever member of the Society he chances to meet.

Second, three or more days later you present him to a priest, to whom you say that you wish to swear in this man, whether what he says about some known matter is true, (and aside so that the priest may not hear) you dictate the oath, and he repeats it three times with a loud voice. Afterwards you ask him in a loud voice, in the rearing of the priest, if those things which he repeated three times are true, and he should reply: they are and they will be true, and as a bond of my promises I swear by the Holy and Sacred Gospel. The priest should then ask him these words, and if once again he replies in this way, the priest puts him on oath according to ecclesiastical law ([which] allows Greeks far from Greece to include in the oath-taking a priest of the Western church, in the absence of an orthodox priest of the Eastern Church).

Third, after the oath you take him to a secret place and question him in detail and with the greatest accuracy according to the appointed way of questioning.

Fourth, you ask him to think carefully if he is suitable and capable of keeping the secret even in danger, if need be, of his own life, because the things he is about to hear are sacred things, on which hangs the fate of the nation itself, and that on joining the Society he should have before his eyes death and all the harsh sufferings, and also the need to which he is subject to kill any traitor to the Society whoever he may be, without the exception even of his closest relatives. Finally he should consider that every other bond or obligation which he might have is as nothing to the bond of the Society and, moreover, if he thinks that he is unable to give a decision about this, it is still within his power to withdraw from being a member of the Society.

Fifth, you explain to him the scope of the Society without loquacity and without any addition. Afterwards you leave him and say to him that on the morrow you will meet to say some articles [of the Confession] to him and that he should not forget to bring a small yellow candle. This should take place at night with extreme care not to give the slightest suspicion. On this day it is not permitted for you to have an extended talk with him.

The First Oath

I swear in the name of the truth and of justice before the Supreme Being to guard (sacrificing my own life, bearing patiently the most harsh tortures), in every respect, the power of the freedom of the secret that is about to be explained to me and that I shall answer the truth to whatever I may be asked.

Confession

(a) How do you live and where do you come from?
(b) What relatives do you have, what is your calling and what is your state [in life] ?

(c) Have you ever quarreled with one of your friends, or anyone else?
(d) Did you make it up and how did these things come to be?
(e) Are you married, have you an inclination to marry?
(f) Are you in love, were you ever in love, did you break this off, and if so when?
(g) Has damage to, or a change in, your state in life occurred?
(h) Are you happy in your calling, and what would you rather do?
(i) Have you some faithful friend, and who is he?
(j) How do you intend to live now, and in the future?

The Object of the Society

The Society consists of true Greek patriots and is called the Society of Friends. The object of its members is the betterment of the nation, and if God permits it, its freedom (the proselyte after the usual confession and sworn catechism is called a ierefs of the Friends).

Part II

After one or two days you come quietly to a safe place and first you put on the table an icon, on which the proselyte leaves his candle. Afterwards you say to him that if he does not consider himself to have sufficient strength, then he still has time to withdraw, and that from the bond he is about to accept only death can free him, and that after a short time repentance will be unforgivable. After this he kneels, on his right knee only, near the table. After he has made the sign of the cross three times to himself, you give him the icon to kiss and you place upon it his right hand, open, and you yourself light the yellow candle and put out every other light. Afterwards you give the candle to him which he, taking, holds in his left hand, and you say to him, 'This candle is the only witness, which our unfortunate country has, when its children swear the oath of freedom,' and as you trace the whole sign of the life-giving cross, you both begin, you to read, he to repeat the great oath, with all the respect appropriate to the holiness and gravity of the matter. When you have finished the oath and its repetition, you place your right hand on his left shoulder and with your left hand you raise up the icon, which he holds with his right hand, and you speak forth the following: "Before the invisible and omnipresent true God, who is the fount of all justice, the avenger of wrongdoing and the punisher of wickedness against the rules of the *Philiki Etairia* [Society of Friends] and, with the strength which the great priests of Eleusis gave, I dedicate ... of ... years old ..., a ... by calling, and I receive him as a member as I was received into the Society of Friends." After the dedication the yellow candle is snuffed out and you command him to guard it well, for straight away it is to be used and further to be carried about with him as the witness of his sworn promises, and [you say] that another time you will explain to him the elements and symbols of the ierefs.

Great Oath

'I voluntarily swear before the true God that I want to be faithful to the Society in every respect and for all time. I will not reveal the least of the symbols, nor of the words, nor will I ever give them to understand that I know anything about these things in any way, neither to any relative, nor to my confessor, nor to any friend.

I swear that in the future I will not enter any other society, whatever it might be, nor into any debt of obligation, but certainly that whatever obligation I might have in the world, including the most irrelevant to the Society, I wish to consider as nothing.

I swear that I will nourish in my heart undying hatred towards the tyrants of my country, their followers and those who think like them, I want to carry out in all ways damage towards them and, when circumstances permit, their complete ruination.

I swear that I will never be over hasty in making myself known to a comrade, but I will use extreme caution lest I be mistaken, and lest anything untoward happen.

I swear that wherever I find a comrade, I will aid and assist him to the extent of my power and situation, that I will offer respect and obedience to him, if he is of a superior grade, and if by chance he happened before to have been an enemy of mine, the more will I love him and help him, the greater was my enmity.

I swear that, just as I was received into the Society, so I wish to receive brethren, (that) I will use every means and every caution until I know whether he is indeed a devoted Hellene, and a defender of our unfortunate homeland, a virtuous and good man, worthy to keep the secret and to catechize someone else.

I swear that in no way will I benefit from the Society's money, but I will consider it as a holy matter and as a pledge, belonging to all my wretched nation, as also the sealed letters that are received and sent.

I swear that I will never ask any member of the Society who received him into the Society, nor will I reveal nor let him know my sponsor, and if perhaps I recognize the symbol in the letters of introduction of someone, I will pretend that I did not know.

I swear that I will always take care to be virtuous in my conduct, I will be reverent in my religion, without despising others, that I will always give a good example, that I will help, advise and assist the sick, the unfortunate and the weak, that I will respect the justice, customs, laws and rulers of the country in which I find myself.

Finally, I swear to you, O holy and wretched Motherland! I swear by your long years of suffering. I swear by the bitter tears, which your wretched children have shed for such centuries! By my own tears, which flow at this minute! To the future freedom of my compatriots I dedicate all myself to you! In the future you will be the cause and object of my thoughts, your name the guide of my actions and your happiness the reward of my efforts! Let divine justice empty over my head all the thunderbolts of its justice, let my name be held in contempt and myself be the object of the curse of anathema of my compatriots, if I should forget for one moment their misfortunes and if I do not fulfil my duty and let death be the inevitable punishment for my sin, so as not to defile the sanctity of the Society with my participation.'

Part III

On the morrow you explain to him the means of recognition, those which are used for the systimenoi, and the symbols of the iereis. You give him to copy the first teaching, the first oath, the articles of the first confession, the objects of the Society, the continuation of the teaching, the great oath. And after the copying, which should be done with the symbols of the priests (*iereis*), in order and with care, and after accurate inspection of the document and confession in Article 5 (of which you should take a detailed and extensive answer), afterwards you say to him that he should offer to the Society a certain amount of money, such as his patriotism would induce him. Together with the money he should give you a letter, addressed to whatever name he wishes, for a distant city (not however such a strange one, that its strangeness could arouse curiosity and suspicion) in which he should reveal his age, calling, his

"The oath of the Philiki." An imaginary depiction of the administration of the great oath of the Philiki Etairia by the painter Theophilos D. Tsokos (1849, National Historical Museum of Athens)

place of birth, and that he has given you this sum to send to his unfortunate friend, or to the newly founded school, or to some monastery, or for the publication of books, or for another reason. Signing and indicating the date and place, he is to write this letter in your presence, and when you see that this [letter] contains all this which should be simply shown, tell him to put on it two signs of whatever kind he chooses, but clearly written, not very small, not very big, the first one to be known as the [sign of] dedication, which he is never to use, the second, [the sign] of his enrollment, he is to use only.

Similarly he folds and seals it in front of you with the prescribed seal, writing the name of the addressee on the outside. The letter should be with double paper, sufficiently thin to be easily posted, but embellished so that the symbols cannot be observed. You give him a letter, [to the effect] that you have received such an amount of money and that you will send them as he directed you with his signed letter, and indicating the date and place.

Second Confession

Article One. Are you, or any friend or relative being sought, by the justice of our homeland, or by anyone else, and for what reason?

Two. Do you have any relative or friend in prison and for what reason?

Three. Has any relative or friend of yours been killed by the government of our homeland, or by anyone else, and for what reason?

Four. Has anything great happened in your life?

Five. Do you know any great secret, or any invention, or anything else great and secret? Whence did you learn it? Do others know it and who are they? Do you have the necessary proofs? And what is it?

Six. Do you have any secret great talent, or any special skill?

Part IV

After copying the teaching up till here you tell him about the systimenoi, whose symbols of recognition were explained to him, that these are a group enrolled in the Society and are called with this name. The only indication of their membership in the Society is a letter of introduction (*systatikon*), that of the iereis is called a letter of supremacy. And they (the *systimenoi*) do not know them (the iereis) save that, being members of the Society, they are charged with the care of introducing patriots to them, so as to watch over the security of members, so as to cherish every beneficial idea. They (the systimenoi) do not know, however, that there exist adelphopoiitoi. The ierefs of the Society must take great care so as not to give these [the systimenoi} to understand anything more, for they know nothing else than that it is a Society concerned with the common good of the nation. And if by the prescribed method, as is explained below, he asks someone he knows to be a systimenos, if he is a ierefs and sees that he does not know anything more, he has a duty in his association with him to lead the talk innocently to learn the name of his mother, which he should imprint firmly in his mind, and after the passage of days he should seek from him the systatikon. This man cannot give it to him without asking him for his letter of supremacy as a ierefs, which he should show from a distance. And later he receives the systatikon so as to inspect it, on the back of which is written the name of his mother, only by the symbols of the iereis, so that the systimenos is completely ignorant of the meaning of these letters, and no one else can know, except the person who wrote them. Further enquiry than this of a systimenos is not permitted to a ierefs, nor is he allowed to speak about the Society with him. If, however, by mischance he meets with someone whose name in the systatikon does not tally with the name he learned from him he should at once suspect a trap, otherwise he has the duty to investigate the whole conduct, state and relationships of the suspect, noting his moral behavior, the sign of the

Nikolaos Tsakaloff, one of the founders of the Philiki Etairia

The seal of the Philiki Etairia

person who signed the systatikon, and with accuracy all that he learned about him, from him and from others, and to send this [information] without delay and safely, by the designated means, to the Society, not refraining subsequently from remarking or informing the same, so that the Society can take the necessary measures and put an end to the situation.

In a word, he has a sacred and essential obligation in such a circumstance to undertake all the necessary measures for the security of the Society. Finally you tell him that it is not permitted to the iereis of the Society to introduce anyone into the Society, for all that they are of much greater value than the systimenoi. Similarly they are not permitted to make anyone adelphopoiitos, except only he whom they know to be worthy to become a ierefs of the Society of Friends, and whom they will afterwards enroll, and thus wish that he be received into the Society, as they were received, or he, who having become a ierefs, did not have the opportunity to become an adelphopoiitos.

Part V

After this you explain to him the calendar of the Society of Friends which you will only use...your introductory letter with which he writes his own, and you sign in the prescribed manner... [The original manuscript is defective here.]

Afterwards you explain to him the symbols and words of the iereis unless... the manner of sending letters and money, from which each one supports his expenses, which he makes for this reason, informing him that if he finds another ierefs, he should explain to him all his written catechism, to check if it is accurate and in order, in order to inform and seek its correction from the beginning if any section is missing. You say to him further that the ierefs may withdraw one who has been catechized and to stop catechizing him and explaining him anything up to the great oath, if perhaps he suspects the faith and healthiness of his views, for all that he has a duty first to confirm his worthiness, he can do this up to and beyond the great oath, without greatly incurring the wrath of the Society. If, however, he finds himself forced to halt the catechism towards the end, on account of the deep wickedness of the person being catechized, which he was unable to know in time, then he should be judged and punished by the deprivation of the privileges of ierefs and should never be promoted to a higher grade. The penalty for the infraction cannot be lessened, nor finally can the ierefs be acquitted, despite the rapid execution. ... He should take certain and decisive measures for the general safety of the Society and particularly of each member, and rapidly informing those above or below, or the arkhi, or in this circumstance another priest, he has an essential duty to support with all his power... the circumstance. In this way the iereis among themselves and the systimenoi in the permitted circumstances help in the uncovering of a trap or deceit, in the ending of any sort of abuse and for whatever benefit to the Society generally and the members of it individually. Finally, you tell him that in whatever situation of worry, success, pursuit or misfortune he may find himself he should be guided by the founding principles which dictated and determined the whole system of the Society of Friends, and which [principles] are great patriotism, virtue, the general and individual safety and benefit of the Society, the complete dedication of all the members in general in it, and [further] the love, togetherness, faith and contribution of all the members between them for the preservation and implementation of these fundamental principles of the Society.

Following that, place him under oath in the known way.

'I swear as an honorable man, wishing the happiness of my fellow countrymen, on which my own happiness depends, in what is sacred and desirable in the world. Since I voluntarily became a member of the Society and I voluntarily gave sworn promises to it that I will keep them unfalteringly, I will be faithful to the end of my life to the whole Society in general and to each of its members individually, and in whatever circumstance of human uncertainty I find myself I will be guided by the fundamental principles which are imparted in the teaching which has been entrusted to me and everything I say I mean with the full meaning of the word.'

After the oath you embrace him and leave him to go wherever fate has decreed.

THE MEMOIRS OF EMMANUIL XANTHOS
A Founding Member of the Philiki Etairia

Following are excerpts from the memoirs of Emmanouil Xanthos, a founding member of the Philiki Etairia. Translated by Richard Clogg for his book The Movement for Greek Independence 1770-1821, *the original text is from Emmanouil Xanthos,* Apomnimonevmata peri tis Philikis Etairias *(Athens, 1845) pp. 1-29.*

Greece, during the whole duration of the Ottoman tyranny, although harshly oppressed on all sides, did not fail to give rise, from time to time, to freedom-loving and daring men, seeking her liberation.

Benakis, Krevatas, Zaimis and other Peloponnesians of blessed memory having failed during the year 1769, at the time a Russian fleet came, sent from the northern ports of that Empire under the command of Admiral Alexei Orlov, having promised to help them in their objective and having abandoned them despite their hope, saw, with deep sorrow in their soul, the destruction of half the Christian population of the Peloponnese and certain islands of the Archipelago. Rigas [Velestinlis] the Thessalian in 1796, encouraged by the promise of help from the French Republic, believed that he could unite Greeks and Turks for the destruction of tyranny. But he, having been betrayed, was arrested at Trieste, with his comrades in Vienna, and they, after being dispatched to Belgrade, were put to death by the Ottomans: But these examples, as also those of Papa Efthymios [Blakhavas] in 1808 and many others, did not discourage the Greeks in any way from imitating their example and benefiting from their failures.

Emmanouil Xanthos, from the island of Patmos, worked as a clerk from 1810 onwards with the wholesale merchant Vasileios Xenos in Odessa, and traded as a merchant. During 1812 he travelled from Odessa to Constantinople for commercial reasons. He founded, with some of the merchants there, Asimakis Krokydas, Khristodoulos Oikonomos and Kyriakos Bitzaktzis, all from Ioannina, a commercial company, leaving for Preveza at the beginning of 1813 to purchase oil. From there he proceeded to Ioannina to seek from Ali Pasa permission to purchase, through the intervention of such powerful officials as Manthos Oikonomos, brother of the above mentioned Khristodoulos, and Konstantinos Marinoglou, among his friends. Travelling later to Levkas, at the suggestion of his friend Panayiotakis Karayiannis, he was initiated into the Society of Freemasons.

Being a freedom-loving man and inspired by a continual hatred towards the Turkish tyranny, he immediately lighted upon the idea that it would be possible to found a secret society on the lines of that of the Freemasons, having as a basis the union of all the kapetanioi of the armatoloi, and other leaders of all classes of Greeks, whether in Greece or in other parts, with the object of bringing about, in time, the liberation of the Motherland.

After carrying out, then, his business undertakings in those parts, Xanthos returned to Odessa towards the beginning of November 1813. He befriended two countrymen who then happened to be there, Nikolaos Skoufas from Arta and Athanasios N. Tsakaloff from Ioannina (of the family, as he said, of the famous Tekelis), young men of patriotic and freedom-loving outlook. During one of their friendly meetings in 1814, these three friends talked about the wretched condition and tyranny to which their fellow countrymen were subject in Turkey, and especially in the Peloponnese, Epirus and some islands, and bewailed the wretched fate of the Nation. They blamed this on the indifference which the Christian rulers at the Congress of Vienna, after the downfall and exile of Napoleon to the island of Elba, manifested towards it [the Greek Nation]. At the same time a learned man in Vienna published a treatise in pamphlet form urging the rulers of the alliance to send their already united and victorious armies beyond the Danube for the liberation of an old and glorious Nation, the Greek, which had for centuries been enslaved by another barbarous and uncivilized nation, the Turkish, etc. But the Austrian Government, informed about this by the representative of the Ottoman Porte, Mavroyenis, prevented this by seizing the said pamphlet and saying that the Greek Nation does not exist in the catalogue of Nations and other such things.

Then Xanthos had occasion to propose to his friends the idea which he had conceived of creating a Society, with the unwavering object of liberating the Motherland. He revealed to them his initiation into the Society of Freemasons and some of their symbols, which could be adapted to this [Society]. He put before them the character of the Greek people and the sources of their strength, the political and moral state of the Turks who tyrannized over them, the efforts of Rigas the Thessalian, the victories of the brave Souliotes, Pargans and other different armatoloi, improperly called klephts, over Ali Pasa, the tyrant of Ioannina, our seaborne victories from time to time under Lambros Katsonis, and on another occasion the general hatred of the fellow countrymen against the tyranny of the Turks, and the inclinations of the different Christian peoples of Europe. And thus the aforementioned decided to undertake the setting up of such a Society and to initiate into it all the chosen and brave men among the compatriots, so as to carry out by themselves, that which for long they had vainly hoped for from the benevolence of the Christian rulers.

It was not possible for a Society such as this, having as its object the rebirth of a nation that had been enslaved for centuries, to exist without leaders. The group of those who were intending to undertake the higher direction of this daring and difficult enterprise was called the arkhi, unknown and invisible to all the enrolled brethren of this Society. For the experiences of the ever to be remembered Rigas and Papa Efthymios, and other good reasons, prompted the leaders to keep the arkhi secret until the beginning of the revolution. For this reason many, misled, took to be leaders different people not only from among the catechized and enrolled brethren of the Society, but also from among those who had no knowledge of, and perhaps no inclination for the undertaking.

The aforementioned three friends, then, planned the so-called Catechism of this Society, and decided, for greater safety in their correspondence, instead of signing with their names, to use, each one of them, different letters of the alphabet. That is to say Tsakaloff took AB, Skoufas AG, Xanthos AD. But afterwards Xanthos, since Galatis who knew of the arkhi through Skoufas in Odessa (as is mentioned later) wished to use these letters, he employed A TH from then on. After this, urgent affairs obliged Skoufas and Tsakaloff to leave, about September of that year (1814), for Moscow where they put the finishing touches to the rules of the Society, which they called the Society of Friends [Philiki Etairia]. About December Xanthos, similarly, was obliged to depart for Constantinople.

Towards the end of October of the same year, the aforementioned two comrades in Moscow decided to attempt to enroll some of the most patriotic of their fellow countrymen, whom they knew to desire the political transformation of the nation. Among these, then, the first to be catechized was the late Georgios Sekeris, a Peloponnesian, young and of good character and education (who truly fought in the Peloponnese and elsewhere, and died for the Motherland).

The two aforementioned leaders, seeing that the catechism made an impression and enthused, as was desired, the first person to be catechized, undertook the catechism of others too, among them Antonios Komizopoulos, from Philippoupolis [Plovdiv]. To [Komizopoulos] (since on testing him they found him of good character and honorable), they revealed that they were themselves the leaders, and thus they received him as a member of the secret arkhi, and he took the initials AE. They catechized others, too, of the Greek merchants to be found there. Some of these travelling to Moldavia and Wallachia catechized several compatriots to be found in these provinces, among them Theodoros Negris, secretary of the hospodar in last, Skarlatos Kallimakhis, and some monks and abbots of Greek monasteries. Leaving Moscow for Paris the aforementioned Georgios Sekeris passed through Vienna where he met the Archimandrite Anthimos Gazis, who was officiating as chaplain, and was about to go to Mount Pelion, his home district, to found a school. He revealed to him that a secret society existed, having as its object the improvement and liberation of the Nation, members of which were to be found in Russia, without enrolling him or telling him any thing more.

Meanwhile, the leaders in Moscow decided that one of them should travel to Odessa, the other two remained in Moscow, and in contact with their comrade in Constantinople, Xanthos, they worked tirelessly and with systematic progress towards this great undertaking.

Then Skoufas went to Odessa towards the beginning of 1816 and carrying out his duties to the Philiki Etairia, enrolled among others Panayiotis Anagnostopoulos, whom he met there for the first time. This Anagnostopoulos enrolled Athanasios Sekeris, to whom Skoufas afterwards revealed the arkhi, adding him to its members with the letters AH. The arkhi was not then revealed to Anagnostopoulos, but he remained a simple member of the Society, the same as others with the grade of ierefs. (For the leaders had created in the beginning four grades: that of the *vlamis* (brother) for the simple and unlettered, that of the *systimenos* (recommended), for compatriots of low estate, that of the *ierefs* (priest) and the *poimin* (shepherd) for the more select and educated. Later, in Constantinople, they instituted two other military grades; those of the *aphieromenos* (dedicated) and *arkhigos ton aphieromenon* (leader of the dedicated), as is later explained.)

It was at this time that a certain Nikolaos Galatis came to Odessa, boasting that he was a relative of Count Kapodistrias, and that he was intending to go to St. Petersburg to meet him on important business. Skoufas, a tireless observer of all his fellow-countrymen, noticed him, and having befriended him, thought to introduce him into the Society. And, indeed, having been initiated into the Society and having learned the arkhi he promised great things, Skoufas therefore supplied him with expenses and with letters of recommendation to Tsakaloff, Komizopoulos and other friends in Moscow. These received him with great attention and introduced him to Prince Alexandros Mavrokordatos the Phyraris, whom he enrolled into the Society, whose secret he learned about with great admiration. Since they facilitated his journey to St. Petersburg, he arrived there, but with his bad and thoughtless behavior he forced the government to expel him from their borders, and he came to Moldavia, where he abused the secret of the Society, for the benefit and satisfaction of his desires.

After this, about the same year, several kapetanioi from Greece, who had served the Russians in the Ionian Islands between 1806 and 1812, during the war against the Turks, came to Odessa, on their way to St. Petersburg to seek, through Count Ioannis Kapodistrias, payment for their services from the Emperor Alexander. These were Anagnostis Papa Georgiou, called Anagnostaras, a distinguished Peloponnesian and enemy of the Turks, and a former companion of the famous Zakharias, the Maniots Ilias Khrysospathis, Panayiotis Dimitrakopoulos, the latter a notable opponent of Ali Pasa of Ioannina. Skoufas and the rest of the comrades in Odessa received and cared for them, initiated and brought them into the Society. Everyone can understand that such irreconcilable enemies of the Turks received such a suggestion with enthusiasm, and thinking that it was something instigated by Russia, showed themselves to be most faithful to their oath. Leaving for Moscow, they took letters of introduction from Skoufas to Tsakaloff and Komizopoulos there. These last received them and cared for them as was proper, and being known to them as simple members of the Society and not as arkhigoi, they introduced them to certain distinguished Greek merchants, and, of course, to the late Prince Alexandros Mavrokordatos the Phyraris. They, in turn, enrolled many of them, so that in Moscow almost all the distinguished Greeks became members of the Society. When the Emperor and Kapodistrias came to Moscow, the aforementioned kapetanoi were introduced to the former through the Count, and, being rewarded, they returned to Odessa during March 1818.

Tsakaloff, in accordance with the opinion of his fellow arkhigoi, having left Moscow at the beginning of July 1817, came to Odessa, and decided to go, with Skoufas, to Constantinople to meet their colleague Xanthos, to whom Tsakaloff wrote on 8 August from there.

The aforementioned two comrades being still in Odessa, Anthimos Gazis came there from Vienna, and met with Skoufas and Tsakaloff. These, testing him and judging him worthy, enrolled him, and revealed to him the arkhi, and thus he became a member and took the initials AZ. Departing from there, he went to Constantinople, where he met with Xanthos and talked with him at length about this great undertaking, leaving for Milies on Mount Pelion to become a headmaster.

About December of the same year Tsakaloff, too, came to Constantinople alone and met with Xanthos, with whom he stayed. And having discussed and considered with him a considerable amount about where they should base themselves, he left about March 1818 for Mount Pelion to meet with Gazis, to persuade him to agree to the arkhigoi meeting there and that Mount Pelion, being safe, be made the place and centre of their activities. But Gazis, feeling that Grigorios Konstantas, being suspect, did not agree, suggested the Mani. So about the beginning of April, Tsakaloff left for Smyrna to seek and meet with certain of his friends; afterwards he returned to Constantinople, where Skoufas was also expected.

About the beginning of the same month of April of this year (1818), Skoufas came to Constantinople, accompanied by Panayiotis Anagnostopoulos and Louriotis, and meeting his colleague Xanthos, he spoke much with him about their future undertakings and about Tsakaloff. They both agreed that the arkhi should be revealed to the aforementioned Anagnostopoulos, as seemingly a youth of good character and enthusiasm. And thus it happened, and he was added to the grade of arkhigoi, and took the initials AI. And after a few days they sent Louriotis, at his request, to Livorno in Italy to enroll those capable fellow countrymen that he might know there. But he, having left for that place and having fallen ill after a certain time, died in Barletta. Anagnostopoulos waited in Constantinople, working together with the two arkhigoi Skoufas and Xanthos, awaiting the return of their colleague Tsakaloff, to whom Xanthos wrote, as he did also to Anthimos Gazis.

Poet and political agitator Rigas "Feraios" Velestinlis, who advocated revolution against Ottoman occupation in the Balkans

After a short time had elapsed the aforementioned kapetanioi, Anagnostaras, Khrysospathis, Dimitrakopoulos and Ioannis Pharmakis, travelled to Constantinople from Odessa with their men, whom the arkhigoi looked after as it should be. By misfortune Skoufas, a few days after his arrival in Constantinople, fell ill and those there were hindered. They awaited his recovery and the return of Tsakaloff from Smyrna (who in fact arrived about the end of June) so as to decide, as the arkhigoi had planned in advance, what directions and instructions should be given to them. But for all the endeavors of the comrades and visits by the doctors Moskhos and Isavridis, it proved impossible for the good Skoufas to recover, and about the end of July he died. Then the remaining arkhigoi gave the appropriate instructions to the said kapetanioi, furnishing them with sufficient money, received from the wholesale merchant Panayiotis Sekeris (brother of the aforementioned Georgios and Athanasios). He had been initiated into the Society by Anagnostopoulos, a few days after he had arrived in Constantinople, very willingly offering ten thousand grosia. They sent Ioannis Pharmakis to Macedonia and Thessaly to proselytize, as he promised, the kapetanioi of the armatoloi and whoever was important or a primate in those parts, which he did. And having travelled to the Holy Mountain of Athos as well, he initiated the Patriarch Grigorios of blessed memory, and Khrysanthos then archbishop in Serres, the virtuous bishop of Ardameri and others. At the same time they sent Anagnostaras to the islands of Hydra and Spetses and to the Peloponnese to enroll those whom he might judge to be worthy and he sent someone especially to enroll Theodores Kolokotronis and other worthies who were then to be found in Zakynthos, which he did. [And they sent] Ilias Khrysospathis, Dimitrakopoulos and Kamarinos Kyriakos to the Mani to catechize its ruler Petros Mavromikhalis and such other kapetanioi of that place, which they did. They sent the Archimandrite Grigorios Dikaios Phlessas, a Peloponnesian enrolled in Constantinople, to Wallachia and Moldavia to enroll those fellow countrymen found there whom he might judge to be worthy. They sent others to different islands of the Archipelago and to the coastal towns of Asia Minor. Moreover, they sent Dimitrios Ypatros to Alexandria in Egypt, and a Corfiot doctor to

Jerusalem to propagate the secret, so that in a short time the secret of the Society had been promulgated in many parts of Turkey, to many kapetanioi on both land and sea, to notables and many of the select of the fellow countrymen, with the greatest speed.

All this, however, demanded great and frequent expenses, and the financial situation of the arkhigoi would not have been adequate to meet these and those that were to occur in the future, if the secret of the arkhi had not included the brave and excellent patriot, Panayiotis Sekeris, who, as mentioned above, having been enrolled into the Society by Anagnostopoulos, gladly offered 10,000 grosia initially and more later.

Petros Mavromikhalis, the ruler of Mani, enrolled there by the aforementioned emissaries, accepted the secret with willingness and enthusiasm and having decided to ready himself, he was in need of money and taking counsel with those that had enrolled him he communicated with the arkhigoi in Constantinople. He sent them his dedicatory letter by way of Panayiotis Dimitrakopoulos, and, at the same time, asked to be sent, by way of his sons then in Constantinople as hostages to the Turkish government, a sufficient quantity of money, so as to prepare war supplies and to pay soldiers obedient to his command. The person who sought this amount was very important, and the Society had need of such a place and Governor, but the arkhigoi did not have the money which he sought. So they turned to the aforementioned Panayiotis Sekeris, seeking the necessary amounts, and this best of patriots willingly paid this amount and others to the arkhigoi. Such generosity was a sufficient guarantee of the character of the man. On account of this, through Anagnostopoulos, the arkhi was revealed to him, and thus becoming a member of it as well and taking the initials AK he worked together with his colleagues, the arkhigoi. From then on he gladly fulfiled the monetary needs of the Society, so that the man had paid a very important amount. The arkhi, for this reason, notified by means of a circular the known members of the Society in different parts, [and asked them] to send to him the dedicatory letters [addressed] to the arkhi, as well as the monetary offerings of all those entering into the Society. But they sent but little money, because most of those joining only promised, without actually offering, money, and because many of the brethren engaged in recruitment spent whatever money they

Ali Pasha of Ioannina, a composition by L. Dupré (Gennadios Library of Athens)

received from those enrolled on travel and on the dispatch of brethren to different parts of Turkey and elsewhere.

Meanwhile, the centre of all the activities of the administration of the Society was in Constantinople in the house of Xanthos. He suggested to his colleagues that a seal be made, bearing on its rim the first letters of the surnames of the arkhigoi and in the middle of it the cross, on which was engraved the E (Ellas) and the number 16, and also [the creation of] a register, in which were noted the names of the members of the Society who had been enrolled, the emblems of their dedication and enrollment, and their contributions, either given or promised. From all sides the arkhi was receiving letters and news about the progress of the Society. As the arkhigoi observed that in Moldavia there was great activity, but that factions and disorders were beginning to manifest themselves among certain members, and indeed suspicions occasioned by the aforementioned Galatis, they decided to send Konstantinos Pentedekas, from Ioannina but then in Constantinople, a simple member of the Society, to observe the disposition of the comrades there and to try, if possible, to bring the aforementioned Galatis back from there, he being a friend of Pentedekas. For this reason the latter, equipped by the arkhigoi with enough money and with introductory letters, left for Bucharest, where as mentioned above the Archimandrite Grigorios Dikaios Phlessas had earlier been sent to recruit.

Since Xanthos also observed that the membership of the Society, which included many men of standing, was rapidly and daily increasing, and that many were displeased by not knowing the secret arkhi, and that because of the abuses of some members of the Society suspicions of deception were aroused, he suggested to his fellow arkhigoi that one of them should go to St. Petersburg to reveal the secret to Count Ioannis Kapodistrias, by this time a man of standing and worthy of the confidence of the Greek nation on account of his important official position in Russia. [The idea was] that the latter should direct this great undertaking and should write to the most important fellow countrymen enrolled in the Society for their support and encouragement. From this it would be believed that the Society would succeed, it being known that Kapodistrias was a patriotic and wise politician, and that the arkhigoi would be able to exploit the popular belief held for centuries by the enslaved Greeks, that liberation from the Turkish tyranny would come from Russia, as a co-religionist. It was decided therefore that Xanthos, who had made the suggestion, should take the necessary measures.

The arkhigoi in Constantinople signed an agreement on this matter and Xanthos, taking all the dedicatory letters of the members of the Society to the arkhi that were there, together with such other documents relating to this matter, left on 23 October 1818. He went first to Mount Pelion, to meet his comrade Anthimos Gazis to discuss this affair with him. He gave him the aforementioned letters, as he was in a safe place, and receiving from him letters of introduction to Kapodistrias and some others, he returned to Constantinople about the beginning of December.

While Xanthos was at Mount Pelion, Pentedekas had returned from Wallachia with the aforementioned Galatis. Tsakaloff, Anagnostopoulos and Sekeris who were there in [Constantinople], received him in a friendly manner, and looked after him well. But he, being of bad character, took advantage of current developments to bother those brethren of the Society that he knew, forcing them to give him money under the threat of denunciation. These men, frightened and justly so, gave to him but were disturbed by such terrible wickedness and many complaints were made against him, with the result that Athanasios Tsakaloff and Dimitrakopoulos (who had returned from the Mani with letters from the Bey Petros Mavromikhalis to the arkhi) persuaded him to embark with them for the Mani, which they did. Reaching Ydra and going from there to Spetses, they both on the one hand were unable to bear his evil behavior and on the other foresaw the danger to which all the members of the Society might fall, and that such a great and difficult work, having made such hopeful progress, could easily be ruined if the necessary discretion was not preserved. With these two unhappy developments in mind they decided, for the safety of the many, to sacrifice one, and in fact they killed him in Ermioni (Kastri), where they had gone to visit certain ruins. They in turn fled to the Mani, but the bey, to avoid dangers consequent on the revelation that the murderers had sought refuge there, and from the planned revolution, advised them to leave for Italy and thus they fled to Pisa, where meeting with the Archbishop Ignatios [Oungrovlakhias] and Alexandros Mavrokordatos, ordinary members of the Society, they revealed to them the arkhi.

Xanthos, returning from Mount Pelion, found Anagnostopoulos and Pentedekas quarrelling, the former wishing to show his superiority over and grumbling about the latter on account of certain peccadilloes. In vain did the other arkhigoi seek to keep the peace between them, for the hatred lasted for ever, and the dissension with Pentedekas was the cause of many disturbances in Wallachia and Moldavia, when Anagnostopoulos went there. He [Pentedekas], scheming and intriguing a great deal against the other, was the cause of many unbecoming things against the interests of the Society. And if Anagnostopoulos had not been obliged to reveal the secret of the arkhi to Grigorios Dikaios Phlessas and Georgios Leventis, the latter a man of great influence there (as is mentioned later), the consequences would undoubtedly have been disastrous.

Since the arkhigoi, as mentioned above, had agreed that Xanthos should go to St. Petersburg, it was decided that Tsakaloff should go to the Mani and remain there. Anagnostopoulos considered going to Smyrna to meet his parents who lived in a small town of that region and [it was decided that] Sekeris should remain in Constantinople and correspond with the other, having of necessity compiled a code to guard their correspondence. But Anagnostopoulos, having learned of the death of Galatis, and having changed his mind about going to Smyrna, left with Xanthos on 19 February 1819. Arriving at Galati, Xanthos, after a few days, went to Tomarovo in Bessarabia to undergo his quarantine, while Anagnostopoulos, after a few days during which he had, as they had planned, set up an ephoreia of the most respectable members of the Society to be found there, to keep watch on the comrades that had been enrolled in the Society so as to receive the dedicatory letters and the contributions of those who by chance wished to be enrolled in the Society, in order to avoid abuses and embezzlement of money first went to Iasi for the same reason, and afterwards to Bucharest to meet the Archimandrite Phlessas. Here he was to rest until he had learned the results of Xanthos' mission to St. Petersburg, and to be guided in his work; but he, finding Grigorios Dikaios Phlessas there, together with Pentedekas, who, as has been mentioned before, hated him, became so involved in such untimely and unseemly quarrels and disturbances that he [Anagnostopoulos] was obliged to seek the protection and help of the powerful member of the Society there, Georgios Leventis, to whom he revealed the secret of the arkhi, and he became a member of it, taking the initials AL. (He [Leventis] benefited the Society greatly and gave financial help to many fellow countrymen before and after the Revolution.) Similar reasons and circumstances also obliged him [Anagnostopoulos] to reveal the arkhi to Grigorios Dikaios Phlessas, who was called Harmodios and took the initials AM to sign by. But since some of the members of the Society there, among them Theodores Negris, first secretary of Kallimakhis (then hospodar in Moldavia) and for this reason very powerful, through the machinations of Pentedekas and some others, acted against and plotted against Anagnostopoulos, the latter being afraid for these and other reasons to remain in these parts or in Bessarabia where after these things he had fled, judging it necessary for his safety to withdraw. Moreover, furnished by Georgios Leventis with several hundred florins for expenses he departed from there, going to Pisa in Italy, and, meeting with Tsakaloff, remained there until the approach of the Revolution.

Xanthos arriving in Moscow in December met with comrade Antonios Komizopoulos and on discussing what one might expect, they judged that the arkhi should also be revealed to the wholesale merchant Nikolaos Patzimadis of Ioannina, a prudent, honorable man, highly regarded in those parts. And so he, too, became a member of the arkhi and took the initials AX with which to sign.

After this Xanthos left at the beginning of January 1820 for St. Petersburg. Two days after his arrival, he was summoned to the presence of Count Ioannis Kapodistrias, to whom he handed over the letter of Anthimos Gazis. He revealed the whole organization of the Society, its arkhigoi, the multiplication of its members, its extent and everything else he considered necessary, and finally that they besought him to direct, as arkhigos, the movement of the nation, either directly or through some suitable plan, and that he should inform the most important of his fellow countrymen who had been enrolled about the most suitable means of beginning the war. But Kapodistrias did not accept, saying that he, being a minister of the Emperor, could not do so, and many other such things. Xanthos repeated to him that it was impossible for the Greeks in the future to remain under tyranny, that the revolution was inevitable, and that because they had need of a leader it was not right for him, as a Greek held in high esteem by them and many others, to remain indifferent, and so on. But the latter repeated that he could not become involved for the above reasons and that if the arkhigoi knew of other means to carry out their object, let them use them, and that he wished God to help. These things took place in two separate meetings.

Xanthos, then, disappointed by the Count, but considering that, for the object of the revolution to succeed with a great outcome, it was absolutely essential to present to the nation one of its most important members for its encouragement, he therefore turned his thoughts to another person as illustrious as Kapodistrias, and more suitable. This was Prince Alexandros Ypsilantis, a general and aide-de-camp to the Emperor and held in esteem and favor by him. He therefore went to visit him and the Prince received him favorably and with great courtesy, and asked where he was from and for what purposes he had come to St. Petersburg. Xanthos replied very cautiously saying that he was from an island, Patmos, and that he had come to St. Petersburg from Constantinople for commercial reasons, and other such things. The Prince asked him how things were with his fellow countrymen in those regions, and if the Turkish government was increasing the yoke of tyranny there too, as in other regions. Xanthos replied that everywhere the Turks tyrannized the unfortunate Greeks, and that the tyranny had become unbearable. The Prince, down-

Panagiotis Sekeris (1785-1846), a member of the governing board of the Philiki Etairia (National Historical Museum of Athens)

cast, said: "Why do the Greeks not try to act, so that even if it is impossible to free themselves of the yoke, then at least they might lighten it?" Then Xanthos replied with much passion: "Prince, by what means and with what leaders are the unfortunate Greeks to improve their political condition?" They have remained abandoned by those who could lead them; for all the worthy fellow countrymen flee to foreign parts, and leave their compatriots as orphans. Look! Count Kapodistrias serves Russia, your late father fled here, and Karatzas to Italy, you yourself in the service of Russia have lost your right arm and others equally worthy, having fled to Christian Europe, remain there without perhaps caring for their unfortunate brethren. The Prince, replying to this said: "If I knew that my compatriots had need of me, and thought that I could contribute to their well-being, I say to you honestly that I would gladly make any sacrifice, even of my wealth and of myself for them." Then Xanthos, getting up and with emotion in his soul, said: "Prince, give me your hand in confirmation of what you have said." The Prince, looking at Xanthos with some admiration, gave him his hand, and the latter said that he had not come to St. Petersburg for commercial purposes, but for another much more important reason which he would reveal to him on the morrow.

The Prince, impatient, sought to know then, but Xanthos begged him to remain patient until the morrow, and thus the first meeting ended. The next day Xanthos went to him, revealed all to him, and the latter willingly and enthusiastically agreed to dedicate himself, with any sacrifice, to the service of his fellow countrymen. Giving to Xanthos a sworn and written statement of his faith and devotion (which Xanthos sent to his comrades in Moscow, Patzimadis and Komizopoulos, among whom it is to be found) Ypsilantis accepted the title of General Commissioner (*Genikos Epitropos*) of the arkhi, taking the name of *Kalos* (Good), and the initials AR to sign by, and thus the objective of the Society was fulfiled through him.

Immediately after this, circular letters were written on behalf of the arkhi by Xanthos (who had the list on which were noted the names of the enrolled members, together with the signs of their dedication and consecration, and also the seal of the arkhi) and by Alexandros Ypsilantis, to the most important known members of the Society in Constantinople, the Islands, the Peloponnese and Rumeli, informing them that Alexandros Ypsilantis, appointed General Commissioner by the arkhi, was to direct the Society and that from henceforth the brethren should communicate with him and follow his orders, and other such things as were suitable for the encouragement of the brethren. These were sent by means of Athanasios and Panayiotis Sekeris, who were in Odessa and Constantinople. Xanthos informed his comrades among the arkhigoi regularly by post about all these activities and acts of his, Athanasios and Panayiotis Sekeris and Grigorios Phlessas in Odessa and Constantinople, as well as Georgios Leventis in Bucharest and Athanasios Tsakaloff and Anagnostopoulos in Pisa, Italy.

Meanwhile Alexandros Ypsilantis discussed the affair of the Society with Count Kapodistrias, urging him to mention it to the Emperor and to seek from him help, if not military, then at least monetary, against the several million grosia which the Ottoman government was obliged to pay the Ypsilantis family. But Kapodistrias refused, repeating what he had earlier told Xanthos. Then Ypsilantis, deciding to carry out with success the movement of the nation, thought to seek facilities from the Nation and the Government of France. For this reason about July of that year (1820) he sought leave of absence for two years from the Emperor, to go to foreign parts, and, receiving this, he left with Xanthos. And they took in their entourage the doctor Petros Ippitis too, who having found himself there, went to Moscow where Ypsilantis, as arkhigos of the future great movement, made the acquaintance of the comrades who were there. Leaving after a few days they arrived at Kiev, where his family lived. There Xanthos received through Aristeides Pappas, one of the fervent comrades of the Society, letters from Count Dionysios Romas of Zakynthos and others, addressed to the arkhi, and different opinions of the success of the work, which were given to Ypsilantis.

On the first of August, Alexandros Ypsilantis, accompanied by Xanthos and the aforementioned P. Ippitis, left Kiev, and when they arrived at Dubossary Ypsilantis, together with Ippitis, headed for Odessa. Xanthos, receiving from him orders and letters to the ephors set up in Bucharest after the departure of Anagnostopoulos, and to Georgios Leventis and other comrades, and to the kapetanioi enrolled there, Georgios Olympics, Savvas Kaminaris, and loannis Pharmakis who had come there from Macedonia a short time before, departed for Bucharest via Ismail and Galata, and discussed with them what one might expect. To encourage and assist them, as they made their preparations, he shared out at their request, to Savvas 500 (five hundred) Dutch florins; to Dimitrios Mousakoff 1000 (one thousand) grosia, to go to Serbia to discuss with its Prince Miles and the other military leaders there; to Khristophoros Perraivos, on the order of Ypsilantis, a bill of exchange of Nikolopoulos for 10,000 (ten thousand) grosia payable in Constantinople by Kyriakos Koumbaris.

Xanthos again from there informed through letters his fellow arkhigoi Panayiotis Sekeris in Constantinople and Tsakaloff and Anagnostopoulos in Pisa of his arrival in Bucharest, summoning them to go to Kishinev in Bessarabia, where Ypsilantis intended to go to meet him, so that they too could cooperate with him further. Panayiotis Sekeris informed Grigorios Dikaios in Constantinople (whom, betrayed shortly before, he [Sekeris] had released from the clutches of the bostancibasi by the payment of a large sum of money), who went to Galati, awaiting Xanthos' return from Bucharest.

Xanthos, returning to Galati about October, and meeting up with Grigorios Dikaios, informed Alexandros Ypsilantis, and the latter, having in his entourage G. Lassanis as his secretary, came from Odessa to Ismail where Xanthos went to do his quarantine, so as to discuss with him his activities in Bucharest. He introduced the aforementioned Dikaios to Alexandros Ypsilantis as a fellow arkhigos and also Dimitrios Themelis, Petros Markesis, Dionysios Evmorphopoulos, Vangelis Mantzarakis, Dimitrios Ypatros, who had returned from Alexandria in Egypt and from Cyprus, and other members of the Society, who came from Galati with Xanthos to become acquainted with Ypsilantis. At the same time Khristophoros Perraivos came there from Bucharest, heading for Constantinople. Ypsilantis gave him and others circular letters and proclamations to the comrades of the Society in Turkey, exhorting and encouraging them in the forthcoming struggle, and giving many other orders. He particularly recommended the aforementioned Dikaios and Perraivos to Panayiotis Sekeris and the ephors in Constantinople, commanding them to give them money adequate to prepare the necessary things for war. Sekeris willingly furnished, with the help of K. Mavros, L. Koumbaris and S. Barb as, ephors in Constantinople, to Perraivos 120,000 grosia, to Phlessas 90,000 grosia and other amounts to others. And these left, and Ypsilantis with Lassanis returned to Kishinev, waiting to collaborate further with Xanthos after his quarantine.

When, after a few days, Ypsilantis arrived in Kishinev, he wrote to Xanthos, still in the quarantine station, sending him certain orders through Lassanis, which it was not appropriate at that time to carry out. Xanthos replied negatively, giving him reasons in writing through the same Lassanis. Ypsilantis was persuaded and was satisfied.

Xanthos was discharged at Ismail, and about 10 November he went to Kishinev and co-operated

The Russian Emperor Alexander I (Athens, Gennadios Library)

with Ypsilantis in the preparation of the revolution. They sent Lassanis to lasi to rest and to await instructions and orders from Ypsilantis, and from Prince Mikhail Soutsos, hospodar of Moldavia, who had been enlisted in the Society, and of his minister lakovakis Rizos. He sent Aristeides Pappas with Petros Psalidas to Serbia with letters from Ypsilantis to Prince Milos and with orders to prepare him to ally with the Greeks.

Meanwhile, Xanthos, aware that Tsakaloff and Anagnostopoulos had been delayed, once again wrote, urging them to hasten their arrival, sending letters for them to Georgios Leventis in Bucharest, to be forwarded. But the latter replied to Xanthos that Anagnostopoulos should not be invited since the tempers of the comrades were excited against him, and that his arrival would once again cause scandal and displeasure, so that it was better he should be far off. For all this, Xanthos, their sincere friend, unwilling to countenance their absence from things and making many recommendations on their behalf to the Prince, once again wrote to them, and they left Italy. But Tsakaloff, falling ill on the way, was stopped at Vienna. Anagnostopoulos came to Bucharest on 30 December, and because Leventis again wrote to Xanthos that Anagnostopoulos should be invited to Kishinev, for it was not in their interest for him to remain there, fearful lest his presence might once again displease the comrades, Xanthos pressed the Prince to invite him there. And thus he arrived in Kishinev about the middle of February 1821, when Xanthos was absent in Ismail, but for reasons which will be made known later, he did not receive a good reception from the Prince.

After his return from Bucharest, Xanthos in Kishinev co-operated, as has been mentioned, with Prince Ypsilantis in the preparation of the revolution. Since it had been planned that the first move would begin in the Peloponnese and the rest of Greece, it was decided that the Prince, as General Commissioner of the arkhi, would go there with Xanthos and the rest, when Grigorios Dikaios and the others wrote from the Peloponnese that all was ready, sending, as they had been ordered, a Greek ship to Trieste to embark them. But before moving the Prince decided first of all some time in March to go with Xanthos to France, with the object, as he said, of carrying out something for the benefit and ease of the movement; and, by means of Lafayette and other important Frenchmen, to raise a loan against the security of his family estates in Russia, and of the three million grosia that the Ottoman Government had then decided to pay him, instead of nine, by the terms of the Treaty of Peace of Bucharest and Akkerman with Russia (as the Russian ambassador in Constantinople, Baron Stroganoff, had written him). He had great confidence, as he said, that the Greeks would be willingly helped by the French nation and its government, as the only nation liberal and honorable enough to assist in the liberation and enlightenment of nations, and particularly the Greek. They would then return to Trieste to embark in a Greek ship and land in the Mani, beginning the war. Simultaneously the brethren of the Society in Moldavia and Wallachia were notified, together with the organized military leaders, Georgios Olympics, Savvas Kaminaris, loannis Pharmakis, Athanasios Touphektzis and many others, to begin the war then. For this reason Xanthos left Kishinev about the beginning of January 1821 for Ismail, where he found his family who had moved there from Constantinople some months before, to put his domestic affairs in order, and afterwards returned to Kishinev about the end of February to accompany the Prince.

In Ismail, Xanthos, being in correspondence with the Prince and others, sent Dimitrios Themelis and Vangelis Mantzarakis to Constantinople and the Aegean, with letters and new orders sent by Ypsilantis, giving to the former six thousand grosia and to the latter eleven thousand grosia. But then the Prince was informed that the Turks, through the treachery of some, had begun to suspect, and-at the same time learned that Dimitrios Ypatros, who had been sent some time before to Niaousta with letters and proclamations, had been betrayed and murdered. It was rumored too that Aristeides Pappas had been arrested by the Turks at Adakale, opposite Craiova. In order to attract all the attention and forces of the enemy to the Danubian regions, so that the Greek lands should remain with only small enemy forces, and for many other reasons, he [Ypsilantis] changed the plan. And he decided to pass into Moldavia, where the hospodar Mikhail Soutsos was prepared to assist with any sacrifice, and to begin the revolution from there. For this reason on 16 February 1821 he wrote to Xanthos, by special messenger, to come to Kishinev. He, starting on the twenty first, arrived there on the twenty-third on account of bad weather, but did not make contact with the Prince, who had left on the evening of the twenty-first with his brothers Nikolaos and Georgios, with Georgios Katakouzinos and some others, and had arrived in lasi on the twenty-second. But he left with his mother a letter for Xanthos, informing him of the revolution which had already been proclaimed, and giving him different orders in connection with the matter and [making clear] his intentions with regard to Anagnostopoulos whom he had left idle and under suspicion. But Xanthos, as a sincere and faithful friend and comrade, was not slow in consoling him in that miserable humiliation, shunned and distrusted by all the household and friends of the Prince, and writing immediately to the Prince in lasi so defended him that he dispersed every bad suspicion against him.

Panayiotis Sekeris in Constantinople, who earlier had undergone many dangers on account of the treachery of a brother of Galatis and other vexations, as soon as the news of the uprising arrived there, was betrayed and sought by the Ottoman Porte but by good fortune was warned and just managed to save himself. So he found himself without money on a boat in which he reached Odessa, deprived of all his property, and leaving his family in the most appaling dangers but which, as by a miracle, was afterwards saved from the tortures of the tyrant.

Xanthos, galvanizing and encouraging his fellow countrymen of these regions, wrote immediately to his emissaries in Greece, Dikaios Phlessas, Themelis and others, about the beginning of the revolution, sending them by sea the proclamations of war with a special man, Stamatis Doukakis, a merchant and member of the Society then in Ismail. He, passing through Constantinople, ran the greatest dangers but succeeded in bringing in time these informatory letters with the proclamations, and the revolution began in the Peloponnese and other parts.

It should be noted that the revolution in the Peloponnese was inspired and encouraged by the proestoi and other landowners and merchants, and these first took up arms and encouraged the people, and almost the whole of the clerical estate, without which the people would never have moved, nor have succeeded. In the islands and Rumeli, on the other hand, the people and the kapetanioi rose up, obliging the proestoi to agree.

A few days after the departure of Alexandros Ypsilantis, his brother Dimitrios came to Kishinev from Kiev and prepared to pass into Moldavia, after he had received from his brother Alexandros letters from the lasi camp, through which he was told to liaise with Xanthos about the uprising. The latter suggested to him that it was essential for a member of the Ypsilantis family to go to Greece for the greater encouragement of those bearing arms and the people there, and for this reason he advised him to go himself. Persuaded of this, he informed his brother Alexandros, to whom Xanthos also wrote about it. Alexandros agreed with this opinion, answering both of them, and urged Xanthos whom he had earlier summoned to his side to accompany his brother Dimitrios, to whom he sent introductory letters to the Greeks, appointing him his commissioner. He also persuaded Alexandros Katakouzinos, who was getting ready to make his way to the Moldavia camp, to go with them to Greece.

When things had thus been arranged, Prince Dimitrios decided first of all to go to Odessa, to cash some letters of credit to the value of eight hundred thousand grosia which his brother Alexandros had received from Andreas Pavlos, a banker in last, and had sent to him, and about which he had written from lasi to the ephors of the Society he had set up in Odessa; and to sell or pawn some jewelry and to take the sums received with him. He left for this place with Xanthos about the middle of March. He spoke to the ephors about the letters of credit, but they did not wish to cash them. Some of them were frightened, as they said, lest they would risk their money if the revolution failed. He pawned the jewelry and received thirty-six thousand roubles, giving a promise of forty thousand for one year (which his mother took, paying in the meantime). He also took eighteen thousand roubles from the subscriptions of fellow countrymen in the treasury of the ephoreia and returned with Xanthos to Kishinev.

During their absence from Kishinev, Alexandros Katakouzinos departed from Greece, accompanied by Mikhail Mikhaloglou from Patmos, Grigorios Salas, Khristos Petalas and some others, with the intention of waiting for Prince Dimitrios at Trieste, which they did.

There flowed into Galati and Pruth many fellow countrymen, who enrolled in a military formation to go to the Greek camp in Wallachia, where they seized fourteen Turkish ships bound up the Danube for Galati, for they had need of war supplies and arms. So it was decided that Xanthos should depart for Ismail, to equip the above mentioned soldiers, to move the ships to the Western shores of the Black Sea, and also to wait to receive such money that was, as they had learned, going to be sent by

Varvakis in Taganrog by means of the ephors in Odessa. For which reason he went there to carry this out. Prince Dimitrios, remaining in Kishinev, was preparing himself, writing on 13 April to Xanthos and leaving 500 florins for him for the expenses of the journey. He then departed, taking in his entourage together with the others Anagnostopoulos, who had been recommended to him by Xanthos and who was afraid to go to Constantinople, as Alexandros Ypsilantis had written [there about him] earlier, and Georgios Typaldos, a doctor.

Xanthos equipped from Ismail the soldiers in Galati and Pruth with such arms as he was able to acquire from General Tuskov, who was there with quite a number of barrels of gunpowder and nineteen cannons, of which sixteen were sent at his order from Odessa by sea, purchased by the contributions of the Muscovite members of the Society. He assisted as well the passage to Moldavia of many other fellow countrymen coming to Bessarabia from different parts of Russia, and many Bulgarians who joined with them at his urging, to go to the Greek camp, equipping them with clothing and arms, and many of them with money to pay the cossacks guarding the banks of the Pruth to turn a blind eye to their crossing into Moldavia. And he sent to Prince Georgios Katakouzinos, who had been sent to lasi from Tirgoviste in Wallachia by Alexandros Ypsilantis to transfer the soldiers concentrated there, and who was seeking financial help, three thousand (3000) Dutch florins and seven thousand mahmudiyes. And at his request twelve thousand (12000) Augustan florins were sent to the merchant loannis Amvrosios in Odessa for exchange, for the ephors in Bessarabia, as they said, had no money. Xanthos decided to send Katakouzinos this amount, so as not to abandon him to the anger of the soldiers who, as a result of the intrigues of Pentedekas, himself seeking to be their leader, threatened to abandon him in the situation in which lasi was threatened by the invasion of Turks approaching from Braila.

Grigorios Dikaios, who used the nom de guerre Papaflessas, was one of the most active members of the Philiki Etairia and died fighting during the revolution (Athens, National Historical Museum)

On carrying out all this Xanthos, learning that Varvakis had sent the promised money with Antonios Komizopoulos (then in Odessa) to Livorno to buy military material to be sent to Greece (which happened), departed from Bessarabia on 26 June for Greece via Hungary, passing, in order to visit the unfortunate Prince Ypsilantis, through Mohacs, where the government of Austria had incarcerated him, together with his two brothers Nikolaos and Georgios, Georgios Lassanis, Gerassimos Orphanos, the Pole Garnowski and one of his servants Konstantinos Kavalieropoulos. Not receiving permission to meet him [Ypsilantis], he headed for Ancona via Pest and Fiume.

The generosity with which Xanthos in Ancona, as well as in transit through the Bukovina, Transylvania and Hungary, assisted the many Greeks who had sought refuge in those regions after the collapse of the army in Wallachia and who were wandering about in distress, is known to many. He gave them money (many of them perhaps are to be found here), taking some of them with him to Ancona and sending them to Greece.

After these things and others about which I remain silent for the sake of brevity, Xanthos went with Tsakaloff to the Peloponnese, disembarking at Tripolitsa, and attached himself to Dimitrios Ypsilantis, fighting with him as far as he was able. He was also appointed a member of the committee to settle a difference between Vristhenis, vice-president of the parliament and some soldiers.

This is the true history and report of all that transpired, from the first founding of the Society of Friends, whose object was the resurrection and freedom of our Greek nation and Motherland, something considered improbable by all the politicians and wise men of Europe. And all this in greatest brevity. [...]

Fight for Faith and Motherland

Following is the full text of Alexandros Ypsilantis' Proclamation of Revolution in the Danubian Principalities, February 24, 1821, translated by Richard Clogg for his book The Movement for Greek Independence 1770-1821. *The original text is from L.I. Vranousis and N. Kamarianos, Athanasiou Xodilou:* I Etaireia ton Philikon kai ta prota symvanta tou 1821 *(Athens, 1964) pp. 24-8.*

Fight for Faith and Motherland! The time has come, O Hellenes. Long ago the people of Europe, fighting for their own rights and liberties, invited us to imitation. These although partially free tried with all their strength to increase their freedom and through this all their prosperity.

Our brethren and friends are everywhere ready. The Serbs, the Souliotes and the whole of Epirus, bearing arms, await us. Let us then unite with enthusiasm. The Motherland is calling us!

Europe, fixing its eyes upon us, wonders at our inertia. Let all the mountains of Greece resound, therefore, with the echo of our battle trumpet, and the valleys with the fearful clash of our arms. Europe will admire our valour. Our tyrants, trembling and pale, will flee before us.

The enlightened peoples of Europe are occupied in restoring the same well-being, and, full of gratitude for the benefactions of our forefathers towards them, desire the liberation of Greece. We, seemingly worthy of ancestral virtue and of the present century, are hopeful that we will achieve their defense and help. Many of these freedom-lovers want to come and fight alongside us. Move, O friends, and you will see a Mighty Empire defend our rights! You will see even many of our enemies, moved by our just cause, turn their backs to the enemy and unite with us. Let them approach with a sincere spirit. The Motherland will embrace them! Who then hinders your manly arms? Our cowardly enemy is sick and weak. Our generals are experienced, and all our fellow countrymen are full of enthusiasm. Unite, then, O brave and magnanimous Greeks! Let national phalanxes be formed, let patriotic legions appear and you will see those old giants of despotism fall by themselves, before our triumphant banners.

All the shores of the Ionian and Aegean seas will resound to the sound of our trumpet. Greek ships, which in time of peace have known both how to trade and to fight, will sow terror and death, by fire and the sword, in all the harbors of the tyrant!

What Greek soul will be indifferent to the invitation of the Motherland? In Rome, a friend of Caesar, shaking the bloody mantle of the tyrant, raised up the people. What will you do, O Greeks, to whom the Motherland, naked, shows its wounds and, with broken voice, calls on the help of its chil-

Alexandros Mavrokordatos, one of the political leaders of the revolution (Athens, Gennadios Library)

dren? Divine Providence, O friends and fellow countrymen, having pity on our misfortunes, has granted the means, so that with a little effort we can enjoy every benefit with Freedom. If then out of culpable stupidity we are indifferent, the Tyrant, become wilder, will multiply our sufferings and we will become for ever the most unfortunate of all nations.

Turn your eyes, O fellow countrymen, and behold our miserable state! See here the ruined churches! There, our children seized for the shameless use of the shameless hedonism of our barbarous tyrants! Our houses stripped bare, our fields laid waste, and ourselves miserable slaves!

It is time to overthrow this insufferable yoke, to liberate the Motherland, to throw down the [Turkish] Crescent from the clouds, in order to raise up the symbol by which we always conquer, I mean the Cross, and thus rid the Motherland and our Orthodox faith from the impious scorn of the heathen.

Among ourselves the most noble is he who bravely defends the rights of the Motherland and works for it in a beneficial way. The nation assembled will elect its rulers, and to this highest parliament all our acts will yield.

Let us move then with a common spirit. Let the wealthy give up part of their own property, let the holy shepherds instill in the people their own example, and let the educated advise what is beneficial. Those fellow countrymen serving as soldiers and civilians in foreign courts, giving thanks to the power for which each works, let them all rush to the great and brilliant career already opened up, and let them offer to the Motherland the debt they owe; and as brave men let us all take up arms, without wasting time, with the unconquerable weapon of bravery, and I promise you in a short while victory, and after victory everything that is good.

What bought and indolent slaves dare to oppose themselves to a people fighting for its own independence? The heroic struggles of our forefathers are witnesses. Spain, who first and by herself put to rout the invincible phalanxes of a tyrant is a witness.

Fellow countrymen, with unity, with respect for holy religion, with obedience to the laws and the generals, with boldness and steadfastness, our victory is certain and inevitable. This will crown with evergreen laurels our heroic struggles. This, with ineffaceable characters, will carve our names in the Temple of Immortality, for the example of future generations. The Motherland will reward her obedient and genuine children with the prizes of Glory and Honor. Those who disobey and turn a deaf ear to this present appeal will be declared bastards and asiatic germs, their names, as traitors, anathematized and cursed by later generations.

Let us then once again, O brave and magnanimous Greeks, invite Liberty to the classical land of Greece! Let us do battle between Marathon and Thermopylae! Let us fight on the tombs of our fathers, who, so as to leave us free, fought and died there! The blood of the Tyrants is acceptable to the shades of Epameinondas the Theban and of Thrasyboulos the Athenian, who crushed the thirty tyrants, to the shades of Harmodius and Aristogeiton, who destroyed the yoke of Peisistratus, to that of Timoleon, who restored freedom to Corinth and Syracuse, certainly to those of Miltiades and Themistocles, of Leonidas and the Three Hundred, who cut down the innumerable armies of the barbarous Persians, whose most barbarous and inhuman descendants we today, with very little effort, are about to annihilate completely. To arms then, friends! The Motherland calls us!

Alexandros Ypsilantis.
24 February 1821

Alexandros Ypsilantis crosses the river Pruth (imaginary composition by P. von Hess, Athens, Benaki Museum)

"Social Banditry"
The Memoirs of Theodoros Kolokotronis

Following are excerpts from Greek Independence key figure Theodore Kolokotronis' memoirs, translated by Elizabeth Mayhew Edmonds, Kolokotronis, the Klepht and the Warrior *(London, 1892) p. 83 ff.*

I was born in the year 1770. It was the 3rd of April, and it was Easter Tuesday. The revolt of the Albanians in the Peloponnesus had taken place in the previous year of 1769. I was born under a tree on the hill called Ramavouni, in the district of old Messenia. My father, Kostantes Kolokotronis, had been a captain of the Armatoli in Corinth, a post which he held for the space of four years. He left Corinth, however, to go to Mani, and whilst at Mani he harried the Turks greatly. [...]

Kostantes Kolokotronis, my father, was wounded by a sword-thrust at the time of the sally, and was afterwards killed through the treachery of a Turkish friend. His head was never recovered. The murderers who slew him concealed his body for the sake of the property which they found upon him. Three years afterwards his body was dug up, and every one knew that it was the body of Kostantes Kolokotronis because one of his little fingers had a crook in it, in consequences of a cut from a Turkish sabre years before. They had hidden him in a hollow between Arna and Kotzatina, and he was afterwards interred again at Melia. My father was exceedingly dark and very thin, so swift of foot that the most speedy stallion could never overtake him; he was thirty-three years of age at the time of his death, and was of middle height, black-eyed, and slim. The Albanians held him in so great a terror that they swore by his name. 'May I be saved from the sword of Kolokotronis!' was their favorite oath. It was said that before he was slain he had killed with his own hand seven hundred Turkish irregulars. [...]

We remained some time at Melia in Mani with my uncle Anagnostes, and I bought back the two enslaved children, my brothers Gianni and Chrestos. One of them had been taken to Hydra; and we stayed in Mani three years. We had sustained many losses, and our other uncles on our mother's side, who were called the Kotsakaioi, came to us and took us away with them to Alonistaina. We managed to get away without being recognized, for we were in great fear of the Turks. My uncle Anagnostes afterwards went to Sampazika, in the district of Leontari, which is at the extremity of Mani. He there allied himself with George Metaxa, a native of the place, and a prefect, and a good shot, to whom he gave his daughter in marriage, and he then built himself a house. Hearing that my uncle had established himself at Akovo, we left where we were and went and settled ourselves there. We stayed there some time, and the submitted Klephts appointed me Armatolos of Leontari to act against the other Klephts, and I managed the province with leniency. I was then fifteen years old.

When I was twenty years of age I married the daughter of the chief primate of Leontari, a man who had been ruined by a Pasha in Nauplia. As I received in dowry both olive-trees and a vineyard, I built houses and settled down as a householder, but I still took care of my Armatolik, and always went about with a gun, for the Turks envied us and wished to slay us all; they were not able to do so because our place was situated on the heights. They therefore kept up a continual warfare against us by craft and subtlety. At one time they sent out one hundred, and upon another occasion two hundred soldiers to attack us, but as these were not able to get us wholly in their power, they did not carry out this attempt. I saw, however, that if they continually found that artifices failed they would at last come against us openly. We received information of this, and fled away from the place. After we had left, the Turks went and destroyed all our possessions, and issued orders that wherever we were found we were to be destroyed likewise.

I now found myself with twelve of the Kolokotroni, all younger than myself, so we took our families to Mani and left them there; and then we rose up openly as Klephts, and got together our soldiers, sometimes sixty in number, and sometimes less. We remained Klephts for two years straight off, and afterwards, when they found they could do nothing against us, they offered us the Armatolik again. I had Leontari and Karytaina given into my charge, and I remained there as an Armatolos four or five years. [. . .]

In the year 1802 a firman came, which commanded that we two, Petimeza and myself, should be killed. This was set in motion by a voivode in Patras. The firman said, 'Either your two heads or the heads of the chiefs.' Whereupon the vizier of Tripolitsa summoned the father of Zaimes and Deligianni. Zaimes obeyed the summons, but Deligianni was very much afraid. He took an oath to them both that it had nothing at all to do with them. I had accompanied Deligianni as far as Tripolitsa, and as we were returning together I said to Deligianni, 'I do not believe that the firman is for us;' and he replied, 'Do not fear.' The Pasha, however, only sent for those two, and he read the firman to them. 'You must give us time,' they said, 'for these are wild men.' Old Zaimes Asemakes, however, had Petimeza quite in his power, because he went down to Kalavryta daily, but for myself I never went to Karytaina. The two primates said that they must make themselves masters of the wild one (Kolokotronis), and that afterwards they could easily get the tame one (Petimeza). Deligianni made two of the primates take an oath that they would kill me. That was rather difficult to manage, because I was always very cautious. They had a conference with Velemvitsa, and swore him in first; but he replied, 'I do not agree with the killing of those men; we shall destroy the province.'

"A War Scene" (Theodoros Vryzakis, 1853 – Athens, National Gallery)

They did not change their minds, however. They then brought one Bouloubases with his Albanians into Karytaina. I had my suspicions about this proceeding, and went to pay a visit to a primate in Stemnitsa. 'What do you want with the Albanian Bouloubases here?' I asked; 'he won't become of your opinion.' The Albanian then came into Stemnitsa, and I went there also, taking with me fifty of my men. I had an interview with Bouloubases, when I said to him, 'They are trying to set us at loggerheads: tame fowl cannot chase away wild ones. Though all fly away, the sparrow still remains.'

That circumstance fortunately brought old Kolias to me, who came with his son Koliopoulos. We now numbered two hundred, and our own men joined us at Magoulia. Anagnostes Bakales, a primate at Garzeniko, derided the Turks and sent me continual information. I wrote to the two primates (before-mentioned) to send me news also, and to advise me what to do, but they only wrote me lies; and I procured some guns and ammunition from Demetri. Bouloubases, with his force of two hundred picked men, surprised us, however, at Kerpeni, when we were only forty altogether. I marched outside the village and shut myself up in a monastery at Kermitsa; but if I had remained there I should have been utterly lost, so I left and got away to the wild parts of the country.

Meanwhile they slew Petimeza in Kalavryta, and sent his head to Tripolitsa. We killed some Turks, however, at Magouliana, and we also burnt some of their villages. The primates whereupon appealed to Kolias, asking him to persuade us to make some agreement, whereby everything might be pacified. I was therefore taken back into the Armatolik service again. Deligianni had been trying for three or four months to effect our ruin, but he had not succeeded.

So, in the month of September, I again entered the Armatolik. Deligianni at this time found an opportunity of wrecking his spite. He had a friend in Lala, one Hassan Aga Phida, and he besought him to slay us—treacherously, of course, because we were Armatoli. We had placed our families now in Palouba, and old Kolias, who had discovered the treachery, sent us information that the Lalians were coming down upon us. I was in a village called Tourkokerpeni when I received this news, and I cast about in my mind how I could unravel this secret movement which was astir for the purpose of overthrowing us, and I thought it over during the whole of the night. The Turks came up and seized upon two roads, sending out two separate bodies, each with two hundred men, in order to entrap me in an ambuscade. I had a traitor about me, and he came to us to see if we were on the move, or if we were sleeping. I had hoped to have been able to send a defiance to them in the morning, but in the morning we found ourselves surrounded in a village. I had given my clothes to an adopted son. We were rejoicing at the return of day, when lo! I saw the Turks drawing nigh. We seized our guns, but as we were endeavoring to get to the back of the hill, my adopted son had eight balls fired into him.

My brother Gianni was also wounded. We then shut ourselves up in three houses, and I stationed myself in the cellar. In all we numbered thirty-eight. The second body of two hundred coming up they surrounded us. We fought through the whole of that day, but at nightfall we sallied forth and fled. This occurred on the 7th of March, in the year 1804.

In the year 1805 I left for Zante. The Emperor Alexander of Russia had sent an invitation to the Greeks to take service in his armies.

All of us, both Souliotes and Roumeliotes and we Peloponnesians, had framed an address to the Emperor to ask him to give us help so that we might set our country free. Anagnostaras was very active in getting up this address. The Souliotes and Roumeliotes were in Parga, but Anagnostaras got together a force of five thousand Peloponnesians for the army at once. I went to Zante. When the answer to the address came – that was in August – I had an interview with the general of the Russian army, and he told me that he had arranged to receive into the Russian service as many Greeks as chose to enter, for the express purpose of fighting Napoleon.

"Then, for my part," I answered, (I shall not enter the service. What concern is it of mine in regard to Napoleon? If you, however, want men for the purpose of aiding us to free our own country, I can promise you from five to ten thousand soldiers. We were once baptized with oil, and we have since been baptized with blood, and yet again will we be baptized in blood for the deliverance of our fatherland!'

"The camp of Georgios Karaiskakis" (by Theodoros Vryzakis, 1855 – Athens, National Gallery and Alexandros Soutsos Museum)

I stayed in Zante a fortnight, but I would not consent to that measure. I left twenty-eight of my comrades behind, and my nephew Niketas, a son of my brother Gianni Kolokotronis. The other Greek soldiers enlisted, and were sent to Naples.

When the Turks saw this movement they sent information to the Sultan, and expressed to him all their suspicions about it. The Sultan thereupon conceived the idea of taking some summary acts of vengeance on the people. The patriarch (of Constantinople) intervened, saying, 'What have the people done? Better that we kill the prime movers and the evildoers;' and so he was turned away from his purpose.

The opinion of the Turks coalesced with the convictions of the French Cabinet, which had advised Turkey to make an end of all those captains called Klephts, and to get rid of the captains of the sea-vessels also, or else at some time or other they would cause a rising.

The Sultan, following this advice, issued a firman to slay all the Klephts. At the same time the patriarch was compelled to issue an excommunication against them, in order to stir up the whole people; and by these means the Peloponnesians, whether Turks or Romaics, were all excited against the Kolokotroni.

I had gone to Zante in August, and I had left it in September, and returned, and in the following January, in the year 1806, came the orders to hunt us all down. Petimeza, Gianni, and Zacharias were already gone from us, and we were now only a hundred and fifty men in all. [...]

The kind of life which we had already led aided us much throughout the war of Liberation, because we knew all the passes on the hills, and we knew the habits and ways of men. We had been accustomed to hold the Turks in contempt, and we were inured to hunger and thirst, suffering, filth, and every other privation. I arrived in Zante in May. After a month's sojourn there I learned that Pappadopoulos, the general of the Russian forces, had come into the island of Corfu, and he sent for me and asked me to enter the service. I replied, 'I do not intend to enter the Russian service, because my purpose is to return to the Morea and avenge the slaughter of my kindred, and the injuries which I have sustained myself. I could not take an oath, and afterwards become a perjurer by fleeing away secretly.' So I returned to Kastro, and remained there ten months without any employment.

The Exodus from Messolonghi by Theodoros Vryzakis

I entrusted a letter to one Rontikes, a native of Magoulia, which he was to take to my family, in order that he should obtain and bring me all the property which I had placed with different men. He took it and went, but he showed it to Deligianni, and Deligianni showed it to the voivode, in consequence of which all my goods were lost. That was in 1807. All the soldiers, and captains, and the Roumeliote Klephts in a body had fled to the seven islands [Ionian Islands] about the same time as my own flight took place. Russia had declared war against Turkey, and commanded all the soldiers to go into Roumeli to attack the Turks. I immediately tried to go to Santa Maura [Levkas], where they were all assembled, and get as many of them as I could for myself and then return to the Peloponnesus. There were two regiments in the service of Russia, one composed of Maniotes, at the head of whom was the son of Pierrakes Samet Bey, and the other was a body of Peloponnesians commanded by Anagnostaras. These were still in Zante. Pappadopoulos had ordered them to fit out a vessel of war. When they had made it ready and I could go in it to Santa Maura, Anagnostaras, the Petimezaioi, Giannaki Kolokotronis, Melios, and others came down to me and said "Do not go, we shall get permission to have a ship for ourselves, and if thou desirest, thou canst go in her." They found a Turkish boat with two cannons, and they bought her and appointed me to be captain.

I took out passports, and went to the government office of the Republic of Corfu, and there they gave me permission to attack the Turks either by sea or land. I took eighty soldiers for land service, and went down to a place called Achaia, near Patras, and burnt the houses, possessions, and magazines of Saitaga, and returned to Zante. The inhabitants of Zante, however, were obliged to import food from the Peloponnesus, and therefore they petitioned the government and begged it not to attack the Morea, as in consequence of that the Turks would not admit any of them who went thither for the purpose of trading. The government prevented me in consequence from making any assaults by land, and ordered me only to carry on the war at Santa Maura.

I met Papadopoulos with Synevi at Corfu. He was making preparations to attack Constantinople in conjunction with the English. I gave him a little of my opinion – namely, that there were twelve hundred Russians and five thousand Greeks in the service of the seven islands, that they had twelve vessels in the Baltic and the Black Seas, and forty other vessels, both brigs and frigates, which had been got together for the purpose of attacking Buonaparte, so that with ten thousand of the islanders we should number altogether twenty-five thousand men with six ships in the Gulf of Corinth, and others at Egina, and that with these forces we could sail away, and then I would undertake that in two months I would free the Peloponnesus.

General Papadopoulos received my proposition, and laid it before Synevi Motzenigo, the national primate, Benakes, the vice-admiral, Deli, and General Atrem. Pappadopoulos took it to the council, and Benakes opposed it, saying "I will not have my country lost a second time even for my father's sake." Motzenigos said "We must go with the English and strike at the head, which is Constantinople, and afterwards, when we have struck the head, all the rest is ours." This opinion was therefore accepted and mine thrown over.

Synevi went to Tenedo, and the English to Constantinople, but rather as if they were going upon an excursion than for any warlike purposes. The Turks were met by the Russians at Tenedo, and after one battle the Turkish fleet was destroyed. [...]

Ali Pharmakes then came to Zante. He had asked permission to go and see his villages until Kolokotronis could come, he said, and he took with him five hundred thousand grosia; and we sent a boat for him, and that is how he got to Zante. We planned to go to Paris together in order to have an interview with Buonaparte, and we went to Corfu in the first instance; but Donzelot, the governor there, prevented us from so doing. 'Stay here,' he said, 'and I will write myself, and state that you require an answer. We must, however, arrange our plans before the answer of the Emperor arrives.' The plan which we made in conjunction with Donzelot was as follows: that Buonaparte should give us the command of five hundred gunners clothed in foustanellas (for there were five thousand Greeks in the French service), and that he should also give us grosia in order to make enlistments in Tsamouria, where there were enemies of Alt Pasha. We crossed over to Tsamouria and got three thousand Tsamides for pay, and then went to Parga and embarked them for Santa Maura. The gathering was intended to take place at Santa Maura and Zante. I crossed over to Santa Maura myself with six hundred men.

At this time (on the 9th) the English came to Zante, and, disembarking, they established themselves there, and sent away the French to Corfu. About four hundred Greeks were put into the boats as prisoners of war. They also took Cephalonia, Ithaki, and Cerigo, and made them their own. General Oswald had orders from the generalissimo of the English forces, who was then in Palermo, to take into the service all the Greeks who were willing to join, and to put Church (who was then ma-

Konstantinos Kanaris blows up the flagship of the Turkish fleet moored in the port of Chios (by Nikiforos Lytras, Athens, Collection of I. Serpieris)

"Hellas on the ruins of Messolonghi." Oil on canvas by Eugène Delacroix (Musée de Beaux-Arts, Bordeaux)

jor) at their head.

When we saw that the English had come into the islands we sent word to Parga to enlist no more soldiers, as our plans were frustrated by their arrival. Our scheme was to get all the forts in Messenia, Parga, and Monemvasia placed in our hands. All the Turkish inhabitants of those places had agreed at a conference we had with them, that we should form a government, consisting of twelve Turks and twelve Greeks - the Turks to be governed with the same impartiality as the Greeks. Donzelot had framed the laws in conjunction with ourselves. Our flag was to have been a cross on one side, and on the other a half-moon and stars. This plan also formulated that when we had secured the Morea we should write to the Sultan to assure him that our action was not against him, but against the tyrannies of Ali Pasha, and Donzelot had already advised with the minister at Constantinople to prevent him from making any movement.

It was my own private intention, however, that when we had got possession of all the forts, we should then make it a more *national* movement, and throw over the Turks; but what I resolved upon doing would have to depend upon circumstances. Our measures would have necessitated raising fifteen thousand of the islanders. Donzelot, myself, Ali Pharmakes, and a secretary were three days and three nights laying out our plans. [...]

---

* *The Movement for Greek Independence 1770-1821 edited and translated by Richard Clogg, (Harper & Row, 1976).*

The naval battle at Navarino, which in effect ended Ottoman control over southern Greece (Watercolor by Martin Verdiot who took part in the battle – Athens, Benaki Museum)

THE 1819 ADDRESS OF COUNT IOANNIS KAPODISTRIAS

Following is the full text of Ioannis Kapodistrias' 1819 address as it appeared in The Portfolio*; a collection of state papers, and other documents and correspondence, historical, diplomatic and commercial, IV (London, 1836) pp. 282-301.*

Sons of our Holy Mother Church, we are all brethren; united by our common misfortunes, we are all bound to lend each other mutual assistance; enlightened by the experience of our errors, henceforth formed in the school of the calamities which have resulted from them, and under which we succumb, we have already arrived at a certain degree of maturity, since we are all equally impressed with the happy conviction that we must give each other mutual aid, but without departing from the principles consecrated by the morality of that holy religion to which alone we owe our existence as a nation, through which we suffer under this title, entertain a profound sense of those sufferings, and experience the necessity of delivering ourselves from them for ever. The march we have for some years pursued with the view of attaining this object is undoubtedly the true one. It is pointed out by the principles of the gospel; it exists in the nature of things.

To do good to our countrymen through the sole love of good, and from no other motive to ameliorate thereby their present lot, and thus to prepare them for the great advantages of moral and Christian salvation; not to trouble ourselves about creating this civilization on the basis of an arbitrary system, or of adventitious circumstances, but to leave this grand work to that Providence, which is alone the arbiter of nations.

Such are in general the directions followed by those Greeks who are called by their devotion to the service of our country; some in employing themselves in the better education of their children; others in promoting, by noble sacrifices, literary views amongst us, and in supporting by their means the less fortunate amongst the young Greeks who frequent the academies of Europe.

But literary education is not the only instruction which we require; our country requires another. It is moral instruction which is wanted.

Moral education ought on the one hand to have for its object to bring into prominent notice men worthy of the respect and the confidence of the nation; and on the other to accustom the nation gradually to respect, to listen to, and to believe in, such men.

If the epochs, in which every thing promised to our country the most honorable and happy future, have passed away, leaving our best hopes unaccomplished, it is because the men of whom that country was to be composed were not yet qualified, either to listen to the august voice of truth, or to be listened to by the mass of our citizens. Scanty intelligence, an entire want of experience, an ignorance of the habits and manners of the world, constituted, in those days, our whole patrimony. Life has no charms amidst such dearth of means, when such is the habitual state of things; how, then, can we hope to escape from it, or to create a happier condition of life?

The man who has shaken off the yoke may rapidly bend his mind to liberal conceptions; but, in order to reduce these ideas to practice, more is required. His heart must be endowed with enlightened benevolence which is taught by the Gospel: out of this sphere there can be no real good.

Either liberal conceptions remain in the world of abstractions, and then they remain without effect, or else they become the instrument of ambition and of personal interest, when they lose all their attraction; instead of securing attachment they draw down the detestation of the people; its civilization cannot advance; it retrogrades. Let us render to ourselves a faithful account of the events which fill up the half of our century; let us examine the depths of our consciences with profound reflection.

Let us scrutinize the consciences of those of our countrymen who have been enabled to render us any service and have neglected the great and splendid opportunities of doing so; and we shall be intimately convinced that, but for ignorance on the one hand, and this want of moral character on the other, the men most distinguished amongst our ancestors, favored by the circumstances of their times, would have bequeathed to us a less equivocal destiny, and a progressive amelioration of our fate.

Nevertheless, this amelioration commences; its principle element consists in the credit which, for some years past, the truths which we have just traced have enjoyed amongst us. It is our duty now to cultivate with method and wisdom this happy tendency of our countrymen, and gradually to lead it to satisfactory results.

One of the means which presents itself as it were spontaneously to the mind, is that of associating in this grand work the efforts of the most enlightened and the best disposed among the Greeks. This association appears to exist; it is in conformity with the letter as well as with the spirit of Christian fraternity; however profane be the character in which attempts are made to clothe it, it is desirable that this association should not deviate from the aim we have pointed out above, and on which it is necessary

General Ioannis Makriyiannis, who fought in many of the major battles of the revolution and later learned to write in order to pen his famous memoirs

again to fix our attention. We repeat, the Greeks must solely and exclusively occupy themselves with moral and literary education; every other object is vain, every other occupation is dangerous.

The point of departure, as the centre of moral education, can only be the institution of the Clergy; ours is not instituted, for want of means; in procuring those means a noble task will be performed. We reduce these means to the following measures:

1. The procuring for the principal dioceses bishops and metropolitans, the most distinguished by their learning and by the exemplary purity of their morals.

2. To engage these prelates indirectly to favor, in the circle of their jurisdiction, public schools; under the title of alms, one might afford them pecuniary assistance.

3. To point out to them the great importance of the service which they might render to their country, in administering justice in their respective jurisdictions with a scrupulous severity and inflexible disinterestedness.

The immense authority of the church, strengthened in this manner, will become the safeguard of the nation. It alone, perhaps, will become the cradle of its future destiny. If we wished to develop this idea, it would be easy to prove conclusively, that it is through the consideration which surrounds the church, and by the salutary influence which it exercises in the internal relations of each diocese, that we shall found the present bases of the regeneration of the nation, and that we shall as it were, hold in hand the thread to which this great event is attached.

It is unnecessary here to observe, that, in the actual state of things, this is the only means by which one can favor, on the one hand, the elevation of men who must be listened to, and, on the other hand, maintain the respect and the confidence of the people towards the latter.

Whatever be the chances of events, whether the present state of our country is to be maintained unchangeable during a series of years, or whether Greece is to undergo a crisis, it is always a matter of deep interest:

1. That the nation should be entirely devoted to its church, and that thereby the people of each country should be led naturally to recognize and to cherish those chiefs who have the most labored for their happiness.

2. That the pastors should be, as much as possi-

ble, the organs of this grand result.

3. That public instruction should be identified with that of the clergy, that the one should never be detached from the other, still less be ever at variance with it.

In favoring the instruction of youth, and in carefully drawing into the bosom of their families men formed in the school of the universities of the world, great care must be taken not to permit them to place themselves in opposition to the church.

This is a grand service, which the Greeks enjoying any credit may and ought to render to their country. They will effect it, in moderation by their ascendancy over the pretensions of the learned, and in neutralizing the prejudices with which ignorance loves to surround itself.

We have said that it is highly important that prelates enlightened, and revered for the purity of their morals, should be placed over the great dioceses.

The second part of moral education should have for its object the formation of men to the affairs of their country. The best school for us is that which is offered by the Christian people of our own religion, and by the free people. It is in Russia that we may perceive how the national prosperity and the progress of civilization is derived from the church.

It is in Switzerland, in England, and in America, where we may learn, by the attractions of example, the science and the art of liberty.

Liberty is a science because it is founded upon principles; it is an art, because the most elevated doctrine is not worth a good action, and because, in affairs, all is action. One must therefore be placed in the midst of freemen to learn to be free, both by the principle and in the fact. One must live some time amidst a nation eminently Christian and religious, and thereby prosperous, to learn to be religious by sentiment as well as by discipline.

The influential men of our country ought, therefore, not to lose sight of these observations, and in adopting them they ought to take care that some of our young people should receive a good education in Russia, in Switzerland, in England, and in America.

Commerce offers them a very propitious opportunity: amongst these young men, one may select those who give the fairest promise by their talents as well as by their morals, and make them travel for a time in the countries which we have just mentioned.

Once formed in these great schools, they must be summoned back and be provided with employment, either by investing them with public duties, or by showing them confidence.

The greater part of the Greeks who have distinguished themselves abroad find themselves, on their return home, out of place and employment;

The murder of first governor of independent Greece, Ioannis Kapodistrias, in Nauplion (Athens, Benaki Museum)

A scene from the battle at Skouleni, where several hundred Greek irregulars faced an army of 8,000 Ottoman troops of whom 4,000 were cavalry (Athens, Benaki Museum

struck with ennui and want of consideration, they grow impatient; they seek elsewhere an existence which they cannot enjoy in their native land; they leave it - they are lost to their country. The grand point is to preserve them, and to make them work for her. This question, in theory, seems immensely difficult; it is easy from the moment it is considered under a practical point of view; man exists but by one interest; the grand art consists in making him find one, and associating this interest with the interest of all.

But there is not a village which does not offer a mass of interests, especially to those who are endowed with strong feeling and much imagination, and when national history can move the one and nourish the other.

In occupying themselves with a part of the service of our country, those who are well disposed may be of great use to her, either in promoting the political education, so to speak, of the young men of great promise, or in making use of those who may have realized those promises by their observations whilst travelling abroad.

These two branches of the national service require a point of contact, a common centre of departure. The enlightened men amongst us who are well disposed and sincere Christians, will be able to form this centre. In constantly giving to all our efforts this straight and moral direction, we fail in none of the duties which each of us has contracted towards the order of things existing in the country which contains our domestic hearths, and the tomb of our fathers; and at the same time we fulfil loyally and honorably all the duties imposed upon us by our holy religion. It commands from us the love of our neighbor, still more that of our countrymen.

On the day when we shall depart from this line of conduct, when we shall embrace a different doctrine, our sacrifices will add to the misfortunes of our country.

It will be, then, no longer the question of the public welfare, but the ambition and the vanity of some individuals, to which the interests of our common country will be made subservient.

We hope to steer clear of this great danger; the consequences of our errors still weigh on our heads.

Θ.Π. Βρυζάκης
Εποιει 1861

THE AMERICAN RESPONSE TO THE GREEK WAR OF INDEPENDENCE

By Constantine G. Hatzidimitriou

This text is part of a book titled: Founded on Freedom and Virtue, *which includes documents illustrating the impact of the Greek war of independence (1821-1829), in the United States. The book is edited by Constantine G. Hatzidimitriou.*

The Greek revolution was a complex affair that lasted almost a decade and had a devastating impact upon the lives and material well being of Greek people. It is difficult for us to imagine the sacrifices and the desperate situation that the fighters of 1821 feed. By 1826 it looked as if the war were lost, and that after five years of struggle the revolution would be over. It is difficult to see how without foreign intervention, the contest would have resulted in the formation of a Greek state.

There is much that remains little understood about the progress of the struggle, the intervention by foreign powers and the motives that contributed to their decisions, that ultimately resulted in the formation of an independent Greek state in 1830. However, it is not my purpose here to go into these details. In this brief overview I will attempt to provide some sense of the role that the United States played in that momentous struggle, and in particular that crucial contribution made by the American people in saving thousands of Greek lives. It is a story that has gone largely unnoticed, but one that deserves to be better known because in a broad sense it has many parallels to subsequent Greek-American relations.

There are three basic components to the American involvement in the Greek War of Independence. The first concerns that official and unofficial role of the American government; the second is the story of the reaction of the American public and its contributions to the war; and the third concerns those of the American philhellenes who actually went to Greece and participated in the struggle. Each of these components relates directly to specific documents in this collection, and it is to these primary sources chat the reader should turn for additional information and documentation.

'Lord Byron Welcomed in Messolonghi" Theodoros Vryzakis, oil on canvas, Athens National Gallery)

The Official U.S. Government Reaction

Most of the attention in the literature has concentrated on the actions and statements of various U.S. government representatives concerning the struggle of the Greek people against Ottoman tyranny. It is important to recall that five American presidents: Jefferson, Monroe, John Adams, James Madison, and John Quincy Adams made very supportive statements concerning the struggle when in or out of office, and that these statements captured the imagination of their contemporaries. It is also significant that the most influential political leaders of early nineteenth century America, men such as Daniel Webster, Henry Clay, Sam Houston and Edward Everett, made strong public pronouncements concerning the official recognition of the revolutionaries and proposals for sending military aid. These federal pronouncements and activities also had their counterparts on the state level where governors and legislators made similar pronouncements and passed supportive resolutions.

The Messenian Senate, one of the earliest self-governing, local bodies set up by the revolutionary Greeks, had addressed an appeal for aid to the American people as early as late Spring, 1821. This was followed by an official request for recognition of the Greek government by Alexander Mavrokordatos in June 1823. The official American reaction was supportive but non-committal. Secretary of State John Quincy Adams counselled the President to be cautious since it was still unclear whether the insurgents would even succeed. Additionally, there were other considerations. The United States wished to avoid European entanglements that might have repercussions in its own hemisphere and had important commercial interests at stake in the Ottoman empire. Thus, a general statement of support for the Greeks was coupled with the famous address of President Monroe on December 2, 1822 in which he declared what came to be known as the Monroe Doctrine, a policy of non-interference in European affairs with a reciprocal non-involvement of European powers in the Western hemisphere.

Despite the cautious stance of the Monroe administration, there were many in Congress and, even in the President's cabinet, who lobbied for an exception to be made on behalf of the Greeks. These lobbyists were informally known as the "Grecians." Their reaction was based on the widespread popularity of the Greek struggle throughout the country and their own set of personal values. Thus, led by Daniel Webster, they precipitated the great Greek debate in Congress in January 1824. The debate was over a resolution to send an official American agent or commissioner to Greece, and it latest for several days. Despite eloquent speeches the resolution was defeated. However, the "Grecians" did not give up, and a secret American agent was finally dispatched to Greece in 1825. Despite a long fact-finding mission, the agent did not accomplish anything that had the slightest influence on American policy .

What was known, except to a few insiders at the time, was that the United States had a secret agent in the Levant who was responding to the President on the Greek war. He was in the region as early as 1820 and did not return to the United States until 1826. Similarly, the American Consul in Smyrna where Americans owned significant property and conducted a large volume of trade, also issued reports to the State Department concerning the Greek war. According to him, any action that compromised American neutrality would have severe consequences for U.S. ships and citizens in the region. Clearly, there were important commercial interests that would be threatened if the Ottoman government perceived any beach of American neutrality.

It was also a well kept secret that Commodore Rogers, the commander of the American Squadron in the Aegean, had been charged by the Secretary of State to expedite the negotiation of a commercial treaty similar to those which European powers had signed with the Ottoman government. Thus, while popular sympathy for the Greek cause was at its height throughout the United States, commercial interests drove the nation's foreign policy towards a course of action that, if it had become public, would have resulted in strong condemnation by the American people. No matter how popular the Greek cause was, or how much lobbying was done by influential citizens and politicians, secret diplomacy, based on the value of Turkish trade and strategic considerations, negated all official efforts to assists the Greeks .

Clearly, even the most ardent philhellenic legislators realized that the United States was not prepared to go to war with the Ottoman empire on behalf of the Greeks. But all of the debates, resolutions and lobbying, with only one exception, did not even result in any official humanitarian aid throughout the 1820s. I will return to this little known exception in the appropriate place below. Let me now turn to the second component of my story, the reaction of the American people .

The Popular American Reaction

To a great degree, the pro/Greek politicians reacted to the unprecedented general outpouring of public support throughout the United States on behalf of the struggling Greeks. This phenomenon was called "Greek fever" or "Greek fire" by the press of the time. Between 1821 and 1830, hundreds of articles were written and reprinted in American newspapers, and thousands of ordinary citizens formed ad hoc local committees and participated in town meetings and fundraising events. Greek personalities such as Ypsilanti, Botsaris, Kolokotronis, Bouboulina and Mavrokordatos and place names such as Souli, Chios and Messologi, previously obscure, now became well-known to the American public. These political and philanthropic actions had their cultural counterparts. As is well known, many of the most significant poets, writers, artists, dramatists, of early nineteenth century. America produced works related to the Greek struggle. It is probably safe to say that Greek personalities did not enjoy the same level of mass recognition again in America until the early 1960's when motion pictures and the Onassis phenomenon captured the popular imagination.

Why did the Greek struggle capture the popular imagination? There were many reasons why America was fertile ground for such a movement. Ancient Greek language and literature were still very much part of its educational system and in both high and popular American culture it was still assumed that Western ideals owed a debt to Classical Greek civilization. Another factor was the fervent Christianity which dominated society. Most Americans perceived the struggle in Greece in religious terms as a

The burning of a 74-gun Ottoman ship of the line by Papanikolis and Patatoukos at the port of Eressos (Athens, National Historical Museum)

battle between merciless Muslims and enslaved Christians who longed for religious freedom. Finally, we must also take into account the fact that most Americans viewed the Greek war as a struggle against tyranny, similar to their own recent national revolution. They considered the Greek revolt a republican struggle against absolutism with democratic goals based on classical models. The revolutionaries helped cultivate these impressions by writing appeals designed to flatter American sensibilities and reinforce their preconceived perceptions. Additionally, a very successful national publicity campaign was orchestrated behind the scenes by well-connected philhellenes such as Edward Everett.

These factors resulted in a popular outpouring of support for the Greek struggle that was unprecedented and threatened the young nation's well established policy of avoiding foreign entanglements. Although "Greek fever" was a national phenomenon it became centered in the northeast, particularly in New York, Massachusetts, and Pennsylvania. Greek Committees were established in many cities and towns, particularly in connection with educational institutions and churches. Many of these groups raised significant funds by holding balls, lectures, theatrical performances and special church sermons. All social classes and ethnic groups participated in these efforts and the newspaper accounts of the time record among others a fund-raising ball held by African-Americans in the New York City on behalf of the Greeks. Elsewhere, a group of young ladies erected a huge white cross in Brooklyn Heights to call attention to their fund-raising efforts, while craftsmen donated a portion of their weekly earnings to the cause.

These funds were sent to Europe through relationship between American and European Greek Committee and up to 1825 were largely used to buy armaments and supplies for the Greek soldiers fighting for their freedom. Obviously, these actions did not comply with the official policy of United States neutrality. However, the government did not dare to interfere and the Ottoman authorities protested in vain at the actions of private American citizens. There is no accurate way to gauge the volume or significance of this private American aid to Greece. It certainly amounted to millions of dollars in terms of present value, and had a very positive impact upon the opinion that the Greek government and public formed of America, judging from the documents that record the gratitude expressed at the time.

This popular outpouring of support also resulted in a brief but important relaxation of official American neutrality that resulted in an American-built warship, the Hope-renamed Hellas- being added to the Greek Revolutionary navy. The American public was both inspired and outraged by the so/called "Frigate Affair." The scandal over the building of two frigates in New York between 1824 and 1826 for the Greek revolutionary government symbolized many of the complexities of the United States involvement in the Greek war. The press eventually exposed the so/called "Frigate Affair" in which certain American commercial establishments had taken advantage of Greek inexperience and desperation to maximize their profits. Privately, even President James Madison acknowledged that their behavior had excited public indignation and involved lamentable abuse.

The scandal pitted those who placed commercial interests and American neutrality above lofty such as freedom and virtue, against American philhellenes such as Everett, Clay and Webster, who would use any possible means to send aid to the struggling Greeks. Although it is clear that the Greek deputies in London who authorized the financing of the enterprise had overestimated their resources, while the conduct of the New York merchants and courts involved in the affair was shameful and embarrassed those Americans who had publicly supported and raised funds for the Greek Cause.

Yet, in the final analysis, despite many twists and turns the scandal brought together a coalition of bankers, merchants, lawyers, philanthropists, and prominent politicians including two American presidents, who helped the Greek government save one of the frigates by persuading Congress to pass legislation that enabled the U.S. Navy to purchase the other. During the summer of 1826, the Hope finally set sail for Greece commanded by an American naval lieutenant at the head of a large group of America volunteers. It was allowed to sail our of New York harbor despite American laws that could have prevented the building and releasing of a warship destined for a foreign nation engaged in a war in which the United States was officially neutral. In this instance the partisans of freedom and virtue were able to prevail over those who argued against antagonizing the corrupt Ottoman regime and on behalf of regional commercial interests.

Eventually, "Greek fever" cooled as news slowly reached America of the disunity and military disasters that took place in Greece by the end of 1826. The character and purpose of private American aid changed after 1826, based on new information about the war that arrived from eyewitnesses. A new wave of support for the Greeks was the result. However, instead of funds and supplies to support the Greek war effort Americans sent ship after ship full of relief supplies to save the women and children of Greece from starvation. It was the first and most extensive example of American philanthropy in United States nineteenth century history and resulted from the deliberate actions of a small number of Americans who knew the conditions in Greece from actual experience. It is now time to turn to the role of these heroic American volunteers.

The American Philhellenes in Greece

In many respects the story of the handful of Americans who participated in the Greek war as volunteers is the most dramatic and interesting component of United States involvement. Although there were many merchants, tourists and seamen who passed through Greece during the war, we know for certain that approximately twenty Americans either fought in Greece or participated in philanthropic activities there. Very little is currently known of the activities of many of these brave men, although future research might bring more details to light. It is interesting to note, that among them was an African American named James Williams of

The tragic epilogue to the revolt in the Danubian provinces was written at the Monastery of Seko, where a band of revolutionaries blew itself up in order not to be captured (composition by P. von Hess – Athens, Benaki Museum)

Baltimore, who although not quite free in his own country travelled to a far-away land to fight for the freedom of others.

Of these American heroes, three individuals stand out for their devotion to the Greek struggle and contribution to stimulating American interest in and aid to the Greek cause. The trio was largely responsible for securing the massive amount of philanthropic aid that was sent to Greece from America after 1826, and in most cases personally participated in its distribution. The first American volunteers to join the Greeks was young George Jarvis, a New Yorker who had grown up in Europe and travelled to the front with other European philhellenes in 1822. Among the westerners who went to Greece he "went native," to a greater degree than the others, a fact that shocked many of his foreign contemporaries. Jarvis not only took the trouble to learn the language well, but he soon abandoned his western mode of life, dress and warfare and became a Greek captain with a band of fighters of his own. He wore a foustanella, lived in the wild Greek mountains and participated in the fighting and factionalism of the Greek klephts (guerrilla fighters) as an equal. He became generally known as Kapetan Zervis of his Greek contemporaries who mention his heroism in their accounts of the war (where he was referred to as to liontari, the lion). Until his death in Argos in 1828, Jarvis served as the guide and authority on whom most of the other Americans in Greece relied. He has left us a remarkable journal written in Greek, English and German in which he describes his experiences, an account full of insights and information not found in any other source. Jarvis also contributed to the appeals for American aid that circulated among the Greek Committees back home and advised that what the combatants needed were funds and supplies not fighting men. The other two Americans of this trio considered him their leader, and if he had survived the war he no doubt would have played a role in subsequent Greek-American relations.

The second American philhellene that must be mentioned was Captain Jonathan Peckham Miller of Vermont, who arrived in Greece in 1824. He was known as the "Yankee Dare Devil" because of his fearlessness in battle. He too learned Greek and wore a foustanella, although he and his colleague, the learned and equally fearless Dr. Samuel Gridley Howe, did not quite go as far as Jarvis in assimilating into Greek society. Howe is probably the best known of the American philhellenes because he continued to be active in Greek affairs after the revolution and became a noted philanthropist in the United States. Both of these volunteers also kept detailed diaries which describe their experiences in Greece and are full of valuable insights and unique information. Both men survived the war and made return trips to the United States, during and after the war, to plead for aid on behalf of Greece. Howe in particular went on a national speaking tour in 1828 for this purpose.

We have several detailed accounts of some of the goods that were collected by these Philhellenes in collaboration with the Greek Relief Committees of New York, Boston and Philadelphia and the manner of their distribution in Greece. For example, Miller published a remarkable book based on his diaries in 1828 entitled: The Condition of Greece in 1827 and 1828; Being an Exposition of the Poverty, Distress, and Misery to Which the Inhabitants Have been Reduced by the Destruction of Their Towns and Villages, and the Ravages of Their Country, by a Merciless Turkish Foe. We know that ten American ships loaded with food and clothing were sent to aid the starving populations of Greece in 1826 and 1827. Their cargoes had a value probably in excess of $100,000 at the time. The number of Greeks saved from immediate starvation based on accounts similar to Miller's are estimated to have been over 400,000 people.

In one of his writings about the Greek struggle, Edward Everett, America's greatest Philhellene, who was also a scholar, a congressman and president of Harvard University, sought to give an answer to the question of why America should send aid. His answer was that it did not matter that the struggling Greeks were the ancestors of the giants of classical civilization, but that Americans should care about them because of their common interest in Freedom and Virtue. Thousands of his countrymen apparently agreed with him and ignored commercial interests and official government neutrality, to send aid to a people yearning to be free.

---

* *[Founded on* Freedom and Virtue, *440 pages, paperback, $30.00. Published by Aristide D. Caratzas, Melissa International Publications, Ltd. P.O. Box 210, New Rochelle, NY 10802. To order: Caratzas/Melissa-SVS Book Services, 575 Scarsdale Road, Crestwood, NY 10707-1699 1-800- 204-2665.]*

1821 "Grecian Fever" Spreads to America

By Steve Frangos

Grecian Fever was the term quickly coined in 1821 for the worldwide excitement caused by the Greek rebellion against the Ottoman Empire. This bid for freedom captured the imagination of the American people still proud of their own revolution. Greek committees spontaneously sprang up all across the country to express solidarity, gather funds, and goods to support the embattled Greeks.

The American people responded as quickly as conditions allowed. Monies, goods and volunteers who fought side-by-side with the Greeks all streamed to the Mediterranean. Yet American politicians, and the interests they represented, were clearly not as interested in such direct action.

Much is made in Greek-American historical accounts of President James Monroe's (1758-1831) passing statements on the Greek rebellion in his sixth and seventh annual messages to Congress. But Monroe's final decision, as presented in his December 2, 1823 address to Congress, was that the United States could not take part in the war. President Monroe saw the avoidance of the Greek rebellion as directly linked to American interests in the western hemisphere. This position became widely known as the Monroe Doctrine. Obviously aware of public sentiments, Monroe quickly added the caveat that America would be among the very first to recognize Greece when she finally became an established and organized state.

President Monroe was nothing if not consistent. The principle events of the Monroe administration were the Seminole war, the acquisition of Florida, the Missouri Compromise, and the clarification of U.S. relations in regard to South American affairs. While the expression of Manifest Destiny and the American president's willingness to ignore European conflicts, such as Greece's War of Independence, is very clear other period specific connections may not be so obvious to contemporary readers.

Aside from the Monroe administration's concerns with annexing land was the explosive issue of slavery. It is not insignificant but rather fundamental that the same Americans who were involved in the Abolitionists Movement, which was then a worldwide effort, saw the Greek rebellion not simply in terms of freedom from political oppression but also as an instance of slaves rebelling against a master class.

On December 8, 1823, a mere six days after President Monroe's speech before Congress, lawyer Daniel Webster, at the time a representative of Massachusetts, introduced a resolution. The resolution answered Monroe's statements and at the same time afforded Congress the means by which to express its own will on the matter of the Greek revolution.

Most people associate the name of politician Daniel Webster with the perennial popularity of a short story, which eventually became a play and later two different movies, titled "The Devil and Daniel Webster." Written by Philadelphia-born Stephen Vincent Benèt (1898-1943), a well-regarded Pulitzer Prize winning author, this 1937 play proved so successful because it displayed Webster's finest qualities as remembered by the American people. A renowned lawyer who presented several famous constitutional cases before the Supreme Court, in the play, Webster offers his defensive before none other than devil himself. In the American imagination, Webster is a man of the people who would protect their best interests against even devil himself.

For modern Greeks, this man's greatest fame occurs right at the moment when the very nation-state of Greece was being born. During what many historians call his finest moments as an orator, Webster defended the Greek War of Independence. His speeches at the House of representatives are without exception always mentioned in published sources on Webster's life. In point of fact they are often cited "as one of the finest displays of Congressional oratory in American history."

On December 8, 1823, Webster moved for the adoption of the following resolution:

"Resolved, that provision ought to be made by law defraying the expense incident to the appointment of an agent or commissioner to Greece, whenever the President shall deem it expedient to make such an appointment."

With the Monroe Administration remaining neutral Webster rose before the Eighteenth Congress in the House of Representatives on January 19, 1824 to state his case. We should be quick to point out that many congressmen, not just Webster, engaged in the 'The Greek Question' debate. Other members of the House such as Henry Clay, Dwight, Poinsett and others spoke for the adoption of the resolution. John Randolph was the leader of the opposition.

The debate lasted several days. Long known as the 'Yankee Demosthenes' here is some of what Webster said: "What [Webster] asked, is this popular assembly? What this free discussion of public measures? What this open, unreserved action, of mind upon mind. What that popular eloquence which, if it were now present, would, on such a theme, shake this hall to its center? What are these but such memorials? This magnificent edifice, these columns, with their stately proportions, this fine architecture by which we are surrounded, what are these, but so many witnesses of what Greece once was, and what she has taught us to be? Yet sir... I have not introduced this resolution, now on your table, with any view towards repaying of the debt, which we, in common with the civilized world, owe to that land of science, freedom, arts, and arms. It is a debt that can never be paid. Whatever may be our feelings of gratitude for these gifts, we are constrained to act with a view alone to the present state of the world, and our relations to it. What I propose, and what I shall say, has reference to modern, not to ancient Greece-to the living, not to the dead.

"I wish to take occasion of the struggle of an interesting and gallant people, in the cause of liberty and Christianity, to draw the attention of the House to the circumstances which have accompanied that struggle, and to the principles which appear to have governed the conduct of the great states of Europe in regard to it; and to the efforts and consequences of these principles upon the independence of nations, and especially upon the institutions of free government. What I have to say of Greece, therefore, concerns the modern, not the ancient; the living, and not the dead. It regards her not as she exists

"The dance of Zaloggo" or "the Souliotisses" (by the French painter Claude Pinet)

in history, triumphant over time, and tyranny, and ignorance; but as she now is, contending against fearful odds for being and for the common privileges of human nature.

"In my judgment the subject is interesting to the people and the Government of this country, and we are called upon, by considerations of great weight and moment, to express our opinions upon it. These considerations, I think, spring from a sense of our own duty, our own character, and our own interest. I wish to treat the subject on such grounds, exclusively, as are truly American. Let it embrace everything that fairly concerns America. Let it comprehend not merely her present advantage but her permanent interest, her elevated character as one of the free states of the world, and her duty toward those great principles which have hitherto maintained the relative independence of nations, and which have, more specially, made her what she is.

"Sir, what has been the conduct pursued by the Allied Powers in regard to the contest of Greece?... They proclaimed their abhorrence to those 'criminal combinations which have formed in the eastern parts of Europe.' Now it must be remembered that Russia was a leading party in this denunciation, yet it is notorious that within the last half-century she has again and again excited the Greeks to rebellion against the Porte, and that she has constantly kept alive in them the hope that she would one day, by her own great power, break the yoke of their oppressor. The Grecian revolution has been discouraged, discountenanced, and denounced, solely because it is a revolution.

"Now it is upon this practical result of the principle of the Continental powers that I wish this House to intimate its opinion. The great question is a question of principle. Greece is only the single instance of the application of that principle. If the principle be right, if we esteem it comfortable to the law of the nations, if we have nothing to say against it, or if we deem ourselves unfit to express an opinion on the subject, then, of curse, no resolution ought to pass. If, on the other hand, we see in the declarations of the Allied Powers principles not only utterly hostile to our own free institutions, but hostile also to the independence of all nations, and altogether opposed to the improvement of the condition of human nature; if, in the instance before us, we see almost striking exposition and application of those principles, and if we deem our opinions to be entitled to any weight in the estimation of mankind-then I think it is our duty to adopt some such measure as the proposed resolution. I close, sir, with repeating that the object of this resolution is to avail ourselves of the interesting occasion of the Greek revolution to make our protest against the doctrines of the Allied Powers, both as they are laid down in principle and as they are applied in practice. I think it right, too, sire, not to be unseasonable in the expression of our regard and, as far as that goes, in a manifestation of our sympathy with a long oppressed and now struggling people. I am not of those who would, in the hour of utmost peril, withhold such encouragement as might be properly and lawfully given, and, when the crisis should be past, overwhelm the rescued sufferer with kindness and caresses. The Greeks address the civilized world with a pathos not easy to be resisted. They invoke our favor by more moving considerations than can well belong to the condition of any other people. They stretch out their arms to the Christian communities of the earth, beseeching them, by a generous recollection of their ancestors. By the consideration of their desolated and ruined cities and villages, by their wives and children sold into accused slavery, by their blood, which they seem willing to pour out like water, by the common faith, and in the name which unites all Christians, that they would extend to them at least some token of compassionate regard."

After this sustained debate the resolution was tabled. To cite but one scholarly evaluation of Webster's stirring oratory Dr. Churchill Lathrop, states that, "The importance of this speech was immediately recognized. It was called 'the best sample of parliamentary eloquence and statesmanlike reasoning which our country can show'. It was translated into every continental language and was read in every capital and court of Europe. To the Greeks it was a most moving and sustaining encouragement. Webster himself was very proud of it. Years later when writing a friend concerning this Greek speech, he said, 'I think I am more fond of this child than any of the family'." (Athene Magazine June 1941).

Yet, at the same time, sustained arguments for the freedom of Greece and the meaning of the struggle to Americans are never discussed in specifics. They are just great speeches. This vagueness is also seen in the biographic accounts on such men who were a part of these notable speeches in one way or another. Representatives such as John Randolph (1773-1833), Henry Clay (1777-1852), and others involved in the extended Congressional debates and in the social and political events surrounding this debate, such as Edward Everett (1794-1865).

Webster had an overwhelmingly distinguished life of public service. His efforts on behalf of the Common American are what were to endear him to so many. This heartfelt attachment to Webster was especially evident at the very end of his life. Webster returned to his home in Marshfield, Massachusetts, in September 1852 and died there on October 24 of the same year.

The general mourning that took place for Webster can only be compared with that which followed the deaths of George Washington and Abraham Lincoln.

POSTSCRIPT: THE TENNESSEE VOLUNTEER

By Steve Frangos

The full roster of American Philhellenes will never be complete until men such as Thomas Setzer Hutchison (b. 1875) are remembered. Hutchison is unique, even among Philhellenes, in that he was one of the American volunteers who went to Greece to fight during the Balkans Wars. A little recalled fact of Greek and Greek-American history is that many American veterans of the Spanish-American War of 1898 went to fight on behalf of Greece during the Balkan Wars, World War I, and even the Greco-Turkish war of 1921-1922. American, Greek, and Greek-American newspapers are filled with stories by and about these American volunteers in Greece.

Hutchison is again unique, even among this singular gathering of Philhellenes, in that he went so far as to author a book on his experiences, An American Soldier under the Greek Flag at Bezanie (Nashville: Greek-American Publishing, Co., 1913). Far from a mere adventurer Thomas S. Hutchison was to maintain his contacts with Greeks in America long after his valiant service in Greece was completed. Unexpectedly, as we learn more about Hutchison's involvement in the military doings of the First Balkan War (1912-1913), we inevitable discover more about the Greek-American community of Nashville, Tennessee.

Thomas Setzer Hutchison began his long military career at the age of seventeen. It was at this young age that Hutchison joined Tennessee State's Washington Artillery unit and saw "hard service in the mountains of East Tennessee during the mining troubles that so frequently occurred." Hutchison's service during the long and bloody mining strikes and riots helped to smash the state's labor movement and was duly noted by his superiors. He was quickly advanced from private to gun corporal, then to gun sergeant, next quartermaster sergeant, until finally he became first sergeant of the battery.

With the approach of the Spanish-American War young Hutchison was commissioned a second lieutenant. With the outbreak of the war with Spain, Hutchison formed his own battery and was quickly commissioned its Captain. Noted for his service in the Spanish-American War, upon its conclusion, Hutchison was appointed by Governor Benton McMillin Captain of Tennessee's Company K of the Fifth Regiment. He was soon promoted to Colonel. Within five years Hutchison completely rewrote the rules and regulations that governed the military forces of Tennessee. His efforts were noted by military experts as one of the best works on military science written up to that time. After nine years of service Hutchison voluntarily went on the retired list as a Brigadier-General.

Hutchison, never one to remain inactive for long, soon became involved with Teddy Roosevelt's Progressive Party in New York City. While Roosevelt's bid for the Presidency failed, Hutchison had the opportunity to witness first-hand the literally hundreds of Greek immigrants as they massed on the city's docks ready to return to fight in the First Balkan War (1912-1913).

For some reason Hutchison began "meeting numbers of [these] Greek volunteers." Taken by the fervor of these ardent patriots Hutchison decided to accompany the Greeks and volunteer his services. On November 13, 1912, Hutchison boarded the Austro-American liner Laura and on the 27th of the same month found himself in embattled Greece.

Given that Hutchison was an experienced artillery officer the Greeks welcomed him with open arms. Almost immediately he was commissioned a major in the Legion of Garibaldi but he never seems to have fought with that special unit. Instead, Hutchison served his entire time with the Greek regular army in the Fifteenth Regiment. While Hutchison was not fated to spend much time at the front, such was the fighting this Tennessee volunteer was to see that he was in no less than eight field batteries.

Hutchison's book provides exacting detail about his participation in the war. Yet it is in his response to an anti-Greek report in the New York Times where we can quickly learn of Hutchison's own experiences in Epirus: "I was with the Greek Army at Fort Bezanie, the Turkish stronghold that guarded the City of Janina, in the mountains of Epirus, and I witnessed the assaults of the Greeks on this seemingly impregnable fortress of snow and ice, defended by 35,000 Turkish veterans and 150 modern Krupp cannons, 6,100 feet above sea level and in the cold months of November, December, January, and February. The Greek army besieging this fort numbered only 60,000 men, and Bezanie seemed a Gibraltar, as I had seen that famous British fortress. But the Greek army, alone and unaided by any of her allies, captured it – one of the greatest military feats ever accomplished (New York Times, Sunday, August 10, 1913)."

It was toward the end of this siege when Hutchison was wounded. As he bent to help a wounded Greek boy, a Turkish shell hit a stone in his vicinity and Hutchison was struck in the head. Although the wound eventually did not prove to be serious, his hearing was forever affected. After his recovery, Hutchison who was still suffering from his head wounds was forced to leave the country.

Upon his return to Nashville the local Greek community gave Hutchison a hero's welcome. As the Nashville Banner reported, "Still nursing an injury he received while fighting under the Greek flag at the terrible eleven-day siege at the bombardment of the Turkish forts of Janina, Col. Tom Hutchison has returned to his home in Nashville, where he was given a hearty welcome by Nashville Greeks, who gathered at the home of his brother, Albert Hutchison."

Among the fifty Greeks was the Greek consul to the port of Nashville Panteles Panagiotopoulos who made a short address. As Colonel Hutchison was still nursing his wound he was not able to entertain the local Greeks and other well wishers for long.

A Cretan fighter in the traditional garb of Sfakia

But the appreciative Greeks could not be put off.

As another of the local newspapers the Nashville Tennessean and American reported: "A beautiful silver loving cup was presented Sunday night to Colonel Thos. S. Hutchison by the Greek citizens of Nashville in appreciation of his services to the Greek cause... The cup, which is large and very artistic token, was presented Colonel Hutchison by Panteles Panagiotopoulos... The presentation occurred at Mr. Hutchison's home on Division street, where about fifty Greek citizens and a few close friends were assembled.

"As he delivered this token of appreciation, Mr. Panagiotopoulos spoke... [in part about the siege and fall of Bezanie]... 'This will only add another chapter to the wonderful achievements of the Greek nation, and in that volume we will see with pride, Colonel Hutchison, your name representing a noble and brave Tennessean of the United States of America, who risked his life in a strange land to help in such a victory. The Greek citizens of Nashville in presenting to you this slight token of their appreciation of your service to their fatherland feel certain that it voices the sentiments of the entire Greek nation. This, Colonel Hutchison, is the meaning of the Greek inscription on this loving cup.'"

But clearly this was not the last time Colonel Hutchison and the Greeks of Nashville ever met. Thomas Hutchison's volume "An American Soldier under the Greek Flag at Bezanie," demonstrates that he was a keen observer of military organization and detail. But it was most certainly not published for that reason alone. Since no records on Greek-American Publishing Company are to be found in the Nashville Room of the Nashville and Davidson County Public Library, the archive where such business documents are now to be found. It seems likely that this publishing company was created solely to publish this single volume as underwritten by the local Greek-American community.

Hutchison did not forget about the Greeks and their cause in the Balkans. While the exact sequence of Hutchison's involvement with the war in the Balkans after 1913 is now uncertain it is clear that the Tennessee Colonel made his way back to Greece. On March 16, 1915, Hutchison returned to the United States from yet another tour in the Balkans. We know that he arrived aboard the steamship Athenai, since the very next day, some few remarks of his on the war appeared in the New York Times— "Says Greeks Are Opposed to War."

Undoubtedly because of the many newspaper articles about Colonel Hutchison's exploits in both the Greek and American press he was a well-known figure to Greeks around the country. As the events leading to the First World War developed, tensions between Mexico and the Untied States grew into a fever pitch. Theodore Saloutos reports in his classic volume, *The Greeks in the United States*, "Colonel Thomas Hutchison ...was invited to come to Chicago and organize a regiment of evzones and lead it into battle against the Mexicans when the need arose (Cambridge: Harvard University Press, 1964: 160)."

Hutchison was to live a full life. A successful inventor, he was married several times, had children, lived at various times in Chicago and near Dallas, Texas and was laid to rest in the city of his birth Nashville at the Spring Hill Cemetery.

Still, more research needs to be undertaken on the lives and exploits of the Philhellenes such as Thomas Setzer Hutchison, the courageous Tennessee Volunteer.

THE DESCENDANTS OF A REVOLUTIONARY CONQUER AMERICA

By Steve Frangos

For the Tsarpalas family the celebrations of March 25th are as much a family observance as a national holiday. At the time of the War of Independence Yiorgos Diakoumogianopoulos and his family were shepherds. Yet as the long-standing troubles boiled over into war Diakoumogianopoulos became such a furious fighter that Theodoros Kolokotronis himself dubbed him Tsarpalas, i.e. the Czar's sword.

As family recollection contends, Diakoumogianopoulos received this paratsoukli (nickname) specifically because of his beheading Turks during battle. While many families proudly recall such oral traditions, the Tsarpalas family also has a metal and certificate of commendation issued on April 19, 1844 by Otto, King of Greece. In the very early 1900s, as the grandchildren of Yiorgos Diakoumogianopoulos began voyaging to America for work when asked their name at Ellis Island, they proudly told the American clerk, "Tsarpalas!"

Now, after more than 100 years in America, the Tsarpalas family still recalls the legends and lore of their 'Papou Yiorgo.' But in a distinctly Greek fashion.

When asked about old Yiorgos Diakoumogianopoulos and his struggles in 1821 they also recount the efforts and hardships of the two other generations that helped establish the family in Pylos and Chicago since the War of Independence ended. Greek notions of soi – the extended family – informs each story. Rather than a simple straightforward account of the times of 1821 we learn also of Papou Yiorgo's descendants and their lives in southern Greece and on Chicago's fabled Halsted Street.

As the annual events of March the 25th arrive each year the family sits together or with close friends and tells stories not just of the War of Independence, although one hears these in song as well as simple stories, but also the family's other heroes their fathers and grandfathers and the struggles, hard as any war, that they too were forced to fight. These are some of those stories.

Many descendants of Yiorgos Diakoumogianopoulos now reside in northern Illinois. One of the family members I spoke with was Angelo A. Tsarpalas (b. November 16, 1924). His father was Adam who arrived in America in 1903. Adam's father was named Angelo. And Yiorgo Diakoumogianopoulos was Angelo's father.

As shepherds, the Diakoumogianopoulos family lived a nomadic life because of the need to find winter grasslands. Simply put, in order to have enough grazing land for thousands of sheep and goats the shepherds needed to have sufficient grassland both in winter and summer. In the old rural lifestyle of Greece St. George's Day (April 23rd) marked the beginning of the summer season. All working contracts between shepherds and landowners were to be signed on this day. St. Demetrios Day (October 26th) marked the beginning of the winter season. Summer contracts and working agreements came to an end and new ones were signed for the winter.

This lifestyle led to the formation of diplokatoikia or multiple residents, which is far from uncommon in the mountainous parts of mainland Greece. The Diakoumogianopoulos family would live with their flocks in the town of Arkodorema during the summer. They would winter their flocks on the island of Sfaktiria, and stay in the village of Kinigou near Pylos. With the advent of spring they would once again take their flocks back up to Arkodorema. And so these shepherds lived until the Great War.

Sometime during the turn of the century the Tsarpalas brothers started to immigrate to America. There were nine brothers Yiorgos, Demetrios, Vasilios, Adam, Pericles, Costas, Sotiri, Yanni, and Nikolas as well as one sister Alexandria.

When asked why they decided to seek out a life in America Angelo A. Tsarpalas told me, "They were coming out of that revolution. They were coming out of the Turkish oppression. The Revolt started in 1821...my dad was born in 1876; something like that...then (immediately after the war) the whole place was chaos. There was nothing there (since it was destroyed during the war) In fact, my great-grandfather, they told him at the time; he could take whatever land he wanted. He could have owned a lot of real estate. He didn't want it. He had his flocks, his religion and his family and that was all he really cared about." By the 1880s-1890s, there was little opportunity for the young men just starting their lives. Temporary work in America seemed the answer.

Sometime in the later 1890s, Costa came first, then Demetri, Adam in 1903, next Yanni and finally Sotiri.

When Costa finally went back, Nick came. So, there were always five out the nine Tsarpalas brothers in Chicago. After working on the railroads and various jobs, all five brothers were hired at the Western Electric Telephone factory, then located at Union and Polk streets, in Chicago's old Greek town district. They were making around $1.00 to $1.25 a day. They all lived together in one house. Demetri the oldest, collected all the money and ran family finances.

One day the foreman took Demetri aside and confided to him, "I know you boys are pretty hard workers. And I know you been saving money. The company is going to build a new plant. In Cicero (Illinois), at 22nd and Cicero.If you have any money and want to make some money go buy some real estate in Cicero.

I understand they had $8,000 saved up which (at that time) was millions. They thought about it and they (instead) gave it to Costa who went back to Greece and bought (them) horafia. Just to show that the Tsarpalas boys were doing good here in America. At the time they could have bought half of Cicero with $8,000."

Life in America was not a paradise. After the First World War serious troubles erupted between the immigrant Greeks and the Irish. Street fights, disturbances at work and worse.

Watercolor on a piece of cardboard by General Makriyiannis and D. Zografos of the battle at Langada and Kompoti (Athens, Gennadios Library)

A cousin of Angelo A. Tsarpalas' was "Notsios Karabatsos, he was a fruit peddler going up and down the alleys peddling fruit. And some young kid (of Irish descent) with a rifle shot him off the porch. And killed him. They went to court and they dressed this kid up in short pants. Claimed he was not right in the head. My father told me the story. They got the kid off. This happened right after the First World War."

As oral traditions recall, the Chicago police, in many neighborhoods, were often faced with large angry crowds few of whom could speak English. This led to the formation of Special Police deputized from among leading figures in a host of ethnic communities. Adam Tsarpalas was one of these men. "This (star) and a gun were given to my father."

The six-pointed metal star has Special Police 2423 Chicago engraved on the front. In, "Buried Unsung, Louis Tikas and the Ludlow Massacre" by Zeese Papanikolas there is a photograph of Tikas himself, with just such a star (c.f. Salt Lake City: University of Utah Press, 1982: 4).

In 1918, faced with local hostilities the Greeks, in a show of solidarity, are said to have held a parade on Michigan Avenue. Adam Tsarpalas was in this parade. The treasured family photograph of him in a fustanella was taken immediately after this parade. The other recollection much often spoken of was his going to the Greek Café on Dearborn Street in the Southwater Market district still in his fustanella. What was a bold public statement of ethnic pride in Chicago, in 1918, was a commonplace back in the village. Adam's father wore nothing but traditional clothes everyday of his life. It was only in America that the fustanella became an emblem of personal honor worn for special occasions. As family recollections convey, the parade had many meanings for Adam Tsarpalas. Aside from the Chicago and American contexts, Adam had returned to Greece in 1911 to fight in the Balkan Wars.

This family story has wider implications. Up until now no Greek-American article or book has noted this parade.

Around 1919, Demetrios started the Apollo Bakery on Green Street, near Halsted and Grand, and soon all the Tsarpalas brothers were working there together. But the brothers never truly believed they would stay in America. None of them initially even bought a house. They were certain they would go back. It was not until America's Great Depression of 1929 with its daily hardships and traumas of being unable to do more than secure a living that they began to change. Added to the economic hardships was the fact of seeing their children grow to young adulthood here. How would the young people fare in Greece? The old dream of returning home slowly, and often very slowly, faded. The Apollo Bakery remained opened until 1942-1943.

The life and exploits of Yiorgos Diakoumogianopoulos are not simply a matter of family history. In *E Kinigiotes stin Epanastasi tou 1821* by Vasilios D. Kaldis we learn much about the Diakoumogianopoulos family and especially Yiorgos' many war exploits and even his doings immediately after the war (Athens, 1984). To cite only one example, sometime after 1839, a considerable number of the Egyptian Muslims were left in the Pylos area. It fell to Diakoumogianopoulos to see that these Muslims were gathered together and placed in their own village, which was given the name Stenhori. Many, many other stories could be told.

Angelo A. Tsarpalas and his extended family are trying to keep up their heritage to pass it on to their children and grandchild as well. Given the grit and determination this family has shown over the last two hundred years, it seems more than likely these memories will be remembered for generations to come.

GREEK HEROES AND HEROINES

By Irene Biniaris

Throughout history, women have played a critical role during wartime in various capacities. Greece's struggle for independence from Ottoman rule in the early 1800s was no exception.

Although many accounts of women 'freedom-fighters' during the Greek revolution have probably gone undocumented, there are several exceptional stories of women that helped Greece, after almost 400 years, finally gain its independence. Among these noteworthy women are Manto Mavrogenous, Laskarina Bouboulina, Evanthia Kairi, and collectively, the women who have come to be known as the 'Souliotisses.'

Manto Mavrogenous (whose full first name was either Mandalena or Magdalena) was born in Trieste in 1796 to an old and distinguished family. Her grandfather, Dimitrios Mavrogenous, was governor of Vlahia and Moldavia.

When the Greek revolution broke out against the Turks, Manto travelled from Trieste to the Cycladic island of Mykonos. Given that in all the neighboring islands the revolution was already fully underway, Manto began to motivate the Mykonian people to act against the Turks.

She purchased two ships and had them specially equipped to chase pirates from the island, as well as to travel to other areas, such as Evia, to instigate the people in the fight for independence there. In addition, she also organized a body of guerrilla fighters, at her own expense, and let then in many successful campaigns against the Turks in the Peloponnese region.

Mavrogenous spent practically all of her personal fortune to contribute to the maintenance of the official Greek army and to providing ammunition for its expeditions. For this service, she was given the title of lieutenant-general.

Her efforts, however, did not end at the financial level. She personally appealed and wrote letters to women in other countries, including England and France, urging for their moral and financial support, and was quite successful in stirring sympathy for Greece.

When Greece finally gained its independence, Mavrogenous withdrew from active life and, largely due to political reasons, lived in solitude on a small pension granted to war-widows by the State until her death in 1848.

The Mykonians, in order to pay homage to the efforts of Mavrogenous, have named the central square of the village of Hora in her honor, and her statue has been erected in the square.

Another very well-known woman in the Greek struggle for independence is *Laskarina Bouboulina*. Bouboulina, the daughter of a sea captain on the island of Spetses took a very active role in the revolution. She was married, and widowed twice, and was the mother of six children. When her second husband died, Bouboulina was

Manto Mavrogenous, of Myconos, who took an active part in the struggle at sea (Athens, National Historical Museum).

50, and the Greek war for independence was just beginning.

It was then that she decided to dedicate, not only her efforts, but her entire fortune as well, to the effort. She financed and equipped four ships for the war and maintained a land army. Most impressively, she herself, took part in the naval blockade of Nauplia–an effort successful in relieving many towns under siege by Turkish forces.

In Tripoli, following a fierce battle, Bouboulina was the first to enter the town on horseback, and she managed to control the rage of the Greek soldiers against the women of the harems. She was also known to ride throughout the countryside encouraging others to take part in armed resistance.

Bouboulina died in 1825 as a result of a stray bullet during an argument with a relative over a family vendetta. Her courage, however, was an inspiration to many, and her life will be forever eternalized in the many folk songs and literary poems dedicated to her honor.

Laskarina Bouboulina, another leading revolutionary figure of the war at sea (Athens, National Historical Museum).

Evanthia Kairi, though not as well known as Bouboulina and Mavrogenous, was also instrumental in helping the effort for Greek independence.

Born in 1797, Kairi is best known as an educator and feminist pioneer of the enlightenment in Greek thought following Greece's liberation from Turkish rule. Though these efforts took place largely following the completion of the revolution, Kairi was also active in appealing for help from various women's groups during the war. It was during those crucial years that she personally contacted several women's organizations throughout Europe, asking for help. Through her many contacts, as well as her intellectual influence, she managed to create a strong philhellenistic movement in Europe and the United States among women intellectuals.

Following the end of the revolution, she returned to her native Andros, and founded a home with the purpose of educating war orphans.

Lastly, another group of women, collectively referred to as the *Souliotisses*, (named after Soulio, the town they inhabited) will always be remembered for their courage and valor during Turkish opposition.

Souli, an area in the northern region of Epirus, operated under a system of self-government which divided their area into 47 groups. Largely due to this construction, the people of Souli, were able to withstand Turkish oppression for several years, and it was not until 1803, that the area finally fell to Turkish forces.

It was in that year that Ali-Passas, the Turkish authority in the Ioannina area, became frustrated by the resistance of the people of Souli and did everything he could to overtake the city.

That year, after the Souliotes resisted Ali-Passas once again under the leadership of 20-year-old Foto Tzavella, Passas became more determined than ever to overtake the territory. As a result, he commanded his forces to surround Souli, so that its people would be forced to surrender their villages rather than die of starvation. Though their water and food supply quickly began to dwindle, the Souliotes could be heard shouting, "We would rather die than surrender."

During one battle, Pelios Gousis, a villager from Souli, betrayed his people and led Ali and his forces into the town. As a result, the villagers divided themselves into three groups and headed in different directions, fleeing Ali's forces.

The first group managed to escape to the area of Parga, which was protected by Russian forces. The second group, which was headed toward Arta, was wiped out near a monastery, and 45 of its members died.

It is the final group, however, and the heroic actions of the women in the group that most people identify with the struggles of the people of Souli. This group, finally surrounded by Ali's forces atop the mountain named Zaloggo on December 18, 1803, decided to adhere to their promise, "We would rather die than surrender."

After fighting continually for two days and nights, some managed to escape while several others died at the hands of the Turks. The women of the group, with many of their men already killed, quickly realized they were also in danger of being killed, or taken by the Turkish forces. Consequently 56 women and children withdrew to the steep top of the hill, overlooking the monastery of St. Demetrios.

There, each of them kissed their children one last time, and then threw them off the cliff. Following, they held hands and began to dance while singing the now-well-known song, "Έχε γειά καημένε κόσμε..." With this, the leader of the circle jumped off the cliff, and each subsequent leader followed suit, until they had all jumped to their death.

Ibrahim Manzur, a Turkish author, wrote and published this account as told to him by Souleiman-Aga, a Turkish colonel, who, under the leadership of Ali-Passas, was an eyewitness of the occurrences. He described the event as follows: "Women of Souli, held their hands and performed a dance, showing unusual heroism and the agony of death awaiting set the rhythm. At the end of each chorus, women expressed a long piercing cry, whose echo died out in the depth of the frightening abyss of the cliff, were they fell off with their babies."

A monument has since been erected upon the cliff of the mountain, as a tribute and symbol in memory of the sacrifices of the courageous Souliotisses. The monument can be reached by climbing 410 steps, which begin from the St. Demetrios monastery.

These women 'freedom fighters,' though all very different, were all crucial in helping make the struggle for Greek independence a success (as was every individual who fought for the cause). Moreover, they served as examples of empowerment for women the world-over, who would, years later struggle in a fight for their own independence.

SOME OF THE PROTAGONISTS OF THE REVOLUTION

Theodoros Kolokotronis

(1770-1834) He came from a family of kleftes and escaped to the island of Zakynthos where he served in the English Army. He returned to the Peloponnese on the eve of the revolution and due to his military experience and knowledge he soon became the leading figure in organizing the Greek forces. He lead the siege of Tripolis and its surrender marked the first success of the Greek revolution. The following year (1822) a small Greek force under his command defeated the army of Dramalis as it was entering the Peloponnese. He was imprisoned by his political opponents but was freed when the Egyptian Ibrahim invaded Greece. Kolokotronis applied guerrilla tactics against the Egyptian Army and was able to inflict major blows to it. He is considered as the most important figure of the Greek revolution.

Georgios Karaiskakis

(1782-1827) He grew up in poverty, the son of a nun who had fallen in love with a klepht, and was forced in his early youth to the mountains as a kleft himself. He was one of the first to take part in the Greek revolution and his military genius became apparent during the last years of the struggle. He was appointed by the first Greek government as chief marshal of Eastern Greece and made Elefsina his headquarters. Following a clash with the Turks at Haidari (an Athens suburb), he planned to cut off Kioutachis supplies, during the siege of Acropolis. His initial failures followed two famous victories at Arachova and Distomo. He was killed in a clash with the Turks at the Athenian suburb of Faliro. Karaiskakis is perhaps the most romantic warrior figure of the Revolution and its most natural leader.

Constantinos Kanaris

(1793-1877) He came from the island of Psara. He blew up the Turkish armada at Chios and at Tenedos and other Turkish ships at Mytilene and Samos (1824). He attempted to burn Turkish ships at the port of Alexandria in order to destroy Mehmet Ali's preparations against Greece and failed only because of the unfavorable wind. He became one of the important naval figures of the revolution. After the liberation of Greece he got involved with politics opposing king Otto. He served several times as a minister and also became prime minister. He was a brave, courageous and modest man.

Papaflessas

(1788-1825) He was born in Messenia, Peloponnese, as Gregorios Dikaios. In his teens he became a monk, but he had the reputation of an opinionated man who was not afraid to use physical force or receive punishment. The Turks, knowing his revolutionary tendencies forced him to leave Greece. In Constantinople, where he went, he became one of the key members of the "Filiki Etairia." Under Ypsilantis' orders he returned to the Peloponnese and started preaching about freedom, paving the way for the revolution. When, in 1825, Ibrahim landed with thousands of French-trained Egyptian forces in the Peloponnese, Papaflessas marched against him in charge of 2000 men. During the battle which took place at a place called Maniaki, on May 20 1825, Ibrahim with 6000 Turks attacked and killed 600 Greeks and their leader, Papaflessas, who fought bravely to the bitter end.

Lord Byron

(1788-1824) George Gordon Lord Byron was born in London. He was of a relatively frail nature and limped slightly in one leg. But he was a brilliant poetic mind and his art blossomed after an erotic disappointment. For a period, Byron, who had inherited a considerable fortune, live a life of debauchery. He visited Greece several times and found inspiration in the Greek revolt against the Ottoman rule, believing that Hellas ought to be independent in order for the ancient spirit to be revived. He supported the revolution even at great personal expense. In his last trip to Greece he decides to remain in besieged Messolongi where he died of a disease on April 19.

Odysseas Androutsos

(1788-1825) One of the acutest military minds of the revolution, Androutsos was active mostly in the region of Central Greece where he and his troops fought several engagements with Ottoman troops. The most famous, was his stand at the inn of Gravia, where Androutsos along with a band of about 100 guerrillas held back for days an expeditionary force of more than 3,000 Turks. Androutsos died in a Greek prison in 1825, a victim if internecine politics.

Andreas Miaoulis

(1769-1835) The admiral was born in the island of Hydra and at age 17 he became the captain of a commercial ship. During the Napoleonic wars he managed to accumulate considerable wealth by running the British blockade in order to resupply France. In the second year of the revolution he was appointed admiral of the Greek fleet. He defeated the Turkish navy near Patra and the Turko-Egyptian navy near Geronda, and on many occasions was able to provide supplies for Greek cities besieged by the Turks (most notably Messolongi).

Athanasios Diakos

(1788-1821) Diakos was born in Mousounitsa. His family was poor and thus his father sent young Athanassios to the monastery of St. Ioannis Prodromos at the age of 12. Five years later, he was made a deacon. Soon however, according to tradition, he was forced to leave the monastery because he was accused of killing a Turk. He subsequently served in the body guard of Ali Pasha of Ioannina, under the command of Odysseas Androutsos, whom he eventually replaced. It was at that time that he joined the Filiki Etairia and became active in the revolutionary war. He died a dreadful death, after his arrest following a battle at the bridge of Alamana in central Greece. His captors impaled him and let him die over a simmering fire.

Ioannis Makriyannis

General Makriyannis was born at Lidoriki in Eastern Greece. When, in June 1825, Ibrahim Pasha attacked the mills of Argos with a force of 4,000 foot-soldiers and 600 cavalrymen from his regular army, Makriyannis, together with Ypsilantis, Mavromichalis, and 300 men defended the position. They had already repulsed four fierce attacks by Ibrahim when, toward the evening, they were reinforced by a detachment of the first regular Greek regiment. Its arrival decided the outcome of the battle and the Turko-Egyptian forces retreated in great disarray with heavy casualties. Makriyannis, who was gravely wounded in the fighting, was invited aboard the French Admiral de Rigny's frigate. At the battle of Faliron on February 5, 1827, Makriyannis commanded the corps of Athenians, under the orders of British General Gordon. He distinguished himself in the defense of his position. Perhaps his greatest contribution is to the memory of the struggle. After the end of the war, the illiterate Makriyannis learned to read and write in order to pen his memoirs which to this day are one of the most moving and valuable accounts of the Revolution.

Patriarch Grigorios the 5th

(1762-1821) Ecumenical Patriarch Grigorios V was born in Dimitsana and was of humble origins. He was, however, one of the most brilliant and active clergymen of his time and after a rapid ascendancy in the ranks of the Church he was named Patriarch in 1797. He was dethroned and exiled twice. In 1918 he is elected Patriarch for the third time. His position became untenable with the eruption of the Greek revolution since he was pressured by the Turks to help put it down and brand the revolutionaries as acting against the will of the Church. His term ended with his martyrdom: on Easter Day, April 10, 1821 he was imprisoned and hanged just a few hours later at the western gate of the Ecumenical Patriarchate. His body remained hanging for three days, exposed to the wrath of the Turkish crowds.

Nikitaras

He was born at Leontari, in the Peloponnese, the son of a poor peasant farmer. He was a nephew of Kolokotronis and he, too, served in the army of the Ionian Islands. In 1821 he became head of a band of "pallikars"—fighters. He fought Kiaya Bey at Kaki Scala and in March and April 1822, at Agia Marina, Nikitas fought successfully under the leadership of Odysseus Androutsos against Dramali, who was threatening Thermopylae. After Dramali's invasion of the Morea, Nikitaras took up a position commanding the narrow passes on his route back to Corinth. There, the Greeks inflicted a terrible defeat on the Turks, killing 3,000 and effectively destroying Dramali's force. The result of this battle won him the nickname *Tourkophagos* (Turk-eater). At the siege of Messolongi, sailors bringing supplies to the besieged town demanded advance payment from the penniless defenders. Nikitaras flung down his sword, a priceless weapon which he had won from a high-ranking Turk, and cried out, "All I have is this sword. I offer it to my country!" His example had an immediate effect. All present stepped forward eagerly to donate whatever they could afford.

The Treaty of London, July 6, 1827

In the Name of the Most Holy and Undivided Trinity.

His Majesty the King of the United Kingdom of Great Britain and Ireland, His Majesty the King of France and Navarre, and His Majesty the Emperor of All the Russias, penetrated with the necessity of putting an end to the sanguinary struggle which, while it abandons the Greek Provinces and the Islands of the Archipelago to all the disorders of anarchy, daily causes fresh impediments to the commerce of the States of Europe, and gives opportunity for acts of Piracy which not only expose the subjects of the High Contracting Parties to grievous losses, but also render necessary measures which are burthensome for their observation and suppression;

His Majesty the King of the United Kingdom of Great Britain and Ireland, and His Majesty the King of France and Navarre, having moreover received from the Greeks an earnest invitation to interpose their Mediation with the Ottoman Porte; and, together with His Majesty the Emperor of All the Russians, being animated with the desire of putting a stop to the effusion of blood, and of preventing the evils of every kind which the continuance of such a state of affairs may produce;

They have resolved to combine their efforts, and to regulate the operation thereof, by a formal Treaty, for the object of re-establishing peace between the contending parties, by means of an arrangement called for, no less by sentiments of humanity, than by interests for the tranquillity of Europe.

For these purposes, they have named their Plenipotentiaries to discuss, conclude, and sign the said Treaty, that is to say; His Majesty the King of the United Kingdom of Great Britain and Ireland, the Right Honorable John William Viscount Dudley, a Peer of the United Kingdom of Great Britain and Ireland, a Member of His said Majesty's Most Honorable Privy Council, and his Principal Secretary of State for Foreign Affairs; His Majesty the King of France and Navarre, the Prince Jules, Count de Polignac, a Peer of France, Knight of the Orders of His Most Christian Majesty, Marechal-de-Camp of his Forces, Grand Cross of the Order of St. Maurice of Sardinia, &c., &c., and his Ambassador at London; And His Majesty the Emperor of All the Russias, the Sieur Christopher Prince de Lieven, General of Infantry of His Imperial Majesty's Forces, his Aide-de-Camp General, his Ambassador Extraordinary and Plenipotentiary to His Britannic Majesty, &c.; Who, after having communicated to each other their Full Powers, found to be in due and proper form, have agreed upon the following Articles:

ARTICLE. I. The Contracting Powers shall offer their Mediation to the Ottoman Porte, with the view of effecting a reconciliation between it and the Greeks. This offer of Mediation shall be made to that Power immediately after the Ratification of the present Treaty, by means of a joint Declaration, signed by Plenipotentiaries of the Allied Courts at Constantinople; and, at the same time, a demand for an immediate Armistice shall be made to the Two Contending Parties, as a preliminary and indispensable condition to the opening of any negotiation.

ARTICLE. II. The Arrangement to be proposed to the Ottoman Porte shall rest upon the following bases: Greece to be a Dependency of Turkey and Pay Tribute. Appointment of Greek Authorities. The Greeks shall hold under the Sultan as under a Lord paramount; and, in consequence thereof, they shall pay to the Ottoman Empire an annual Tribute, the amount of which shall be fixed, once for all, by common agreement. They shall be governed by authorities whom they shall choose and appoint themselves, but in the nomination of whom the Porte shall have a defined right.

Greeks to become Possessors of all Turkish Property on Payment of Indemnity.

In order to effect a complete separation between the individuals of the two nations, and to prevent the collisions which would be the inevitable consequence of so protracted a struggle, the Greeks shall become possessors of all Turkish Property situated either upon the Continent, or in the Islands of Greece, on condition of indemnifying the former proprietors, either by an annual sum to be added to the tribute which they shall pay to the Porte, or by some other arrangement of the same nature.

ARTICLE III. The Details of this Arrangement, as well as the Limits of the Territory upon the Continent, and the designation of the Islands of the Archipelago to which it shall be applicable, shall be settled by a negotiation to be hereafter entered into between the High Powers and the Two Contending Parties.

Following are excerpts from the text of the Treaty of London for Greek Independence, July 6, 1827. The text was titled, Treaty Between Great Britain, France, and Russia for the Pacification of Greece.

ARTICLE IV. The Contracting Powers engage to pursue the salutary work of the Pacification of Greece, upon the bases laid down in the preceding Articles. and to furnish, without the least delay, their Representatives at Constantinople with all the Instructions which are required for the execution of the Treaty which they now sign.

ARTICLE V. The Contracting Powers will not seek, in these Arrangements, any augmentation of territory, any exclusive influence, or any commercial advantage for their subjects, which those of every other nation may not equally obtain.

ARTICLE VI. The arrangements for reconciliation and Peace which shall be definitively agreed upon between the Contending Parties, shall be guaranteed by those of the Signing Powers who may judge it expedient or possible to contract that obligation. The operation and the effects of such Guarantee shall become the subject of future stipulation between the High Powers.

ARTICLE VII. The present Treaty shall be ratified, and the Ratifications shall be exchanged in 2 months, or sooner if possible.

In witness whereof, the respective Plenipotentiaries have signed the same, and have affixed thereto the Seals of their Arms. Done at London, the 6th day of July, in the year of Our Lord, 1827.

(L. S.) DUDLEY, (L. S.) LE PRINCE DE POLIGNAC, (L. S.) LIEVEN

ADDITIONAL ARTICLE. In case the Ottoman Porte should not, within the space of one month, accept the Mediation which is to be proposed to it, the High Contracting Parties agree upon the following measures:

I. It shall be declared to the Porte, by their Representatives at Constantinople, that the inconveniences and evils described in the patent Treaty as inseparable from the state of things which has, for six years, existed in the East, and the termination of which, by the means at the command of the Sublime Ottoman Porte, appears to be still distant, impose upon the High Contracting Parties the necessity of taking immediate measures for forming a connection with the Greeks. It is understood that this shall be effected by establishing commercial relations with the Greeks, and by sending to and receiving from them, for this purpose, Consular Agents, provided there shall exist in Greece authorities capable of supporting such relations.

II. If, within the said term of one month, the Porte does not accept the Armistice proposed in Article I of the patent Treaty, or if the Greeks refuse to carry it into execution, the High Contracting Powers shall declare to either of the Contending Parties which may be disposed to continue hostilities, or to both of them, if necessary, that the said High Powers intend to exert all the means which circumstances may suggest to their prudence, for the purpose of obtaining the immediate effects of the Armistice of which they desire the execution, by preventing, as far as possible, all collision between the Contending Parties; and in consequence, immediately after the above-mentioned declaration, the High Powers will, jointly, exert all their efforts to accomplish the object of such Armistice, without, however, taking any part in the hostilities between the Two Contending Parties.

Immediately after the signature of the present Additional Article, the High Contracting Powers will, consequently, transmit to the Admirals commanding their respective squadrons in the Levant, conditional Instructions in conformity to the arrangements above declared.

III. Finally, if, contrary to all expectation, these measures do not prove sufficient to produce the adoption of the propositions of the High Contracting Parties by the Ottoman Porte; or if, on the other hand, the Greeks decline the conditions stipulated in their favour, by the Treaty of this date, the High Contracting Powers will, nevertheless, continue to pursue the work of pacification, on the bases upon which they have agreed; and, in consequence, they authorize, from the present moment, their Representatives at London, to discuss and determine the future measures which it may become necessary to employ.

The present Additional Article shall have the same force and validity as if it were inserted, word for word, in the Treaty of this day. It shall be ratified, and the Ratifications shall be exchanged at the same time is those of the said Treaty.

In witness whereof the respective Plenipotentiaries have signed the same, and have affixed thereto the Seals of their Arms. Done at London, the 6th day of July, in the year of Our Lord, 1827.

(L. S.) DUDLEY, (L. S.) LE PRINCE DE POLIGNAC, (L. S.) LIEVEN.

ST.
5TH AVE
QUEENS
MIDTOWN
TUNNEL

Epic in America: The early immigrants

Favorite.

Greek Americans hail the arrival in New York harbor of the training ship 'Miaoulis' of the Hellenic Navy from the decks of the 'Favorite', on September 14, 1900

THE GREEK AMERICAN MOSAIC

*By Charles C. Moskos**

The Greek immigrant experience in the United States is a story with many chapters. It includes Greek indentured servants arriving in British Florida in the late 18th century. It is the saga of several score Greek orphans brought to this country by American philhellenes following the Greek War of Independence in the 1820s. It is a story of Greek merchants and sailors who arrived in small numbers in the years after the American Civil War. It is the still unfolding story of the yesterday's arrivals from Greece.

But the heart of the story starts in the 1890s and ends in the 1920s with those Greeks who came over in the era of mass migration. The struggles and successes of this pioneer generation shaped Greek America permanently. The world of the Greek peasant at the turn of the century was desperately poor. Whatever the glories of its classical monuments and the beauty of its seas and mountains, Greece was a harsh land from which to wrest a living. The overriding motive for Greek migration to the United States was economic gain. The intent of the vast majority of immigrants was to return to Greece with sufficient capital to enjoy a comfortable life in their home villages.

It is hard to recapture the power of the lure that was America. But a sense of the times can be gained by a Greek account in 1909: "In every village the farmer deserts his plow, the shepherd sells his sheep, the artisan throws away his tools, and all set aside the passage money so that they can take the first possible ship to America and gather up the dollars in the streets before they are all gone."

In the early decades of the 20th century whole villages were stripped of their young males. When sons went driven by the hope of escaping a limited existence, there was the tearing away from distraught mothers and grim fathers. When husbands went it was with the promise that they would soon return after making their fortune. At the least, they expected to insure the proper marriages of their daughters and sisters by building up dowries – the prika – with their American earnings. Because so few young men remained in the village, however, dowries became exorbitant in order to attract the eligible males still living at home. By the time the men who had emigrated to America were themselves ready to marry, they sought girls younger than the ones of their own generation left behind. It was a cruel piece of irony that precisely because so many men went to America to insure their sisters marriages, many young women in Greece had to face the probability of remaining single or marrying old men.

During the 1880s about 2,000 Greeks came to America, mostly from Sparta. During the 1890s more than 15,000 Greeks, coming mainly from the Peloponnesos, departed for the United States. There was a flood of Greek immigrants in the first two decades of the 20th century drawing from a wider regional base. Between 1900 and 1910 some 167,000 Greeks came to these shores.

From 1911 through 1920, despite the interruption of World War I, more than 180,000 Greeks migrated to America. These figures refer only to Greeks born in Greece proper and, therefore, do not include immigrants of Greek stock who came from outside the Greek state. We do not have accurate statistics as to how many Greeks came from such "unredeemed" areas, but all in all, around 500,000 Greeks – the vast majority males – arrived in the United States between 1890 and 1920. Probably about a third went back to resettle in Greece.

After the initial immigrants had settled in America, they wrote to their home villages, usually with passage money enclosed, to encourage their male relatives to follow. Those without relatives in America to bring them over were often recruited by labor agents scouring the Greek hinterland with promises of jobs in America. However he acquired his passage money the immigrant's trauma began before he arrived in America: wrenched from familiar surroundings, consigned to the nether regions of an oceanic ship, crossing in cramped quarters, fearing that a cough or blemish might cause him to fail the physical examination required for entry into America.

Once through the processing of Ellis Island, the newly arrived immigrant would head by train toward his destination. The flood of Greek immigrants can be traced along three major routes: Greeks going to the western states to work on railroad gangs and in mines; Greeks going to New England mill towns to work in the textile and shoe factories; and Greeks who went to the large northern cities who, in addition to working in factories, found employment in the service trades. Although each of these movements shared many similarities, each requires separate comment.

The first sizeable group of Greeks to arrive in the American West came as strikebreakers. A 1903 strike of coal miners in Utah was broken by Greeks brought in from the East. Though the Greeks in the main were not stirred by the workers movement that was gaining strength in the West in the years before World War I, they did take a leading role in some strikes: notably, the 1912 copper strike in Bingham Canyon, Utah, and the 1913-14 coal strike at Ludlow, Colorado. By the time of World War I there were at least 50,000 Greek workers in the mines and smelters and on the railroad gangs throughout the West. An explosion in 1913 in Dawson, New Mexico killed 263 miners of whom about a hundred had identifiable Greek names; another explosion in 1924 near Price, Utah, caused the death of 172 men, including 50 Greek miners.

As in other parts of the country, the Greeks in the West were to confront a virulent nativistic reaction. But it was in the West where their relative numbers made them more visible, that the Greeks faced the most serious incidents. In McGill, Nevada three Greeks were killed in an anti-foreign melee in 1908. The most publicized anti-Greek assault took place in 1909 near the city of Omaha, Nebraska, on whose southern outskirts was a shantytown of several thousand Greek laborers. Following a shooting incident between a Greek and a policeman, a mob, with the acquiescence of local authorities, rampaged through the Greek quarter, burning it to the ground and driving all the Greeks from the city.

A second major destination of Greek immigrants was the textile and shoe factories in the mill towns of New England. In the first decades of this century sizeable Greek colonies could be found in Manchester and Nashua in New Hampshire; Bridgeport, New Britain and Norwich in Connecticut; Chicopee, Haverhill, Lynn, Peabody, New Bedford and Springfield in Massachusetts. Early on there was a major Greek concentration in Boston. The settlements of Greek workers in New England had counterparts in the factory towns of Ohio, Pennsylvania and upstate New York. But for Greeks the foremost mill town was Lowell, Massachusetts, a community that has a special significance in the history of Greek America. In 1906 the first Greek Orthodox church in America with a Byzantine motif was erected in Lowell. By 1910 Lowell, with a total population of about 100,000, had at least 20,000 Greeks. Even as late as 1920 Lowell was the third-largest Greek city in America, trailing only New York and Chicago.

The living conditions of the early Greek immigrants in the mill towns were, to say the least frugal. The object was to save as much money as possible to send back to Greece. Usually a half dozen or so men would rent a cheap apartment and collectively share expenses. Modern hygiene and a balanced diet were not commonly practiced. Tuberculosis was a frequent scourge. Most of the Greek immigrants in New England were to remain in the mills for at least a decade or two, many for their entire working lives.

The third major destination of the Greek immigrants was the big cities of the middle Atlantic and Great Lakes states. On the eve of World War I

A Greek immigrant dressed in traditional costume

there were at least several thousand Greeks in such cities as Philadelphia, Pittsburgh, Buffalo, Cleveland, Toledo, Detroit, Gary and Milwaukee. But the preeminent Greek American cities were to become New York and Chicago. By 1920, New York and Chicago each possessed at least 50,000 Greeks. Chicago's "Halsted Street Greektown" was the most geographically concentrated of any in the country and developed into a distinctive ethnic enclave.

Along with those who found work in meat-packing plants and steel mills, many Greek immigrants in the big cities started out as busboys, pushcart vendors and peddlers of fruit candy and flowers. Unique to New York City was Greek involvement in the fur industry. A mainstay in the early immigrant economy was the shoe- shine or bootblack business. There were literally scores or even hundreds of Greek-owned shoeshine parlors in each of the big cities. Some of the owners of these parlors employed a 'padrone' system, which was little more than indentured labor for recently arrived boys from Greece. For many years bootblacks and Greeks were synonymous in our large urban centers.

Only a small number of Greek immigrants headed toward the South. Of all the Greeks who came to America before 1920, fewer than one in 15 settled in the states of the old Confederacy. There is a small community in the South, however, which does occupy a singular position in Greek America-Tarpon Springs, Florida. In 1905 more than 500 Greek spongers from the Dodecanese Islands were brought to Tarpon Springs. From that time until World War II, Tarpon Springs had a majority Greek population, a situation without parallel in any other town in the United States.

Immigration officials examine immigrants on Ellis Island

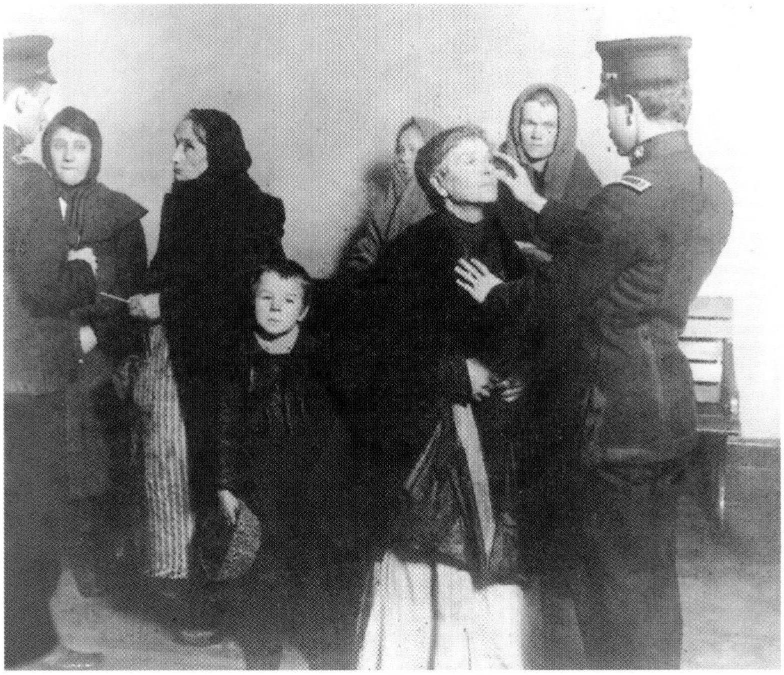

The beginnings of a Greek American middle class can be detected by, say, 1910. The entrepreneurial capacity of the Greek immigrant was remarked upon by almost all American observers of the early immigrant scene. In 1911, a Yale professor noted: "Give a Greek a start in business and he will do the rest. He can buy a pushcart or even a small tray hung over his shoulder, on which he can place a small stock of candy or fruit. However small his earnings, he manages to save a part of them. He gets control of a sidewalk space and puts up a little stand. Very soon he is able to rent a small store, and it is only a matter of time until he is operating a finely appointed store on one of the best streets in the city."

The new businesses tended to concentrate in certain enterprises: confectioneries or sweet shops, retail and wholesale produce, pool halls, floral shops, hatters, dry cleaners and shoe repair shops. The Greek presence in America was putting down commercial roots.

But it was in food service that the Greek immigrant would make his most enduring impression on American society. The first recorded Greek-owned restaurant was the "Peloponnesos," which began operation in the 1880s and was located at 7 Roosevelt Street on the lower East Side of Manhattan. An American commentator described it as "a poor, forlorn affair; yet to the lonely immigrant it meant comradeship and a breath of home. Here the Greek peddlers found cooking and manners of home." By 1910 there were several hundred Greek-owned eating establishments throughout the country. By 1920 there were thousands of Greek-owned restaurants – over 800 in Chicago alone. The expression became popular that "when Greek meets Greek they start a restaurant."

The arrival of large numbers of Greek women in the 1920s anchored the Greek community in this country. Before the turn of the century only a few Greek women entered the United States; each must have been a heroine in her own right. Between 1900 and 1910 women made up less than one in twenty of the Greek immigrants, and only one in five between

1910 and 1920. The preferred way for a Greek woman to come to America was to be accompanied: if married, with her husband; if single, in the company of brothers or male cousins. But since marriages were frequently arranged across the ocean, many "picture brides" had to travel to America on their own.

By and large, Greek immigrant women did not work outside the household. There were, however, important exceptions to the general pattern. For a woman to work in the family store was acceptable, though even this was not a rule. In the West in the early years, moreover, many married women ran boarding houses for Greek laborers. But it was in Islew England where the likelihood of women working was highest. A large proportion, some say a majority, of the Greek immigrant women in the mill towns were operatives in the textile and shoe factories. But even there many women did not continue working once they were married or after their husbands had secured a modicum of economic stability. The clearly dominant standard-and the one that was in the main adhered to-among early Greek immigrants was for women not to be in gainful employment.

The 1920s also saw the transformation of the Greek immigrant colony into a Greek American community. By 1918 there were already over 100 Greek churches in the United States. The significant point of the appearance of Greek Orthodox churches in America was that they originated from the actions of the immigrants themselves. The Greek Orthodox Archdiocese was founded in 1922. The early history of the Church in America was marred by squabbles between royalist supporters of King Constantine and liberal backers of Greek statesman Eleftherios Venizelos. With the arrival of Archbishop Athenagoras in 1931 the Royalist-Venizelist conflict was eventually defused and the Church took firm root in America.

The political events occurring in Greece were mirrored in the Greek American press. The Greek American press was quick to take sides between contending factions. With origins going back to the first waves of mass migration, the Greek-language press in this country was to have it golden age in the decade following World War I.

Two newspapers in particular, both dailies and both coming out of New York City, were destined to play a powerful role in the immigrant community for many decades. The Atlantis was ardently royalist while The National Herald supported Venizelos. At their peak circulation, each had daily press runs of around thirty thousand. To read either the Atlantis or The National Herald was to choose sides on the issues dividing the Greek American community.

No treatment of the early Greek community would be complete without mention of the kafenion or coffeehouse. Almost from the time of the first arrivals, an enterprising Greek would rent a space in a cheap location, install a few tables and chairs, purchase a dozen decks of playing cards and serve sweets and thickly brewed coffee in the manner of the old country. Though sometimes frowned upon by established Greeks who saw the coffeehouse as a place for idlers and gamblers, it was the kafenion where Greek men could find a respite from this strange land

The pattern of fragility and localism of Greek American associations was broken in 1922, when a group of Greek businessmen founded AHEPA – the American Hellenic Educational Progressive Association. AHEPA was to become the leading Greek American fraternal association and represented the social aspirations of a growing Greek middle class. Most important AHEPA acknowledged the wrenching reality that most Greeks were in this country to stay. An AHEPA president in 1925 could finally state the unthinkable: "Today ninety per cent of our compatriots have definitely decided to remain in America. This is the country where they will die-the country where their children will live."

The close of the 1920s was also the end of the

Paying tribute to Greek American who fought in WWII

Scene from an AHEPA event on Ellis Island

first cycle of Greek American history. Greek American folk heroes had begun to appear: Nick "the Greek" (Dandalos) gained a national reputation at the gaming tables and race tracks. Jim Londos became the world heavyweight wrestling champion at a time when that activity was still sport rather than theater. The Skouras brothers – Charles, George and Spyros – were starting a movie business that would culminate with their becoming titans of the Hollywood entertainment industry. Dimitri Mitropoulos was already well into a musical career which would bring him into the very apex of symphony orchestra conductors.

The '30s were grim Depression years for most Americans and Greek Americans were no exception. World War II revived prosperity and continued the Greek advance into the middle class. In time many of the progeny of the immigrants would become prominent in business, science and the arts. For their numbers, Greek Americans have done exceptionally well in national politics. Two – Paul Sarbanes and Paul Tsongas – have been elected to the U.S. Senate, and another nine have served in the House of Representatives. Some would even say we had a Greek American Vice President.

But the true meaning of the Greek American experience is found in that pioneer generation of Greeks who came to these shores over half a century ago. They came without the English language. They were not well educated even in Greek. They worked incredibly hard. They were devoted to their families. They brought Greek Orthodoxy to a new country. They were good American citizens, yet they never forgot the old country. They were our parents and grandparents. We shall never see their likes again.

---

* *Charles C. Moskos is a professor of sociology at Northwestern University and the author of* The Greek Americans: Struggle and Success *(Prentice Hall). This article first appeared in the July/August 1985 edition of the Greek Accent.*

Arriving in the New World

FIRST WAVE
18TH CENTURY SETTLERS IN FLORIDA

*By Mary Evans Andrews**

They came by moonlight from villages of Mani, treading corkscrew trails down the wild mountains o southern Greece. That September in 1767, Yannis Giannopoulos and 400 of his fellow Maniots were leaving their homeland forever.

They were accepting the offer of the English doctor, Andrew Turnbull, a Scot, whose ships awaited them across the Gull of Messenia. The doctor promised freedom from Turkish tyranny in a far off, peaceful land called Florida. There, after working a few years to pay for this new start in life, every man would own 50 acres of fertile soil blessed by water and sunshine.

Yannis could scarcely imagine one stremma (half an acre) of rich land. Mani had no farm fields, only patches of dusty earth. Each scrawny olive tree clinging to the slopes needed a stone all to buttress the pocket of soil around its roots.

The Maniots loved this land as fiercely as they loved liberty. But the Turkish occupation of southern Greece had become a reign of terror. Charging their leader Bishop Ananias with inspiring revolt, the Turks had arrested and beheaded him. A few weeks earlier, Turkish soldiers had ambushed a group of Maniots returning from a religious festival without their warriors. The entire party of men, women and children was slaughtered.

While Mani was in mourning, news of Turnbull's offer had reached the villages. Yannis' parents agreed he should take this chance for a better life. At 18, he was lean, tough and eager. Used to little food and hard work, he was the ideal immigrant for the doctor's Florida colony.

At Koroni they learned that Turnbull had bribed the Turks and they could sail without fear. Greek priests gave the signal for departure. Over and over they made the sign of the cross, blessing ships and all on board. Soon the priests were tiny black figures against the white stone buildings of the port. Yannis watched Koroni's stark castle and Mani's blue Taygetos range fade in the distance. Now all he had of home were memories and his lumpy bundle.

That winter Doctor Turnbull sailed the stormy Aegean collecting colonists from Greek islands and Asia Minor. It was at Smyrna, years earlier, that Turnbull had married his Greek wife. He would christen the Florida colony New Smyrna in her honor.

At Mahon, capital of the British-ruled island of Minorca, Turnbull found 70 colonists from Corsica and 110 more from Italy. Some had waited so long they had acquired Minorcan wives. The hope of owning land tempted even more Minorcans than Greeks. Three years of famine was helping to drive these farmers from their home. Turnbull's description of Florida attracted more people than he could pack into his six ships.

Minorca's British governor persuaded the captain of a Danish vessel to take the overflow as far as Gibraltar. That he was bringing 800 more people than were expected in Florida seems not to have troubled Turnbull. Rather, he was elated. He had been granted 20,000 acres of land, but one third of the area had to be settled within three years or the whole grant would be forfeited. Hence, the more settlers the better.

For the last time the Minorcans saluted their famous harbor. Four days later the ships arrived safely at Gibraltar. Here Turnbull was lucky. Captains of two smaller British vessels agreed to take his extra colonists to Florida. On April 17, 1768, eight ships cleared Gibraltar for the open Atlantic. They bore westward 1403 passengers – and as many dreams.

On board were five newborn babies, children, poorly nourished adults and old people who could not be left behind. Soon it became evident that every ship carried an unseen passenger – Death. Crammed together below decks, their food a thin stew and hardtack, their only means of sanitation buckets of seawater – all could not possibly have survived. But no one had expected the 148 burials at sea that haunted the terrible 10-week voyage.

Nor could the eight vessels keep together. Finally, on June 26, 1768 the first four reached Florida. At the sight of white beaches and green shores, the bone-weary passengers cried for joy. Men pushed out on deck and climbed the rigging to cheer the pretty town of Saint Augustine, with its guardian fortress.

Only when Turnbull was rowed ashore did Governor James Grant learn the shocking news. Instead of the expected 500 Greeks, these ships and four still en route carried 1,255 settlers in need of food and shelter. Provisions had been made 75 miles to the south, the site of future New Smyrna. There a four-month supply of corn and some "great huts" had been provided, but for only 500 people.

Some of the men volunteered to hike the last 75 miles. To Yannis and the Maniots, Florida must have looked incredible. No mountains, no hills, not a piece of stone. The soil was obviously rich to produce this green jungle. "Dragons!" they cried at the sight of alligators. "Saint George protect us!"

When they reached their future home, the men were enthusiastic. A short way inland, the Hillsboro River, running south, met the Halifax River, forming a safe and pretty harbor on the Atlantic. No one considered its name – Mosquito Inlet – ominous. The mosquito-malaria connection was still unknown.

Immigrants crowd the deck of a steamship on its way to America

Around the harbor the land lay low, but the west bank of the Hillsboro was a shelly bluff. There, beneath spreading live oaks, the ground was clear. Spanish moss hung from every tree. Inland the newcomers could see the glossy dark green of a wild orange grove. But in July there was no ripe fruit.

On the high ground stood a few palmetto-thatched huts, too few to shelter even half the new arrivals. Yannis, apprentice carpenter, surely helped to fell pines and build frames for more dwellings. Other men stripped fronds from palms to thatch the roofs. Laid thick and neatly trimmed, the fronds made a surprisingly sturdy shelter. Unfortunately the thatch also sheltered vermin, including mosquitoes and oversize cockroaches called palmetto bugs. Thatch was a fire hazard too. Many families brought holy pictures. Vigil lamps burning before them swayed in the wind and could set a house ablaze in seconds. Cooking and washing were done in a separate lean-to. Everyone lined up at a drum signal for food ladled out of community kettles. Given no chance to recuperate from their ordeal at sea, the colonists were immediately set to work clearing land for vegetable gardens.

Fresh food was desperately needed to combat scurvy. Without fruit or vegetables on the long sea voyage, many settlers already showed symptoms of the disease which caused spongy gums, loose teeth, diarrhea and exhaustion. The settlers' staple diet was a food most had never tasted – corn. Lumpy white hominy or finer-ground grits, with fish or a bit of pork, were all they could count on until their gardens ripened.

They toiled in gangs, urged on by former British Army corporals. They had no experience clearing tropical undergrowth and in the sultry heat of Florida in summer one can imagine their misery. Heavy rains were another source of astonishment. Mediterranean skies are nearly cloudless from May to October.

Once the gardens were planted, the work of clearing ground continued. The settlers would raise something called indigo. The bushy plants produced a blue dye that sold for a great price in England. In exchange for indigo, the colonists were told they would have everything they so desperately needed: food, clothing, bedding and tools.

For seven long weeks the people endured hardship and hunger. Already their labor was changing the face of the wilderness. On August 18 Dr. Turnbull drove through the fields with visitors from South Carolina. These well-fed, well-dressed people traveled at ease in horse-drawn carriages. The strangers' approval was obvious. Dr. Turnbull took the trouble to translate what they were saying. "Experienced African slaves could not accomplish more than these newly arrived Europeans... If they went on as they had begun, this must turn out to be the best settlement in America!"

That evening, when the visitors left, a pleased Andrew Turnbull rode with them. He planned to go as far as St. Augustine, where his wife and four children were living until their home at New Smyrna was ready. Unsuspected by Turnbull or his overseers, the settlers' attitude had changed. These were Europeans, accustomed to independence, self-respect and even a modest degree of comfort. They had not come to Florida to be driven like slaves. Underfed and overworked, many had become ill, only to be accused of laziness. Some felt they had been tricked with lies about Florida. The more rebellious decided to escape.

Carlo Forni, an Italian who had been made a foreman, declared himself their leader. A supply ship had just unloaded provisions for New Smyrna. Carlo and about 20 others decided to grasp this rare opportunity. On the morning of August 19 everything appeared normal. The men began working as usual. About 11 a.m. the word was passed. Everyone quit and gathered at the center of the settlement. Forni harangued the crowd, citing their grievances. Urged on, the men broke into the storehouse and began taking food, clothing and blankets. Then someone opened a cask of rum. As it was passed through the crowd, more than 200 men joined Forni. Seizing weapons, they agreed to commandeer the supply ship and sail it to Havana, sure the Spanish would protect them from their mutual English enemies.

Several overseers, led by the cruelest, a man named Cutter, tried to stop them. An Italian settler, Guiseppe Massiadoli, swung a cutlass, taking off Cutters ear and two fingers. Also wounded in the groin, the hated overseer was locked in a storeroom where he bled to death. As the mob swarmed down to the ship, two loyal settlers slipped away to warn Turnbull, who lived four miles off. But he had left for St. Augustine with his guests. A rider was sent galloping to the plantation where they had stopped for the night.

News reached Turnbull about midnight and he set out at once for New Smyrna. First he dispatched a rider to St. Augustine asking Governor Grant to intercept the ship and put down the revolt. Grant acted promptly, but it was two days before the provincial frigate East Florida could sail south.

Meanwhile, the rebels had loaded their captured vessel and should have escaped handily. However, a premature celebration delayed their departure. By morning of August 22 they had sailed only to the mouth of Mosquito Inlet. As they waited for high tide to lift the ship over the bar, the East Florida appeared. Frantically they threw supplies overboard to lighten the ship, but the East Florida was too close. A cannon shot across their bow frightened most of the rebels into flying white rags. About 30 men made off in a stolen sailboat heading south down the coast. Soldiers boarded a smaller vessel sailing with the East Florida and chased the fugitives for days. In the Florida Keys, less than 100 miles from Havana, the rebels were captured.

In wretched condition, they were taken to St. Augustine. At the trial, in January 1769, three were sentenced to death: Fomi for piracy, Massiadoli for murdering Cutter and Elias Medici, a Corsican Greek, for killing the cow the rebels had stolen for meat. The rest were acquitted. No one had escaped, so Governor Grant doubted there would be another revolt. Moreover, Turnbull could ill afford to have many of his workers executed.

Turnbull counted up his losses–stolen goods thrown overboard to lighten the schooner – as "four to five hundred pounds, at most." The colonists paid a far higher price. Numb with hopelessness, they returned to their life of hard labor, scarce food, primitive living conditions and millions of mosquitoes. After the escape attempt, Anthony Stephanoli, a Greek survivor related, "the people being starved, they began to die 10 or 11 a day, some days 15."

In December 1768, Governor Grant solemnly reported the death toll to Lord Hillsborough, British Secretary for the Colonies. In the eight months since 1,403 colonists had left Gibraltar, 450 people had perished. Something had to be done quickly to save the colony.

New Smyrna was purely a business venture, the investment of Turnbull and two wealthy British nobles. The settlers had contracted to work for six or eight years (both figures are recorded) to repay the original costs, though a copy of the contract at Mahon, signed only by Turnbull, gives a term of ten years. When the land began producing, a 50-50 share crop was planned. The plan was never carried out.

Each of the London partners had received a land grant of 20,000 acres from the British throne. Their original cash investment of 9,000 soared to 28,000 and finally reached 52,000. The project had grown too large for private enterprise. Even when granted more acreage, the partners could invest no more capital. Governor Grant appealed to the British Colonial Office, which appropriated 2,000 to avert starvation.

For the colonists, production of a cash crop was literally a matter of life or death. The answer was indigo. However, indigo production required tremendous labor. First, the swamp had to be made into clean and level fields. Next, tiny seeds were sown. Planted from early March through May, the crops were harvested and processed every ten weeks through October. When the lacy-leafed indigo burst into blooms, the plants were cut with reaping hooks and thrown into large vats of water. Held down by heavy timbers, they began to ferment. After eight to 10 hours, the water turned purple-blue. Holes in the vats were unplugged and the liquid drained into beating vats. After it was churned, the sediment was allowed to settle for another eight to 10 hours. Then it was strained, bagged and hung up to drip. Finally the bags were emptied and the indigo was cut into bricks. Open sheds were built to keep the sun from fading the dye. The stench drew swarms of flies which the children had to shoo away.

A brochure of the steamship 'Acropolis', which carried thousands of immigrants from Europe to America

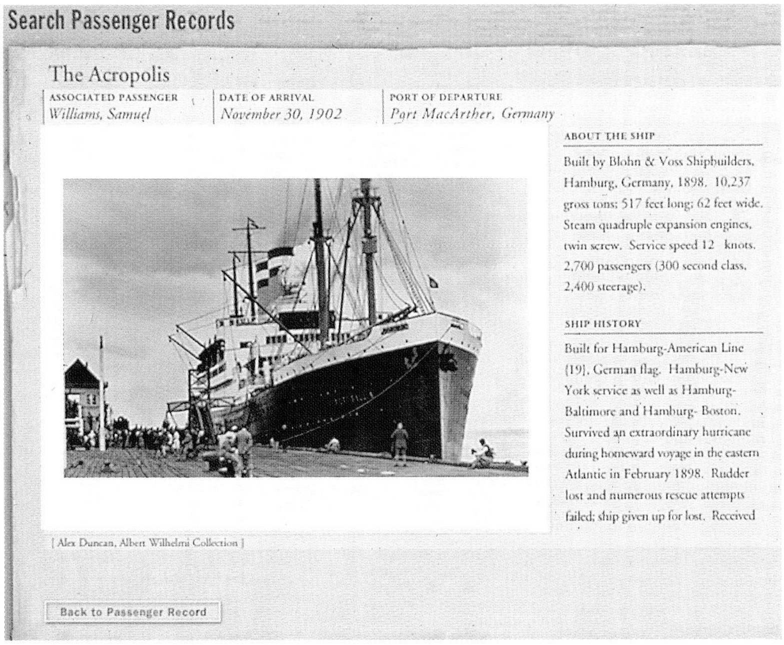

Search Passenger Records
The Acropolis
ASSOCIATED PASSENGER
Williams, Samuel
DATE OF ARRIVAL
November 30, 1902
PORT OF DEPARTURE
Port MacArther, Germany
ABOUT THE SHIP
Built by Blohn & Voss Shipbuilders, Hamburg, Germany, 1898. 10,237 gross tons; 517 feet long; 62 feet wide. Steam quadruple expansion engines, twin screw. Service speed 12 knots. 2,700 passengers (300 second class, 2,400 steerage).
SHIP HISTORY
Built for Hamburg-American Line (19). German flag. Hamburg-New York service as well as Hamburg-Baltimore and Hamburg- Boston. Survived an extraordinary hurricane during homeward voyage in the eastern Atlantic in February 1898. Rudder lost and numerous rescue attempts failed; ship given up for lost. Received
[Alex Duncan, Albert Wilhelmi Collection]
Back to Passenger Record

After nearly three years' labor, in April 1771, New Smyrna shipped its first indigo – 2,420 pounds – to London via Saint Augustine. This was the 1770 crop. In November 1771 Turnbull shipped another 9,138 pounds to England through Charleston. Production continued high – 9,065 pounds in 1772.

Meanwhile, the settlers were building their own large wharf. First they had to quarry slabs of coquina, a conglomerate of shell fragments and coral that is Florida's only native stone. By December 1773 the colonists shipped 10,262 pounds of indigo from their new port.

From natural sources the colonists were producing other exports. Oakum, a ship-caulking material, was stripped and dried from palmetto trees; pine-tar and turpentine were processed from the abundant pine forest These naval stores were in constant demand by British shipyards. Another source of income was barilla, a soda needed by Europeans to manufacture glass, paper and soap. It was extracted from the ashes of seaweed the children gathered.

And what of Yannis Giannopoulos, apprentice carpenter? After helping to build palmetto huts for the extra settlers he would have worked in the fields, like everyone else. Later he must have helped to replace the huts with board houses, and since no one could bring furniture on the crowded ships, perhaps Yannis learned to make that too.

Sometime during his nine years at New Smyrna, Yannis married. Only one Greek woman is known to have emigrated, so his wife was Minorcan. Typically she would have been dressed in a tight bodice, full skirt and scarf.

Spiritual help came from Father Pedro Campos, a Minorcan priest who shared all the hardship and privation of his parishioners. Father Campos recorded the few highlights of their lives. We know Yannis married because records show that by 1777 he was a widower.

One of the few ills the colony escaped was an Indian raid. Governor Grant had treated the neighboring Creek Indians fairly. Knowing the Indians hated the Spanish, Grant took care to explain that the Mosquito Inlet colonists were not from Spain but were British subjects who had come to cultivate new lands. Unhappily for Florida, Governor Grant retired to England in May 1771.

The same month about seventy Indian braves appeared near New Smyrna. Armed for war, they roughed up the crew of one of Turnbull's boats. The terrified men escaped to warn the settlement.

News of the raid reached Turnbull at Saint Augustine. He rushed home to parley with the chiefs. The Indians left peaceably, but the incident set off a series of events that would lead to the downfall of New Smyrna.

The settlers, struggling to stay alive, knew nothing of Florida politics. Turnbull had been deeply disappointed when Governor Grant did not appoint him acting governor. Grant had considered Turnbull, but wrote to London that "his constant residence at New Smyrna is...indispensable." Instead, Grant appointed an Irishman, John Moultrie, "the best planter in the province."

However, Turnbull had powerful friends including Florida's Chief Justice, William Drayton, who thought the Doctor should be interim governor. He and several other leaders developed into a political bloc opposed to Moultrie and all his policies.

When Turnbull reported the Indian raid to his London partners, he went over Governor Moultrie's head. Claiming they were a serious threat to New Smyrna, he asked that his letter be shown to Lord Hillsborough. Moultrie was rightly indignant. The action came as a complete surprise, as he and Turnbull had previously agreed that the Indian danger was slight.

Next, the Florida Council, of which both Turnbull and Drayton were members, met and decided that soldiers were needed at New Smyrna to discourage future Indian raids. Moultrie dutifully forwarded their request to the commander of British forces in Florida. The officer, stationed in St. Augustine, curtly informed Moultrie that he must apply to the British general in New York, a procedure requiring about three months. Such treatment further belittled the acting governor's authority.

These incidents multiplied. What began as personal dislike and jealousy of Moultrie grew into a catastrophic struggle between the Governor and the Drayton-Turnbull faction. On the defensive, Moultrie grew more and more arbitrary. Many citizens, Drayton and Turnbull among them, began to agitate for the election of a representative legislature. When the colony was formed such an elected body was promised. But now rebellion against England was brewing in all the American colonies and Moultrie feared that an elected legislature would become the focus for anti-British sentiment in Florida. In March 1774 the new governor arrived. An Irish colonel, Patrick Tonyn had orders to stamp out revolutionary activity. Tonyn ruled with iron will. Opposition to his policies was interpreted as disloyalty to England.

Six months after Tonyn took office the first Continental Congress convened in Philadelphia. Georgia and Florida were the only colonies not represented. Meanwhile, Moultrie lost no time prejudicing the governor against Drayton and Turnbull. They were carefully watched. Within the year an attempt by Drayton to buy land directly from the Indians aroused Tonyn's suspicion. No such private deals were authorized. A wealthy Georgia man had initiated the project; Turnbull was included due to his connections in London. The Governor saw the deal as a conspiracy.

Drayton was visiting Turnbull at New Smyrna when both were warned that Tonyn planned to arrest them. Late in March 1776 both fled to England. Drayton was soon reinstated as Chief Justice and by September he was back in St. Augustine. Turnbull, however, remained in London trying to have Tonyn replaced. But the Governor had proved devoted to British interests. By now, Georgia had joined the American Revolution. Tonyn was the only governor south of Canada who had succeeded in keeping his colony loyal to Britain. Tonyn was reprimanded for his action against Drayton and Turnbull but was not removed from office.

The Declaration of Independence had been signed on July 4, 1776. Britain and the American colonies were at war. Ships to New York were scarce, so Turnbull had to wait another two months for passage. He arrived, "after a most tedious convoy," in September 1777. During the year and a half he was away conditions at New Smyrna had changed.

At first, under management of Turnbull's nephew, also named Andrew, the colony prospered. In the fall of '76 New Smyrna shipped 6,390 pounds of indigo. That winter Saint Augustine suffered a food shortage and New Smyrna actually had 5,000 bushels of surplus corn to sell there. Out of a semitropical wilderness the settlers had created a small town. They built 145 houses, wells, lanes, bridges, canals, indigo works, storehouses, mills and a church. New Smyrna was well on the road to economic success but at an incredible cost in suffering and death. Official reports show that within two years, 627 of the 1,255 colonists who landed in Florida were dead. If those who died at sea are in-

A mother with her children immediately following their arrival on US soil

cluded, more than half of the original 1,403 colonists had perished. Though some casualties were unavoidable, the heavy toll must be blamed on those in control, who used these people as if they were livestock. Turnbull was all powerful at New Smyrna. Mrs. Turnbull, a tender mother to her seven children, showed not the slightest interest in the welfare of her Greek countrymen. Most of Turnbull's overseers were former slave drivers with orders to get the utmost out of the captive workers. Even before Turnbull left for England, the six-year term of the colonists' indentures had expired. Those who dared ask him for release were punished or jailed. When Anthony Stephanoli reminded Turnbull that he had fulfilled the terms of his contract, he was "put in stocks" and forced to sign for four more years of service. Petros Cosifachis, on making a similar request, was forced to prolong his service by six years. Louis Marquand, master blacksmith, having served five years, asked for his discharge. Instead he received 50 lashes, was put in irons and jailed with grits and water. Marquand, "seeing the miserable condition of his wife and child, ... was forced to sign a paper to serve Dr. Turnbull five years longer."

On March 25, 1777, three men got permission to go up the coast turtle hunting. Once out of sight, they took the coastal road to Saint Augustine. Their route required them to swim the dangerous Matanzaw River. They made the crossing safely and went to the Governor to appeal for justice. Tonyn promised with alacrity that their rights would be protected. Satisfied, they returned home.

In New Smyrna they spread the news. Secret plans were made for a mass exodus. When all was ready, one evening in late April whole families slipped away to rendezvous on the road to Saint Augustine. The strongest men, armed with wooden spears, marched front and rear.

The next morning, when the overseers realized what had happened, the settlers were long gone. Turnbull's nephew rode after them, overtaking them before they reached St. Augustine. His appeal to return fell on deaf ears.

When they arrived, Tonyn himself received them. They declared they had fulfilled their contracts and should be released from bondage. It was decided that they should make depositions; 90 statements were dictated to a clerk of the Attorney General. Eighteen men were chosen to stay and represent the grievances of all. The majority, at Tonyn's request, went back to New Smyrna long enough to secure the crops. Tonyn was concerned not for Turnbull's welfare, but by Florida's growing food shortage. Due to the revolution he could not obtain shipments from Georgia or South Carolina. Loyalist refugees from the colonies had swollen the population of St. Augustine, causing acute shortages of both food and housing.

By mid-July 1777 the courts had released all the colonists from their contracts. They were offered ownership of the land on which they had slaved so long. But they suspected some trick to get them back into Turnbull's hands. Not one colonist returned to New Smyrna.

The people of New Smyrna continued their struggle to survive. Governor Tonyn finally gave them small plots of land outside the city wall. Hastily they built shelters against the torrential rains and high winds that struck the city that autumn. During their first eight months in overcrowded St. Augustine 34 Greeks and 69 other colonists died.

When the American Revolution ended, England had lost not only her American colonies, but her French as well, which in 1784 was returned to Spain. The survivors of New Smyrna faced a new dilemma. Governor Tonyn, determined to depopulate the province, offered everyone free passage to the British possession of their choice. Few New Smyrna people accepted his offer. Once Father Campos decided to stay, most of his parishioners followed suit.

Their first, anxious petition to the new Spanish Governor was for confirmation of their property rights and freedom of movement. These he granted at once.

Like his fellows, Yannis Giannopoulos had arrived in St. Augustine that summer of 1777 with little more than the rags on his back. He was a widower, aged 27. After a year he seems to have had something to offer a wife, for he married a widow from Minorca. He and Antonia were an industrious couple. Within five years Yannis had built a house near the Minorcan Chapel and rented five acres of land which he farmed with the aid of three slaves and two horses. In 1787 Yannis' wife died. Four years later Yannis married another Minorcan woman. But within two years he lost his third wife.

When he married a final time, he had found an American girl, 24 years his junior. Ann Maria Simpson was born in Saint Augustine of an American mother and a British father. Perhaps she had some education and helped Yannis educate himself. Though still known as a carpenter, he had acquiree enough book learning to open a school.

Florida was purchased by the United States and organized as a territory on March 3, 1821. So Yannis Giannopoulos, from the remote mountains of Greece, became one of the earliest teachers in the oldest city of the young United States of America. Tradition has it that the original Giannopoulos school is the one now pointed out as the oldest wooden schoolhouse in the U.S.

Happily, the story of Yannis' success is one of many among the New Smyrna settlers. Another, Miguel Costa, became a doctor of sorts. Gaspar Papi, from Smyrna in Asia Minor, began his free life as a farmer, acquired acreage and cattle and died a wealthy storekeeper. Yannis' neighbor Petros Cosifchis, once nearly starved and watching in anguish as others died of malnutrition, also became a storekeeper. Eventually he acquired a schooner, hauling his goods in Florida's beautiful coastal waters.

In 1821 when they applied to the U.S. government for confirmation of their land titles, the former settlers of New Smyrna owned an impressive 48,956 acres.

To those nameless settlers whose unmarked graves darken the sands of New Smyrna, there is at last a fitting tribute. The Avero property on St. George Street, site o the Minorcan chapel, was recently purchased and restored by the Greek Archdiocese of North and South America. A memorial shrine was built on the location, the first known site where Greeks took part in public worship in the Untied States. With solemn and beautiful ceremony, it was dedicated on february 27, 1982.

This American Greek Orthodox shrine has at its heart the gemlike Chapel of Saint Photios. Unknowingly perhaps, Yannis Giannopoulos had been his humble and distant follower, for Saint Photios was an educator.

---

* *This article first appeared in the July-August edition of the Greek Accent.*

Typical 18th century neighbor in Florida

ELLIS, THE ISLAND OF TEARS

By Irene Biniaris

Approximately 12 million immigrants from throughout the world entered New York harbor, sailed past the Statue of Liberty, and finally made their way to Ellis Island from 1892 to 1954.

Designated by President Benjamin Harrison in 1890 as one of the first sites of federal immigration stations, Ellis Island served as the door to 'the promised land' to approximately 71 percent of immigrants who entered the U.S.

Contrary to popular belief, however, upon entering New York harbor boats did not first stop at Ellis Island, but rather at the Hudson or East River piers. There, first and second class passengers disembarked, never having made their way through the inspection process of Ellis Island. Immigration officials felt that if a person could buy a first or second class ticket, they were less likely to become a burden, whether for medical or legal reasons.

Immigration offficial checks the papers of recent arrivals

However, third class passengers or "steerage," as they were more commonly referred to, often made the long voyage in very crowded and often very unsanitary steamers. Following disembarkment at the New York City piers, these passengers were put on either ferries or barges and transported to Ellis Island for legal and medical inspections, before they could set foot on American soil.

If an immigrant's papers were in order and there were no signs of bad health, chances were that the inspection process – which usually took place at Ellis Island's Great Hall – would last approximately three to five hours. Those with problems, however, were detained on the island for some time (usually no longer than a week), until their ailment was cured or their papers were put in order. Only two percent of those who tried to enter the country were excluded, usually due to a dangerously contagious disease, or because it was thought they would become a public charge.

This was the common practice for immigration until the conclusion of World War I. As the U.S. emerged as a superpower, American embassies were established worldwide, giving the opportunity to foreigners to apply for their visas at the consulates and also have their medical inspection finalized there.

By the early 1920s, Ellis Island served only as a home to those immigrants who had still not sorted through their immigration papers, as well as refugees of war. It did remain open, however, for several more years, mostly serving as a detention center for enemy seamen and a training spot for the United States Coast Guard.

In 1954, over 60 years after it became an immigration port, Ellis Island was officially closed. It was not until 11 years later, in 1965, that President Lyndon Johnson declared Ellis Island a branch of the Statue of Liberty National Monument. Though the island was open to the public on a limited basis for a number of years following the decision, it wasn't until 1982 when easier access was made possible. In 1982 President Ronald Reagan requested of Lee Iacocca, then Chairman of the Chrysler Corporation, to head a private sector effort to raise the funds necessary to pay for the restoration and preservation of the Statue of Liberty as well as Ellis Island, since both monuments were greatly in need of repairs.

As a result, the Statue of Liberty-Ellis Island Foundation was established, and in close cooperation with the National Park Service, has since led fundraising drives for the monuments. Since then the foundation has managed to raise over $500 million for the project, making it the most successful public-private partnership in the history of the United States.

Many funds used to complete the project were raised through donations to the American Immigrant Wall of Honor, the Foundation's tribute to America's immigrant heritage, which is found on Ellis Island.

Many Greek Americans have chosen to honor their ancestors on the American Immigrant Wall, including Telly Savales, most well known for his television role as "Kojak," and Michael Dukakis, former Massachusetts governor and presidential candidate.

Among the famous Greek immigrants who passed through the immigration port of Ellis Island is Spyros Skouras (1893-1971), producer and former president of 20th Century Fox, who immigrated from Greece in 1910, and his brothers Charles and George, who joined him to form 20th Century Fox.

One of the major contributors to the Island's monument restoration efforts was the American Hellenic Educational Progressive Association, AHEPA.

Since more than 500,000 Greek immigrants came to the U.S. through Ellis Island, a long time symbol of America's immigrant heritage, AHEPA decided that the reconstruction effort was vital and merited its full support by raising over $400,000 for the cause. As a result, the U.S. Department of the Interior named AHEPA an official underwriter of the Ellis Island restoration project.

"AHEPA has been actively involved in both the

INS agents interrogate immigrant family

Statue of Liberty and Ellis Island restorations because we believe these monuments should be revered as central components of the American dream," then AHEPA President James S. Scofield had said.

As a result of its contributions, AHEPA was also given the exclusive use of Ellis Island for a celebration honoring the Greek immigrant experience, which was held on April 20, 1991.

The "AHEPA Evening on Ellis Island," as it was called, honored several prominent and successful Greek Americans, and also served to honor the courageous immigrants who came to America many years ago.

With the help of generous donations from private individuals as well as large companies, restorations on Ellis Island were complete by 1986. They

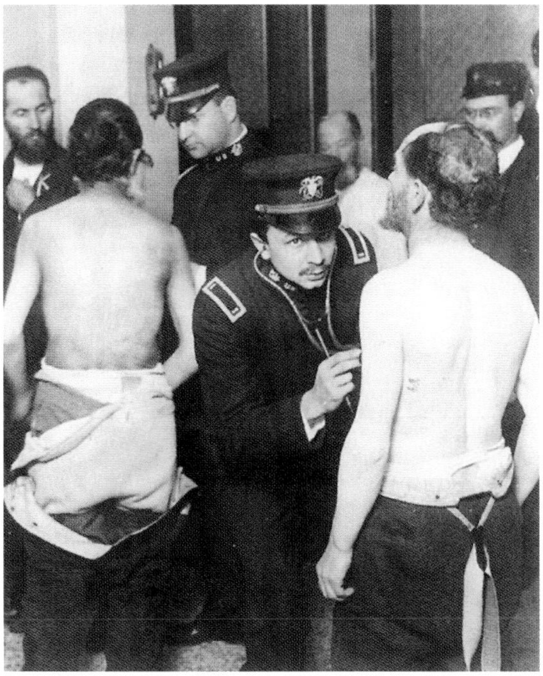

Immigrants undergo medical examination

included the restoration of many rooms in the main building, which now look as they did during the height of the immigration processing, while other rooms were transformed into theaters or as housing for libraries and collections.

The Ellis Island Museum was officially opened in September 1990.

It was around that time that the Ellis Island Foundation also undertook an even greater task.

The names of each and every immigrant that stepped through the doors of Ellis Island had been transcribed by immigration officials on large sheets called "manifests." These manifests usually included the name of the immigrant, their age, gender, occupation, ethnicity, name of vessel, port of departure, port and date of arrival, marital status and possibly even the names of relatives or friends in the United States. At some point, these manifests became stored on microfilm, and many of the original paper manifests were sold in the 1950s.

In 1993, the Church of Jesus Christ of Latterday Saints, in conjunction with the foundation, began the process of transcribing the ship passenger manifests from 1892 until 1924. The volume was incredible. In fact, if stacked flat, the 3,685 rolls of microfilm that were eventually transcribed by Church volunteers would exceed three times the height of the Statue of Liberty, from the hem of her flowing robe to the very top of her torch.

But after 5.6 million hours and with the help of over 12,000 Latter Day Saint Church volunteers in 2,700 congregations throughout the nation, the task was finally complete.

Disembarkation in New York

These names have since become the focus of the latest development of the Statue of Liberty-Ellis Island Foundation, named "The American Family Immigration Center," (AFIHC). The names currently comprise a database including more than 22 million immigrants, passengers and crew members who entered through the port of New York during the height of immigration at Ellis Island.

Subsequently, AFIHC opened a center which is housed at the Ellis Island Museum, as well as a website on April 17 of this year. At the museum, visitors have the opportunity to use computers and other multimedia technology to print out materials and investigate their own family immigrant history. It is also possible to search for relatives who may have passed through Ellis Island through the AFIHC website at www.ellisisland.org.

Another highlight of this new development is that through the use of this new program, people also have the unprecedented capability to create their own family history scrapbooks with personal family documents, records and photos. In addition, upon completing such a scrapbook one may choose to purchase a copy on CD-ROM or a printout of the book.

Maria Antenorcruz-Lee, the public affairs coordinator for the Statue of Liberty-Ellis Island Foundation, notes that the scrapbooking process also allows "children to offer their expertise in using the technology, and the adults can contribute their stories," thus making the process of completing the scrapbook a time for families to bond and learn about their history.

Among the official sponsors who helped AFIHC get started are the Church of Jesus Christ of Latterday Saints, Compaq, Discover Card, the Eastman Kodak Company, Genealogy.com and the Oracle corporation. Other contributors include the Xerox Corporation, Salomon Smith Barney, the Andreas Foundation, Pricewaterhouse Coopers, and Goldman, Sachs & Co.

"We are gratified to have such tremendous technology-driven companies supporting our effort," Stephen A. Briganti, president and CEO of the Statue of Liberty-Ellis Island Foundation, Inc. told The National Herald recently. "Not only have they played a major role in making the Center a reality, but, they will ensure its continued growth and expansion in the future," he added.

And it is clear that upon launching the center, and especially its web site, the foundation was ready to grow and expand.

"Within one week of opening the site, I believe that Lycos reported that we had jumped from nothing to the number one site in the world," Jack Hagouel, president of Zeky Consulting Services, a consultant firm used by the Statue of Liberty-Ellis Foundation and AFIHC, told the Herald.

He noted that the web site currently hosts 640,000 registered users, with an average of 57,000-60,000 visitors per day, and over 80 percent of users are able to log onto the site without encountering any difficulties due to the high traffic volume. Since its launch in April, he added, there have been more than 676 million hits.

It is estimated that there are 100 million living descendants of the Ellis Island immigrants, representing nearly 40 percent of the United States population.

"I think it is really exciting because I do a lot of projects for a lot of companies, and I've been in business for a long time. But this particular project has a personal touch, an it's amazing... it touches a very sensitive chord in the American psyche because a lot of us are immigrants," Hagouel noted.

Hagouel, himself an immigrant from Thessaloniki who came to study as an undergraduate student, received his Ph.D. from Columbia University. As such, he also serves to exemplify the common success story of many immigrants, including Greeks, who came to the U.S. After working for IBM, ITT and ohter well-known corporations, he opened his own consulting firm in 1986.

"Greek Americans have been very successful, and I think as Greeks we have a lot to offer, because Americans grew up knowing that Greece was one of the roots of civilization," Hagouel noted, adding that the challenge of retaining the rich Greek culture in a foreign land is a difficult task. "You are no longer a Greek in the Greek sense and you cannot take that away, but nevertheless there is a Greekness in you, and a desire for it," he said.

This Greekness, Hagouel discussed, has certainly not been lost within this melting pot of the nation. The Greek immigrants who travelled through Ellis Island often left their homelands fleeing hardships, in hope that America would serve as a new beginning for them. With this new beginning, however, did not come the end of old traditions.

Rather, traditions – Greek language, religion, and customs – have thrived through several generations of Greek Americans–proof that what these immigrants have brought with them to this country will never be lost.

A scene from Ellis Island

In Search of a Better Life

Following is the transcript of an interview with Panagiotis Chletsos, born in 1888, an immigrant who came to the United States in 1904 at the age of 15. The interview, conducted by Nancy Dallett, was recorded on November 26, 1985, at Chletsos' home in Philadelphia, Pennsylvania. He came to America aboard a Cunaro Line ship, exact name not recalled. Transcripts such as this are kept at the Oral History room at the library of the Ellis Island Museum.

My name is Nancy Dallett, and I'm speaking with Panagiotis Chletsos on Tuesday, November 26, 1985. We are beginning this interview at 12:30 PM and we are about to interview Panagiotis Chletsos about his immigration experience from Greece in 1904. This is the beginning of side one of Interview Number 85. Okay, we are about to begin. Can you take me back to the beginning of your story and tell me where you were born.

CHLETSOS: I was born in Turkey. It was, uh, it was not Greece then. We only got free about 1912, when Greece took it back.

DALLETT: And what year were you born?

CHLETSOS: 1888.

DALLETT: 1888. Tell me what it was like as young boy in Turkey at that time.

CHLETSOS: Well, I guess it was a school, that's all.

DALLETT: Tell me about your family. Tell me about your father. What did he do in Turkey?

CHLETSOS: My father was a, he had a garden. He was working on his father's garden.

DALLETT: What was in this garden? Do you remember his garden?

CHLETSOS: Oh, yes. I was there myself. I was eight years old when I lost my father.

DALLETT: And so, do you, how was it that you lost your father?

CHLETSOS: Well, he left by the, what they call the – *(Wife speaks.)* lightening.

DALLETT: Lightening.

CHLETSOS: It was a raining day. He used to go to grab the lamb, he was wearing a belt to pass back the water. At the same time he got hit, the lightening.

DALLETT: So he was struck by lightening.

CHLETSOS: By the lightening.

DALLETT: And he was killed.

CHLETSOS: He was killed, yeah.

DALLETT: And tell me about your mother.

CHLETSOS: My mother was living until she was around 90 years old, I guess.

DALLETT: Do you remember her as a young child in Turkey? Did she come to this country?

CHLETSOS: No.

DALLETT: No.

CHLETSOS: No, she was, I left my mother and three brothers and a sister.

DALLETT: And why is it that you left home? When you say you left, you meant to come to this country?

CHLETSOS: Well, when I come to this country, yes. I had, my brother was here, and I come – *(Wife speaks.)*

DALLETT: You had a brother that already lived in this country. Brother-in-law.

CHLETSOS: Brother-in-law.

DALLETT: And your sister, I assume, then, lived in this country. Is that right?

CHLETSOS: Well, I had a sister, yeah.

DALLETT: And do you remember when she left Turkey to come to America?

CHLETSOS: My sister?

DALLETT: Uh-huh. Your sister and your brother-in-law?

CHLETSOS: Oh, I guess about two years before I left.

DALLETT: And so once they were in this country did they write to you and say that you should come to America?

CHLETSOS: That's right.

DALLETT: What did they tell you about what life was like in America, can you remember?

CHLETSOS: Well, like (?). When I come in this

country –
DALLETT: Did you have an idea, uh, what it was going to be like for you to come to this country?
CHLETSOS: No, nothing. *(He laughs.)*
DALLETT: But, did you want to leave Turkey and come?
CHLETSOS: Well, we had to leave Turkey, yes. I had to go find something to do for help my mother and brothers.
DALLETT: So you thought if you came to this country you could raise some money and send it back to your mother and brothers?
CHLETSOS: Yeah, My two brothers in this country back, and my younger sister.
DALLETT: Uh-huh. Do you remember actually coming, packing up, uh, your belongings and saying goodbye to your mother then, the first time you came to this country?
CHLETSOS: To do what?
DALLETT: Do you remember when you left?
CHLETSOS: Oh, yes.
DALLETT: How did you feel about saying goodbye?
CHLETSOS: About two months I was driving from home to come to this country. I arrive on the Fourth of July in New York.
DALLETT: You came on the Fourth of July. And what year was that?
CHLETSOS: 1904.
DALLETT: 1904. Um, do you remember how you made that trip from, Turkey to New York?
CHLETSOS: Oh, yeah. *(He laughs.)* We had an awful time, driving from one place to another.
DALLETT: What were you, you were driving? What were you driving?
CHLETSOS: Well, it seems like, in Europe you had to walk to get the train from one place to another.
DALLETT: Uh-huh. So you took a series of –
CHLETSOS: Not so easy.
DALLETT: Right. So you took a series of trains?
CHLETSOS: Yeah. We, we took a train to go to, one train from Italy, another train from, uh, France or something. We had to change, a lot of trains, you know.
DALLETT: Uh-huh. And then, eventually, you, you

Immigrants greet the Statue of Liberty from the deck of their arriving ship

took a boat?
CHLETSOS: Then we took the boat from, uh, Belgium.
DALLETT: The boat was from Belgium. Is there any way you remember what the name of the boat was?
CHLETSOS: I can't –
DALLETT: Can't remember that.
CHLETSOS: Cunard Line.
DALLETT: But it was the Cunard Line.
CHLETSOS: That's all I know, was the company.
DALLETT: Okay. Do you remember anything about the trip itself on the Cunard Line ship?
CHLETSOS: Yeah. *(He laughs.)* The first night, see, they had some spaghetti, macaroni or something and everybody get sick at night. So the next day I went up all the way on the top of the boat. When the food was coming in I was leaving I was going up to, I couldn't stand it, so I had –

Sometimes I used to pass by the bar and they had some kind of fish on the table. The first day I took some money, I handed the man to get the food on the spot. So the next day I went there, there was nobody there, and I took it, and I used to run all the way up to the top, to sit there for a couple of hours, and then go down.
DALLETT: So you ate fish and never ate that, that macaroni again.
CHLETSOS: I never go back at that table again.
DALLETT: So did you find that you had plenty to eat?
CHLETSOS: Oh, yeah. *(He laughs.)*
DALLETT: And how about sleeping accommodations? Do you remember, were there bunks or, where did you sleep on the boat?
CHLETSOS: Over the, all the way down, one bed on another on the top.
DALLETT: With a group of other people.
CHLETSOS: Oh, yeah.
DALLETT: And were there any other people that were traveling on that boat from your town?
CHLETSOS: Yeah, I had two cousins.
DALLETT: Two cousins.
CHLETSOS: Was, one of my father and the other cousin from my mother's.
DALLETT: Uh-huh. Um, I'm sorry, I never asked you the name of the town where you were born, the town where you were born.
CHLETSOS: Lemnos. Lemnos. The island was Lemnos and the town was Lihna.
DALLETT: Would you know how to spell that?
CHLETSOS: Yes. Lemnos is L-E-M-N-0-S, and Lihna is L-I-H-N-A.
DALLETT: Um, okay. So back to the boat. You were traveling with two cousins and they were also coming to America for the first time?
CHLETSOS: That's right.
DALLETT: How long did the voyage take? How long was the boat ride?
CHLETSOS: I think it was, uh, we left Friday and we was, uh, back to America on Saturday, next Saturday.
DALLETT: Uh-huh. So about a week.
CHLETSOS: About a week. Seven days, I think.
DALLETT: Do you remember when you came into the New York harbor and you were about to land?
CHLETSOS: Yeah. I was, uh, sleeping in Ellis Island for one night.
DALLETT: What was that like on Ellis Island?
CHLETSOS: On the Fourth of July, it was the day, and I come out the next day.
DALLETT: Were there lots of other people there?
CHLETSOS: Oh, yes. A lot of people, yeah. Except my two cousins, they left the same day.
DALLETT: Oh, how was it that they left and you stayed behind?
CHLETSOS: Well, the people, they come in, they took them out. But brother-in-law didn't come in the same day, he come in the next day.
DALLETT: So you had to wait until your brother-in-law came to pick you up.
CHLETSOS: Yeah. I had breakfast on Ellis Island. Stewed prunes and, uh, oatmeal. *(He laughs.)*
DALLETT: Were you used to eating stewed prunes and oatmeal? Had you ever had those before?
CHLETSOS: No, I never had oatmeal.
DALLETT: No. Do you remember actually having that oatmeal? Did you like it?
CHLETSOS: I didn't. *(He laughs.)* No.
DALLETT: Didn't like it. How about, where did you sleep in Ellis Island?
CHLETSOS: Well, they had beds. Nice beds.
DALLETT: And did the people, did the officials there ask you a number of questions about why you were there?
CHLETSOS: The next day the, my brother-in-law come in and they asked him questions, what's he going to do with me. And he was telling him they was going to put me in school because 15 is all, you're not supposed to have a, you can't get a job.
DALLETT: And that's how old you were when you came, 15?

CHLETSOS: Fifteen.
DALLETT: Um, so I imagine you were, you were speaking, would it be Turkish or Greek that you were speaking when you came?
CHLETSOS: Turkey. I mean, Greek, yeah. Greek. Not Turkey.
DALLETT: Okay. Um, did you understand what the people were saying at Ellis Island?
CHLETSOS: No.
DALLETT: So, how did you manage to, to figure out what to do there?
CHLETSOS: You see, they had a man, he was talking Greek. Every nationality had their own people that was asking questions.
DALLETT: So they could help interpret for you. Um, were you nervous when you were there? How did you feel? *(They laugh.)* You just thought your brother-in-law would come?
CHLETSOS: Was like a (?) man, what nervous could I –
DALLETT: So then your brother-in-law came and picked you up?
CHLETSOS: Yeah.
DALLETT: And what happened next? Did he bring you to Philadelphia?
CHLETSOS: Well, I had a job in New York. I worked in the factory, Notaros Brothers. They was making Nectar cigarettes. I worked there for two months, and then they brought me here, Notaros Brothers. They had a factory, they had a store at 12th and Chestnut. They used me like a, a sawboy. They dressed me up with a Turkish suit, a Turkish cap and everything. Just to walk around the store there, just for show.
DALLETT: And you, and they were making cigarettes there.
CHLETSOS: They was making cigarettes.
DALLETT: And, I'm sorry, was this in New York that this was happening, or, no, this was Philadelphia, 12th and Chestnut.
CHLETSOS: In Philadelphia, yeah.
DALLETT: Okay. Um, where did you live then? Where did your brother-in-law bring you to live?
CHLETSOS: Well, we had furnished room. We used to live in the furnished room. Couple of dollars a week.
DALLETT: And how did you feel about Philadelphia, coming here from, from the islands?
CHLETSOS: We had a Greek restaurant. I used to go there, in the Greek restaurant, I used to eat for 10 cents. Maybe, night, 15 cents for my dinner.

An immigrant to America, poses for a commemorative picture

DALLETT: Ten cents would buy a meal.
CHLETSOS: Yeah. Good meal for 10 cents.
DALLETT: Were there a lot of other –
CHLETSOS: You could eat stew, like Russia. Except the roast lamb used to be 15 cents. Stew you could buy for 10 cents
DALLETT: And were there a lot of other Greeks who lived in your community?
CHLETSOS: It didn't, there was not so many Greeks then, when I come in. There was only about five families in Greek but a couple of hundred, uh, more people, young people that used to work there. Just five families in 1904. Today we have, uh, five churches. *(He laughs.)*
DALLETT: How was it that you managed to send money to your two brothers to bring them to this country? How did you do that?
CHLETSOS: Uh, used to, used to send, uh, five dollars in English money, that's all.
DALLETT: So you'd send money and they saved up and then, how –
CHLETSOS: Once in a while I used to send about five dollars, that's all I could afford to send them.
DALLETT: And how many years later was it that they joined you in this country, your two brothers?
CHLETSOS: Well, in two years later, I think, I got my first brother and, uh, every two, two years they

Portrait of a Greek immigrant family

come other, four years different.
DALLETT: And did you stay in the Philadelphia area?
CHLETSOS: Yes. In Atlantic City sometimes.
DALLETT: And then how was it that you met your wife?
CHLETSOS: My wife, she was in New York. And I got married, I took, from New York we went to Atlantic City. I was working in Atlantic City then.
(We go off record.)
DALLETT: Did you ever have to go through any kind of examination before you could come into the country, either in Belgium or...
CHLETSOS: Yes. I was all right everywhere. *(Wife speaks.)* Except in, in Belgium, before we went to the boat. There was a doctor, he was looking in your eyes, and he find that something wrong with my eyes. It was like a, I don't know, was a...

So he took me back. So he, he start with the next man. But my oldest cousin, he was the first one, he was passing by, he was waiting for me. Instead of me it was the other cousin he was passing by. And so he asked him, "Where is Panagiotis?" And I slipped out.
DALLETT: What did you do?
CHLETSOS: I passed by the (?).
DALLETT: You passed by?
CHLETSOS: Before the doctor see me I went up to the boat.
DALLETT: Ah, so you snuck by the doctor.
CHLETSOS: Yeah. I ran away.
DALLETT: So he didn't catch you. You just were able to get on the boat.
CHLETSOS: He didn't catch me. No.
DALLETT: Good. How about Ellis Island? Did you have to see a doctor there?
CHLETSOS: No.
DALLETT: No one looked at your eyes at Ellis Island.
CHLETSOS: I don't think so. No, I don't – They didn't have anybody. Nobody paid –
DALLETT: So they only, at Ellis Island, they were only asking questions about what you were going to do here.
CHLETSOS: That's all. That's all.
DALLETT: Um, I'm sorry to jump around in time so much, but could you just tell me something about your family now, your children?
CHLETSOS: My oldest daughter, here, I've got the second daughter, a son, third one, I got a daughter in the fourth, and the fifth is a boy, and the sixth a girl.
DALLETT: Six children.
CHLETSOS: Six children.
DALLETT: Are they in Philadelphia?
CHLETSOS: Yeah. They're all here, Philadelphia, except my son. He's in, uh, here, what they call that, *(wife speaks)*, Levittown. He has, uh, he has a pharmacy.
DALLETT: And you have grandchildren?
CHLETSOS: Yeah, I got 10.
DALLETT: Ten!
CHLETSOS: Ten grandchildren and two great-grandchildren.
DALLETT: Two great-grandchildren.
CHLETSOS: Two.
DALLETT: Well, I'm glad you're telling me your story, for your grandchildren and your great-grandchildren. And thank you very much. That is the end of side one and the Interview Number 85.

---

* *Recording engineer: Kimberly Haas; transcript originally prepared by Nancy Vega in 1986; transcript reconceived by Chick Lemonick in January 1996 – Oral Historian's Note: Chlestos is the husband of Marianthe Chlestos, Interview Number Akrf-86. Paul E. Sigrist, Jr., Director of Oral History, 1/17/96.*

Passage to America and Life in the New Land

By Irene Biniaris

First I wanted freedom, because we weren't free... While I was going to school I always used to tell my friends and classmates, 'I'm going to go to America. I'm not going to stay here. There is no progress here'," Dukenie Babayanie Bacos, who came to the U.S. from Kirk Klisse, Turkey in 1919 remembers.

Bacos, whose first name Dukenie means duchess, in honor of her great grandfather who was a duke in Turkish-occupied Constantinople, was only 14 years old when she made the long voyage from Greece to America.

Born on December 12, 1905, Bacos lived in the town of Saranda Klisse in what was formerly a part of Thrace, until Turkish forces took over and renamed the area Kirk Klisse, meaning "church."

As a result of the Turkish occupation, the people of Kirk Klisse lived in fear, and Bacos describes Thrace's people as being enslaved–living in fear of being forced to convert, or having their children kidnapped at any moment, especially the girls.

It was in this town gripped by fear that Bacos lived with her parents and sister in a rather large home. The stone house, with its four bedrooms, two kitchens and large yard filled with beautiful trees, flowers and vegetable gardens, was often the site of many celebrations and dances. It was a home, she says, that her father worked very hard to acquire. He too, like his daughter, had an adventurous spirit and when he was quite young travelled to Russia and then Bulgaria to work, but only after having two wives die–one of appendicitis, and another of tuberculosis.

Her mother's first marriage was also met with great misfortune. She was married to a man who sold horses and made quite a handsome living. Upon making a very lucrative deal one night, however, one of his guards cut off his head in a jealous rage.

Upon hearing of his villager's tragic story, Bacos' father, Dimitrios Babayiane returned from Bulgaria and asked for the widow's hand in marriage. The two were married in 1900, and Dukenie Bacos was born five years later; four and a half years later, the couple had another daughter.

Meanwhile, Bacos' father learned that while he was in Greece, his brother had sold his business in Bulgaria leaving him practically penniless. But determined to make a good life he worked in the mills and maintained vineyards, which produced wine he sent to Constantinople. He was also a sheriff. And so, initially, the family lived a comfortable life until 1912 when World War I began. In 1915 Bulgaria invaded their area and though Bulgarian forces only remained in their village for only a matter of nine months, the villagers suffered greatly from this foreign occupation. And when they left, things became even worse. "We didn't have to eat... the Turks used to sell us bread, they used to mix bread with sand, just to kill us... they closed the schools for a while..." Bacos recalls.

Babayanie, a self-made and determined man, schooled his two daughters at home during this terrible time.

As the years went by, it became clear to Bacos that not having a son was difficult on her family. Remembering her father say in a private conversation, "only if we had a boy," so that he could take on the family's responsibilities, Bacos approached him and said, "Don't worry, Dad. Someday I'll become your son, and I'm going to help you. Don't worry about the future." Her father, regardless of his worries, would reassure the young girl, telling her, "Don't worry, dear. God gave me two girls. God will provide for everything."

But Bacos was determined to help her father and used to stay up late dreaming of travelling to America to become a successful doctor and help her family.

In 1918, her prayers were finally answered. She was home one day when a man knocked on their door and asked for her mother. When her mother greeted the man, he told her he had a correspondence from [Bacos'] mother's brother who at the time was living in America. Along with the letter was $25–quite a large sum of money at the time.

A few days later, a young Bacos decided to write her uncle a thank you note, but also wrote him of her dream of travelling to the U.S. to finish her studies, since her family could not afford to send her to Constantinople to study after high school.

Her uncle, who, as she later learned, was an avid gambler, received the letter and decided to play the fate of the young girl's dream in a card game. One night he announced, "We'll play one ticket for my niece," and luckily he won. He then played for her expenses, and once again won.

One month later, Bacos received a letter from her uncle, along with her ticket to freedom. Just as quickly as her dream had come true, however, it was nearly shattered. "Never will a child of mine go away from my arms. I went to Russia, and I know what I went through. I went to Bulgaria and I know what I went through. Child, 15 years old, never," Bacos recalls her father telling her upon hearing the news.

But Bacos was determined and nothing would stand in her way. She remembered hearing that a classmate of hers had plans to travel to America with his family, and so she asked them to take her with them, to which they agreed. The Floridas family, with whom she would be travelling, was a distinguished family in Kirk Klisse, and so her father agreed to allow her to make the voyage in their company, although strongly advising her not to "ever dirty my forehead. I raised two sisters and they are pure. They went pure married."

Residents of Kastelorizo bid farewell to fellow islanders departing for America

Bacos remembers packing only a small valise in which she carried a few undergarments and stockings. She also took with her a coat and her beloved mandolin.

The long-awaited day finally came and Bacos boarded a train set for Athens, with her acquaintances' family. It was only when the train began to pull from the station and she watched the white handkerchiefs in her family and villager's hands bidding her farewell that she began to realize the magnitude of her actions.

When in Athens, the family stayed all together in one room of a very poor hotel, and quickly realized that they were not going to be on their way to America as fast as they expected.

They had been scheduled to depart on the Megali Hellas (literally translated, Great Hellas), but due to mechanical problems the boat would not depart on time. Moreover, Bacos, then a minor travelling alone, also encountered many problems because of her age. More determined than ever, the young girl boarded a train to Piraeus all alone, and there she managed to have her travelling papers signed. She and her companions were to travel on the King Alexander, a brand new ship from Germany set to leave Athens in 40 days. Until then, Bacos continued to live with her classmate, his sister and mother in Athens.

Forty days finally passed and the King Alexander docked in Piraeus. Bacos remembers the ship being beautiful. Initially the four of them slept in a one-room second class cabin. The mother of the family, however, became ill during the trip and the family upgraded to a first class cabin, where Bacos shared a cabin with three other girls.

Bacos, a carefree, lively girl spent her days on board the ship playing her mandolin and having a grand time. In total the trip lasted 13 days, and was a relatively calm voyage.

As the ship sailed into New York harbor fear gripped the young girl. Sailing past the Statue of Liberty she remembers praying that she too would be accepted into the U.S. as had many immigrants before her.

"Lady, you're so beautiful. You opened your arms, and you get all the foreigners here. Give me a chance to prove that I am worth to do something, to become somebody in America," she recalls saying to herself.

Fear of being apart from her family, but also the frightening thought of being unable to pass through customs (she had heard rumors on board that she would be sent home because her uncle was a bachelor and she was underage) was paralyzing.

True to her worries, upon arriving at Ellis Island, customs officials realized that her uncle and sponsor was a bachelor, and detained Bacos on the island for three days. Many people came and went through the immigration port in those few days which seemed like an eternity to Bacos as she continued to be detained not knowing what her future held. And though she states that she was treated quite well during her stay at Ellis Island, even having seen a ballet company perform, she also remembers feeling as if she was on a road with many thorns, not knowing whether she would overcome her troubles and be allowed into America or forced to return home.

But three days later, her uncle returned having found a family willing to sponsor his niece. She was finally officially allowed into America, and settled in the lower part of Manhattan, where many other Greek immigrants lived at the time. It was December when she first arrived and the apartment in which she lived faced a big school and windows, but nothing else. She remembers that it was Christmas time, but she also recalls not leaving the house for an entire week, and not even knowing what New York looked like or if there were roads (they had made the trip from Battery Park to the apartment by subway).

But weekly gatherings of Greek immigrants who would join to exchange letters and news from the homeland and reminisce about old times were a great relief to her. Although she was excited to be in the US. Bacos was also nostalgic of her home. Living in lower Manhattan, she would often go to the harbor, sit and lament for hours that she had left her home and her family.

One day, soon after her arrival, a Greek woman, whom Bacos called "thea," took Bacos to visit a nearby Greek family, who happened to have several sons. Upon entering the home she remembers seeing seven boys sitting around a table, and another sitting on the side.

Although the one off to the side, whose name was Michael Bacos, seemed shyer than the others (she later found out) that when he saw her he said, "You see that spring chicken over there. That spring chicken is for me." And so, "this spring chicken will be for me," became the first English words Bacos learned.

As time went by, the young Greek girl became more acquainted with her admirer, and things were going rather well for Bacos, who was also doing quite well in school. But one day her uncle approached her with the terrible news that he would no longer be able to send her to school because he had gambled away his money–$10,000–in one night. He informed her she would either have to return to Greece or be married. (All the while he was determined to wed her, often bringing home different men, many of them wealthy in the hopes that she would marry one of them.) But Bacos, a true romantic at heart, was determined to marry a man she loved and refused to have an arranged marriage, especially under such circumstances.

But as her uncle continued to pressure her, Bacos informed Michael Bacos that if he didn't act soon she would be forced into marriage with a man selected by her uncle. And so, one day the two met and got married in New York's City Hall. They did not live together, however, until six months later when they were able to have a proper Greek Orthodox wedding. Her Greek friends, who had not forgotten her, sent her a special wedding gift. Before leaving for America, Bacos had been working on a

A Greek couple of the liner 'Saturnia'

tapestry, which she was forced to leave behind. Her former classmates, however, completed the work for her, placed her name and date on it, and sent it to their friend in the U.S. To this day the tapestry, which depicts the dance of Zallogho, hangs in the family room of Bacos' daughter, Hope Bazaco's home in Purcelleville, Virginia.

Together, Michael and Dukenie Bacos raised Hope, who is now 76 and three sons, one of whom lives most of the year in Greece, and another who is a practicing cardiologist in Washington, D.C. All the children were raised to speak Greek and following many Greek traditions. Their youngest son, who suffered from cerebral palsy, died at the age of 52.

Bacos also spent years trying to fulfill the promise to her father that she would help support the family. To earn money, especially during the period of the Great Depression, she sold 'piece work,' or sewed and repaired clothing. She saved money by sewing the family's clothing, as well as growing vegetables and flowers in the family garden. She was also of great assistance to her husband, who owned a concession stand in a theater owned by George Skouris, one of the most well-known Ellis Island immigrants, who became president of 20th Century Fox.

Scene from a Greek American baptism celebration

Bacos also found the time to study the stock market and even prospered from it as a result. In fact, to this day Bacos follows the stock market faithfully, and is still the family's "favorite stock broker."

Bacos never did become the doctor she had dreamed of, but there is no doubt that she did succeed in life. Sadly, however, her father, Dimitrios Babayanie died before she had the chance to bring him to the United States like she did with her mother and sister.

Through all their hardships, Dukenie and Michael Bacos continued to keep their home in New York City, where they were members of the Zoodoho Pigi Greek Orthodox Church. There Dukenie Bacos is still remembered to this day for the multitude of plays, poems and songs she composed for the parish's children.

After her husband's death, Bacos lived alone, until a year ago when her children decided it was best that their aging mother live closer to them. Consequently, her home in New York was sold and she moved to Virginia to live on a 300-acre farm with her daughter. There the family often hosts wine tastings and is currently in the midst of building a winery.

One of the traditions Bacos has passed on to her daughter Hope is her traditional Greek cooking. "My pastry [baklava] has become very well-known in the area, and people who come to wine tastings, then come to the house (for) a piece of baklava. Everybody leaves this house with a piece of baklava," Hope Bazaco told the Herald.

Bacos and her children are now members of a Greek Orthodox parish in Winchester, Virginia. She and her daughter often spend their nights with their grandchildren telling stories and teaching them Greek.

They proudly admit that they have excelled quite a bit, having gone well beyond the elementary level of the language.

Since leaving her homeland in 1919, Bacos has had the opportunity to travel to Greece many times, but hasn't been there in the last 20 years.

The Greek immigrant, now 96, who admits to having "had a good life," has also had the opportunity to visit Ellis Island, an area now home to a museum honoring America's immigrant heritage, and walk its halls reminiscing about how it felt as a young girl wandering those very same halls.

GREEKS BUILT OLDEST SCHOOL IN U.S.

By Steve Frangos

In 1768, over 1,200 Mediterranean colonists arrived in eastern Florida. These hardy individuals helped to establish the New Smyrna Colony, some 70 miles south of St. Augustine. More than half of those who arrived were Greek. The history of this ill-fated colony is well documented in New Smyrna and in the book *An Eighteenth Century Greek Odyssey*, by the late E. P. Panagopoulos (Gainesville, University of Florida Press, 1966).

With the failure of the New Smyrna Colony in 1777, the surviving colonists moved north to St. Augustine. In the old section of St. Augustine several streets are named after those Greek settlers with Genoply Street being, perhaps, the most well-known. Numerous National Historical Registry plaques can be found on buildings throughout Old St. Augustine attesting to the long-term presence of those colonial Greek immigrants. Perhaps no such structure is more famous, in American historical accounts, than the 'Oldest Wooden Schoolhouse'.

This small wooden building still stands at 14 St. and George Street, just south of the original city gates. It is a quaint little clapboard structure of hand-hewn red cedar planks. Today, this building is a tourist site, although no one is allowed inside the school. Historical documents confirm that this building was the property of Ioannis Giannopoulos, one of the New Smyrna Colony survivors. Since Giannopoulos bought the lot in 1778, and was by trade a carpenter, it seems likely that he built the schoolhouse himself.

According to documents held in Florida archives, Giannopoulos, born in Skoutari, Mani, was the son of George and Maria (Canelas). He was around 18 years old when he left Greece to join the New Smyrna Colony. By 1783, he was farming on three acres of land he rented from an Englishman for "72 1/2 pessos". At this time, Giannopoulos also owned three slaves, two horses, and his own house, which was "situated further up than the Minorcan chapel." Today, this Minorcan chapel, which was also known as the 'Greek chapel', is the site of the St. Photios National Shrine.

Widowed several times, Giannopoulos married Ann Maria Barbara Simpson on December 2, 1793. Within five years they had three children, George Pedro Pasqual (Oct. 23, 1794), Maria Manuela Barbara (Jan. 1, 1796), and Manuel de Jesus Domingo (Dec. 25, 1798). Concerned for his children's education, "Giannopoulos began teaching them, thus becoming one of the first teachers in the 'oldest city' of the United States. Though no details are know about this school, receipts of tuition paid by his pupils indicate that he might have had a sizable income from it" (Panagopoulos 1966: 183).

Giannopoulos appears to have also hired other teachers. The oldest existing schoolhouse receipt is dated 1810. This document shows Giannopoulos paying William Lawrence the balance due for a year of teaching.

Given the haphazard way records of everyday life were preserved, the history of the Giannopoulos schoolhouse is still open to debate. However, we do know that Giannopoulos' son George kept the school in operation. Three advertisements were placed in the St. Augustine Examiner on May 11, 18, and June 15, 1867.

The advertisement read: "Encouraged by solici-

One of the oldest schools in America convened at the home of Ioannis Yiannopoulos in St. Augustine, Florida, which was built in 1777.

tations of several citizens I will establish a School on St. George Street, near the house of Wm. Rayes, to be opened on the 13th of May. All the branches of a through English education will be taught, and it will be my aim, by strict attention and discipline to lead the pupils to a fast advancement in their studies. Fees for tuition will be, for beginners, $4 per quarter; for advanced pupils $6 per quarter; for Latin and Spanish lessons $2 per quarter at the beginning and the other half at the end of each quarter. A subscription is opened at the store of George Greeno and R. V. Balsam. George Genople, St. Augustine, May 11, 1876."

In 1821, Florida became a part of the United States. At this time, the once destitute New Smyrna Colonists were among the wealthiest members of the St. Augustine community. The U.S. Land Commissioners confirmed the claims of the New Smyrna colonists to the titles for 48,956 acres of land.

Among those holdings was what is said to be the oldest wooden schoolhouse in North America. Whatever the exact details of the schoolhouse origins, Giannopoulos, a Greek immigrant prompted by his concern for the welfare of his children, saw to the establishment of this school.

THE GREEK GRAVES ON TARPON SPRINGS

By Steve Frangos

Among the many documented customs modern Greeks continue to practice as they have since classical times, are those related to observances for the dead. Yet in all the accounts written about Greeks in North America none mention, let alone describe in any detail, the cemeteries established or sought out by the early pioneers and how they have been maintained by their descendants.

One especially noteworthy gathering of historical monuments are those found in the Cycadia cemetery of Tarpon Springs, Florida. Named after the cycadia palms, first planted to mark the cemetery grounds, this community institution was founded around 1886; one year before the city of Tarpon Springs was incorporated. It was at this time that two early pioneer women Liola Beekman and Amilia Meres began to care for the then small gathering of graves. In November 1904, these ladies saw to the establishment of the Cycadia Cemetery Association.

In 1905 John Cocoris, a sponge industry entrepreneur, his brothers, and 500 Greek spongers from the Aegean and Dodecanese islands came en masse to western Florida. Others soon followed. Sadly, the inherent dangers in driving more than 10 fathoms down for the best deepwater sponges soon resulted in deaths. As befits those daring sponge divers, their gravestones, mausoleums, and large family plots are among the most unique and artistically distinctive to be found anywhere in the nation. The overall Greek presence at the Cycadia cemetery is in direct measure to their demographic standing along the Gulf coast of Florida.

By 1940, there were well over 1,000 men actively engaged in the sponge industry. With their families these men constituted roughly 2,500 Greeks in a town of 3,402. By the late 1970s, with the town of Tarpon Springs proper numbering some 13,000 individuals, an estimated one-third were Greek or of Greek descent. Today the total number of Greeks along the western coast of Florida has unexpectedly grown. Retired Greeks from all around the country have flocked to towns along the north, south and west of Tarpon Springs. In turn, while no reliable statistics are available, the general impression is that the Greek presence in the Cycadia cemetery is growing apace.

What is so striking about the Greek grave sites is their pronounced individuality. Folklorists as well as historians of popular culture have long recognized connections between cemeteries and other areas of American design. In the Victorian era when houses and public buildings were elaborate structures, with a strong emphasis on decorative detailing, so were the average gravestones. In the period following World War II, as suburban track housing with its utilitarian square-shaped structures began to encircle urban centers, the designs in gravestones followed suit with cubes of marble surrounded by cleanly cut lawns of grass.

Greek graves at the Cycadia cemetery, however, did not follow this national trend. The Tarpon

Springs Greek tombstones and grave sites differ in a number of distinct ways from those that surround them.

As one would expect, many headstones show nearly photographic carvings of spongeboats and deepwater diving helmets. Classic Greek columns, urns and crosses with intricately carved reliefs document in stone the identification Greeks felt and continue to feel with their ancient ancestors. Also to be expected are the highly accurate carvings of the home island on a number of these tombstones. In one particular case not only is a carved map of Rhodes shown but the two villages from which the couple immigrated are specifically noted. In fact, the strict sense of home all Greeks feel can stiil be read even on the latest inscriptions.

No single style or dominant motif runs throughout the Greek graves. In the earlier stones one can see art deco-inspired headstones with majestic sweeps of curving stone, tree trunks wrought from sandstone, large and small urns, along with photographic ovals of the deceased; each with a judicious employment of colored marble. The sepulchral monuments for children are among the most unique and heartfelt. In the statuary for the graves of babies we find beautifully carved angels before red marble gates, small lambs, and even the profiles of faces.

In the gravestones for teenagers and young adults sometimes only a name will appear as "Nicky" does in carved script or the simple epitaph "Free Spirit." Individuality is the only common element among the Greek graves. Musical notes adorn the impressive tombstone dedicated "To Our Sweetest Mother." One recent grave is marked with a large wooden cross with not only the deceased's name and dates of birth and death in large scrolling script but also striking carvings of baskets, wreaths, and sheaves.

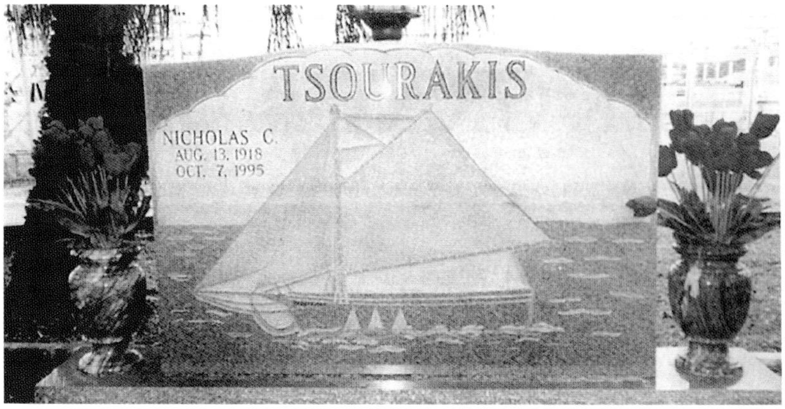

The grave of a Greek American seafarer in Tarpon Springs

Aside from the tombstones, a number of other means are used to clearly demarcate the grave site. At times the border of the plot is marked by low rough-cut granite or marble. For other sites elaborate ironworked fences, marble posts with chains, or even low-block walls with the family name carved in a stone set at the foot of the grave. Other grave sites have the entire top of the plot covered.

Again, the coverings of these graves vary, ranging from a thick cover of white stones, to a carefully laid field cement or baked-clay tiles, or even massive slabs of three inch to four inch granite or imported marble. With the usual individual grave plot measuring four feet by nine feet, family sites can be huge expanses of granite or marble.

The large family plots are also the areas that prominently features statues, benches, large urns, for burning incense, memorial candles, trellis, intricate plantings of flowers, and quite often wind chimes.

Such costly and artful arrangements of space clearly are meant as places where the living can come together with the dead. Gatherings of relatives who come to honor and remember the best of those who have passed on can be seen in any cemetery where Greeks have come to rest.

THE HUMBLE BEGGININGS OF INDIANA' S GREEKS

BySteve Frangos

In 1906, a man by the name of Mihalis Magremes rode from south Chicago to Gary, Indiana on horseback. He had a crate of oranges tied behind his saddle and a four-foot stalk of bananas across the horn. The blowing sand from the dunes made his horse difficult to handle, so Magremes decided to stop by a large tree near one of the entry gates to the area's steel mills. Tying the stalk of bananas to a low branch and piling the oranges on top of the crate, Magremes sold his fruit to the steel workers.

Many senior generations of Greeks in Indiana still recall this story of the first Greek immigrant in northwest Indiana as a reminder of their humble origins and later achievements. The timing of this story is itself significant since the city of Gary, Indiana, and all of its steel mills, first opened in 1906.

Other Greeks followed Magremes to Gary and in the spring of 1912 the first formal meeting for building a church was held. Although at this time there were only 10 Greek families in Gary, the new community, which was the first Greek Orthodox community in all of Indiana, decided to built a church and establish the parish of Saint Constantine and Helen.

The first services were held in 1913, in a rented building at 1259 Madison Street. For the next three years, as the small collective of faithful grew, the parish moved to 1235 Madison Street where visiting priests held irregular services.

Later in 1913, with the congregation still growing, the Gary Greeks started negotiations for the purchase of a parcel of land at 14th and Madison Streets. Then in 1915, the first permanent priest arrived, Archimandrite Nicholas Mandilas of Corfu. With a full-time priest the community continued to grow so it was decided that a still larger site, this time at 13th Street and Jackson, would better serve the community.

In 1917 the property was purchased for $3,500 which was paid out of a $10,000 loan secured by community leaders. The 14th and Madison Streets property was sold for $3,000 at that same year. Ground breaking ceremonies took place as soon as the community secured the property. However, with the outbreak of World War I construction was delayed.

Easter Sunday 1919 marked the first service held in the newly completed church. On September 27, 1919, the new SS. Constantine and Helen Church was dedicated in what one Gary newspaper described as, "the most pretentious celebration among foreign-born citizens ever held in Gary." It was also in 1919 that, in true Greek business fashion, the loan for the new property was fully paid off.

Yet all too soon events in Greece were to have a direct influence on the Gary Greek community. During the 1920s, as with many other Greek communities across the United States, the parish of SS. Constantine and Helen became caught up in the controversy over the Greek political battles between Eleftherios Venizelos and King Constantine. In 1922 families who supported the policies of the King established a new parish, the Holy Trinity at 11th Street and Jackson.

This arrangement was not meant to last long. In 1931 the two groups reunited when, in the darkest hours of the American depression period, the mortgage for SS. Constantine and Helen was almost foreclosed. The parishioners of Holy Trinity sold their church building and used the proceeds to pay the outstanding debts of SS. Constantine and Helen. Slowly, the parish flourished again.

From the 1930s through the 1960s, the Greeks in Gary rose from poor immigrant laborers to educated and propertied citizens. Most were second and third generation, but new immigrants from

Scene on the deck of an immigrant ship

Greece periodically supplemented their ranks.

In the 1960s when urban decay drove residents away from Gary, many Greek Americans initially found the idea of relocation unthinkable. Ultimately, a sermon delivered by Father Evagoras Constantinidis fuelled their determination: "You left your homes in Greece without fear to start a new life and you must do that again," he told his parishioners.

In 1967, after extensive study, 37 1/2 acres were purchased for $200,000 at 8000 Madison Street in Merrillville, Indiana, which is now a suburb of Gary.

Ground was broken on September 20, 1970 for the new church and buildings. On Thanksgiving Day 1971, the Cultural Center was formally opened and Rev. Bishop Timotheos of Chicago held church services in the Great Hall. Not long after, on May 14, 1972, Archbishop Iakovos conducted the dedication of the Complex. On April 12, 1976, it was Archbishop Iakovos once again who proclaimed the new SS. Constantine and Helen parish of Merrillville, Indiana a Cathedral.

However, with second and third generation Greeks an active part of the Cathedral's life, and mixed marriages a common place, it is difficult to arrive at accurate community demographics.

During the 1970s, it was estimated that some 7,000 Greeks lived in and around Gary. To be sure this was a vast increase from the 1,392 in 1920 or again in the 1930 Census when 3, 344 Greek-born residents were identified along with their 730 American-born children.

The 1980 Census only indicated that in the two counties immediately around Gary there were 4,430 self-identifying Greeks in Lake County and 481 in Porter county. While these were the largest population figures for Greeks in Indiana many feel that more of an effort should have been made to contact second and third generation Greeks. A servable record of the history of the Gary Greek community and its eventual move to the nearby suburb of Merrillville, is recorded at considerable length in the community's own historical album, "The First Sixty-two Years of Saints Constantine and Helen Greek Orthodox Church of Merrillville Indiana 1913-1975."

A Greek celebration in Gary, Indiana

There is also a complimentary reference. In 1984, Tina Bucuvalas and this author were awarded an Indiana Arts Commission grant to conduct a folk arts survey of the Greek community in the Gary/Merrillville region.

Initially fieldwork began with the idea of mounting a museum exhibit at Indiana University's William Hammond Mathers Museum. Eventually the exhibit was to tour to Saints Constantine and Helen for exhibition in their cultural center.

Unfortunately, the inexperience of Geoffrey Conrad, the newly arrived museum director, resulted in a lack of promised funds for the proposed exhibit. It was Bucuvalas' idea that we take the written material intended for the museum labels and expand that text into a booklet. The result was *Techne Traditional Arts in the Calumet Region* (Bloomington, IN: Cultural Research Associates, Inc., 1984). The field recordings, photographs, and other documents, gathered during the course of the project were all deposited at Indiana University's Archives of Traditional Music in Bloomington. Today, these materials are available to the general public.

THE FIRST GREEKS OF MASON CITY, IOWA

By Steve Frangos

James Chimbidis, retired filmmaker, is the unofficial historian of Greeks in Mason City, Iowa. A native Iowan, Chimbidis, is systematically and painstakingly gathering the historical documentation, interviews, and photographs necessary for a full-length documentary on the history of the local Greek community.

With over half a century of filmmaking to his

credit, Chimbidis is treading the fine line between an ethnic documentary and a community biography.

At the turn of the century, Mason City was an ideal location for any newly arrived immigrants. As the seat of Cerro Gordo County, this town in north central Iowa is situated on the Winnebago River, 130 miles N.N.E of Des Moines. Founded by Freemasons in 1851, by the time of the new immigrant's arrival, Mason City was a nationally recognized hub of transportation and commerce.

Mason City was the location for six railroad trunk lines and was in fact the largest railroad facility between the Mississippi and Missouri rivers. The town was also the setting for the Northwestern States Cement plant; the Portland cement plant, the world's largest producer of cement; the Decker Meat Packing Plant along with nine brick and tile plants, and a highly productive farming community that surrounds the town to this day. Yet, even with all this commerce, this town is no more than 16 blocks north and 20 blocks south.

In 1931, two-year-old Chimbidis and his family arrive in Mason City where his maternal grandfather James Nickolaou (d. 1937), the owner of the Garden City Fruit Market, a pool hall, and two homes on Van Buren Street South, was already a noted member of the Greek community. Chimbidis' father, Nick, worked at the Mason City Brick and Tile Company and later in the Decker Packing Plant.

A family from Thebes, Greece, poses for the lens in Milwaukee

As this film project is a labor of love, he has taken his time to systematically comb through Mason City business directories, immigration records, and the back files of all local newspapers, including The Times, and the Globe Gazette. He has managed to locate every newspaper story written on Mason City Greeks from 1909 until the present. Early Greek pioneers were often accused of crimes such as bootlegging, gambling, knifings, shootings, and even drugs and prostitution. Soon it became commonplace to see the phrase "Crazy Greek(s)" used in the local press.

Chimbidis' collection of these stories is certainly a professional's desire for historical completeness. However, he is also keenly aware that these stories, with their uninhibited racist ovetones, report upon not simply the local news but the despair, loneliness, and rage many of these young men were experiencing.

In 1898, the first known Greek, Gus Skoundas arrived to town to manage the Mason City Candy Kitchen, which in 1902 became the Olympia Candy and Ice Cream Parlor. Not long after Skoundas' arrival, Greeks from all over the world started coming to Mason City.

In time, chain-migration led to the vast majority of the local Greeks, hailing mainly from the village of Aghios Loukas in Northern Greece and from the island of Euboea. At its peak, some 200 Greek families lived in Mason City numbering near 3,000 people. Many of the early Greek men were the fabled transient 'Birds of Passage.'

The unprecedented arrival of all these foreigners did not go unnoticed. In 1920, individuals from the Iowa State University conducted a census of Mason City's ethnic make up. Of the 2,665 immigrants surveyed, Greeks were demographically the largest foreign group. This is all the more significant when we realize that at this time 55 ethnic groups called Mason City their home and that the city's total population was some 20,000 individuals which ranked it only second to Los Angeles in terms of racial mixture.

Although, not all new immigrants in Mason City were Greeks (the four or six block district near the Mason City Brick and Tile Company running on the north side of the Milwaukee Railroad line was known locally as "The Balkan Ghetto") many of them, Austrians, Bulgarians, Croatians, Lithuanians, Montenegrins, Rumanians, Russians and Serbians, were Eastern Orthodox.

The harsh labor conditions and the directionless lives of many of the local Greek youth led to the formation of a church. In 1914, James Farmakis, Peter Karamitros, Elias Manis, James Nickolaou, and Basil and George Tsirikos founded the charter for the Transfiguration of Our Lord parish. It was the second Greek Orthodox Church in Iowa. In this early period, church services were held in private homes, the Carnegie public library, and the Salvation Army hall.

Groundbreaking took place in 1916, but even with the wholehearted support of the community, the necessary funds for the building of a Church were difficult to gather. Eventually a $2.00 tax was levied on each Greek resident to raise the necessary funds. Nevertheless, the church building, at the corner of North Washington Avenue and 14th Street Northwest, was not completed until 1920.

By 1922 the church's Greek language school was established with Father B. Pantazopoulos serving as its first instructor. Classes, which included Greek history, were held three nights a week from 5:00 pm to 7:00 pm.

The growing needs of the church were such that in 1927, Father D. Loukas found it necessary to organize a catechetical school. Soon the church became the center for many of the social and education Greek groups founded in the United States, including AHEPA, the Daughters of Penelope's Helios Chapter, GAPA and the Hellenic Orthodox Youth Club, which preceded GOYA in 1942.

While Greeks first came to Mason City as laborers, they quickly moved up the social ladder into owning retail businesses, such as shoeshine parlors, pool halls, grocery stores, and restaurants. Slowly, the town boasted such Greek establishments as: The Princess Cafe, The Soda Girl, The One-Minute Lunch, The Green Mill, The Popular Cafe, The Wander Inn, and The Royal Roost.

Chimbidis recalls, "I took it for granted, as a kid, when I walked down the street that I could go into a place of Greek business within five doors of any place in the city...they were everywhere...I didn't realize it then that these people must have mortgaged their life savings and probably borrowed from the bank to establish themselves."

By 1942 parish membership reached 558. Still, in the late 1940s planing was underway for a new church. On June 22, 1952, the cornerstone was laid for the new building with Archbishop Michael officiating at the services. In April 1953, the new church at 1311 Second Street SW was completed at a cost of nearly 1.4 million dollars.

Between 1956 and 1966, new Greek immigrants began to arrive in Mason City. These immigrants were known as "Jet-immigrants" after the manner of transportation said to have brought them to the rolling prairies of Iowa.

On August 14-16, 1998, some five hundred individuals were invited to the Centennial Orthodox Reunion, held at the Hartford Inn.

During the three-day events, the Reunion honored the local Greek community and its church. Clearly, however, much had changed. Today, Father Mirowski, and American-born priest of Russian-Ukranian ancestry, "refers enthusiastically to his parish as a 'beautiful example of Pan Orthodoxy'." Most of the community is comprised of second and third generation Greeks. Yet, some 40 percent of the congregation is composed of the descendants from other turns of the century Orthodox immigrants such as Arab-, Bulgarian-, and Russian-Americans. As with Orthodox parishes around the nation converts are included in the overall mix.

Aside from other films, Chimbidis recently completed, "It's Yesterday, Once More," a documentary on the history of Mason City. While the city gratefully accepted the finished commercial film, in the preview stages of production, they asked Chimbidis to take out some of the material that was "too ethnic." While he would be the first to admit that the history of Mason City is more complex than just what can be learned about the local Greeks, the city's full-story can never be truthfully told without acknowledging the full cast of its citizens.

A significant problem Chimbidis faces is that he may have too much material. In terms of photographs, he has numerous images he has carefully collected and taken over the years. Complimenting his personal collection are some 200 photographs of local Greeks available at the Mason City Public Library. The library is home to many thousands of photographs drawn from the collections of several local professional photographers Stafford Lock, Carl Wright, and Elwin Musser that span over 100 years of life in Mason City.

Still, with the weight of years of research and a lifetime of experiences Chimbidis is not about to falter. The film is ready, he just has to give images and order to the lives and experiences of over 100 years of Greek life in Mason City. A challenge worthy of its subject.

THE GREEKS OF CHICAGO

*By Katina Alexander**

GREEK PEOPLE BEGAN settling in Chicago in 1882. Today, four generations later, you can still find a Cretan in Chicago who owns a grocery store and dreams of going back to Greece someday.

That was the idea in 1907. The Socrates School of the Holy Trinity Church taught only Greek because nobody expected to stay in America long. But 10 years later, Chicago's first Greek school began teaching English. The Chicago Daily Journal wrote in 1924 that by the' 20s, only five percent of an estimated 50,000 Greeks went back home. Exact population figures are hard to determine, since many laborers based in Chicago shipped out on jobs in the railroad industry. One preliminary count by Jane Addams' Hull House lists only 1,467 Greeks in the 19th ward of the Halsted Street area, which later became known as the 'Greek ghetto' of the 20s, 30s and 40s.

Holy Trinity was the first permanent Greek Orthodox church in 1898. Chicago police were often called to prevent the fighting and bloodshed from power struggles there. Those disputes ended with the establishment of two more churches, St. Constantine-Helen and the Annunciation. There are now 21 Greek Orthodox churches in Chicago, and a population roughly estimated at 200,000.

Thomas Burgess wrote in "Greeks in America," published in 1909 that it was "an almost impossible task for American Protestants to proselytize Eastern Orthodox churches here," meaning Chicago.

The Greek people also had their own coffee houses, newspapers, and bank. For many, it began with a train ride from New York City to the end of the line. The men worked project by project on the railroads. One labor agent from that period was quoted by Burgess as saying he rarely used Greek men on jobs more than two or three times, because once they had a little money, they went into business for themselves. Chicagoans were said to view the Greeks as hot-headed and independent, like the Irish.

Some Greeks opened shoe-shine shops and peddled fruits and vegetables. They saved their money and opened grocery stores, flower shops and restaurants; they built larger commercial concerns; ice-cream and candy companies like the "Temptation Chocolate Factory" at Halsted and 19th Streets, and they bought real estate. By the 1920s, at least 10 real estate companies were listed as owned by Greek people. There were also many Greek doctors, lawyers, dentists and pharmacists.

In his contributing chapter to Ethnic Chicago, Andrew Kopan wrote that "the Greeks gained virtual control of Chicago's wholesale food industry at the Randolph and South Water Streets commission markets."

Chicago's Greeks gave America the first ice-cream sundae and soda shop. Their restaurants were noted in the 1920s for cleanliness, service and fine surroundings. Chicagoans were said at that time to "delight to eat in the magnificent Raklios establishments" scattered throughout the Loop area. The Greeks also opened two grand ballrooms, The Aragon and the Trianon. The Aragon, on Lawrence Avenue, is owned by Willie Miranda, a non-Greek, and features rock 'n roll concerts and boxing matches.

But all was not confection and spice in the immigrants' early days. Many young Greek boys serving under a peonage system suffered at the hands of their elders. They lived in barns, stables, or crowded rooms above shoe-shine parlors and groceries. They earned an average of $10 a week and were charged $30 a month rent. Burgess wrote in 1909 that cases of physical abuse were often reported to the League For The Protection of Immigrants.

My own grandfather was one such boy, and he lived above a stable until he had saved $50 to buy a blind horse that nobody wanted. He led that horse through the streets and sold potatoes. When the influenza epidemic hit Chicago in 1918, his father, sister and a baby in the family died. My grandfather caught the fever and he locked himself in a room with three bottles of Metaxa to reckon with it. He always said it was the Metaxa that saved his life. (And a good thing it did. My mother wasn't born yet.)

Jane Addams of Hull House kept a watch over many Greeks in her settlement house, co-founded by labor-activist Ellen Gates Starr. Hull House was a complex of 13 buildings in the middle of what historian Perry Duis calls "one of Chicago's most squalid slums." In Duis' "Chicago, Creating New Traditions," a Hull-House map of that area in 1895 listed immigrants of Irish, French, German, Dutch, Russian, Polish, Italian, Swiss, French-Canadian, Bohemian, Scandinavian, Chinese and Black descent. The Greeks settled in one of America's most ethnic cities, a city Duis says was fighting its image as "an unsophisticated, overgrown village."

Addams wrote in the early 1900s that "a number of Greeks come to Hull-House, where they have various clubs and undertakings, and we are quite devoted to them." When Jane Addams died in 1935, the Greeks closed more than 1,500 shops in mourning.

The Halsted Street area was the largest Greek neighborhood in Chicago from Randolph to Harrison Streets. There were an estimated 60,000 Greek people living there until the 1960s, when most of the area was razed to make room for the University of Illinois Chicago Circle Campus. Halsted Street is now a tourist attraction near downtown Chicago. The strip is lined with Greek restaurants, specialty stores, bakeries, groceries, and butcher shops.

Most of the restaurateurs come from Peloponesos, which is why James Ward, the food critic of the Chicago Sun-Times, calls Greek food in Chicago "Pelopponesian cookery."

To many Chicagoans on Halsted Street, Greek people represent lots of food, wine, merrymaking and gyros stands. But that idea is changing.

Greek culture is scattered throughout Chicago. Some intense fragments are isolated, others connected. The churches and the nightclubs appear to have the power to pull the students, working people and professionals together. Most Chicago Greeks would say they love their religion or their music, or both. And most would bow to the power of an education – whether they have one or not.

It would be an ordinary June night in Chicago for those who gathered, as usual, in a coffee shop, a rented apartment for students' political discussions, a church auditorium, or a nightclub. But it would become an extraordinary journey if one person were to enter each of those worlds on the same night, each group a planet of its own, orbiting around a Greek center.

Greek immigrant family in Chicago

A cab driver who likes to talk, but doesn't like to give his name, comes to a coffee shop most every night and weekend afternoons, to see his friends, speak Greek, and not spend too much money. He can't afford the more expensive nightclubs with drinks and bouzouki music.

He thought he'd spend just five years in America, but this is his seventh. "If they say they come here to stay," he says, "they're a liar." But he likes it here. America is more "convenient," and here, "you get the freedom." Freedom for this man means freedom from relatives. The only way to be truly free in Greece, he says, "is to be orphan." On his last visit, he fought continually with a thrifty female relative who kept shutting off the hot water – even when he was in the shower. He says all he talks about with his friends is politics. "You name it," he says. "about any country, Greece or America." He also says he can tell an educated Greek in these discussions, because he is the one who is quiet, listening.

The cab driver goes to church on the big holidays. He knows where to pick the best grapevine leaves (in Schaumburg, Illinois). He has a religious candle in his home, and believes fervently in the healing power of the "vendouza" as well. He is very polite, and there is a sense that he is very lonely. That is why he comes here.

Members of the Progressive Greek Students Association of Chicago are gathering in the small apartment they rent for discussion forums. They meet here about four times a week. The old immigrants came to Chicago to return to Greece with money, but the members of this club will return with diplomas. There is a lot of secrecy here. The students say they have no political affiliations, though they have a great interest in films by Eisenstein and Charlie Chaplin. A large young man with a handlebar mustache is standing while the others are seated in folding chairs arranged in a circle. His arms are folded across his huge chest, and he is not smiling. He stands there all night, watching.

There is a female student here, who is also a member of the Greek Women's Group. "We speak Greek here," she says, "whoever can, can join." She says the Greek schools in Chicago do not represent Greece as she would like. "And there is too much emphasis on religion." she adds. A young man with bright eyes and curly hair speaks up, and says the Greek American schools are a "rip-off" of immigrant parents, and provide "unqualified teachers." And as far as Greek school after American school goes, the students say "what child wants to go to American school all day long, and then spend more hours at a Greek school?" The young man says the children "hate it, and they don't want to learn."

Their solution to the problem as they see it, is to get the "American state" to offer Greek electives in Greek communities, as well as other ethnic electives in Spanish, Polish and other languages.

They also voiced objections to the Greek parade, calling it "Greek Orthodox, nationalist and male chauvinist." When the Greek Women's Group attended the open committee meeting for the parade, their ideas were rejected, though the young man reminded the girl student that they weren't well prepared in offering alternatives.

"When you clear the smokescreen," said one Progressive student about the parade. "It's a big commercial show for the restaurants – the gyro and hamburger places. The self-appointed parade committee calls the restaurant owners for their own advertisements. You've seen that 'cheezeborger, cheezeborger' routine – [by the late John Belushi on Saturday Night Live] – c'mon! enough is enough!"

The Progressive students are well informed as to what's happening and where in many parts of the Greek community. Some remembered the concert by Mikis Theodorakis at the Auditorium Theater in 1977. The curly haired student still gets excited: "My hands hurt from clapping, and I couldn't speak from yelling so loud."

They recently rented a film from the library on pollution in Greece, and followed it with hours of discussion. It appears these students, about 12 of whom meet here, support Greek – the language, music and arts – but not the church. And always, they talk of going back to Greece.

It is still the same night, and the night is long. Deni's Den at 2941 N. dark Street has a four a.m. liquor license. A handful of young adults from St. Andrew's are going there, too.

Deni's has a rich history behind it. When the junta took over the Greek government in 1967, repercussions were felt 5,445 miles away in a tiny place called Deni's Den, then on Lawrence Avenue.

Most of the patrons were university students, who came to hear the partisan music censored before and during the dictatorship. Much music had been forbidden in Greece, from the post World War II "andartika tragouthia," or songs of the guerrilla movement, to the music of the artistic revolt in the 1960s called "neo kyma," or New Wave. That music was heard in Chicago, in a small, dark room that was almost always crowded. Many conservative Greek Americans avoided it then, as they do now.

Deni's began as a "boite," or small club where the owner sings and plays for quiet, listening audiences. They came to hear a message, not to party.

There were only two places in Chicago for free Greek expression at that time, Andonis Kanakis' WOJO-AM radio show and Deni's Den.

Then-owner Deni Demitrais has since returned to Greece, but in those days his audiences heard Theodorakis; readings by Kimon Friar, the translator of Nikos Kazantzakis; Gregory Bithikotsis, the first man to sing Theodorakis' music; Marinella, the singer; and Harry Kline, the comedian.

The New Wave, the artistic revolution against big-name artists and music companies, has since died. But the artists of Neo Kyma, who presented a different view of life than the old, heavy songs about disasters, immigrants and sailors, remain. Michalis Violaris, Yiannis Poulopoulos, and Giorgos Zographos are examples of those artists. They want to create a more optimistic view of life, to make the music uplifting, spiritual – something to ease the soul, rather than repress it with laments of the past.

With that legacy behind it, Deni's today is a large white room, and still crowded. Owner Chris Verdos and his wife, Georgia, have changed it from a center for Greek protest music to a successful restaurant and nightclub. But the musical guide of Deni's is Vasilios Gaitanos, who started with Deni on Lawrence Avenue 12 years ago, after touring with Theodorakis. "He is my musical father," said Gaitanos of Theodorakis, "and he allows me to be his spiritual son. I will follow him always."

Back in the early 1970s, Gaitanos would leap on top of his piano and lead the audience in the andartika, or protest songs. Like a possessed preacher of the gospel, he would whip his audiences into a frenzy of believing, with choruses of "elephteria!" freedom. The singing went on past midnight, into dawn.

A longtime ago, Gaitanos was a merchant marine. He says he heard about the new wave music "while on the waves." He was once an immigrant dishwasher, but has become an important artistic figure in the Greek community, though his politics are controversial to some.

"I try for 37 years to be communist," he says. "but I'm not one yet. But politically," he explains. "I am left." Gaitanos says he loves Chicago because the city "started the first revolution May Day at Haymarket Square." That was in 1886 and is now celebrated as a worker's holiday around the world. Those police riots began with a protest for the eight-hour work day.

Gaitanos doesn't follow the Greek political organizations so much because he says "I live in the

A crowded inner-city marketplace

United States. But one of the most important things I keep is my religion. If you lose the church, you lose a very big part of your Greek nationality, and that is one of the most important things for my roots."

Stavros Papaioannou, a linguistics student at Northeastern University (Chicago) and a lover of Greek music, also traces Greek protest music through the "art engage" movement in France in the 1960s young people's music devoted to a political purpose. "I think Vasili's is the only place you can hear that music," said Papaioannou, "and now he has to adjust to all the levels of expectation that people have. But late at night, you can still hear him do the 'oldies' of Neo Kyma."

Papaioannou made no mistake when he called Deni's "Vasili's place." Gaitanos and his band now play everything from the Jewish "hora" to the fox trot, mixed in with Greek music. The band pulls together many musical styles for an international audience at different times of night. The dinner crowd wants slow dancing, and the late night people want to dance the syrtaki, zeimbekiko and hasapiko.

They still smash plates here, and throw money over the dancers. Spyros Panaoussis, the pianist who alternates with Gaitanos on Deni's stage, explained the showering of dollar bills on the dance floor: "They are so happy that they don't count the money."

Gaitanos has already performed Vangelis' "Chariots of Fire" theme song at Deni's, but he is also working on what he calls "my new style." His music will have English lyrics about "all the problems of minorities in North America."

Vasilis Gaitanos has found a home in Chicago, on the stage of Deni's Den. If you go there, you will find a shaggy-haired, charismatic performer bent over his keyboards. And each night he plays and sings, he leaves one sailor/dishwasher another day behind him.

Deni's closes when most of Chicago opens its eyes. The musicians and waiters will be sleeping by time the Randolph-South Water market starts selling vegetables and fruits across town.

The United Hellenic American Congress, although the most powerful national Greek organization in Chicago, is not the only Greek organization in Chicago. In 1909, Burgess wrote that some 20,000 societies were formed by Greek people in Chicago.

On June 25, 1946, they held their first "Unity Conference" involving 10 parishes and over 200 voluntary associations. That effort collapsed from lack of agreement.

On May 28, 1982, the Consulate General of Greece in Chicago made the second effort in 36 years to unite the Greeks again. The small room of the Consulate above the National Bank of Greece on 168 N. Michigan Avenue was filled with more than 100 people. Two men shared the same chair. Others filed off into a side corridor at the front of the room.

Then Consul General Emmanuel Vlandis addressed his eager audience in Greek, saying "we are not just souvlaki and syrtaki." In his soft voice, he suggested the formation of a committee from those present.

There was an explosion of shouted opinions, interruptions, hissing for silence, applause, and a sea of red faces. It was highly probable that the objectives of this meeting would also fail, and there were about 35 reasons why. One or two representatives from each organization came to support his or her own group. Some of those represented were from The Messinian Association, The Calavritan Society, The Federation of Greek American Organizations of Illinois, The Elyian Society, The Hellenic Medical Association, The Tripoli Association, the Greek press and media, Hellenic Council on Education, Cephalonian Brotherhood, Zakinthian Society, Hellenic American League. Loukaitan Society, United Hellenic American Voters, The United Hellenic American Congress, Pan-Hellenic Socialist Movement, Pan Arcadian Federation, Hellenic Association, Greek Popular States, Carpathian Society, Justice for Cyprus Committee, Congress of American Hellenic Organizations, Spartan Society, Greek Teachers' Association, Pontian Association, Cyprion Brotherhood, Athanasios Diakos Society, Rumeli Society, The Federation of Rumeli, Gramos Society, Tsipiana Society, Nafpaktiaki Society, Greek Dental Association.the Corinthian Society, and the Distomo Society, among others.

The diplomacy of Consul General Vlandis was probably never as strongly tested as it was that evening. But he never raised his voice and remained calm through the most vociferous interruptions.

Father Isaiah is the immediate assistant to Bishop lakovos at the Diocese headquarters in Chicago at 40 E. Burton Place, a beautiful stone building on the north side. Their function together, says the Father, "is to see a harmonious family" in all 58 parishes of the Midwestern United States.

"You will see a different make-up from parish to parish," he says. "indicating the reality that Greek is not that much spoken." He also noted that parishioners of the Assumption Church at Harrison and Central don't live anywhere close to that church, which is in an all-black area, but they go for sentimental reasons.

The tall, vigorous looking Chancellor pointed out that, unlike the Catholics and Protestants, the Greek Orthodox Church relies more on tradition than on rules. "We do not take an issue on anything that smells of political football." he said, and cited the abortion issue as an example. "Abortion has been with us as long as humanity someone is for or against something to collect votes, not because they are sincere."

But, "When Turkey invaded Cyprus there was a united and concerted effort, an outcry, and that was the last time everyone got together. The Church and fraternal organizations met, and decided how to make Washington aware of it. The outcome of that, because of our strong lobbying efforts, is that Congress stopped aid to Turkey for a few years."

The reception room at the Diocese is hung with colorful icons and photographs of the Bishop with parishioners. One shows the Bishop flanked by Chicago's Mayor Jane Byrne and Evangeline Gouletas-Carey, the wife of New York Governor Hugh Carey.

The life of the Bishop is one of telephone calls, meetings and travelling. Father Isaiah says his presence is requested at church building programs, consecrations, ordinations, festivities, banquets and annual church events.

His Grace glides into the room, and the whiteness of his full head of hair is startling. He has very graceful hands, which he folds on his lap of black robes. He talks about his concern for youth programs and establishing a cultural center, library and museum of Greek culture in Chicago's downtown area.

Bishop lakovos is a newcomer to Chicago, here three years, and has served in Boston and Detroit. When pressed to make a comparison, he says Chicago is more active as a community.

But here, he says the mission is more difficult. He talks about the separateness of Greek worlds in Chicago, and why you will not see him in the caffeneio. "The rich may not understand the caffeneio," he explains, "It is a conception, a part of life. The bachelor comes here and tries to associate with someone. He has nowhere to go. The newcomer needs help. He must be embraced by someone and try to make the best. The truth is, he reacts negatively to any approach.

"If a priest would go to the caffeneio, they would see him as being in a strange place, and think he is there to do something against them. In Greece it is not that way, but here, we would be heralded by bad criticism of the priest in the caffeneio. If they spend too much time there, they cannot progress, learn the language. "You can go to the caffeneio, speak Greek and love the motherland, but you must explore opportunities in this country."

The Bishop defines the mission of the church to teach the Orthodox religion, and then to teach the Greek language, history and ethos. When he spoke with Dr. Angeline Caruso, former acting head of Chicago's Board of Education, they both thought two Greek high schools would be an asset to the Greek community, "Now," he says, "the child who wants to play after American school has to go to Greek school, so both in one day-school is best, like Holy Trinity." He believes the Greek education will not deprive them of being good American students.

"Without the unity of church communities, people would be dispersed and lost," continued the Bishop, and here he struck the armrest of his chair, with a delicate hand. "If the church was not the center of the Greek community, Greek Americans would not succeed as the dynamics that they are. Professors, doctors, lawyers all these come from within the Greek Church community. It grew out of that and will continue."

"The Greek covers the universe. Speaking Greek and eating souvlaki does not make you Greek. One should carry out and promote what pertains to the whole world, not only to Greeks."

Three churches in Chicago have full-time Greek schools from kindergarten through eighth grade. Koraes of St. Constantine Helen is on the south side of Chicago, Plato School of the assumption is in the downtown area. To the north is Socrates School of Holy Trinity Church, the oldest Greek school in Chicago.

The gymnasium/lunchroom at Socrates at 6041 W. Diversey is littered with paper plates and milk cartons. All the children have run out to play. About 18 teachers are still seated at their table, picking over macaroni and munching apples. The principal, Elias K. Politis, sits at the head of the table. Politis has been principal since 1955, at Socrates' first location near the early Greek settlements in Chicago.

There are 417 students here, whose parents pay a yearly tuition of $1,200 including bus fare and meals. Politis says the community "likes to spend a lot of money to give the best to our kids." The parents, he says, also like a strict school, "because in the public schools they have trouble every day." Politis says they are taught "to respect the law, the property of other people."

All 21 teachers at Socrates must have at least a degree from an American teacher's college, or a certificate from the Greek academy. The students learn Greek in the morning and English in the afternoon.

In the classrooms of the younger grades, the Greek alphabet is lettered across one side of the room, English on the other. Greek and American flags are criss-crossed in each room, and Greek heroes of the revolution share wall space with American presidents and Jesus Christ. The rooms are bright, cheery, and full of colored decorations. The students wear uniforms, and stand at attention whenever the principal enters the room.

In the eighth grade classroom, a celebration is on for upcoming graduation. Beatles music is blaring on a phonograph, and the kids are eating pizza. Most of the students will go on to St. Patrick high school, Notre Dame, or Steinmetz. a public high school.

Their teacher, Voula Alexakou-Sellountos, sits

with her students over pizza. She teaches humanities, modern Greek literature and ancient Greek history. Alexakou-Sellountos is from the National University of Athens. She looks like a student herself, and she is. She's working on another degree in Linguistics at Northeastern University (Chicago).

A tour through the other classrooms shows the children reading Greek and English. When asked which language is easier, the majority of the students say that Greek is. Politis says the kids are very happy here. They are especially excited today, because tomorrow they go on a bus trip downtown, to the Museum of Science and Industry.

Although most universities in Chicago offer the Greek language as an elective, the only modern Greek studies program is at the University of Illinois, Chicago Circle. Fotis Litsas, director of that program, says they offer a full curriculum, including Greek culture and folklore, literature, and poetry. Every year, the Hellenic Club at the U. of I. offers two big celebrations, including the "Hellenic Letters," where speakers have included Helen Kazantzakis; Nestor Matsas, the documentary writer; and Constantine Trypanis, Secretary-General of the Academy of Athens.

Litsas plans to publish Greek works by students,, and has written his own book, The Greek Folk Wedding. What he'd like to do first is a volume of Greek verse. He is especially enamored of Greek folk poetry, his favorite program in the culture series. In bi-lingual texts, his students also read Angelos Sikelianos, John Ritsos and Odysseus Elytis.

The Greeks in Chicago are a tenacious people with a strong sense of the Protestant work ethic. They also have a sensitivity and awareness to all ethnic groups in Chicago, one of the most ethnic cities in the world. They may feel they cannot afford the risks of isolation and failure to become artists, and maybe that is why there are so few of them here. But their craving for artistic expression has not died.

You can find it in the Greek – young or old – dancing the zeimbekiko, arms circling close to the body, like a bird that wants to fly, but the air heavy around him. Many say Greek music in Chicago is better than in Greece. Maybe the reason why is that it is in Chicago, and not Greece. It is needed here. Any night of the week, one may get the urge to visit Deni's Den, Vrahos at 3256 W. Lawrence, or Psistaria at 2412 W. Lawrence.

These places also attract a large number of non-Greeks, drawn to the power of the bouzouki, clarinet or keyboards. At Vrahos on Saturday night (their only music night) you may find Josh Dunson there, who is Jewish, and more Greek than many Greeks, filling his ears with the "clarino" or clarinet music he loves.

"The clarinet is a very special instrument," said Dunson, who writes about Greek clubs for Chicago Magazine. Dunson is table-hopping and his face is flushed with excitement. He truly enjoys himself here. "At this place," says Dunson, "the Greeks keep their roots without those costumes'"

A young Greek is doing backflips, one hand anchored around the white handkerchief his very strong friend is holding. There are whoops, hollers, whistles, clapping and clinking glasses.

Clarinetist George Panopoulos closes his eyes while he plays, leading the crowded room like a Pied Piper, somewhere beyond the Acropolis-like structure of the Museum of Science and Industry, the Hancock Building and the Sears Tower; and somewhere back in time, hundreds of years before the day the first Greek set foot in Chicago.

---

* *This article appeared in the September 1982 edition of the Greek Accent.*

Immigrant workers in Mason City

THREADS OF TRADITION: WEDDING

Early Greek immigration to the United States was mainly a male phenomenon. Men escaped the poverty of Greece to earn money to pay off family debts and provide dowries for daughters or sisters. Most had no intention of staying permanently in the United States. Some 40 percent did return to Greece – one of the highest repatriation rates.

Those men, if they did marry, married mainly Italian and Irish women because of their associations where most were employed. After the first generation, their offspring became totally assimilated into the American milieu.

Greek women began to slowly arrive after 1905. The first Greek woman in Chicago was Mrs. George Bitzi Pooley, who came with her Corfiote husband in 1885 and established the first Greek family in Chicago. She was responsible for founding the Greco-Slavonic Society which organized the first Greek Orthodox religious services in Chicago and other charitable associations which provided social services to young Greek immigrant bachelors.

Initially these women were brought over by fathers or brothers who preceded them to America for the purpose of marrying them off to immigrant men. These women were able to contrive marriages with similar-aged men due to the fact that their male relatives sought their welfare and arranged such marriages. In the beginning there were some dowry arrangements, but gradually the custom died out.

Eventually, fathers in Greece with marriageable daughters contracted with marriage-brokers in America who, for a commission, would arrange marriages with Greek immigrant men. These arrangements eliminated the need for dowries. This resulted in the "picture-bride" phenomenon, in which pictures (sometimes false ones) would be shown to these men and a marriage contract would be arranged. This procedure often resulted in much dissatisfaction and unhappiness, for both parties. Overaged women were fenced off as maidens, and more likely, extremely young Greek women would be married to men 15 to 25 years older than themselves. This "father-husband" relationship was the cause of much unhappiness and stress among these women, resulting in what has been described as the "Persephone Syndrome" – a resentment against their parents for arranging such a marriage. But worse yet, this practice resulted in young Greek girls being sent to America alone, defenseless and at the mercy of strangers and ruthless exploiters. The experiences of the exposure to men not related to them, travelling steerage, sharing living quarters

A groom and bride with their families after their New York wedding

with strangers, travelling by train in strange lands unescorted did much to traumatize them. This was a great contrast to the close-knit family life in Greece where the female's role was highly restricted and circumspect. Helen Zeese Papanikolas gives a poignant account of such an incident in her book *Toil and Rage in a New Land*.

Another procedure that evolved to facilitate marriages for the many Greek immigrant men in America was the development of mass excursions to Greece. These were organized by the order of AHEPA, which was founded in Atlanta, Georgia, in 1922 and became the largest fraternal organization of Greek Americans. The first excursion took place in 1928 and was followed by several others. It was the first time in the history of Hellenism in America that an organized group of nearly 1,000 men travelled on one ship to visit their homeland. The 1930 AHEPA excursion sailed aboard the SS Saturnia from New York City and the New York Times writer Dorothy Dayton had this to say about the occasion:

"Helen launched a thousand ships, but it takes 1,000 Penelopes to launch the good ship Saturnia... on which 1,000 modern Ulysses sailed for the fair land of Hellas. Nevertheless, not the beauteous Helen remains the national ideal of the young men of Greece. Ah, no, but rather the homekeeping Penelope who learned the gift of waiting. At least so say the young men who were standing in line these days at 59 Washington Street to receive passports and tickets for the Third Annual Excursion of the Order of AHEPA. One thousand bachelors are making the trip.

If every one of them doesn't return with a bride, it's not because he isn't open-minded. N. Lambadakis, chairman of the excursion farewell committee, fully excepts the trip to result in five hundred wide-eyed brides returning to New York sometime this spring and summer. Ask any of the young men waiting there, investing ten years of savings in the excursion, with a neat sum set aside for setting up housekeeping later, and he'll tell you the reason that he is going to travel 4,000 miles isn't because there aren't plenty of Helens in American but because Penelope is to be found only across the seas."

A Greek wedding in Utah

By far, however, the arranged marriage was the most common practice among Greek immigrants. This took place not only with the original first generation immigrants who came from Greek lands but also with their American-born children. The practice lasted down to World War II and even beyond. It wasn't until the postwar period with the formation of Greek youth organizations such as the Orthodox Youth and the Greek Orthodox Youth of America, GOYA, when young men and women would freely mingle and start to date, that the practice began to disappear.

The position of the second generation girl was not an enviable one, especially if she was the first child born into a family with little money and much respect for tradition. The girl had always been a source of worry to parents in Greece, and she continued to be so in the U.S. Her plight was aggravated by the greater degree of subservience to which she was subjected. As a rule the U.S. opened the matrimonial frontier. The demand for wives of Greek background was greatest in the earlier years when the ratio of females to males was small. The opportunities were so abundant that anyone unable to acquire a husband under such condition was deemed as being deficient.

The arranged marriage thus became a reality to many girls of the second generation. When women of Greek birth or parentage were scarce and demanded a premium, parents of an eligible girl found themselves in a very favorable bargaining position. The theory behind the arranged marriage was based on the belief that the parents knew best. They knew poverty first hand and they craved economic security, which to them was synonymous with happiness for their children. They made diligent efforts to find a groom with whom their daughter would neither starve or suffer and welcome the well-established man who sought her hand. A daughter might be promised comforts hitherto unknown, financial security and perhaps wealth, plus a certain amount of social prestige. It sometimes has been charged that parents arranged such marriages without consulting their daughters. But it s difficult to believe that much could have been accomplished without some degree of assent on the part of the girl.

There does not appear to have been any fixed rule on how such marriages were arranged, although a pattern of sorts did emerge. Sometimes a potential groom of Old World vintage would ask a third man to approach the parents and ask for the hand of the girl. In most cases the initiative was assumed by the men, either the potential bridegroom or the anxious father, which as a rule meant that a third party became convenient, if not indispensable. This intermediary could have been a relative, a koumbaros or "best man," a parish priest, or a close friend of the would-be bride or groom. After a sufficient amount of exploratory work had been done, arrangements would be made for the perspective mates to meet at a social function, a family gathering, or even a specially devised meeting. Sometimes the meeting was arranged to the complete innocence of the potential bride or groom; sometimes it was known to both and sometimes only to one. After a sufficient amount of confidence had been gained by both sides, a direct inquiry would be made into the prospects for marriage.

Once a matrimonial understanding had been reached, the bride lived a sort of Cinderella existence. She was showered with gifts, clothing, and personal accessories, and made her appearance at social functions with her future husband. Unlike the custom in Greece, the bulk of the expense was shouldered by the groom-elect, who often made a conspicuous display of his capacity to spend. In many instances he could afford it, but often it was made possibly only through borrowing from friends, relatives, or business associates. The expenses of the parents were at an absolute minimum and far cry from what they might have been in Greece. Often the go-between was rewarded in one way or another by the groom and the parents. This was especially true when he had been produced by the bridegroom to find him a wife.

The arranged marriage made less headway among the second generation males. In fact, a boy of this group was more likely to despise and ridicule it as something barbarous and uncivilized. Often he would tease a youthful friend with a query about whether his parents had "lined up" some girl from the Old Country for him. The resistance and rebelliousness of the boy meant that arranged marriage was less common among the members of his sex. By the same token, the male was more likely to marry outside his group than the female, especially in the earlier years. The double-standard conduct of the Greek boy compared to the Greek girl and his aggressive independence contributed to this. So did the fact that he was more likely to go to college where romances frequently blossomed into marriages. The college boy tended to view arranged marriages as the product of a backward society. The fact that he wanted to divest himself of all traces of foreignism probably was another reason for wanting to marry outside the group. It was by no means uncommon for these men to be reminded that they should have married a girl of their own background.

---

* *This narrative was part of an exhibition at the Hellenic Museum and Cultural Center in Chicago, Illinois, titled* Threads of Tradition: The Wedding *which was on view from October 18, 1996 until January 31, 1997.*

Scene from a wedding

GREEK WOMEN'S FABRIC ART IN AMERICA

*By Artemis Leontis**

Diaspora is the Greek word for human scattering: people leaving their place of birth in search of more ample resources elsewhere. Diaspora has delivered people to all corners of the earth. Diaspora brought my two grandmothers to the United States. Both came in 1916 for the same reason: to meet "a good fate," which meant for a Greek woman to marry a Greek man who would help her make a good home. A good fate was a woman's most precious resource at that time, something that had become so scarce in the war-torn homeland of the early twentieth century that many Greek women had to travel to the far ends of the earth – where Greek men had already spread – to meet their fate.

Diaspora deposited not only my grandmothers in the New World, but also their trunks full of valuables. Of course these are not the kinds of valuables one stores in a safety deposit box. They are everyday items used to make a home, what one needs to ease the difficult transition to a new place of dwelling.

A set of circumstances, some tragic, allowed my paternal grandmother's immigrant trunk to remain intact, safely preserving all that she had brought with her. Much of what the trunk contains might have belonged to any comfortably established European woman of the astiki taxi "urban middle class." Even the designs and techniques we find in her handwork conform with a late-Victorian sensibility. There are all kinds of white work, including, cut work, eyelet, different kinds of needle lace, tatting, interesting combinations of lace, ribbons, and embroidery, and elaborate patterns of couching and laid work on cotton, linen, and home-grown silk. One pair of exquisitely embroidered, monogrammed silk karré 'square table runners' incorporates several techniques.

The point is that the trunk might have filled a comfortable, middle-class European home but didn't. Poulheria Ioannidou was forced to flee her homeland in Eastern Thrace, Turkey in 1909. She stayed in Alexandria, Egypt for seven years before coming to the U.S. to marry Neocles Leontis, her fiancé of nearly a decade. Once a successful confectioner in New Jersey, he died of tuberculosis in the 1920s after gambling away the family business. She lived the unhappy life of a refugee who had seen a change in fortunes for the worse. For decades she moved from one dingy apartment to another, until her son was able to buy them their first home. All the while she continued to make handwork from the parakatathiki "stock" of designs circulating at the time.

As a girl I occasionally witnessed the following scene in our midwestern household. Admiring friends would prompt my mother to pull out the handwork she had collected. As my mother would show and tell, visitors would comment on the pieces' materials, techniques, and travels. This scene repeated itself in other homes. Everywhere, it seemed, handwork generated stories about women's education, rites of passage, relatives in other lands, and the trials of immigration or the challenges of growing up in America. From this I surmised that handwork was not only an essential frill in Greek American homes, but also a swift key to memory retrieval. I could see that embroidery, lace, and woven textiles offered in some cases the only thread women had leading them through the labyrinth of time passed and geography crossed to homelands left behind. There was a strong connection between women's handwork and their lives, and handwork could trigger a story under many circumstances.

This observation became useful to me one day as I pondered how to document a collection for a college folklore class. My solution was to go through handwork given to my mother by her mother, mother-in-law, and several other relatives, and to inquire of her, as others had done in the past, whence each piece came. Gaps in my mother's accounts led me to my maternal grandmother, the only surviving link to immigration. Then a youthful 82, she told me what she could not recall today at a feeble 102, and I am grateful for having had the foresight to record her account while I had the chance. I learned about the women who had passed in and out of her life. I developed in my mind's eye an image of girls' life in her village on the island of Cephalonia during the early part of this century. I heard about the early immigrants' struggles. I visualized the homes they might have made before and after World War II. In the process I learned what the first generation born in this country did or did not value. At the same time, I thought long and hard about my own uncomfortable position at an even greater distance from immigration. The history of several generations of women became embodied for me, too, in those family heirlooms, which were acquiring new layers of meaning with each day that passed.

As I finished that project, I longed to give it a wider frame of reference. Immigrant histories are community narratives, never just personal stories of private lives. And so it happened that in 1994, almost 20 years later, I took the opportunity to organize an exhibit of "Women's Fabric Arts in Greek America" for the annual Greek festival in Columbus, Ohio. The sponsoring organization was the Hellenic Heritage Foundation, a non-profit cultural organization incorporated in central Ohio. The Ohio Arts Council provided partial funding.

To complete this project, I interviewed 13 individuals (12 women and one man), who invited me into their homes, pulled out materials from trunks and drawers, and recounted the story of each piece. Thus I spent many delightful afternoons studying handwork and recording stories. As I reflected on the information I had collected, I thought about the connections between handwork and the narratives Greeks produce to account for their presence in America.

At the heart of my research lies the question, what does women's handwork represent, that is to say, what does it stand for in a Greek American home? Behind this lies another question, how does handwork speak to us? We can begin to answer this through a process of elimination. Handwork is not a representational art form, which means that it does not speak directly through images or words, even if it incorporates an image or a message. Expressions like kai afto tha perasei "this too will pass" or kalos orisate 'welcome' are formulaic. They are not personal statements. Even if a piece involves an original synthesis of designs, techniques, and colors, it represents a period and, if traditional, a region more than it does a private sensibility. Handwork reflects the fashions that gave it form, the milieu that gave it value, and the education that made it possible. It does not allow us to identify individual points of view. Furthermore, the excellence of a piece is measured by the precision of its execution or by the successful combination of pre-existing motifs. At best, it is one of a kind in a class of similar works.

A Greek immigrant woman

When studied anonymously, a piece of handwork tells us little about its origins, history, or uses. Yet it stands for a great deal more than the designs and materials themselves can suggest. In the context of the home that claims it, handwork evokes specific memories. It awakens certain emotions. It reconnects people to places and events. Even the most typical work – the one mass–produced, frequently copied, and therefore found in many homes – may embody a personal story. Informants frequently commented on the personal significance of handwork they possessed. A piece reminded them of a beloved person, an important event, a feeling that possessed them as they began their journey to the United States. As Evgenia showed me a cross-stitched semen 'rectangular table runner' with a neoclassical design, she recalled the feelings she had during the summer months when she was waiting to learn the results of her entrance exams to junior high school: "While I was making this piece, I cried, I laughed, I visited with my friends, and I listened to people talk. Into it I put all my dreams for the future." Because the pattern was widely circulating in the 1960s, some Greek women who saw it exhibited found nothing original in this piece. But for Evgenia it still represents her crossing an important threshold in her life.

Let us consider the following example. Sotire, an American-born son of immigrants showed me several pieces made by his wife, mother, mother-in-law, and maternal grandmother, each with its own story. As he displayed the handwork, he narrated the story of his parents' emigration from the Turkish island of Tenedos to Toledo, Ohio.

My father left Tenedos to avoid a seven-year conscription in the Turkish army. He sent a letter to my mother's father asking for her hand. Her father accepted on her behalf. She immigrated in 1921. At first we lived around Greeks. But Mother wanted to get away. She was very progressive. She wanted to learn English. She always kept busy. She worked the yard and cooked. Before the War we had a garden and we had animals: chickens, goats, pigeons. Mother crocheted all the time. She knew how to embroider, but crochet was her specialty. Whenever she'd be sitting down she would crochet or read the paper. Every space in the house was covered. All the Greek women in Toledo did handwork together. They would pick up pictures of doilies from newspapers. My mother never sent for patterns. She could figure them out.

A family in Greece pose just prior to their departure for Calgary, Canada

The story of Sotire's parents' immigration is closely tied to a curtain Sotire's mother crocheted to decorate the back door window of the family home in Toledo.

This curtain is a piece she crocheted before the war. She crocheted thousands of pieces at that time. During the war years she slowed down some, because she had to keep up with so many things. The curtain hung on our back door from 1937 to 1985. When my father died, I brought it here and framed it and put it in my bedroom.

Though a commonplace American ideal, the word "liberty" formed through the pattern of openwork was charged with special significance for his family, as Sotire explained to me. Kemal Atatürk's resounding defeat of the Greek army in Anatolia in 1922 brought an end to the Greek presence in Asia Minor just one year before his mother's departure for the U.S. Greeks living on Tenedos and Imbros became part of an exchange of populations. Those who remained on Tenedos saw their movements greatly restricted: "When Greeks leave Tenedos, they cannot return. There were only a handful of octogenarians left on the island when I visited in the 1980s," Sotire informed me. For his parents, the U.S. symbolized not only economic opportunity but also the freedom of movement lost in the homeland. For years the curtain indicated the values held by those who lived inside the home where it hung. One could expect to find a resourceful homemaker who solved her decorating challenges herself. She never let her hands rest. She could make something out of nothing. Sotire described her as "progressive": she learned English, she read newspapers daily. Her message to the world outside was that she valued what it had given her. The liberty she had lost in the old world she had found in the new. Today the curtain represents this story.

And so my approach to learning about handwork has been one of eliciting stories from materials. From interviews, I pulled the information I needed to write an exhibition catalog, organized, like the exhibit, according to individual collections. Every piece was accompanied by extensive documentation identifying the maker, the collector, the materials, place and date of origins, date of collection, a detailed description of the techniques and materials used to make the piece, a summary of its contextual history that brought the piece to central Ohio, and oral commentaries. There were also biographies of each collector.

As I step back from the work of collecting materials and stories, I am now able to find new sense in all that I have learned about women's handwork in Greek America. While certain patterns take shape in my mind, I also recognize the time warp of historical writing. Conclusions I draw about the past depend on present recollections. Immigrants who arrived during the early part of this century, as well as the mothers and grandmothers left behind by immigrant women who spoke to me, have no voice in this story, even though they are frequently its subject. Whatever we know is contained in the materials we now possess and the memories these materials evoke. Yet I find it useful to call attention to certain patterns we find in women's changing attitudes toward handwork, on the one hand, and expanding work opportunities, on the other.

The first wave of Greek women immigrants crested in the 1910s and broke with the tightening of U.S. immigration policies during the 1920s. Most early women immigrants brought a trousseau with them when they immigrated, whether their country of origins was Greece, Turkey, Egypt, Albania, or any other country in Europe or the Middle East. This fact is a very important condition of their homemaking in America. Handwork is part of a Greek woman's prika "dowry", specifically the prikia, "little dowry or trousseau" composed of bedding table settings, home decorations, and personal items. Many women who immigrated to the U.S. as part of this first labor migration came here precisely because their families could not provide them with the immovables or cash needed to "marry well" at home. It is one of the ironies Greek-American history that the prikia is an important legacy of women's immigration, given that the lack of a prika was a determining factor. Perhaps the point is that a Greek woman could marry a Greek man in the U.S. without a prika, but without her prikia she could not make a home.

Nothing resonates with an aura of familiarity so resoundingly as the theme that this generation of "picture brides," as we often call them, arrived with nothing but a trunk full of things, many of them "useless," and managed to make something out of nothing. Resourcefulness was a basic measure of a woman's value in an era when public education for girls in the Greek world stopped with grade school, when private gimnasia "junior and high schools" for wealthy young ladies in urban centers were essentially finishing schools, and when handwork was an essential element of every woman's education, whether this took place in school or at home. Thus the typical story that handwork from this era elicits is of an undereducated Greek women who came to the U.S. to marry someone laboring abroad and managed to make a good home by putting to use whatever fit and storing the rest for a rainy day.

Greek-style embroidery from America.

I heard the following story from Despina, the daughter of Greek immigrants from Kastoria who settled in upstate New York. It not only describes how life in the U.S. determined what her mother did or did not use; it also explains how it happened that the first generation of children born in the U.S. – Despina's generation – undervalued the "old things" that their mothers had hidden away. It closes with Despina's revaluation of these "old things."

My "mother was 10 when she embroidered the mantelpiece. She used it to decorate the mantel in her parent's home in Kastoria. Then it decorated one of the five fireplaces in our home in New York. It was cold there, too. She also used her mother's woven pieces. But there were things she didn't use. Do you know what these are? Slippers! She never finished them. Every so often we would go through her trunk. When mother was still living, she would sometimes show someone her things. I didn't pay much attention. We would say "Oh! look at that!" She would say "Palia pragmata 'old things'. Oh, this is something I've had for a while." It was a time when you were not proud of your ethnicity. You wanted to be like everyone else. It didn't seem like it was anything special to be Greek. Now things have changed. When mother died, they said on the farm, do you want the trunk? They just didn't have an interest. Maybe they would now. It's really hard to say. The lovely woven and embroidered pieces have much significance for me. These pieces decorate my home, bringing into my home part of my mother and her heritage and her love for this form of art. My ability to do this type of handwork is nil. Although Mother tried to teach me stitches, etc., her efforts did little to inspire me in that direction. However, her beautiful work has instilled in me a love for Greek art," Despina said.

The same inter-generational differences to which Despina refers also organize stories told to me by two women of Despina's generation who were born in Greece. Both are city-born, both aspired to higher education, both felt deeply ambivalent about what their mother's world could offer them. They tried hard to transcend the limits that had held their mothers back while they also gave them a framework for their artistry. Neither made an investment in acquiring the skills of making beautiful handwork, yet both valued what their mothers had given them. Here is the story told to me by Anna, a sculptress who immigrated to the U.S. with her husband in the early 1960s.

Anna says: "My mother was an embroidery artist. She had the most expressive hands. They never stopped. She could do anything. She embroidered this mandilothiki 'handkerchief holder' to make this piece, she probably combined different motifs that she had seen. She balanced the design. She was capable of making her own designs. Her favorite time of day was the early evening, when women of her generation would have finished their housework and gone to visit one another. It was the hour of the kendi 'embroidery time'. Have I told you about the kendi? They would sit and embroider and talk. There was a polite competition. They would pick up designs and techniques from one another. They would try to improve them.... I never wanted to embroider. I had better things to do. I loved books. I studied drawing, painting, and sculpture. I completed a program in foreign languages and I was very advanced in piano. But my mother kept pressing me. One day I said to her, 'do you want me to prove to you that I can embroider?' I found a black and white floral design in the newspaper. It was so tiny, then itan tipota 'it was nothing'. I gave it my own colors. I embroidered in on the finest petit point canvas. Then my mother said, entaxi, se parathehome 'fine, I take my hat off to you'."

Immigrant family

This story gives us insight into the generation of women who matured in Greece after World War II. We find uncanny similarities between women born in the U.S. and those who grew up in Greece's larger cities – despite the obvious difference that women in Greece were trained in handwork while their Greek-American counterparts were not.

For women in Greece, passage to America was an outlet of rebellion. Odd as it may seem, some women saw an arranged marriage with an immigrant laborer as a ticket to freedom from a world that would limit them to working with their hands. Litsa, a woman who immigrated in 1959, said that in the 1950s America symbolized for her the place where she could make something of herself not by creating a home but by acquiring a real education. Her story of frustration begins one generation before her:

"Mother had wanted to become a teacher, in fact she attended sholarhio, something our high school, but she couldn't continue because her sister married and then divorced. This was considered such a source of shame that she and her sister secluded themselves at home when she was 15, they wouldn't go anywhere. Embroidering other people's dowry was a way to make money while secluded in the home. So she became an asprokendistra 'white embroiderer'."

In spite of her own disappointment, Litsa's mother determined to make a modistra "seamstress" of her younger daughter. Litsa rebelled:

"I didn't want to pick up a needle. We had to embroider this sampler when I was in the second year of gimnasio 'junior high school'. Mother had to help me. You can tell what she has embroidered. Every year mother would say, 'Next year you're leaving school,' so I would study harder to pass my exams. She would say, 'All right, one more year'."

Litsa now proudly displays the sampler and apron she embroidered in school. These pieces stand for all the pain that she endured as she tried to escape the future that her mother had laid out for her.

Most remarkable of all, Litsa is an avid collector of handwork. But I would venture to say that the collector's mentality is found in many Greek women in the U.S. today. It seems to defines the present. Research shows that women's handwork in Greek America has been undergoing an interesting change in status. Since the 1970s, the traditions of making and using handwork, particularly the European whitework once dominant in Greek women's trousseaus, have been vanishing. Furthermore, handwork no longer comprises an important part of women's work or defines a woman's value. Instead, textiles and fabric arts from previous eras are finding new value as objects of art, embodiments of tradition, or, in this country, testimonies of Greek immigrant experience. They are taking their place in collections marked for study, reproduction, and display.

Women of my own generation have been developing mechanisms for collecting traditional designs as well as preserving and displaying family heirlooms. Here again we may draw parallel lines that ally immigrants of the past few decades with women several generations removed from immigration. Pamela, whose great-grandmother arrived in Arkansas in the early 1900s, uses her mother's collection of handwork to study her family history and to explore her ethnic heritage: "It is very strengthening and affirming for me to look beyond the immediate past of my lifetime, to bring forward the richness of how my family before me has lived." Fay, who immigrated with her family in 1967, took every opportunity to travel to Greece during summer vacations. "I was lucky because my parents let me hold onto whatever was Greek. Every summer, three months in Greece... That is how I got to know Greece." She has collected handmade textiles from all over Greece. In addition, she has made an effort to learn about traditional designs and techniques. Once she purchased a slide reproduction of a traditional work found in the Benaki Museum of Folk Culture in Athens. She started the piece in Greece and completed it in Columbus. "The karavaki 'little boat' is a design from the Ionian islands. I wanted to make something traditional. Shades of blue dominate. I am very proud of this piece."

The bestowing of new uses and meanings to Greek women's handwork coincides with a rise in cultural activism in ethnic America. Like other ethnic groups, Greek Americans have been making a concerted effort to chronicle their past even as they ponder an uncertain future. In this effort, women's fabric arts may serve as a remarkable tool for retelling histories. At each stage in its travels from the old world to the new, handwork accumulates history, which can be recalled when attention is drawn to a piece. Handwork has the power to awaken memories, elicit narratives, and so to help us reconstruct the otherwise elusive stories of women who immigrated to the United States and applied themselves to making their home here.

---

* *Artemis Leontis is presently Adjunct Associate Professor of Modern Greek at the University of Michigan. In 1994, she received grants from the Ohio Arts Council and from the Modern Greek Program at the Ohio State University to organize an exhibit of Women's Fabric Arts in Greek America for Hellenic Heritage Foundation, an Ohio non-profit cultural organization dedicated to preserving and developing the Hellenic heritage in Ohio.*

Artemis Leontis

GREEK AMERICA AT WORK

*By Dan Georgakas**

The affluence that now characterizes Greek America has tended to blur the economic realities faced by most Greek immigrants in the years preceding World War II. Like most immigrants who arrived in America between 1900 and 1924, Greeks were poorly educated and rarely possessed skills that commanded high wages. Their subsequent move up the American social ladder has been extraordinary, capped by their children becoming among the most highly educated and prosperous of all second-generation Americans. That very success has sometimes dimmed the memory of how hard Greeks had to struggle for success in America. Many aspects of that story are unknown even to Greek Americans.

One of the most interesting Greek enclaves formed in Tarpon Springs, Florida, a Gulf port just north of St. Petersburg. When John Cocoris, an immigrant from the Dodecanese islands, first visited the area in the late 1890s, he observed that American sponge fisherman still used a hook-and-pole method instead of the pressured diving suits already used in Greece. In 1905, Cocoris arranged for six divers from Aegina to use their gear on a Tarpon boat. Within a year there were 50 Greek sponge boats operating out of Tarpon Springs.

American spongers, who considered Greeks to be racial inferiors, fought on land and sea with rifles and flaming torches to protect their monopoly and methods. The Ku Klux Klan and local police often aided them, but within a year, the Greeks had asserted themselves. From then on, Greeks dominated the sponge industry in what became an upward wave of prosperity that defied even the Great Depression of the 1930s. At its height, the Greek fleet boasted over 200 boats with a thousand full-time seamen. The pay for workers was a share of the catch with each worker's percentage based on his particular task. Divers got the biggest share for good reason. The U.S. Department of Labor listed sponge-diving as among the most dangerous jobs in America.

The Greek-dominated natural sponge industry was brought to an end in the late 1940s by two factors. First, a sea fungus devastated the Gulf sponge beds in 1947. This was followed by Du Pont marketing its first synthetic sponges. The industry never recovered, but the Greek community did not dissolve. Benefiting from nearly four decades of prosperity, the Tarpon Greeks transformed a still infant tourist trade into a major industry. The close-knit community has since managed to retain considerable ethnic authenticity with dance groups, Greek language classes, and other cultural endeavors. An intriguing aspect of community life involves the role of women. Because men were in the Gulf for weeks at a time, Tarpon women played a major role in maintaining family and community institutions. Women often possessed shares in boats and associated business endeavors.

More typical of the Greek experience was the pattern in New England where Greeks worked in the textile and shoe industries. In 1912, Lowell, Massachusetts, was home to 10,000 Greeks, making it the third largest Greek center in the United States. Given the miserable working conditions and pay of the era, it is not surprising that between 1900 and 1920, there was rarely a year in which Greek workers in Lowell did not strike one or another textile mill. They sought to abolish child labor, to raise wages, and to improve conditions that kept the average life span of mill workers to under 30 years.

In the historic Lawrence strike of 1912 that involved some 20,000 workers of all ethnic groups, the Greeks were specifically lauded in the marching songs. Shortly thereafter, Greek textile workers were critical in winning a crucial follow-up strike at Lowell. A key event in that strike was a mass meeting of Greeks held at the local Greek Orthodox church. The long-term effect of the two strikes was to bring vastly improved pay rates and working conditions to a quarter of a million textile workers.

Contrary to popular assumptions, many Greeks remained in the textile and shoe industries for most of their working lives. A particularly bitter strike occurred in 1933 at shoe factories located in Peabody. Although one of the factories was owned by a Greek, some 220 Greek merchants proprietors, civic leaders, and clergy backed the strikers. A few years later John Poulos organized unions with large Greek memberships in the Lynn area and was a delegate to the founding convention of the CIO (Congress of Industrial Organization). In 1955, James Ellis (Boutsellis) who had begun his work life at a Lowell mill became state director of the CIO.

Greek women arrived earlier in New England and in greater numbers than in other regions. Many found employment in the mills, but their greatest impact was in family-related concerns characterized by a keen sense of civic involvement. New England became a bastion of Greek American culture with a high circulation of Greek-language newspapers, a plethora of community organizations, and a Greek Orthodox seminary. Greeks also were heavily involved in American politics. Michael Dukakis and Paul Tsongas would win personal national fame in the 1980s, but their careers also reflected a massive Greek political infrastructure at every level of state and local government.

The gateway to America, of course, was not Massachusetts or Florida, but New York. Those who did not immediately depart for work elsewhere usually found employment as shoeshine boys, fruit vendors, candy-makers, floral workers, street peddlers, waiters, or common laborers. Working and living conditions were so arduous that poor personal health capped by premature death was not uncommon. One of the few vehicles available for building a better life was the trade union movement.

Greek ownership of eating places is such a well-recognized fact of American life that it usually obscures the reality that many more Greeks have been employed as cooks and waiters. From the early 1900s, Greek food workers in New York city tried to organize unions. They were heavily involved in a major hotel strike in 1912 and thereafter were mainstays of the food unions. As late as the 1950s, 10 percent of waiters in all American hotels and prestige restaurants were Greek. The head waiter at for the Congressional dining room in Washington and the head waiter at the major dining room for the New York Stock Exchange are still Greeks.

The struggle for a respectable conditions and wages was not easily won. A tragic spotlight fell on Greek food organizers in 1930 when Steve Katovis, a foodhandler and union militant was killed by New York police during a strike. Some 50,000 workers from all ethnic groups demonstrated at Union Square in protest. Greeks remained at the heart of various food-related unions that ultimately achieved organizational stability during the New Deal era of President Roosevelt.

The fur industry also had a significant Greek component. Although some 70 percent of the shops were owned by Jews from Eastern Europe, another 20 percent were owned by Greeks who often hailed from Northern Greece, home of the Greek fur trade. Nearly 2,000 Greeks, about a quarter of them women, worked in the Greek shops. During the 1920s, the mainly Jewish workers in the Jewish shops and the mainly Greek workers in the Greek shops came together to form a single fur workers union. This organizational effort involved battles with Jewish gangsters hired by the employers to break the union. After bloody street fights that included some deaths, the union prevailed. By the end of the decade, the fur union had organized every fur shop in the region.

The fur workers union was especially known for

Greek miners in Utah

the spectacular gains it won for its members. This success inspired the failing leather workers to affiliate with them. The International Fur and Leather Workers Union came into being in 1939. This union was always led by Jews, but Greeks were prominently involved. Tom Galanos, the Greek leader of the Newark, New Jersey local was especially famed for his militancy and success. The fur workers sponsored numerous cultural events in the Greek community, including English classes and stage plays.

Other areas of the East and Mid-South with considerable Greek populations had similar patterns of Greek participation in large unions. In the 1920s numerous Greeks were employed at cigarette-making factories in Philadelphia and in auto assembly in Maryland. One of the auto locals in Baltimore continued to hold meetings in Greek as late as the 1950s. The Greek workers would also be a key base for the distinguished senatorial career of Paul Sarbanes.

The extent to which Greek workers were organized can be assessed by examining the record of the Greek American labor Committee set up in 1940 to agitate for Greek War Relief and for assistance to the anti-Nazi partisans in Greece. The Committee included delegates from 22 CIO and AFL (American Federation of Labor) affiliates that had a combined membership of 100,000. These unions represented clothing workers, musicians, bakers, confectionery workers, barbers, chefs, shipping clerks, fur workers, typographers, hotel employees, painters, restaurant workers, seamen, journalists, bridge painters, paperhangers, waiters, and waitresses. Another 10 unions, including the Greek Maritime Union, were non-voting associates.

Half of the Greeks in America have remained in urban centers and the second most intense concentration of Greeks in America is in the industrial Midwest. Chicago has long been the second largest urban center of Greek America and large Greek communities are found in and around Pittsburgh, Buffalo, Cleveland, Toledo, Detroit, Gary, Akron, Youngstown, and Milwaukee. As elsewhere these Greeks have been highly visible in the food industry, but they have also played a largely unnoticed role in the basic manufacturing activities which made these areas prosperous.

Chicago in the early 1900s was similar to New York City in that many new immigrants found their first employment as bootblacks, fruit peddlers, waiters, and hatters. By 1908 there were already over 200 Greek confectioneries and by 1913 several hundred Greek-owned luncheonettes. Fully as many Greeks, however, were employed in the steel industry. One of the novels of Harry Mark Petrakis, "Lion At My Heart," deals with the life of a Greek steelworker in Gary, Indiana. Another Chicago-based author, Theano Papazoglou-Margaris also wrote (in Greek) about Greek workers in her popular newspaper columns. Her other artistic activities included involvement as an actress/organizer in various progressive movements in the 1930s.

The phenomenon of the shoeshine parlor has passed from the American scene, but in the early 1900s, every America city of over 10,000 population had such establishments. A large number were run by Greeks and were often linked in regional chains. The workers were young Greek boys brought from the old country. They often lived in unsanitary rooms, worked marathon hours, had no free time, were denied education, and were exposed to hazardous chemical fumes. The Chicago Greeks, led by lawyers and doctors, were among the first to put ethnic pressure on Greek owners to make reforms. They were able to enlist the Greek Counsel in a successful effort to end the worse abuses.

Less public attention was subsequently given to the number of Greeks in basic industry. Nevertheless, whether one looks at coal mines in Pennsylvania and West Virginia, tire factories in Akron, auto plants in Toledo and Detroit, or steel mills in Youngstown, East Chicago, Gary, and Pittsburgh, large numbers of Greeks are found struggling their way into the new world. The community usually rallied to trade union activities. In places such as Akron, Greek Orthodox churches were often strike centers. Although the children of these immigrant workers usually gravitated to professions or public service, a percentage remained in basic industry, their presence strengthened by Second Wave immigrants in the 1970s. Greeks, for example, remained part of the Youngstown steel-working labor force until the day the steel mills were closed, and they were among the new autoworkers hired by General Motors in the 1970s when GM established a new state-of-the-art factory in Lordstown, Ohio.

The region has other fascinating configurations. In the town of Campbell, a suburb of Youngstown, Greeks from the Dodecanese were painters of industrial bridges, a trade to which new York City Greeks were also drawn. The industrial painters of Campbell often spent months away from their homes while working on specific bridges. As in Tarpon Springs, this resulted in Greek women playing a more visible role in community and family affairs than is usual in Greek American society. Another characteristic of this region is that it is home to a large number of Pontic and Anatolian Greeks.

At the far western end of Lake Superior where the Mesabi iron range is located, Greeks first immigrated to work as miners and were involved in the organizing drives of the late 1910s. Greek seamen also worked in the Great Lakes region. Their numbers grew with the eventual opening of the St. Lawrence Seaway. Most of these post-World War II immigrants settled in Canadian cities such as Toronto and Montreal.

During the early decades of the last century, some 30,000-40,000 Greek males worked in the far west. They were part of a virtual army of itinerant workers then dominating the American labor scene. Most of these Greeks were in the lumbering, mining, construction, and railroad industries. For a brief period, Greeks were concentrated in the laying of railroad tracks. By the late teens, they made up 20 percent of the work force of the nine western railroads. Wages at this time were so poor that some itinerant workers may had count it a good month when they did not accumulate more debt.

An additional problem for Greeks in the West was racial discrimination. This occurred in other regions as well, being most severe in the American South. Among the best known of large-scale anti-Greek actions are the burning of the Greek section of south Omaha, Nebraska, in 1909 and the expulsion at gunpoint of Greek lumber workers from Grays Harbor, Washington, in 1912. More common were restrictive local ordinances that lumped Greeks, Mexicans, Asians, and African Americans as undesirables.

Greek workers in the West soon fashioned a reputation for their militancy, fighting by whatever necessary to push forward the social agendas they favored. Greek workers were particularly prominent in mining disputes involving copper and coal workers, but they were also active in lumber, agricultural, and railroad unions. An early peaking of this kind of involvement came in 1912-1914.

In 1912, Greeks were present at an attempt to organize agricultural workers in Wheatland, California. In a physical confrontation between workers and company guards, two lawmen and two strikers were killed. At Bingham, Utah, the fighting was more formal with Greek strikers holding the mountainside as the company tried to bring in replacement workers under armed guard. The Greeks, mainly Cretans, employed the guerrilla-warfare savvy they had learned in the liberation struggles against the Ottomans in their homeland. At Wheatland, the strikers lost their organizing effort, but at Bingham they prevailed.

A year later, a massive coal strike began in Colorado. Louis Tikas and a core of fellow Cretans played a leading role in the Ludlow region. On April 21, 1914, when company guards opened fire on a tent city of strikers, Tikas was killed trying to bring families to safer ground. The final death toll was 30 and virtual civil war was averted only by the intervention of a federal commission to investigate the killings. The Ludlow Massacre has remained a key event in American labor history. On the official monument at the site of the murders, the first name is that of Louis Tikas. A dozen years after Ludlow, the coal miners again felt the need to strike in Colorado. Greeks, now making up 10-30 percent of the work force at some mines, were a highly visible element in the upsurge.

One difficulty in determining the longer-term impact of Greek miners in the Southwest is that few permanent Greek communities came into existence. The main reasons for this was the lack of Greek women. While some brides were imported from Greece, most Greek men who wanted to marry Greek women moved to other regions or even back to Greece. A large number also married non-Greeks. The children from these unions usually did not preserve their Greek identity.

The Greeks of the Intermountain West have had the good fortune of having their history brilliantly recorded in the fiction and historical writing of Helen Papanikolas. Harry Mark Petrakis has written a novel about Cretan coal miners in Utah titled "Days of Vengeance," and Zeese Papanikolas has told the story of Louis Tikas in "Buried Unsung."

The West Coast is home to about 15 percent of the Greeks in America. There are numerous studies of specific communities, but no regional or industrial overviews, a problem that also exists for the relatively small Greek population of the South and agricultural Midwest. Existing local studies suggest that the same patterns prevail as those in the industrial East and Midwest.

In San Francisco, Greek restaurants arose with

the arrival of Greek maritime and railroad workers. As in the East, the workers in these restaurants and the region's many hotels first created all-Greek unions and then affiliated with larger AFL units. Just as a Greek food handler in New York was killed by police in the 1930s, a Greek cook was killed by police in the historic San Francisco General Strike of 1934. Some 20,000 workers marched in the ensuing funeral cortege. The continuum of labor militancy among Greeks was evidenced 14 years later when Brooklyn-born Alexis Georgiadis organized the California CIO-Political Action Committee, one of the first in the nation. In 1956, George Christopher became the first Greek to be elected mayor of a major American city. His father had worked on a railroad gang in Sacramento before resettling in San Francisco.

California, of course, is home to the movie industry, and Greeks were active from its onset as exhibitors. Alexander Pantages, based in Seattle, owned some 80 theaters by the early 1920s. Later, the three Skouros brothers of St. Louis would own 400 theaters. This ownership became the basis for Spyro Skouros becoming president in 1942 of Twentieth Century Fox, one of the largest Hollywood studios. How many Greeks worked in the hundreds of Greek-owned theaters is unknown, but Greeks have had an impact in Hollywood far out of proportion to their percent of the general population. A sense of that involvement is seen in the contributions to scores of Hollywood classics by Dean Tavlouris (set design), Hermes Pan (choreography), Theoni Alredge (costume design), Dimitri Metropoulos (music) and Elia Kazan.

Greek immigrants preferred shopping in Greek owned stores

The Greek community is no longer industrially oriented as it was in the pre-World War II years. Nonetheless, considerable numbers of Greeks remain in working class jobs, particularly in the skilled trades. Greeks also continue to hold office in major unions. In New York City, for example, in the past 20 years, Greeks have been officers in unions representing steel workers, sign fabricators iron workers, bridge builders, industrial painters, teamsters, butchers, clothing workers, commercial film and video technicians, teachers, supreme court officials, sanitation workers, plumbers, waiters, police officers, civil servants, electricians, and gas fitters. Most prominent among these local officials have been Arthur Cheliotes, President of the Communication Workers of America-Local 1180, and Nick Hambas, who headed the New York Joint Board of the Amalgamated Clothing and Textile Workers Unions. The highest placed Greek American labor leader at the national level has been George J. Kourpias, past president of the powerful International Association of Machinists and Aerospace Workers. Representative of the huge presence of Greeks in the field of education was the naming of Mary Bicouvaris as American Teacher of the Year in 1989.

Over the past hundred years, the patterns that dominated Greek communities have changed dramatically. As have-not newcomers, the immigrants of the Great Migration were drawn to reform movements of the kind characterized by Roosevelt's New Deal and militant trade unions. They were determined to create an even better America than the one they found. While succeeding in that effort they forged a hardworking and patriotic public image that has accrued to their children, grandchildren, and subsequent Greek immigrants. Our present relative comfort derives from this history of struggle that was unaccepting of America's shortcomings. It is one of our most precious legacies.

---

* *Georgakas is a labor historian currently teaching at New York University.*

EUTERPE DUKAKIS

The story of an Immigrant Woman who lived the American dream

Following is the transcript of an interview with Euterpe Boukis Dukakis, born September 4, 1903, in Greece, an immigrant who came to the United States in 1913 at the age of nine. The interview, conducted by Debby Dane, was recorded on November 21, 1985 at Dukakis's home in Brookline, Massachusetts. Dukakis does not recall the name of the ship which brought her to America. Transcripts such as this are kept at the Oral History room at the library of the Ellis Island Museum.

This is Debby Dane and I'm speaking with Euterpe Dukakis on Thursday, November 21, 1985. We are beginning this interview at 3:30. We are about to interview Euterpe Dukakis about her immigration experience from Greece in 1913. She was nine years old. Mrs. Dukakis, if you could tell me the day you were born and the name of the town in Greece.
DUKAKIS: I was born on September the 4th, 1903, in the city of Larisa, which is in northern Greece.
DANE: Will you describe the type of town it was, the size, what people did for a living?
DUKAKIS: It is, and it was, one of the largest cities of Greece. It's a military, uh, not exactly a post but, shall I say, a military center. It always has been. Because it is in northern Greece and it is in the city. And the, and, particularly in those days, the borders were not terribly far away from Turkey and the Balkan states. It is now over 200,000. It is one of the, probably about the third city in size. It's still a great military center for Greece. Uh, we were, my father was a bookkeeper in a big market. Ah, we were not rich. We were, in fact, fairly poor. But as far as I was concerned, I was, I had all I needed as a child and it never occurred to me that we weren't. As it was Greece, as it is now and as it was then, uh, the young people, unless they have a great deal, if the family has property and money, the future is not a very bright one. And at that time, everybody was going to America, and so my older brother, I had two brothers and four sisters, my older brother, Nicholas, was 18 and decided that Greece didn't have very much of a future for him at the time, at any rate, so he decided to go to the United States, to come to the United States. We had, my father had a, a cousin here who lived in Manchester, New Hampshire, with whom my brother got in contact and he sent the money for him to, to, uh, come to the United States. So he, he left, came here, was on his own, could speak no English, and found a job in a shoe factory. In two years he sent enough money so that my younger brother could join him, my brother Adam. And in another, must have been, four years they sent money for the six of us to come. At that time, in 1912, 1913, the, uh, steamship companies were carrying on a great deal of competition to bring, uh, immigrants to the United States because there was a great need for them in building the railroads out toward the west and our factories, shoe factories, textile factories, steel factories, all that. And so the companies, the steamship companies, proceeded to, uh, entice the, uh, young, young men, particularly from southern and central Europe to come to the United States. And, in fact, the competition was so strong that my brothers got the tickets for us to come and they cost 80 dollars for the six of us.
DAME: For all six?
DUKAKIS: All six of us. So we came on a boat that had been a coal ship, coal freighter. Had been very quick, hurriedly dressed, changed to an immigrant boat. And the conditions were very, very bad, so bad that my father protested to the administration of the boat that he would not have his family housed around the hold of the ship. That's where the tiers of bunks were one on top of the other for the men and the quarters for the women were not much better. At any rate we did get better quarters and we

did the best we could. The weather was terrible. It was in March, the end of March, the beginning of April. The food was worse. But we managed to get here. And when we arrived in New York, uh, I did not see the Statue of Liberty, incidentaly. It must have been at night and I never, I didn't know anything about it. I learned about that much later. Uh, we were in quarantine in New York for a day, and then we were allowed to go to Ellis Island and we were herded there like sheep and there we were to be examined, and all very fearful that we might not be found healthy enough and might be sent back.

My father referred to the Ellis Island as the Place of Tears, or sighs, because everyone was so fearful. Ah, my youngest sister and I were very, very innocent. We didn't know what was going on. We went wherever we were told. But we didn't like it when the doctor stuck his finger in her eyelid and turned it up for a very bad disease that was communicable and infectious, contagious. So we didn't, uh, we got through all right. And we did find our brother Nick down at the pier looking for us, and my sister Helen remembered him and recognized him and started yelling and calling, "Nick, Nick, Nick, Nico. Nico, Nico."

And we did, he received us, and had rooms for a found, uh, I had, uh, uh, reservations for the, us to go on the Fall River Line to Fall River and then to Brockton, and from Brockton by, by train to Haverhill, Massachusetts. Uh, I cannot say that I, I found everything ready for us, a house, furniture, food, my first real meal other than the box which had been given to us on Ellis Island as we left it, a sandwich and a banana, the likes of which we never seen before and didn't know how to eat.

But my first real meal in the United States was, uh, lamb chops and French fried potatoes. (She laughs.) Which was, fortunately, kind of indicative of my life in the United States. My brother said that, had all the knocks. I, we were settled in Haverhill, I went through the public schools. I was very fortunate in having wonderful teachers who were interested in me and in my progress. I went through Haverhill High School and then to Bates College. Taught four years in two small towns, one in New Hampshire, and one in, uh, Massachusetts. And then I was married to my husband, to Panos, P-A-N-0-S, Panos, who was a young physician trying to make his way in Boston. We had one child Stelien [PH] in due time and, uh, then Michael came and that is my life. The United, America has been truly the promised land for me.

DANE: I have a few questions for you.

DUKAKIS: Very well. Shoot.

DANE: Back in Greece, when your brothers were here, did they write home?

DUKAKIS: Oh, yes. Very Often.

DANE: Did they paint a picture of America for you?

DUKAKIS: Ah, they sent us cards and they also told us that houses could be moved from place to place and I didn't believe such a thing. Of course we thought of houses being built, by stone, and you don't move a stone house. And we didn't, there were many things that they would write to us that we couldn't believe because we had no background or knowledge to believe such things. Ah –

DANE: Was their life hard for them?

DUKAKIS: My older brother went through a great many knocks because he came in 19, uh, '07, and soon after he arrived here there was the big panic, as they called them. We call them a depression. In those days they called them a panic. And he lived on bake, on boiled beans for quite a while because they were, factories were closed. Uh, he saved some money and had to use that up to live from day to day. Fortunately, that was over and then things straightened out and he was able to work and, uh, gather enough dollars to send for my younger brother.

DANE: Did he ever consider coming back to Greece, going back to Greece?

DUKAKIS: I think that when he first started, I remember when, uh, uh, he was about to leave to come to the United States and my mother was, uh, he waited so that my mother could be delivered of our youngest sister. And when he, uh, went to see her after the baby was born, see, there were three of us, three girls already and, uh, she looked up at him and she said, "Oh, Nico, another girl." And he said, "Mother don't you worry I'll stay in the United States another two years for her." What he meant was he was going to the United States and he was going to work hard to make dowry for his sisters so that they could be married. Because in those days, and the custom isn't too far from there today, but not so bad because the girls become, are educated now in Greece and go into careers. Ah, what he meant was that he would gather enough money so that they could be given a dowry to marry. Instead we all came here. (They laugh.) And I was the first one to go back to Greece on a trip. In 1936, yeah,

my husband and I and my mother-in-law went to Greece to, the summer of 1936. It was a wonderful return, and I've been there six more times, and I've enjoyed every trip, but I, this is home.
DANE: Yeah. Then your older brother went. Was it hard for your mother to let her other son go?
DUKAKIS: My mother cried all the time. There was, if a letter didn't come when she expected it she cried, too.
DANE: Uh-huh. Was she anxious to come here, or did she just wish they'd come home?
DUKAKIS: She, she, no. She never, in fact, we used to tease her. She never considered, never wanted to come visit the old country. And we used to say to her, "Mother, everybody wants to go to Greece. Don't you want to go and see your sisters?"
"Go back to Greece? What for? All that I love, all that I treasure, is here. What do I want to go back to Greece for?" She never did.
DANE: And your father, was he, did he want to leave when it came time to go?
DUKAKIS: Oh, yes. He was ready to, yes, yes. The boys were here and they wanted us to come. It was, uh, uniting the family again. My mother wanted it very much. That was it. We got along very well. My brothers did well in the United States. My sisters married by the old custom, into very good marriages, my two sisters. We lived, this was the place for us, and we never wanted to go back to live there.
DANE: Did you ever hear the stories, probably your brothers blew that balloon as far as, the gold in the streets and opportunity?
DUKAKIS: Oh, yes. Oh, yes. Of course. Yes. Those stories were but we knew it wasn't so because my brothers told us of the difficulties they had. They didn't complain, they were just simply stating facts.
DANE: Uh-huh. And on Ellis Island, can you remember as if you were a television camera, what it looked like? Were there lots of people there in 1913?
DUKAKIS: It was crowded because it was, ours was not the only immigrant ship that had docked and was being processed. Many, there were several at the same time. I think it's very difficult for people to understand what was happening in those days. People were coming to the United States in droves from everywhere, even from the West Coast where the Oriental people, the Chinese, particularly, and the Japanese. Because this was the promised land. This was the land that was advertised and also that we heard about that this, this were opportunities that we didn't have in the old countries.
DANE: Uh-huh. When you came to Haverhill and brought with you your Greek culture, did you maintain certain holidays and customs?
DUKAKIS: Oh, yes. We always have.
DANE: What are some of those?
DUKAKIS: Well, we have, of course, Christmas and we have easter, although Christmas is not the, it is now for us, because we are here, we are Americans. We, in Greece, Christmas is a religious holiday, not a folk holiday. Uh, Easter is the, rather, the

Greek Americans in Lowell, Mass. welcome Metropolitan Germanos of Seleukeia.

New Year is the time of exchanging gifts and, uh, celebrating parties and that sort of thing. Uh, Easter is the very, the holiest time of the year. It starts 40 days before Easter and the fasting of the days and the preparing the house and the, uh, preparing for Easter the last week with all the wonderful, uh, celebrating, shall we call it, of the Passion during, the week before Easter and then the, going to church constantly of that week and then, finally, the, uh, Good Friday, which is very sad, because it's the reenactment of the Passion of Jesus, and then, uh, the Saturday midnight mass when everyone goes and has a candle. There is the joyous declaration of "Christ Is Risen," you know. And then the next day when families get together out of doors and they roast lambs out of doors and the dyeing of red eggs and the, it's, it's a very festive time. It was then and I suspect it still is. It was very nice, and we do as much of that as we can. I used to, in the, in the, uh, when the boys were very young we, the calendar, in the Greek church, was still the Julian calendar whereas we go by the Georgian now, as you know. And so we have two Christmases, two Easters. We still have two easters occasionally. I used to say to the boys, "See how lucky we are." You know, "We have two Christmases and we have two Easters." And we still do, of course, occasionally, every four years, I think, we have the same date, but usually – So we celebrate both.

DANE: Uh-huh. And food? How about food? Did your mother bring over –

DUKAKIS: Oh, well, we always know she didn't bring over food, they had regular food here. (Voices garbled.) Yes, but there were, of course, all the traditional dishes that we have like lamb for Easter and, uh, there was no particular food for Christmas but, of course, we'd have, uh, turkey or chicken mostly. In those days, when we were young, there weren't very many turkeys being raised and it wasn't advertised the way it is now. And turkey was very expensive, incidentally, then, because there weren't so many. Now, of course, everybody has turkey and we, when we gather for Thanksgiving and Christmas we're about 25 now. (She laughs.) Not with my own family, because now I, see, I got with my Kitty and Michael, and wherever they go I go, too. And it's Kitty's family that we get together, we have a very large family with all the different ones involved.

DANE: Uh-huh. When you first came, of course, you spoke Greek, because you were a Greek girl. How do, did you learn English? I know you went to school when you got here.

DUKAKIS: Well, as you know, my family didn't speak English. My brother spoke English, but it was very, a broken kind of ordinary street English. Um, my father and mother couldn't speak, my mother never spoke English. She was at home all the time. If she ever went out, we took her out ourselves, we girls took her into town and we did all the talking for her. And, uh, her life was, of course, among Greeks, some Greek neighbors and the church and the family. So that I heard English almost only at, at school. And I learned my English from teachers, mostly. Uh, at first, I couldn't speak it at all and my sister who is, uh, three years younger than I, uh, couldn't either. Could hardly say more than yes or no and hello and how do you do. And my younger brother was very cross and he said to my mother, "What's the matter with these girls? Are they stupid? Why can't they, here they've been all these months and they haven't, they don't know how to speak English yet." Well, at six months, and it happened to me, it happened to Effie, it was like the coming down of the Holy Spirit to the, apostles and the disciples of Jesus, we spoke English, just like that.

DANE: That's wonderful. Amazing.

DUKAKIS: That's why I don't understand this bilingual thing, this English as a second language. But things are different now. There weren't any Greek children in school, so that I was forced to speak, for me to speak, uh, Greek with. And there weren't any children in my neighborhood. I had one other little Greek girl with whom I was friends and still am. Uh, so that I'd learn my English from, in school. Of course that's a different story. You take all the children here who are Hispanic, and the whole school is full of Hispanic children. How are they going to learn to speak English? The teacher isn't enough. So maybe it is useful. Maybe it's as it should be.

DANE: You started to speak English and then in school you started to learn how to read English also.

DUKAKIS: It was no problem because I could read Greek, and all I had to do was to learn the pronunciation of syllables and the letters, and that's all it was. It was no problem. Mathema –, uh, arithmetic was, I knew arithmetic from the Greek school. I had gone two years, full years, in Greece, and part of one year into the third grade. There was no problem at all in that way. As long as I just learned the pronunciation there was no problem.

DANE: And your principal, he was very helpful to you?
DUKAKIS: Oh, he was wonderful to me. I was one of the few immigrant children and I happened to have one very, very thick, long braid of black hair down my back. And that was very unusual and it was noticeable. So from that he made it. He was so wonderfully helpful. He was like a second father to me. He was sort of an intellectual father. And he was, he made a great deal of the American life available to me which I would not have had and I had very fine American teachers, Yankee, shall I say, who, uh, invited my sister and me to their homes. And we had wonderful taste of the real American life, which was very, it was really, I was very fortunate.
DANE: As far as education goes, I mean, you went off to college. Was that unusual for, I mean, coming from Greece, didn't women stay in the home?
DUKAKIS: It was very unusual. In fact my, the Greek people of Haverhill thought, my parents were out of their minds when they let me go, not only to college, which no other Greek girl had done in Haverhill, a community of 3,000 Greeks, but that I went away to school 160 miles away and co-educational also. (She laughs.) It was really quite a shock.
DANE: Was it your idea? Did you want to?
DUKAKIS: Oh, yes. Yes. And I have a feeling that if, if we had stayed in Greece that my brothers would have seen to it that there were enough funds in the family so I could have gone on to more than just the common, the, uh, the elementary school. And that I should go to the, uh, (?), it was called and probably have graduated so I could teach in Greece. So I worked. Oh, I worked summers, I worked Friday afternoon and Saturday, all through high school and saved my money. I knew that I would have to do that and show that I really wanted to go to college. My brothers helped me, but I worked every summer. I worked in the shoe factory and earned, uh, enough for my tuition, at least. And, uh, I had a very small scholarship in college, every year, which wasn't very much but it was helpful. And, uh –
DANE: Were they supportive, your parents?
DUKAKIS: Oh, yes. Very, very supportive.
DANE: When you first came in school and you were the only Greek, one of the only Greek girls there, did you ever feel like an outsider in the first years that you were here?
DUKAKIS: I was too young to be an outsider, to feel an outsider. My life was very busy. You know, I was, I didn't feel an outsider because, uh, I had everything. I had my family, I had my school. I played games outside, my sister and I were, playing together, and I had a very good friend, Felksi, who is still my friend, and we see each other every year. When I go back to Lewiston, Maine, she still, the college. She lives in Auburn, which is just across the river. Um, I didn't feel an outsider at all.
DANE: And what was your maiden name? What did you come over?
DUKAKIS: Boukis. Euterpe Boukis, B-O-U-K-I-S.
DANE: How did you meet your husband?
DUKAKIS: Uh, let's see, how did I meet Panos. Uh, my sister, my older sister, married Tom Nucas who was, uh, was to be, he wasn't then, who was to be a lawyer in Lowell, Massachusetts. And, uh, they, uh, were friends with the Dukakises. And I met my husband just because the, the two families were friends. Then my husband went to Bates for a year. He went to Boston University for a year, uh, but didn't like it, because he wanted some campus life. He had done his college preparatory work at the American International College in, uh, Springfield. It was then a, uh, a school, a preparatory school, particularly for foreign born and they stressed this because the teaching of English. And he was very happy there. He, too, was taken under his wing, under the wing of one of the professors there who encouraged him a great deal and invited him to their home and would invite him for Thanksgiving, for instance, at their home, and that sort of thing. Uh, and, uh, he liked the campus life, you see, and so when he went to Boston University, granted that he, it was very cheap and he could live very cheaply, uh, in the city, still he wanted some campus life. And so he transferred to Bates and, uh, was very happy there and did a great deal of work, extra work there. And, uh, was, uh, ready to go, in those days the, uh, graduate and undergraduate degree was not, was not, uh (a telephone rings.)
DANE: This is the end of side one, Euterpe Dukakis, Interview Number 91, I don't know what time it is.
DANE: This is the beginning of side two, Euterpe Dukakis, Interview Number 91, it's 4:05.
DUKAKIS: Where were we?
DANE: We were, you were talking about, um, your husband, and he was at Bates.
DUKAKIS: Yes, he went there. In fact, he graduated, he left Bates, and was accepted at Harvard Med-

Former Massachusetts governor and presidential candidate, Michael Dukakis

ical School. And, in those days, they did not require an undergraduate degree. But he had, he really had about three years of college, preparatory, medical, uh, what they call it, medical, pre-medical courses. And he had enough of it. Anyway, he was accepted at Harvard Medical. He graduated in 1924.

DANE: And you married –

DUKAKIS: 1929. He'd had a great deal of, uh, hospital training, so he was able, in those days it wasn't quite as specialized as it is now and he was able to, he had good gynecological and obstetrical preparation at the hospital, at the Lying In Hospital, that was, also, he trained at the Providence City Hospital, was very good for pediatrics. And, uh, he was, his first internship and residence was at the, uh, Boston City Hospital in surgery. And so he, really did, and he was very good. He was one of the early, first, one of the very early Greek doctors in, uh, in, uh, Boston. And, uh, had a very good reputation among non-Greek people. And, in fact, Michael used to say he won his first term for Governor because everybody been, had either been operated on by his father or somebody in the family or, had been, because he was very well known, you see.

DANE: And for you to marry another Greek, he had come from Greece, I take it, or –

DUKAKIS: Yes, he was an immigrant too. He came when he was 16.

DANE; Uh-huh. Did you think you'd grow up and marry a Greek when you were here?

DUKAKIS: Oh, yes. I never was interested in any – It was early, then. You see, we were brought up in a Greek environment. And it was right because I think that I would have, uh, uh, my generation, perhaps, of girls anyway, because the Greek young men did marry non-Greeks. But, uh, in my generation I, I think it was the best thing.

DANE: You lived in a Greek community in Haverhill.

DUKAKIS: Yes.

DANE: Was it a very tight community, or –

DUKAKIS: Well, we, we had the friends. You see, we knew what other people (a telephone rings.) (Break in tape.)

DANE: We were just talking about, um, the Greek community in Haverhill. Was it a very tight community? Did people know each other –

DUKAKIS: Oh, yes. We knew each other. Of course, the church was a center, a religious as well as a social center. We had other friends as well. Once I graduated from high school I didn't go back, I went back home only for vacation. I taught away from home and then, on, after four years of teaching I was married, lived in Boston and then in Brookline, so we're, I really didn't go back to Haverhill very much and I don't know, occasionally. Although I have two sisters there, but they come here more than I go there. So, I really –

And here my connections are with the whole community. I mean, the larger community as well as with the Greek community. Our church, of course, is a Greek church, and then I belong to Greek organizations, but I belong to American organizations, woman's club, junior league, I mean League of Woman Voters, uh, what else. All sorts of things.

DANE: Were there Greek clubs? I understand, uh, who was I just talking with the other day, German, a German woman who came, and they were in Baltimore, and they had lots of German clubs and they, was it the same with the Greek community?

DUKAKIS: Yes. We had some. I belonged to the, I still do belong to the Greek college club, University Club. That was one of the first organizations I joined when I was married in Haverhill. We didn't have anything like that. But, uh, in Boston it was a very thriving club. It still is. I can't attend meetings any more because they meet at night and I can't go out at night, of course. When my husband was living I, we went to, we went together to all the meetings. There is a Hellenic Medical Society, and there is also the Norfolk Medical Society, to which my hus-

band and I would go. And, uh, we did, and it's just, again, you cannot, if you drop everything of your own kind it's like cutting off part of you. You may be able to do without your arm, but is it the best thing for you to do? You need both arms, both hands. There are people who just, they feel they are Americans and want to be, but it isn't. My son, Michael, he, he brings up his Greek background all the time. He speaks Greek, he reads Greek and, uh, he speaks Spanish, he reads Italian speech before Italians. He's really a wonderful guy. Don't you think so, Dane? I say that objectively. In fact, I've always been able to look at my children objectively.
DANE: Like every mother. (They laugh.) Um, let's talk about that just for a few more minutes about, um, well, first we'll go in though your citizenship. Did you have, you came at nine, did you have to go through getting papers and everything?
DUKAKIS: Yes. I went to apply for my citizenship papers, uh early. I applied when I was 18 or 19, I think. Uh, I had, of course, plenty of years here, so I could. But I would not have been able to get, uh, to get them, or at least I wouldn't have been able to afford. How was that, why did I wait till after, uh, something about the laws then which have changed, on citizenship. At any rate, I went to, uh, signed up, when I was about 18 or 19 at the county courthouse. And the officer there, the clerk, said, "Why do you do this? You're going to marry an American anyway, so what's the sense of this?" I said, "I want to get my own citizenship for myself." As it happened, when I did get my citizenship, ready to get my citizenship, uh, the law had changed so that women could get it, uh, would not have their own citizenship if they married somebody. They have to go through the process themselves. Anyway, I became, uh, they, uh, on this, I was more than 21 because my, uh, it was my first year teaching and I had to come back from Nashua, New Hampshire, to go and get my papers. And that was all right. I got my citizenship, voted as soon as I could. I've never failed to vote.
DANE: Was that a happy day to become an American?
DUKAKIS: Oh, yes. Very much so. Very proud.
DANE: Uh-huh. Did your parents get citizenship?
DUKAKIS: My parents did not. But all, my sisters and brothers did. We all did, became citizens.
DANE: And then a little discussion about that, about being an American of Greek heritage. You were born in Greece and became an American citizen. Two questions. One is when did you feel like an American?
DUKAKIS: Well, of course, when I was young, those things didn't really matter when I was very young, didn't come up. Uh, afterwards , well, I, it's hard, how do you acquire these things, it's hard to say. But I know one thing now, I'm an American in America, in the United States, where there's everything that has to do with life in the United States. And when something is Greek, the Greek comes out in me. I speak Greek with those who speak Greek to me. In the church it's Greek. We have certain things, certain customs which we celebrate. And that is, I feel Greek then.
So that I'm really part of both lives. I, should I throw away my Greek-ism? When I marry, do I forsake my family? I don't. All that my family has meant to me continues to mean to me, but I take on a husband and his family also, and I expect that he has his family. And it's part of our lives, it's part of my roots. Otherwise, I couldn't be a whole person. Michael and I have discussed this and he himself, he feels that Greek in him, his Hellenism. He feels it very strongly. And he's, uh, it adds, it has added and it is a big dimension in his life. And it should be that way. How about Michael's children? Even they have a little feeling and knowledge. Of course, I have tried to give them as much as of a background because I feel it's a strength to know your background, it's a strength to know your roots. It gives you that, a sense of, uh, uh, security, shall we say, which, the past is part of you. None of us are born suddenly. We're born with what has come before, in back of us. I don't know.
DANE: I think that's wonderful.
DOUKAKIS: How do the rest of your prospects feel about this? Have you had any, have you had any other interviews?
DANE: Yes, some say, uh, mostly, people that came because of persecution don't look back. Most of them that I've talked to-
DUKAKIS: They can't. If they do it's bitterness, it's horrible, it's misery.
DANE: So they started here. But they bring, and most of these, of course, they're Jewish people. They bring their religion, they bring their culture, that, as we know, is all over the world. And that's what gives them strength. Um, and it's their heritage in the word, um, but not tied to a country any more at all.
DUKAKIS: No, it isn't a country. It's an idea. It's a

feeling. It's an emotion. You take that with you always.
DANE: But this German woman, I'm trying to think of, without the religious, she, um, she pretty much left Germany behind except, except for some – But she, I think because of World War Two and the cultural reasons there, she wasn't as outspoken about how, what she was tied to her country.
DUKAKIS: I, of course, I was very young but whatever I, the life I had in Greece was a very happy one. I was very sorry to leave my grandmother. She wouldn't come with us. She was 80 years old and she said she was too old to change her life. So she went back to the village in the mountains of Epirus. Fortunately she had a daughter there who took care of her until she died when she was 95. But, uh, it was very, I had a happy childhood. I had a happy childhood here.
DANE: This is one thing, I mean, people will know this, but for the future generations, you represent, really, I'm sure everyone's told you this and it's paved some campaign trails, the American dream from, from another culture. Went to college here, which you might not have done, raised two sons. And one of them has grown up to be an American citizen who is now the governor of the state of Massachusetts. Do you feel like you represent –
DUKAKIS: It was really a, uh, it was, if it was a dream I did not, I always said to myself I must not dream the dreams for my children, for my sons. They were to do the dreaming themselves. They should make their own dreams. Uh, but, uh, it, it couldn't have been a happier life. We've had our sorrows, we lost a son, grown up, who was struck by a hit-and-run driver and left a vegetable, lived for about four and half months between life and death. Uh, it's, it's a constant pain, a sad memory. But everybody has to, if you live long enough you go, everybody will have sorrow, will have some misery, some, perhaps some people have more than others. But I, I for myself, I feel that I have been, uh, whatever you want to call it. God or luck or whatever, I have, living, coming to the United States and living here has really been a, a, uh, reality of the promised land.
DANE: I think that's great.
DUKAKIS: I was very fortunate and I think our, all my family have been fortunate in having come to the United States.
DANE: Would you do me a favor, because my voice will be taken away, when, in the future on the tape, if you could say your full name, first name, maiden name, last name, married name, and then say your son's name and say what year he was elected governor, and say that he is the governor of Massachusetts.
DUKAKIS: I thought we said that.
DANE: But they won't hear that on my side.
DUKAKIS: Oh, I see, you didn't say that. Oh, I was born Euterpe Boukis, and I'm now Euterpe Boukis Dukakis. I, uh –
DANE: Had Michael.
DUKAKIS: I've married Panos Steelan Dukakis who was a physician, a very well-respected physician. We had two children. We have only one now. Our older boy was, unfortunately, hit by a, struck by a hit-and-run driver and was left very, very ill and died. I have one son now, and he's the governor of Massachusetts. The United States has been to me a very wonderful country.
DANE: Thank you. Thank you.
DUKAKIS: Okay? I hope you'll edit that.
DANE: This is the end of side two with Mrs. Euterpe Dukakis, Interview Number 91. It's 4:21.

A postcard sent by a Greek immigrant depicts the Lowell City Hall in 1907

* *(Recording engineer: Dean Cappello; transcript originally prepared by Nancy Vega in 1986; transcript reconceived by Chick Lemonick in January 1996).*

GREEK AMERICAN PATRIOTISM

*By Andrew T. Kopan**

Πατρός τε και μητρός, και των άλλων προγόνων τιμιωτέρον εστί και αγιωτέρον η πατρίς

" One's country is more honorable and more sacred than one's parents or ancestors."

Socrates (469-399 B.C.)

This ancient injunction that one's country is to be revered above one's parents and ancestors has been an ideal which Greek immigrants kept close to their hearts. The Greeks, founders of democracy 2,500 years ago, have always been imbued with its defense during their long and glorious history. Defense of country and democracy was a trait of Greek immigrants in whatever country they emigrated to. This is especially true in the United States where despite their small number in total population, Greeks served in practically all of America's wars.

Indeed, the fire of patriotism of Greek Americans was exemplified in deeds of unequivocal meaning. Early historical accounts and newspapers in the United States extolled Greek American patriotism. There was not a more loyal and patriotic class of people in this country than were the American Greeks. A great percentage of them served in the armed forces of America (a proportion believed to be greater than that of any other ethnic group in the United States). The great majority of them who came within the draft early ages flatly refused to claim exemption.

The greatest majority of those who enlisted or were drafted served in the Civil War battles, in the American Expeditionary Force during World War I and military campaigns in Africa, Europe and the Pacific southwest in World War II. Many of them paid the supreme sacrifice on the battlefields of France, in the South Pacific and in Vietnam. Some of them attained the rare distinction of receiving high honors for bravery. Among them were George Dilboy in World War I and Chris Carr in World War II, who were awarded the highest honor within the power of the Republic – the Congressional Medal.

An extraordinary example of Greek patriotism was the voluntary return of Greek immigrants to their homeland to fight in the Greek-Turkish War of 1897 and in the Balkan War of 1912-1913. So strong was their sense of obligation to their mother country that they felt compelled to leave the safe haven of their new-found home in America to return to Greece at their own expense and fight the Turks in defense of freedom and the homeland. Several thousand did so, especially those from large urban areas such as Chicago.

Greek men and women who were left behind also contributed to the cause in other ways, especial in proportion to their means and power. They subscribed generously to the various Liberty Loans and Red Cross during World War I and were among the heaviest buyers of defense bonds during World War II. In fact, the AHEPA, the largest Greek fraternal organization in America, was one of the largest sellers of American defense bonds. Similarly, Greek Americans rushed to relieve the sufferings of Greece after its fall to the Axis Power in 1940 establishing the Greek War Relief Association, a national group with the late John L. Manta of Chicago as its head, providing succor and international relief for the starving people there.

America's Wars

Among the Greeks who were known to participate in the wars fought by the United States in defense of freedom and democracy, are the following:

Pre-Revolutionary Activity

Greeks are known to have served in the military service of Spain and in English and Dutch expeditions, seeking to explore and colonize the New World. This was especially the case since the fall of Constantinople to the Turks in 1453 resulted in a flood of Greek soldiers and sailors to the West seeking employment on expeditions exploring America.

Indeed, according to the ship manifest of Columbus there were three recognizable Greek names, identified as "Griego" who sailed with him in his discovery of America in 1492. Such was also the case with Hernando Cortez, who had several Greeks in his expedition which conquered Mexico in 1519, and Francisco Pizarro in his conquest of the Incas in Peru in 1538. In fact, his chief gunnery officer was Pedro di Candia from the Greek island of Crete.

The first authoritative reference to a Greek in the New World is mentioned by Cabeza de Vaca. A Greek called Don Teodoro served in the expedition of Panfilo de Navaez which explored the Gulf of Mexico area in 1528. While on a land mission, Teodoro was captured by Indians and lived among them in the area that is now Mobile, Alabama. De Soto learned about this when he explored the central Mississippi area during 1538-1542. Of some 200 men listed in the military roster of Coronado's expedition that explored the American southwest in 1542, some 40 men are listed as being "Griego."

Interestingly the word "gringo" is derived from "Griego" and was used pejoratively by the Spaniards to denote strangers.

A Captain named Thomas Grecian in command of a British ship that explored the New England area, is known to have settled in Boston in 1660. A John Dye or Dervish, served in a Dutch expedition that explored the New York bay area in 1689. During the colonial period the best known Greek in America was John Paradise, who lived in Williamsburg. He was a friend and later a military advisor to Thomas Jefferson and introduced him to Adamantios Koraes, the intellectual father of the Greek Revolution, while in France. In the Pacific Northwest, an entrepreneur specializing in furs, Eustrate Delarof, who had migrated from Greece to Moscow, became director of the Russian American (Fur) Company in 1783 and subsequently served as the first Russian governor of Alaska until 1791. At the southeastern end of the continent in 1767, a mass migration of Greeks landed in New Smyrna, Florida. They were on eight ships carrying nearly 1,500 Greeks, Italians and Minorcans. It was the largest importation of white settlers ever brought to America, larger than Jamestown in 1607 and that of Plymouth Rock in 1620.

THE UNITED STATES OF AMERICA
TO ALL WHO SHALL SEE THESE PRESENTS, GREETING:
THIS IS TO CERTIFY THAT
THE PRESIDENT OF THE UNITED STATES OF AMERICA
HAS AWARDED THE
PURPLE HEART
ESTABLISHED BY GENERAL GEORGE WASHINGTON
AT NEWBURGH, NEW YORK, AUGUST 7, 1782
TO
PRIVATE HARRY J. PAPPAS, UNITED STATES ARMY
FOR WOUNDS RECEIVED
IN ACTION
EUROPEAN THEATER OF OPERATIONS 21 JANUARY 1945
GIVEN UNDER MY HAND IN THE CITY OF WASHINGTON
THIS 5th DAY OF February 1988

A Purple Heart for Harry Pappas, who was wounded in 1945, while fighting in the European theater.

War of the American Revolution

During the American Wars of Independence, Demetrios Ypsilanti, a scion of a mercantile Greek family and grandfather of the Greek revolutionary hero of the same name, reportedly outfitted a small ship and came to the new land with a band of followers to fight in support of America. Some sources claim that his group participated in the Battle of Monmouth, New Jersey, in 1778, under the command of General Lee. The city of Ypsilanti, Michigan was reportedly named after him in 1823.

War of 1812

Alexander Dimitry (1775-1852), was born on the island of Hydra in 1775 and emigrated to New Orleans in 1799 where he met Michael Dracos, a wealthy Greek merchant and an influential citizen. Dimitry won Draco's favor and assistance and received the hand of his daughter, Marianne Celeste Dracos. With such a family connection, Dimitry soon became wealthy and influential and distinguished himself in many fields. He was a private in the Louisiana militia and took past in several battles in the War of 1812, between the United States and Great Britain, including the crucial Battle of New Orleans in 1814. Dimitry held various important offices with honor and distinction, including that of a newspaper editor in New Orleans and first superintendent of Public Instruction in Louisiana from 1847-1841. In acknowledgment of his distinguished services the American government honored him with a grant of 1,000 acres on the Gulf Coast of Mississippi where he built his famous villa, 'Dimitry Point'. When he died in 1852 the firing of American canons and muskets saluted this distinguished citizen.

War with Mexico

Charles Monahan or Demetrios Koroneos (1805-1905), was born on the island of Skopelos in the northern Aegean Sea. As an adult, he joined the British Navy, then patrolling the sea during the War for Greek Independence. On one of his trips to America, he settled in New Orleans becoming a permanent resident. He participated in the Mexican War during 1846-1847 and later in the Civil War with the Confederacy. He died in New Orleans in August, 1905 at the age of 100 years, leaving behind him a progeny of 21 children.

Colonel Lucas Miltiades Miller (1824-1902), served in the American army and fought in the Mexican campaign from 1846-1847, reaching the rank of colonel. He was born in Levadia, Greece, the son of a Greek chieftain who was killed in the War of Greek Independence. He was brought to the United States by Colonel L. P. Miller, an American who was then fighting in the Greek army. Miller gave his adopted son his name and a home in Montpelier, Vermont, where he was educated. He studied law, and after being admitted to the bar, he moved West to Oshkosh, Wisconsin, where he became one of the most influential men in the city and state. In 1853 he was elected to the Wisconsin State Assembly, served as Commissioner of the Wisconsin Board of Public Works and also served 10 years as chairman of Winnebago County and donated the lot upon which the court house now stands. In 1891, Colonel Miller was elected by the Democratic Party to the 52nd Congress (1891-1893), having been nominated without his knowledge and against his wishes. He was the first Greek American to serve an elected position in congress.

Civil War

Among the many Greek Americans who served in the Civil War on both sides of the conflict, the most famous was George Mousalas Calvocoressis (1816-1872). Born on the Greek island of Chios he came to the United States on an American brig together with nine other boys whose families had been massacred by the Turks during the Greek War for Independence. The ship arrived in Baltimore where the residents showed great interest for the orphaned children's welfare. George attracted the attention of Captain Alden Partridge, director of the military academy of Norwich, Vermont, who offered to care for and educate the child. George consequently attended the military academy from which he graduated in 1838. Thereafter he was admitted into the U.S. navy and later took part in the Wilkes naval expedition to explore Antarctica. During the American Civil War, he was promoted to commander and served as an executive officer of a warship and was later honored for his distinguished service to the nation. Later, during a conflict between Spain and Chile, he protected American citizens and their interests as a commander of an American warship, whereupon he was promoted to the rank of captain in the Navy. He retired from active service in 1865 and died in 1872.

Evzones of the Greek Presidential Guard march up New York's Fifth Avenue

Like his father, Alexander Dimitry, John Dimitry or John Bull Smith (1835-?), was a historian, master of languages and a statesman. He was born in Washington, D.C., where his father was serving in a government post, and was educated at College Hill in Mississippi. When the Civil War broke out he joined the Confederate army and fought in the Battle of Shiloh in Tennessee, where his hip was shattered while rescuing his company commander. Returning to civilian life after the war, he settled in Louisiana where he became the secretary to the state superintendent of education, and wrote his "History of Louisiana," publishing it in 1899. It became a valuable textbook in the state's public schools for many years. It is not known when he died.

Charles Patten Dimitry (1837-1910), was another son of Alexander Dimitry and brother to John Dimitry, who was also born in Washington, D.C. With the beginning of the Civil War he went into the confederate army like his brother and served in the army of Tennessee until 1865. During 1864 while stationed in Richmond, Virginia, the capital of the confederacy, he wrote and published serially a novel entitled "Guilty or Not Guilty." He also wrote a series of short genealogical sketches that were later bound into a book entitled "Louisiana Families," which included the genealogy of the Dimitry family. He was married to Ann Elizabeth Johnson in 1871 and had one son who preceded him in death.

George A. Perdicaris (1803-1872), came to America in 1823 when he was 20 years of age. He was the first consul of the United States in Athens, Greece, in 1837, and remained in that post for 10 years. Upon his return to America in 1847, he recorded his studies and impressions of Greece in a two-volume book entitled "The Greece of the Greeks."

He was married to an American woman from South Carolina and had a son, Ion. With the outbreak of the Civil War he joined the United States Navy where he was awarded the title of a lieutenant, serving honorably for the rest of his life. In 1861, he was promoted to commander and participated in various naval expeditions all over the world. Later, during the war he commanded the U.S.S. Supply and later still, the U.S.S. Saratoga where he won the praise of his admiral and was commended by the Secretary of the Navy for his "zeal and good service to the country." In 1867 he was retired with the rank of captain and lived with his family in Litchfield, Connecticut, where he met an untimely death by highway robbers in 1872.

George Papadakis or Patterson (1828-1901), was born in Boston and after completing his studies there in 1852, went to Plymouth, North Carolina to study for holy orders. He was later ordained a deacon in a Protestant denomination and served in the southern states. During the Civil War he served as a chaplain in the confederate army. After the war he became the Rector of Grace Church and after a long active life died in Memphis, Tennessee, in 1901. Bishop Gailor wrote: "Dr. Patterson was very proud of his Greek descent" and that he was a noble Christian Gentleman.

Another chaplain in the Civil War was Photios Fisk who was also one of the orphans of the Greek War of Independence brought to America in 1823. He served in the United States Navy as a chaplain for many years. He was an early staunch advocate for the abolition of slavery and by his last will and testament, bequeathed most of his fortune for the anti-slavery cause.

George Sirian was a gunner in the United States navy. He too was born on one of the Greek islands, probably the island of Syros in the Aegean Sea. During the Greek revolution he was set adrift in a boat by his mother to escape a band of Turks. She remained behind to await her fate. The boat was picked up by one of the United States cruisers which brought the boy to America. Growing up and educated in the United States, he subsequently entered the Union Navy and later became a warrant officer. Later, he married the daughter of one George Marshall, who was also a Greek and the first one to publish a manual of naval gunnery used in the United States naval service. Little else is know about them.

Other known Greek Americans who participated in the Civil War are: John Valsamos who came from the island of Cephalonia in the Ionian Sea off the western coast of Greece and who died in 1896; John Christy from Dayton, Ohio; Thomas Kaffeges of Boston; Vasilios C. Tsiros from New York; and Sam Carsoneas, the "Spartan" who fought in the Civil War and is later believed to have participated in the Battle of Santiago in Cuba during the Spanish-American War.

Spanish-American War

George Partridge Calvocoressis (1847-1932), was born in Norwich, Vermont, the son of Captain George Mousalas Calvocoressis and like his father made an enviable record in the United States Navy.

He participated for two years in the Civil War, serving on the battleship commanded by his father. In 1865, he entered the United States Naval Academy at Annapolis, Maryland, graduating in 1869. He was promoted to ensign in 1870, to master in 1872, to lieutenant in 1875 and to lieutenant-commander in 1897. In the Spanish American War he was the executive officer of the U.S.S. Concord at the Battle of Manila Bay in the Philippines. He was "advanced five numbers" for his conduct in this battle. He was awarded a Congressional Medal for bravery in 1900 and was promoted to commander. He was promoted by Admiral Dewey to executive officer of his flagship the U.S.S. Concord and was commander of the Olympia battalion in the ovations of welcome for Dewey in New York, Washington and Boston. He served as head of the Navy Yards in New York and was commander of the naval station at Key West, Florida. He also served as commander of the U.S.S. Enterprise as well as other ships. He resigned after 48 years of active service with the rank of Rear Admiral. He died at home in Litchfield, Connecticut and is buried in that town's New East Cemetery. He was married to Mary D. Baldwin and had two sons and a daughter; both sons following their father's footsteps as officers in the United States Army.

World War I

Of the several thousands of Greek Americans that served in the American Expeditionary Force during World War I, many of whom served with high distinction, one was singularly honored by the American Government for making the supreme sacrifice in the war that was fought "to make the world safe for democracy." He was George Dilboy, born in the town of Alatsata in Asia Minor on February 5, 1896.

After the Balkan War of 1912-1913, his family fled to America to avoid persecution from the Turks and made their home in Keene, New Hampshire.

During the Mexican Border trouble of 1916, the young hero joined the National Guard and served under General John Pershing with Company H, First Infantry Regiment. Then the family moved to Massachusetts and settled in Somerville. It was there that Dilboy was called into service on July 25, 1917 and was assigned to Company H, 103rd Infantry, 26th Division. He was sent with his company to France and took part in the Champagne-Marne counter offensive. He was killed on the battlefield near Belleau, France, July 18, 1918 and was post humously awarded the Congressional Medal for Bravery, the highest medal of the Republic. The official citation reads:

"Dilboy, George, Private. Deceased, Company H. 103rd Infantry. For gallantry and intrepidity in action above and beyond the call of duty near Belleau, France, July 18, 1918. After his platoon had gained its objective along a railroad embankment, Private Dilboy, accompanying his platoon leader to reconnoiter the ground beyond, was suddenly fired upon by an enemy machine gun from one hundred yards. From a standing position on the railroad track, fully exposed to view, he opened fire at once, but failing to silence the gun, rushed forward with his bayonet fixed through a wheat field toward the gun emplacement falling within twenty-five yards of the gun with his right leg nearly severed and with several bullet holes in his body. With courage undaunted he continued to fire into the emplacement from a prone position, killing two of the enemy and dispersing the rest of the crew."

In a ceremony on the Boston Commons where many dignitaries were present including Governor Calvin Coolidge, future President of the United States, the Medal of Honor was pinned on the coat of Antonios Dilboy, father of the hero, in the presence of thousands of people. General Clarence R. Edwards addressed the aged father thusly:

"Your boy was born in a foreign land, and like you he spoke the Greek language and with you came to his adopted country. You taught him of Flag and what American citizenship means. You made him appreciate the blessings afforded to all aliens. You told him it was the greatest honor on earth to be chosen to defend with his life the freedom that you enjoy, and you so developed his character and instilled into him this pride in your adopted country that no American boy excelled this boy in the supreme sacrifice that he made. He was almost superhuman. He achieved things supposed above the limit of mental and physical endurance. His act cleared the way for his platoon to break through; that he died, a splendid example."

The remains of George Dilboy were removed form France to his birthplace in Asia Minor but because of the desecration of his grave by the Turks they were finally removed from there to the United States and were interred in the National Cemetery at Arlington. Besides a number of American Legion Posts which bear the name of this hero, the George Dilboy Memorial Foundation with headquarters at Hines, Illinois, was chartered on January 25, 1935 and an imposing George Dilboy Memorial was erected in the George Dilboy Plaza on the grounds of the Hines Veterans Hospital in that Chicago suburban community.

World War II

While many thousands of Greek Americans served in the armed forces of the United States, many of them second and third generations of the original Greek immigrants, and with many of them receiving accolades and citations for their bravery and accomplishment, one in particular stands out for his heroic exploits on the field of battle, for which he was also awarded a Congressional Medal of Honor by a grateful nation. He was Chris Carr (name legally changed from Christos H. Karaberis, under which the medal was awarded). Karaberis was a second generation Greek American, born in Manchester, New Hampshire, of parents who emigrated from Greece. It was here that he entered military service, becoming a member of the United States Army, Company L, 337th Infantry Division ending up with the rank of Sergeant. During the Italian campaign near the town of Guignola, Italy, on October 1-2, 1944, he performed action beyond the call of duty for which he was awarded the Medal of Honor.

The citation reads as follows:

"Leading a squad of Company L, he gallantly cleared the way for his company's approach along a ridge toward its objective, the Casoni di Remagna. When his platoon was pinned down by heavy fire from enemy mortars, machine-guns, machine-pistols and rifles, he climbed in advance of his squad in a maneuver around the left flank to locate and eliminate the

enemy gun positions. Undeterred by steady fire that ricocheted off the barren hillside, he crept to the rear of the first machine-gun and charged, firing his submachine-gun. In this surprise attack he captured several prisoners and turned them over to his squad before striking out alone for a second submachine-gun. Discovered in his advance and subjected to direct fire from the hostile weapon, he leaped to his feet and ran forward, weaving and crouching, pouring automatic fire into the emplacement that killed four of its defenders and forced the surrender of alone survivor. He again moved forward through heavy fire to attack another machine-gun.

When, close to the emplacement, he closed with a nerve-shattering shout and burst of fire. Paralyzed by his whirlwind attack, all four gunners immediately surrendered. Once more advancing aggressively in the face of a thoroughly alerted enemy, he approached a high ground occupied by two machine-guns which were firing on his company on the slope below.

Charging the first of these weapons, he killed four of the crew and captured three more. The six defenders of the adjacent position, cowed by the savagery of his assault, immediately gave up. By this one-man attack, heroically and voluntarily undertaken in the face of tremendous risks, Sgt. Karaberis captured five enemy machine-gun positions, killed eight Germans, took 22 prisoners, cleared the ridge leading to his company's objective, and drove a deep wedge into the enemy line, making it possible for his battalion to occupy important commanding ground."

The citation which is dated November 1, 1945, has an Olympian ring to it and is reminiscent of the heroic exploits of our forebears in the ancient battles of Thermopylae and Marathon.

Archbishop Michael with President Harry Truman on January 21, 1950

World War II was different from previous wars insofar as for the first time women were permitted to enter into armed forces in defense of our country. Greek American women, despite restraints of growing up in a patriarchal society, were no laggards in coming to the defense of their country. Among the first were Hon. Adeline J. Geo-Karis of Chicago. Born in Tegea, Greece, she came with her parents to the United States while at a very young age. She was educated in the Chicago public schools and at DePaul University where she earned a law degree. In 1942 she enlisted in the United States Navy serving throughout the war in the WAVES (Women Accepted for Volunteer Emergency Service) – doing legal discipline work for the navy. She was among the very first Greek American women serving in the armed forces along with those who joined the WACs (Women's Army Corps).

Upon her honorable discharge in 1946, she moved to Zion, Illinois, where in 1972 she was elected to the Illinois House, serving one term. In 1987 she was elected mayor of Zion for one term. Her strong policy of advocacy for the people soon resulted in her election as State Senator in 1978 where she served for 19 years.

In brief, this has been the illustrious history of Greek Americans in the service of their country in defense of freedom. America's more recent wars such as the Korean Conflict, the war in Vietnam and the Gulf War have had their share of Greek Americans participating in them.

Of special note is the singular role of Lt. General Gus Pagonis in the Gulf War and that of Vice Admiral Michael P. Kalleres. But the story of their participation has yet to be fully written. When it is, it will undoubtedly be revealed that their participation was no less glorious than their predecessors, and another golden page will be added to a long and illustrious history of Greek Americans in defense of freedom. In so doing, they remained faithful to the Socratic injunction of honoring their country above that of parents and ancestors.

---

* *Andrew T. Kopan, a historian and veteran of World War II, researched and wrote this narrative for an Exhibit at the Hellenic Museum and Cultural Center in Chicago, Illinois, titled* Defenders of Democracy: Greek Americans in the Military *which was on view from February 20, 1998 until June 30, 1998.*

RAPHAEL
SANTIVS
PINX